EMPIRES AT

Empires at War, 1911–1923 offers a new perspective on the history of the Great War. It expands the story of the war both in time and space to include the violent conflicts that preceded and followed the First World War, from the 1911 Italian invasion of Libya to the massive violence that followed the collapse of the Ottoman, Russian, and Austrian empires until 1923. It also presents the war as a global war of empires rather than a European war between nation-states.

This volume tells the story of the millions of imperial subjects called upon to defend their imperial governments' interest, the theatres of war that lay far beyond Europe, and the wartime roles and experiences of innumerable peoples from outside the European continent. *Empires at War* covers the broad, global mobilizations that saw African solders and Chinese labourers in the trenches of the Western Front, Indian troops in Jerusalem, and the Japanese military occupying Chinese territory. Finally, the volume shows how the war set the stage for the collapse not only of specific empires, but of the imperial world order writ large.

Robert Gerwarth is Professor of Modern History at UCD and Director of UCD's Centre for War Studies. He is the author and editor of several books on the history of violence, including a biography of Reinhard Heydrich (with Donald Bloxham, 2011), *Political Violence in Twentieth-Century Europe* (2011); and *War in Peace: Paramilitary Violence after the Great War* (with John Horne, 2012).

Erez Manela, Professor of History at Harvard University, is the author of *The Wilsonian Moment: Self-Determination and the International Origins of Anticolonial Nationalism* (2007) and co-editor of *The Shock of the Global: The 1970s in Perspective* (2010). He is currently completing a book on the global eradication of smallpox in the Cold War era.

THE GREATER WAR

General Editor ROBERT GERWARTH

The paroxysm of 1914–1918 was the epicentre of a cycle of armed conflict that in some parts of Europe began in 1911 and continued until 1923. Taken together, the volumes in this series recognize not only that the Great War has a greater chronological dimension, but also that it has a greater territorial reach than the well-published struggle on the Western Front.

Empires at War

1911–1923

Edited by
ROBERT GERWARTH
and
EREZ MANELA

OXFORD
UNIVERSITY PRESS

OXFORD
UNIVERSITY PRESS

Great Clarendon Street, Oxford, OX2 6DP,
United Kingdom

Oxford University Press is a department of the University of Oxford.
It furthers the University's objective of excellence in research, scholarship,
and education by publishing worldwide. Oxford is a registered trade mark of
Oxford University Press in the UK and in certain other countries

© Oxford University Press 2014

The moral rights of the authors have been asserted

First published 2014
First published in paperback 2015

Published in the United States of America by Oxford University Press
198 Madison Avenue, New York, NY 10016, United States of America

British Library Cataloguing in Publication Data
Data available

Library of Congress Cataloging in Publication Data
Data available

ISBN 978–0–19–870251–1 (Hbk.)
ISBN 978–0–19–873493–2 (Pbk.)

Acknowledgements

This present volume is the result of collaborative efforts over several years. Most of the authors assembled in this volume met at two themed conferences in Dublin in 2010 and 2012. The editors would like to thank the participants and commentators, who provided extensive critical input. Neither the conferences nor the publication of this book would have been possible without the generous funding provided by the European Research Council (ERC) for the Dublin-based 'Limits of Demobilization' project, and it is with profound gratitude that we acknowledge the ERC's critical financial support.

We are also immensely grateful to our editorial team at OUP—notably Christopher Wheeler, Robert Faber, Cathryn Steele, and Emma Slaughter—for the enthusiasm with which they have seen the book through from conception to production. Three anonymous reviewers for OUP went beyond the call of duty in providing critical input, and we thank them immensely for their helpful comments.

Finally, we wish to thank our contributors, whose abiding commitment to the project made our work intellectually fulfilling and even—despite the grimness of the topic—eminently enjoyable.

Robert Gerwarth and Erez Manela

April 2014

Contents

List of Contributors	viii
List of Maps	xi
List of Figures	xii

Introduction 1
Robert Gerwarth and Erez Manela

1. The Ottoman Empire 17
   Mustafa Aksakal

2. The Italian Empire 34
   Richard Bosworth and Giuseppe Finaldi

3. The German Empire 52
   Heather Jones

4. Austria–Hungary 73
   Peter Haslinger

5. The Russian Empire 91
   Joshua Sanborn

6. The French Empire 109
   Richard S. Fogarty

7. British Imperial Africa 130
   Bill Nasson

8. The Dominions, Ireland, and India 152
   Stephen Garton

9. The Portuguese Empire 179
   Filipe Ribeiro de Meneses

10. The Japanese Empire 197
    Frederick R. Dickinson

11. China and Empire 214
    Xu Guoqi

12. The United States Empire 235
    Christopher Capozzola

13. Empires at the Paris Peace Conference 254
    Leonard V. Smith

Index 277

List of Contributors

Mustafa Aksakal is Associate Professor of History at Georgetown University. He is the author of *The Ottoman Road to War in 1914* (Cambridge University Press, 2008) and is currently working on a book about military and civilian life in the Ottoman Empire's final decade.

Richard Bosworth is Professor Emeritus of the University of Western Australia and a Senior Research Fellow at Jesus College, Oxford. He is the author of several books on modern Italy, notably of a critically acclaimed biography of Mussolini. His last book was *Whispering City: Rome and its Histories* (Yale University Press, 2011). His next book, also with Yale, will be *Awash with its Pasts: Italian Venice—a History*.

Christopher Capozzola is Associate Professor of History at MIT. His research interests are in the history of war, politics, and citizenship in modern American history. His first book, *Uncle Sam Wants You: World War I and the Making of the Modern American Citizen* (Oxford University Press, 2008), won the Lois P. Rudnick Book Prize of the New England American Studies Association. His current research project, *Brothers of the Pacific: Soldiers, Citizens, and the Philippines from 1898 to the War on Terror*, is a transnational history of American soldiers in the Philippines and Filipino soldiers in the USA in the twentieth century.

Frederick R. Dickinson is Professor of History at the University of Pennsylvania. He is the author of *War and National Reinvention: Japan in the Great War, 1914–1919* (Harvard University Asia Center, 1999), *Taisho tenno* (Taisho Emperor, Minerva Press, 2009 [in Japanese]), and *World War I and the Triumph of a New Japan, 1919–1930* (Cambridge University Press, 2013).

Giuseppe Finaldi is an Associate Professor of History at the University of Western Australia. He is the author of *Italian National Identity in the Scramble for Africa: Italy's African Wars in the Era of Nation-Building, 1870–1900* (Peter Lang, 2009) and *Mussolini and Italian Fascism* (Pearson, 2008). He is currently working on a history of the modern Italian empire.

Richard S. Fogarty is Associate Professor of History at the University at Albany, State University of New York. He is the author of *Race and War in France: Colonial Subjects in the French Army, 1914–1918* (Johns Hopkins University Press, 2008). He is now working on a study of North African prisoners of war during the Great War, with special attention to the place of Islam and Muslims in France and the French colonial empire, as well as in the wider military and ideological struggle in Europe and the Middle East.

Stephen Garton is Professor of History and Provost and Deputy Vice Chancellor at the University of Sydney. He has written on the history of psychiatry, incarceration, masculinity, social policy, eugenics, and Harlem. He has also written extensively on the history of demobilization and repatriation, including *The Cost of War* (Oxford University Press, 1996), and more recently co-authored with Peter Stanley the chapter on the 'Great War and its Aftermath, 1914–23' in the *Cambridge History of Australia*.

Robert Gerwarth is Professor of Modern History at University College Dublin and Director of UCD's Centre for War Studies. He is the author and editor of several books on modern Germany and the history of violence, including a biography of Reinhard Heydrich

(Yale University Press, 2011); (with Donald Bloxham) *Political Violence in Twentieth-Century Europe* (Cambridge University Press, 2010); and (with John Horne) *War in Peace: Paramilitary Violence after the Great War* (Oxford University Press, 2012).

Peter Haslinger is Professor of East-Central European History at the University of Giessen and Director of the Herder-Institut for Historical Research on East-Central Europe in Marburg. He has published widely on nationalism in the late Habsburg Empire including, most recently, *Nation und Territorium im tschechischen politischen Diskurs* (Oldenbourg, 2010).

Heather Jones is Associate Professor in International History at the London School of Economics and Political Science (LSE) and a member of the Board of the International Research Centre of the Historial de la Grande Guerre, Péronne. She is the author of *Violence against Prisoners of War in the First World War: Britain, France and Germany, 1914–1920* (Cambridge University Press, 2011) and co-editor of *Untold War: New Perspectives in First World War Studies* (Brill Academic Publishers, 2008).

Erez Manela is Professor of History at Harvard University, where he also directs the Program on Global Society and Security. He is the author of *The Wilsonian Moment: Self-Determination and the International Origins of Anticolonial Nationalism* (Oxford University Press, 2007) and co-editor of *The Shock of the Global: The 1970s in Perspective* (Harvard University Press, 2010).

Filipe Ribeiro de Meneses is Professor of History at the National University of Ireland Maynooth. He is the author of, among other works, *Portugal 1914–1926: From the First World War to Military Dictatorship* (University of Bristol, 2004); *Salazar: A Political Biography* (Enigma, 2009); and *Afonso Costa: Portugal* (Haus, 2010).

Bill Nasson is Professor of History at the University of Stellenbosch, South Africa. His works include histories of the British Empire (Tempus, 2006), the Anglo-Boer War (NB Publishing, 2010), as well as the South African experience in the First World War (Penguin, 2007) and the Second World War (Jacana, 2012). His latest book (co-edited with Albert Grundlingh) is *The War Comes Home: Women and Families in the Anglo-Boer War* (Tafelberg, 2013). He is currently writing a history of the British Empire during the Great War for Oxford University Press.

Joshua Sanborn is Professor and Head of the Department of History at Lafayette College. He is the author of *Drafting the Russian Nation: Military Conscription, Total War, and Mass Politics, 1905–1925* (Northern Illinois University Press, 2003) and co-author (with Annette Timm) of *Gender, Sex, and the Shaping of Modern Europe: A History from the French Revolution to the Present Day* (Bloomsbury, 2007). More recently, he has written several articles and essays on Russia's experience in the Great War. His next book, *Imperial Apocalypse: The Great War and the Destruction of the Russian Empire* will be published by Oxford University Press.

Leonard V. Smith is Frederick B. Artz Professor at Oberlin College. He is the author of *The Embattled Self: French Soldiers' Testimony of the Great War* (Cornell University Press, 2007); *France and the Great War, 1914–1918* (with Stéphane Audoin-Rouzeau and Annette Becker) (Cambridge University Press, 2003), and *Between Mutiny and Obedience: The Case of the French Fifth Infantry Division during World War I* (Princeton University Press, 1994). He also co-edited *France at War: Vichy and the Historians* (Berg, 2000; French edition 2004).

Xu Guoqi is Professor of History at the University of Hong Kong. He is the author of *Strangers on the Western Front: Chinese Workers in the Great War* (Harvard University Press, 2011); *Olympic Dreams: China and Sports, 1895–2008* (Harvard University Press, 2008); *China and the Great War: China's Pursuit of a New National Identity and Internationalization* (Cambridge University Press, 2005, 2011); *Chinese and Americans: A Shared History* (Harvard University Press, 2014). Professor Xu is currently working on a book *Asia and the Great War* (Oxford University Press, forthcoming).

List of Maps

1. Europe in 1911 — xiii
2. Europe in 1920 — xiv
3. A World at War, 1917 — xv
4. Global territorial changes, 1918–1922: The Middle East — xvi
5. Global territorial changes, 1918–1922: Africa — xvii
6. Global territorial changes, 1918–1922: China and the Pacific — xviii
7. Portuguese Africa at War — 178

List of Figures

1. Refugees in Thrace, *c.*1915 (Georgetown University, Washington, DC)   22
2. Locust burning in Palestine, *c.*1915 (Library of Congress)   30
3. Italian soldiers dancing during time off in Tobruk, May 1914
    (Editori Riuniti, Italy)   39
4. Italian residents in Eritrea give thanks for Italy's victory, November 1918
    (Archivio della Società Africana d'Italia, University of Naples 'l'Orientale')   49
5. Wilhelm II in Warsaw (Mary Evans Picture Gallery)   58
6. Imperial PoWs (Heather Jones Private Collection)   66
7. Embattled imperial borderlands I: Austro-Hungarian trenches in the formerly
    West Russian province of Volhynia, 1917 (Herder-Institut for Historical Research
    on East-Central Europe, Marburg)   84
8. Embattled imperial borderlands II: the destroyed market square of the city of
    Ostrołęka, formerly part of the Russian Empire, in May 1916 (Herder-Institut
    for Historical Research on East-Central Europe, Marburg)   84
9. Kazakh laborers at the Eastern Front (Florence Farmborough)   100
10. Soldiers recruited from German POW camps training as the new
    1st Division of the Ukrainian Army, 1918   103
11. French Poster advertising a war loan in the colonies
    (Hoover Institution Archives)   116
12. 1918 French poster advertising a war loan (Library of Congress)   126
13. General Louis Botha (TAB archive, South Africa)   141
14. Botha's opponents: Imperial Germany's African troops (Bundesarchiv, Berlin)   146
15. Irish recruitment poster, 1915 (Everett Collection)   157
16. Camel Corps, 1918 (Imperial War Museum)   163
17. Australian soldier in Egypt (Australian War Memorial Collection)   164
18. Afonso Costa (UNOG Library, League of Nations Archives)   182
19. 'Qingdao', cover of *Tōkyō Puck*, 1 October 1914. (Courtesy of Shimizu Isao)   202
20. 'The European Girls Still Courting the Japanese Soldiers', cover of *Ōsaka Puck*,
    15 September 1917 (Kyoto International Manga Museum)   207
21. A parade of Chinese volunteers before their departure for France (Prichard
    Collection; Leeds University Library)   230
22. Chinese labourers in France (Prichard Collection; Leeds University Library)   231
23. Territory of Hawai'i registration day, 31 July 1917 (Library of Congress)   242
24. Marines landing at Santo Domingo during US occupation of the
    Dominican Republic (US National Archives and Records Administration)   249
25. Empire in action: British checkpoint in Palestine, 1920 (Library of Congress)   268
26. Empire under siege: removing a French mailbox in wartime Turkey (Library of
    Congress)   272

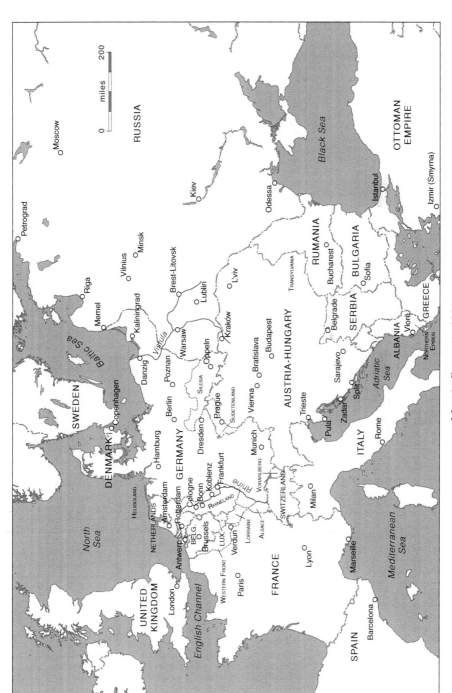

Map 1. Europe in 1911.

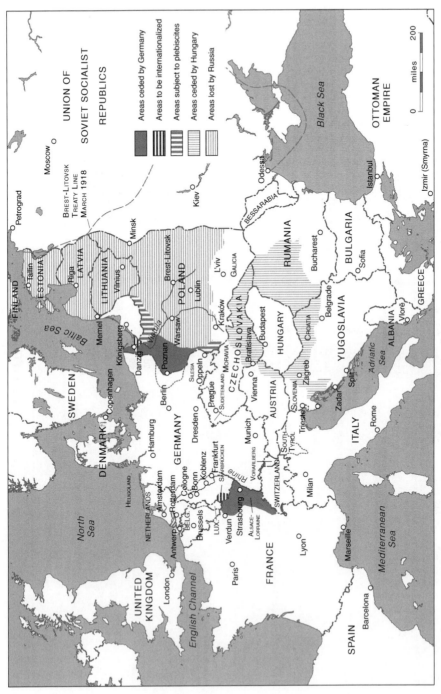

Map 2. Europe in 1920.

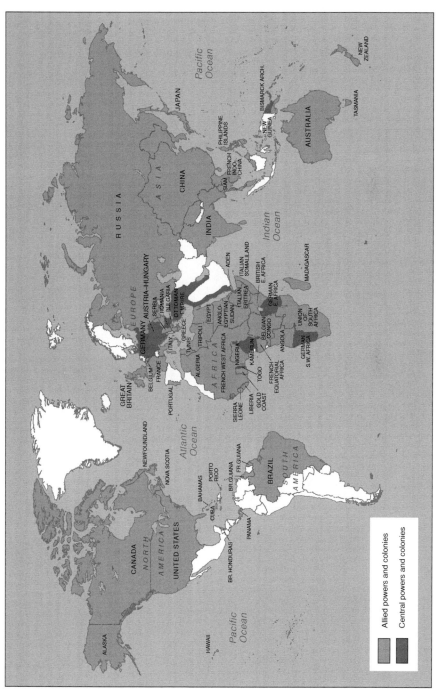

Map 3. A World at War, 1917.

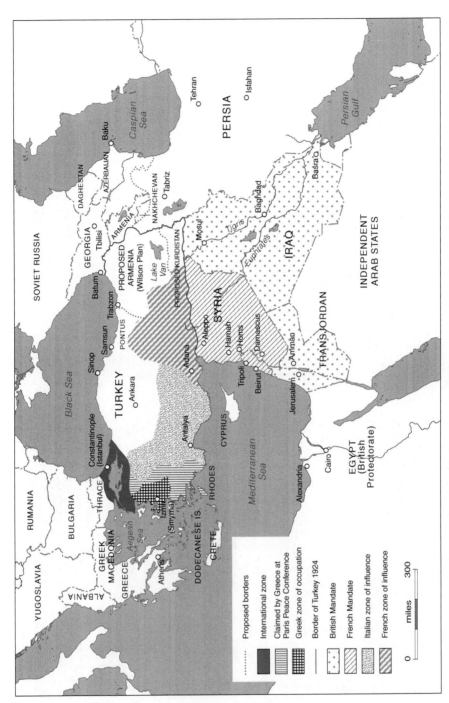

Map 4. Global territorial changes, 1918–1922: The Middle East.

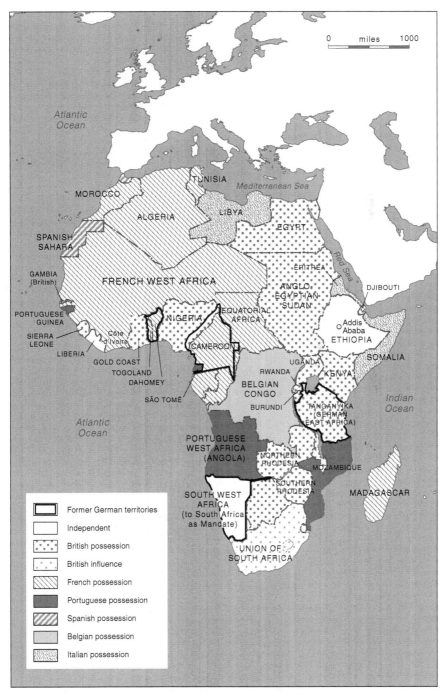

Map 5. Global territorial changes, 1918–1922: Africa.

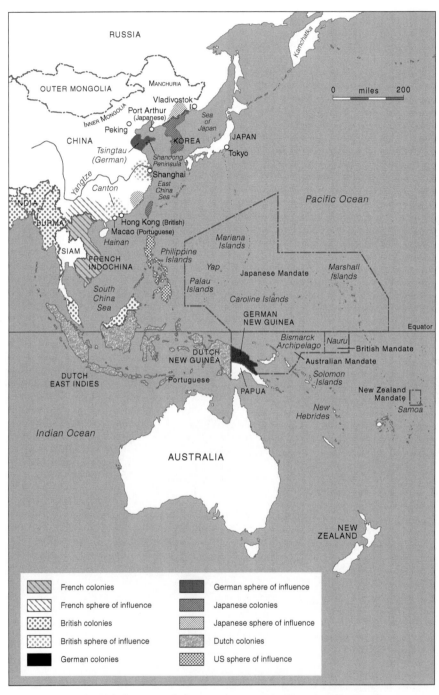

Map 6. Global territorial changes, 1918–1922: China and the Pacific.

Introduction

Robert Gerwarth and Erez Manela

The First World War formally ended in late 1918 with an Allied victory. In its wake, three vast and centuries-old land empires—the Ottoman, Habsburg, and Romanov empires—vanished from the map. A fourth—the Hohenzollern Empire, which had become a major land empire in the last year of the war when it occupied enormous territories in East Central Europe—was significantly reduced in size, stripped of its overseas colonies, and transformed into a parliamentary democracy. The victorious West European empires, despite their significant territorial gains at the Paris Peace Conference, were not unaffected by the cataclysm of war either: Ireland gained independence after a bloody guerilla war against British forces, while, in Egypt, India, Iraq, Afghanistan, and Burma, London responded to unrest with considerable force. France fought back resistance to its imperial ambitions in Algeria, Syria, Indo-China, and Morocco. Even further from the main theaters of the Great War, Japan did the same in Korea.

Benito Mussolini famously commented on the disintegration of the great European land empires and the new challenges confronting the blue-water empires with a surprisingly nervous reference: neither the fall of ancient Rome nor the defeat of Napoleon, he insisted in an article for *Il Popolo d'Italia*, could compare in its impact on history to the current reshuffling of Europe's political map. "The whole earth trembles. All continents are riven by the same crisis. There is not a single part of the planet [...] which is not shaken by the cyclone. In old Europe, men disappear, systems break, institutions collapse."[1]

For once, Mussolini had a point. For centuries, European history, and indeed the history of the world, had been a history of empires, both within the European continent and in terms of maritime exploration, expansion, and conquest of overseas territories. Imperial players such as the United States, Japan, and the Ottoman Empire had carved out their own respective spheres of influence and colonial domination. At the peak of such unprecedented imperial expansion, on the eve of the Great War, much of the land mass of the inhabited world was divided into formal empires or economically dependent territories. That world unraveled dramatically in the twentieth century, as these vast empires either collapsed or came under great strain in the cataclysm of the First World War.

---

[1] Mussolini as quoted in: R. J. B. Bosworth, *Mussolini* (London: Arnold, 2002), 121.

Neither the First World War nor its effects on Europe's political landscape are neglected subjects of historical research. Yet—understandably perhaps, given the imprint of the fighting on Western Europe—most of the literature produced since 1918 has focused on the events on the Western Front and their impact on metropolitan Britain, France, and Germany. Most of these histories are framed within two "classic" assumptions: first, that the war began with the sounding of the "guns of August" in 1914 and ended with the Armistice of 11 November 1918 and, second, that the war was primarily one of nation states and that it was largely a European affair. Meanwhile, ethnic minorities, imperial troops, and East European or non-European theaters of fighting, conscription, and upheaval have remained at best sideshows in general history accounts of war and peace on the Western Front.[2]

Both of these assumptions have dominated and defined the Western historiography of the Great War for decades. And, while the literature based on these assumptions has produced many valuable insights into the causes and consequences of that conflict, this book seeks to expand the canvas on which the history of the Great War is written by proceeding from two premises that diverge from these assumptions. The first premise is that it pays to examine the war within a frame that is both longer (temporally) and wider (spatially) than is typical. The focus on the period between August 1914 and November 1918 makes more sense for the victorious Western Front powers (notably Britain and France) than it does for much of central-eastern and south-eastern Europe or for those colonial troops whose demobilization did not begin in November 1918. The paroxysm of 1914–18 was the epicentre of a cycle of armed imperial conflict that in some parts of Europe began in 1911, with the Italian attack on territories in Northern Africa and the Mediterranean previously controlled by the Ottoman Empire, and the Balkan Wars, which broke out the following year.[3] Moreover, the massive waves of violence triggered by imperial collapse continued until 1923, when the Treaty of Lausanne defined the territory of the new Turkish Republic and ended Greek territorial ambitions in Asia Minor with the largest forced exchange of populations in history until the Second World War.[4] The end of the Irish Civil War in the same year, the restoration of a measure of equilibrium in Germany after the end of the Franco-Belgian occupation

[2] Hew Strachan, *The First World War*, i. *To Arms* (Oxford: Oxford University Press, 2004), the magisterial first volume of his planned three-volume history of the Great War, gives an indication of the possibilities of a global approach. For a primarily European-focused transnational history of the Great War, see Alan Kramer, *Dynamics of Destruction: Culture and Mass Killing in the First World War* (Oxford: Oxford University Press, 2008). Recent works that survey the war from a global perspective include William Kelleher Storey, *The First World War: A Concise Global History* (Lanham, MD: Rowman & Littlefield, 2009), and Michael S. Neiberg, *Fighting the Great War: A Global History* (Cambridge, MA: Harvard University Press, 2005). For the global ramifications of the Paris Peace Conference, see Erez Manela, *The Wilsonian Moment: Self-Determination and the International Origins of Anticolonial Nationalism* (Oxford: Oxford University Press, 2007).
[3] Richard Hall, *The Balkan Wars, 1912–1913: Prelude to the First World War* (London, 2000). Donald Bloxham and Robert Gerwarth (eds), *Political Violence in Twentieth-Century Europe* (Cambridge: Cambridge University Press, 2011), 1–10.
[4] Ryan Gingeras, *Sorrowful Shores: Violence, Ethnicity and the End of the Ottoman Empire, 1912–1923* (Oxford: Oxford University Press, 2009).

of the Ruhr, the stabilization of the Bolshevik regime in Russia with its decisive victory in that bloody civil war and the confirmation of the New Economic Policy on Lenin's death in 1924, and the reconfiguration of power relations in East Asia at the Washington Conference two years earlier were all further indications that the cycle of violence, for the time being, had run its course.

The second contention of this book is that we should see the First World War not merely as a war between European nation states, but primarily as a war of multi-ethnic, global empires. Charles Maier has defined empires as supra-national entities characterized "by size, by ethnic hierarchization, and by a regime that centralizes power but enlists diverse social and/or ethnic elites in its management."[5] In this volume we use "empire" as an inclusive and open concept that describes a polity whose territories and populations are arranged and governed hierarchically in relation to the imperial center, which is precisely how most of the polities discussed in this volume viewed themselves at the time. Thinking about the Great War as a war of empires rather than of nation states allows us to see, as many of the chapters that follow show, how the various contenders mobilized, deployed, and demobilized different imperial populations in differential ways and why this mattered both to the general history of the war and to the mobilized groups themselves. Moreover, if we take the conflict seriously as a *world* war, we must, a century after the event, adopt a perspective that does justice more fully to the millions of imperial subjects called upon to defend their imperial governments' interest, to theaters of war that lay far beyond Europe including in Asia and Africa and, more generally, to the wartime roles and experiences of innumerable peoples from outside the European continent.[6]

The mobilization of millions of imperial subjects on both sides of the conflict proved essential for all combatant states, from Germany to the Ottoman, Habsburg, and Romanov empires and, of course, the Entente powers. Indian, African, Canadian, and Australian soldiers among others all served on the Western Front, as well as in a range of ancillary theaters, and hundreds of thousands of them died. Non-combatant laborers—notably from China—also proved vital to the conduct of the war, as did the involvement of the Japanese Empire, which, as Frederick Dickinson shows in his chapter, used the war as an opportunity not only to try to penetrate further into China but also to stage an extensive occupation of Siberia that lasted until 1922. The involvement of imperial troops, Chinese laborers, and others in the Great War turned what had begun primarily as a European conflict into a world war and marks what has long appeared as mainly a conflict between states as an imperial war. Fighting also took place outside Europe—from Siberia and East Asia to the Middle East, from the South Pacific to the protracted campaigns

[5] Charles S. Maier, *Among Empires: America's Ascendancy and its Predecessors* (Cambridge, MA: Harvard University Press, 2006), 31.
[6] For a more detailed discussion of competing definitions of "empire" and its usefulness as an analytical concept, see, e.g., Joseph W. Esherick, Hasan Kayalı, and Eric Van Young (eds), *Empire to Nation: Historical Perspectives on the Making of the Modern World* (Lanham, MD: Rowman & Littlefield, 2006), and Jörn Leonhard and Ulrike von Hirschhausen (eds), *Comparing Empires: Encounters and Transfers in the Long Nineteenth Century* (Göttingen: Vandenhoeck & Ruprecht, 2011).

in East Africa. The impact of the war was profoundly felt by hundreds of millions living across the imperial world, as the war brought conscription, occupation, inflation, and economic dislocation, while also in many instances kindling new opportunities, ideas, plans, and hopes.

It is only when the war is viewed though this expansive set of lenses that its scope, significance, and implications can be grasped in their fullest sense. Viewing the Great War as a war for imperial survival and expansion helps to place the conflict into a broader spatial and chronological context, one that began with the 1911 Italian invasion of Ottoman territories in North Africa and the Balkan Wars of 1912–13 and that launched a process of imperial decline, which would ultimately lead to the violent collapse of a global order based on territorial empires and replace it by one predicated on the nation state as the only internationally legitimate form of political organization.

The imperial frame also makes it easier to see that the mass violence of war did not end with the Armistice of 1918 and to see how the violence that preceded August 1914 and continued after November 1918 was in fact part of the same process of the realignment of global patterns of power and legitimacy. Large-scale violent conflict continued for years after 1918, as the Great War destroyed the dynastic empires of Russia, Austria–Hungary, and Ottoman Turkey and created a heavily contested border in Germany's East, thereby leaving "shatter zones," or large tracts of territory where the disappearance of frontiers created spaces without order or clear state authority.[7] Revolutionary regimes came to power and then fell amidst great violence in the East and Central European shatter zones of the dynastic land empires. The massive carnage of the Russian civil war continued unabated, as did a number of large-scale but hitherto little studied relief projects. And, of course, civil war accompanied by massacres and population transfer of unprecedented scope raged in Anatolia. The large-scale violence did not come to an end until the Treaty of Lausanne in 1923, which stabilized, at least temporarily, the post-imperial conflict in south-east Europe and Asia Minor.

But the conflict had dealt a substantial blow even to those empires that emerged victorious. As early as the spring of 1919 Britain was facing major civil unrest in Egypt and the Punjab. By May, British forces were engaged in the opening stages of the Third Afghan War, and Ireland was beginning its descent into an extended period of insurgency that would lead to the establishment of the Irish Free State. The British Empire deployed extreme and widespread violence, including civilian massacres and aerial bombardment to quell revolts in Ireland, India, Iraq, and

---

[7] See Gordon East, "The Concept and Political Status of the Shatter Zone," in N. J. G. Pounds (ed.), *Geographical Essays on Eastern Europe* (Bloomington: Indiana University Press, 1961), and Donald Bloxham, *The Final Solution: A Genocide* (Oxford and New York: Oxford University Press, 2009), 81. For an overview of the ethnic violence attendant on the collapse of the multi-ethnic empires, see Aviel Roshwald, *Ethnic Nationalism and the Fall of Empires: Central Europe, Russia and the Middle East, 1914–1923* (London: Routledge, 2001). For the chaos and violence in the Russian countryside, see Joshua Sanborn, *Drafting the Russian Nation: Military Conscription, Total War, and Mass Politics, 1905–1925* (DeKalb, IL: Northern Illinois University Press, 2003), 170–83. See also Omer Bartov and Eric D Weitz (eds), *Shatterzone of Empire: Coexistence and Violence in the German, Habsburg, Russian and Ottoman Borderlands* (Bloomington: Indiana University Press, 2013).

elsewhere, and they were not alone in doing so. The French fought viciously to beat back fierce resistance to their expanding rule in the Levant and Indochina; the Japanese struggled to contain challenges to their empire on the Korean peninsula, even as they sought to expand their influence deep into Siberia. Indeed, the entire edifice of the imperial world order was convulsing violently in the aftermath of the Armistice even as it reached its greatest territorial extent. The organized mass violence of the war had not ended; it had only shifted its modes and focal points.

MOBILIZING EMPIRES FOR WAR

When Europe went to war in 1914, it was—and had been for centuries—a continent dominated by dynastic empires with vast territorial possessions both within and outside the continent. When the cataclysm of industrial warfare ended, three of these empires had collapsed and faced territorial dissolution, while others were confronted with major problems of what Paul Kennedy called "imperial overstretch." Yet, some of the contestants had faced imperial decline for much longer, notably the Ottoman Empire, under strain since the Eastern Crisis of the 1870s. Drawing on the opportunities provided by the Ottomans' inability to prevent gradual disintegration, Italy—a newcomer on the imperial stage—declared war on the Ottomans in September 1911. Originally conceived as a war to occupy Ottoman provinces in Tripolitania and Cyrenaica, in the tradition of nineteenth-century European colonial conquests, the Italian campaign against the Ottoman forces quickly escalated in intensity, ambition, and geographical scope, fueling racial and religious hatred around the eastern Mediterranean and Balkans.[8]

Just over a year later, on 17 October 1912, Serbia, Montenegro, Greece, and Bulgaria declared war on the Ottoman Empire and achieved a decisive victory.[9] The Balkan Wars had an immediate knock-on effect. When the Balkan League began its war against the Ottoman Empire, challenging the status quo in the Balkans, the Danube Monarchy found itself forced to rethink its Balkan policy. Serbia was the most victorious state with the greatest territorial expansion in both Balkan Wars. After the defeat and withdrawal of the Ottoman Empire from Europe, Austria–Hungary, a multinational state with a slight Slav majority, was concerned that it was the next "sick man" and a target of a future Serbian attack, which helps to explain Vienna's uncompromising position in the July crisis of 1914.

As soon as a wider European war was deemed inevitable, it was clear that all combatants would call upon their imperial subjects to take up arms. For the entire course of the Great War on the Eastern Front, the imperial belligerents fought with multi-ethnic armies in colonized spaces. In August 1914, Russia conducted a general mobilization, calling on reservists to join the army in the west. The composition

[8] On the Italian–Ottoman war, see Timothy Childs, *Italo-Turkish Diplomacy and the War over Libya, 1911–1912* (Leiden: Brill, 1990).
[9] On the Balkan Wars, see Richard Hall, *The Balkan Wars, 1912–1913* (London: Routledge, 2000); and William Mulligan and Dominik Geppert (eds.), *The Wars before the Great War Conflict and International Politics before the Outbreak of the First World War* (Cambridge and New York, 2015).

of the army roughly reflected the country's multi-ethnic make-up. If the ethnic Russian population in the empire in 1897 was about 44 percent of the overall population, Russians contributed an estimated 50 percent (75 percent if one adds together Russians, Ukrainians, and Belorussians) of the vast imperial army, with over 11 million men under arms in 1917, while the rest came from the more than 150 ethnic groups of often less than 5 million people inhabiting the territories of the Romanov Empire.[10]

Russia's principal opponent on the Southern Front, the Ottoman Empire, also relied heavily on the conscription of ethnic and religious minorities, as Mustafa Aksakal demonstrates in his chapter. While the commonly used figure of Arab conscripts is 300,000 (or 10 percent of the total number of men mobilized), more recent estimates suggest that recruits from the empire's Arabic-speaking provinces may have comprised over 26 percent. Furthermore, of the 49,238 men who deserted in Aydın province between August 1914 and June 1916, about 59 percent were Muslim and 41 percent non-Muslim, indicating that the Ottomans drew heavily on their Christian minorities (mainly Greek, Armenian, and Assyrian).[11] Over the course of the war of 1914, however, the state increasingly questioned the loyalty of the empire's non-Muslim and non-Turkish populations, suppressed them violently, and thereby ended the empire's viability.

The war also reinforced inter-ethnic tensions in the Austro-Hungarian Empire, the subject of Peter Haslinger's contribution to this volume and arguably the most ethnically diverse of the land empires, with more than ten ethno-linguistic communities living within its borders.[12] The Habsburg army drafted its soldiers from all of these communities, which, according to the official census of 1910 contained 23% German-speakers, nearly 20% Hungarians, 16% Czechs or Slovaks, almost 10% Poles, and nearly 9% Serbs, Croats, or Bosnians, 8% Ukrainians, 6% Romanians, and a whole host of smaller ethnic communities.[13]

Even the German Imperial Army—seemingly the most ethnically homogenous of all combatants—drew heavily on the country's substantial ethnic and religious minorities, notably those from the borderlands (even if they were rarely used as soldiers in the borderlands they originated from).[14] Excluding the German use of Askaris in Africa and General Lettow-Vorbeck's African carriers (which were a separate force), some 10 percent of the German army was recruited from the minorities, including some 850,000 Poles (6 percent of total manpower),[15]

---

[10] Sanborn, *Drafting the Russian Nation*.

[11] See Mustafa Aksakal, Chapter 1, this volume. See, too, Mehmet Beşikci, *Ottoman Mobilization of Manpower* (Leiden: Brill, 2012).

[12] Helmut Rumpler, "Grenzen der Demokratie im Vielvölkerstaat," in Helmut Rumpler and Peter Urbanitsch (eds), *Die Habsburgermonarchie, 1848–1918*, vii. *Verfassung und Parlamentarismus*, pt I: *Verfassungsrecht, Verfassungswirklichkeit, Zentrale Repräsentativköperschaften* (Vienna: Verlag der Österreichischen Akademie der Wissenschaften, 2000), 1–10, here p. 1.

[13] Robert A. Kann, *Geschichte des Habsburgerreiches 1526 bis 1918* (Vienna and Cologne: Böhlau, 1990), 581.

[14] Leszek Belzyt, *Sprachliche Minderheiten im preußischen Staat 1815–1914: Die preußische Sprachenstatistik in Bearbeitung und Kommentar* (Marburg: Herder-Institut, 1998).

[15] Alexander Watson, "Fighting for Another Fatherland: The Polish Minority in the German Army, 1914–1918," *English Historical Review*, 126 (2011), 1137–66, esp. 1138 n. 6.

400,000–500,000 Alsatians and Lorrainers (3–4 percent),[16] some 100,000 Jews (<1 percent),[17] as well as 26,000 Danes[18] and a small number of Sorbs, Sinti, and Roma.[19] The German case, discussed in Heather Jones's chapter, illustrates that there was more than one way to be an empire: it was the only one of the combatants to define itself as both a European land empire, significantly enlarged after the Treaty of Brest-Litovsk, and an overseas empire with global ambitions.

As the European land empires mobilized their multi-ethnic imperial troops in early August 1914, the British and French also called upon their empires to assist in the war effort. In 1914, London and Paris controlled the two largest colonial empires in the world, and they would draw on them extensively during the war for both human and material resources. For France, the empire played an integral role in its efforts and ability to fight a war against Germany. The war was a testing ground for General Mangin's plea for the mobilization of "la force noire," a large reserve of African troops to counter France's demographic disadvantage vis-à-vis Germany.[20] In addition to the 90,000 *troupes indigènes* already under arms when the war started, France recruited between 1914 and 1918 nearly 500,000 colonial troops, including 166,000 West Africans, 46,000 Madagascans, 50,000 Indochinese (plus an additional 50,000 laborers from this French colony), 140,000 Algerians, 47,000 Tunisians, and 24,300 Moroccans.[21] Most of these French colonial troops served in Europe.

As Richard Fogarty demonstrates in his chapter, mobilization of imperial resources included not only manpower reserves but also the drawing on the economic and financial resources of the colonies. And the total contribution—measured in tons of goods, francs, laborers, and soldiers—loomed even larger in the French imagination than mere numbers would suggest. In the cultural mobilization that was so important in this all-consuming conflict, the colonies were especially visible, and the war also left deep imprints upon the empire itself and its peoples. In the end, although it was the Second World War that truly inaugurated the process of decolonization, this earlier war played a significant role in destabilizing French rule in its overseas possessions, and in undermining the colonial relationships upon which that rule rested.

[16] Christoph Jahr, *Gewöhnliche Soldaten. Desertion und Deserteure im deutschen und britischen Heer 1914–1918* (Göttingen: Vandenhoeck & Ruprecht, 1998); Alan Kramer, "Wackes at War: Alsace-Lorraine and the Failure of German National Mobilization, 1914–1918," in John Horne (ed.), *State, Society and Mobilization in Europe during the First World War* (Cambridge: Cambridge University Press, 1997), 105–21.

[17] Jacob Segall, *Die deutschen Juden als Soldaten im Kriege 1914–1918* (Berlin: Philo-Verlag, 1922); Tim Grady, *The German–Jewish Soldiers of the First World War in History and Memory* (Liverpool: Liverpool University Press, 2011).

[18] Claus Bundgård Christensen, *Danskere på Vestfronten 1914–1918* (Copenhagen: Gyldendal, 2009).

[19] Hansjörg Riechert, "Im Gleichschritt...: Sinti und Roma in Feldgrau," *Militärische Mitteilungen* 53 (1994), 377–97.

[20] Charles Mangin, *La Force noir* (Paris: Hachette, 1910); Richard Fogarty, *Race and War in France: Colonial Subjects in the French Army, 1914–1918* (Baltimore, MD: Johns Hopkins University Press, 2008), 15–54.

[21] Fogarty, *Race and War in France*, 27.

The same applies to the British Empire, although in a more uneven way, as the two chapters by Bill Nasson and Stephen Garton suggest. Garton's chapter focuses on those parts of the empire that contributed the most considerable manpower, financial, and material resources to the war effort: the Dominions, and particularly Canada, Australia, and New Zealand, as well as Ireland and India (the latter proving a particularly rich source of manpower, as approximately 1.4 million men were enlisted up to December 1919). The chapter examines the impact and consequences of participation on these parts of the empire and explores the social, political, and cultural tensions that emerged around mobilization for war, tracing the gradual transition from "innocent enthusiasm" to increasing ambivalence and even outright resistance to the war effort.

Britain's initial mobilization of African troops, by contrast, was relatively modest, and it led to somewhat different results, as Bill Nasson's chapter attests. Following the pre-war template laid out by the Committee of Imperial Defence, governors and their military advisors looked first to the security of their own colonies and then to seizing Germany's African ports and wireless stations in Togoland (Togo), Kamerun (Cameroon), German South-West Africa (Namibia), and German East Africa (Tanzania). The initial focus of British colonial mobilization was to raise sufficient local forces to seize the coastal regions of German Africa as rapidly as possible. This appeared to be a relatively easy proposition in southern Africa, where Louis Botha, the first Prime Minister of the new Union of South Africa, gladly accepted London's "invitation" to seize strategic points in German South-West Africa in September 1914.

But the often arbitrary recruitment practices in British Africa led to at times violent resistance.[22] In South Africa, too, resistance flared up, spurred by the deep resentment that many Afrikaners still felt towards the British Empire after the Boer Wars.[23] The vast majority of Africans recruited during the First World War were not, however, combat troops. Instead, they served as laborers or carriers in the African theater of war. Up to 200,000 of them died (mostly as a result of diseases such as Malaria and the most fatal of wartime illnesses, dysentery, rather than combat), and among the laborers serving in Africa the death rates may have been as high as 20 percent.[24]

Matters were somewhat more straightforward with regards to the white settler dominions. When London declared war in 1914, it did not see fit to consult Dominion prime ministers. Yet, most dominion leaders and commentators enthusiastically embraced the call to arms, pledging to support Britain down to the "last man and the

---

[22] G. Shepperson and T. Price, *Independent Africa* (Edinburgh: Edinburgh University Press, 1958), 235.

[23] Bill Nasson, *Springboks on the Somme: South Africa in the Great War, 1914–1918* (Johannesburg: Penguin Books, 2007).

[24] Strachan, *First World War*, 497; Melvin E. Page, "Black Men in a White Men's War," in Melvin E. Page (ed.), *Africa and the First World War* (Basingstoke: Macmillan, 1987), 14. Richard Fogarty and David Killingray, "Demobilization in British and French West Africa at the End of the First World War," *Journal of Contemporary History* 50 (2015), 100–123.

last shilling" or in Canada the "last dollar."[25] Canada, South Africa, Australia, New Zealand, and Newfoundland contributed some 1.3 million men to the British war effort.[26] In proportionate terms, New Zealand made one of the largest contributions in the British Empire (with 5 percent of its men aged 15–49 killed), while Australia (with 300,000 troops sent overseas, of whom 60,000 were killed and 150,000 returned wounded, disabled, ill, and psychologically scarred) suffered a casualty rate of nearly two-thirds—the highest of any force serving the Allies.[27]

Mobilization in a colonial context was delicate. Though the British Empire had regularly used colonial troops in the imperial realm, it had not done so in Europe against other white people. After all, a war fought on both sides with native auxiliaries was likely to undermine the very principle on which colonialism rested: the notion of white racial superiority. If a "colored" man was trained to kill other Europeans, what guarantee was there that he would not one day attack his own colonial masters? However, after the heavy casualties suffered by the British Expeditionary Corps in August 1914, two Indian divisions were diverted to France. The French, for their part, had to persuade the men of North Africa to make war on Germany, a country with which they had no quarrel, in defense of an empire that had reduced them to second-class citizens in their own homelands. The task was made all the more difficult by German propaganda that played on Islamic loyalties to turn the Muslims of North Africa against the French.[28] Still, in France imperial troops were used in Europe right from the start. The North African troops were dispatched to the Belgian frontier, where they first saw battle in Charleroi on 21 August. Battalions of 1,200 infantrymen were cut down to less than 500 in a single day's fighting—initial casualty rates ran to 60 percent dead and wounded. In all, some 6,500 North African soldiers died between August and December 1914 alone, and thousands more were wounded.[29]

Imperial mobilization became ever more central to the Allies' war effort from 1915 onwards. After losing decisive battles against the Germans on the Eastern Front, a decree of 25 June 1916 called upon previously exempt men from Central Asia to serve in labor battalions, sparking unrest and resistance throughout the region. For Britain, too, mobilizing imperial manpower became a greater strategic necessity. Having suffered nearly half a million casualties at the Battle of the

---

[25] The "last shilling" reference was made in a speech by Andrew Fisher, leader of the Australian Labor Party, and soon to be prime minister, on 31 July 1914. The "last dollar" comment was made by popular Canadian Prairie novelist C. W. Gordon, quoted in John Herd Thompson, *The Harvests of War: The Prairie West 1914–18* (Toronto, McLelland and Stewart, 1978), 32.

[26] Figures quoted in Santanu Das, *Race, Empire and First World War Writing* (Cambridge: Cambridge University Press, 2011), 4.

[27] Stephen Garton, "Demobilization and Empire: Empire Nationalism and Soldier Citizenship in Australia after World War I," *Journal of Contemporary History* 50 (2015), 124–143.

[28] Jacques Frémeaux, *Les Colonies dans la Grande Guerre: Combats et épreuves des peuples d'Outre-Mer* (Paris: 14–18 Éditions, 2006); Leonard V. Smith, Stéphane Audoin-Rouzeau, and Annette Becker, *France and the Great War* (Cambridge: Cambridge University Press, 2003); Alice Conklin, *A Mission to Civilize: France and West Africa, 1895–1930* (Stanford: Stanford University Press, 1997); Fogarty, *Race and War in France*.

[29] Gilbert Meynier, *L'Algérie révélée: La Guerre de 1914–1918 et le premier quart du XXème siècle* (Geneva: Librairie Droz, 1981), 271–4.

Somme in 1916, and faced with imperial commitments stretching from India to Mesopotamia to the Dardanelles, the coalition government in London broke with the revered English tradition of voluntary military service and introduced universal conscription in Britain in March 1916. London's attempt to convince Ireland and the self-governing white dominions to follow suit sparked intensive political controversy and met with limited success. Under these circumstances, raising more troops became paramount, which led imperial strategists to reconsider their views on the military value of subject Africans. In many of the colonies, there was a political calculation on the part of those who chose to enlist or those who encouraged others to do so. Leaders of the Indian National Congress or many "Home Rulers" in Ireland supported the war in the hope of greater political autonomy, perhaps even national independence. Mohandas K. Gandhi, who returned to India in 1915 from his long sojourn in South Africa, famously campaigned to recruit his fellow Indians to fight for the empire, in the hope that their participation in the imperial war effort would place India within the imperial structure on a par with the white dominions and advance its claim for home rule. London encouraged this line of thinking, making wartime promises of a greater participation of Indians in their own government.[30] This strategy of promising some measure of post-war self-determination in exchange for wartime support was applied elsewhere as well, most famously perhaps in the incompatible wartime promises made to Arabs and Jews over the disposition of Ottoman Palestine.[31]

Nor was this logic limited to formal colonial contexts. As Xu Guoqi shows in his chapter, newly republican China also came to see support for the Allied war effort as the price for a seat at the table in the post-war settlement and a place as an equal within international society. Beginning in summer 1915, Beijing allowed the Allies to recruit as many as 140,000 Chinese laborers to the European front, and in 1917, despite weakness and internal division, the Chinese Republic officially joined the war on the Allied side. In this respect, the war proved a great disappointment for many who had hoped to parlay support for the Allied war effort into advances in claims for self-government. This result set the stage of anti-colonial conflict for decades to come, not least in making the radical promises of the Bolshevik Revolution in Russia all the more attractive for those seeking to throw off the colonial yoke.

DISMANTLING EMPIRES, EXPANDING EMPIRES

The announcement of the Armistice on 11 November 1918 augured a new world of sharp contradictions. Empires both disintegrated and expanded, and, while violence ended on the Western Front and in some other theaters, it continued unabated and sometimes even intensified elsewhere. This was notably the case in the

[30] See Shane Ryland, "Edwin Montagu in India, 1917–1918: Politics of the Montagu–Chelmsford Report," *South Asia*, 3 (1973), 79–92.
[31] See, e.g., David Fromkin, *A Peace to End All Peace: Creating the Modern Middle East, 1914–1922* (New York: Henry Holt, 1989).

former lands of the Russian Empire, which, as Joshua Sanborn's chapter argues, experienced a moment of "decolonization" when the imperial structure, flawed but relatively stable in 1914, collapsed as a result of the Great War. The crisis of empire began in 1914, when the imposition of martial law in the borderlands crippled governmental authority and led to profound insecurity for the many different ethnic groups living in these war zones, and intensified with the military defeats of 1915 and the massive anti-colonial rebellion that rocked all of tsarist Central Asia the following year, and as the political elites turned on one another. Decolonization culminated in the revolutionary year of 1917. New plans for the structure of the state proliferated, eventually leading to movements for autonomy and/or independence in all of the imperial borderlands.

As a consequence of imperial collapse and the rise and clash of violent Bolshevik and anti-Bolshevik movements, an extensive arc of post-war violence stretched from Finland and the Baltic States through Russia and Ukraine, Poland, Austria, Hungary, Germany, all the way through the Balkans into Anatolia, the Caucasus, and the Middle East, and even Czechoslovakia, long thought to be an island of peace, experienced significant inter-ethnic tensions and violence. The death toll of the period between the Great War's official end in 1918 and the Treaty of Lausanne in 1923 was extraordinary: including those killed in the Russian Civil War, well over four million people lost their lives as a result of civil wars or inter-ethnic struggles, not counting the millions of expellees and refugees that fled the havoc unleashed in Eastern and Central Europe.[32]

In imperial domains beyond Europe post-war violence, while not nearly as massive as it was on the Continent, was nevertheless widespread. Indeed, the years immediately after the war saw widespread upheaval across much of the Middle East and Asia. In Egypt, the "1919 Revolution" that erupted against British influence in the spring following the Armistice included mass street protests in the cities and widespread acts of sabotage in rural areas, targeting telegraph lines and other symbols of imperial authority. Egyptian nationalists, who saw the peace conference as an opportunity to be rid of British meddling, grew frustrated as their hopes for a hearing evaporated and mobilized forcefully against the British presence. Though London managed to stave off the internationalization of the Egyptian question, the continuing instability eventually led it to give Egypt its independence unilaterally in 1922, while keeping for itself the "core interests" of defence and the Suez Canal. But Egyptian nationalists grew increasingly assertive in the post-war years, and a tense relationship persisted until the final liquidation of British power in Egypt in 1956.[33]

In India, too, the spring of 1919 saw widespread disturbances, as Gandhi and others mobilized Indians against Westminster's decision to extend wartime emergency measures into peacetime, an imperial effort to stem resistance that begat greater resistance still. The killing of hundreds of unarmed protesters who

---

[32] Robert Gerwarth and John Horne (eds), *War in Peace: Paramilitary Violence after the Great War* (Oxford and New York: Oxford University Press, 2012).

[33] Selma Botman, "The Liberal Age, 1923–195," in M. W. Daly, *The Cambridge History of Egypt*, ii. *Modern Egypt* (Cambridge: Cambridge University Press, 1998).

broke curfew in the Panjabi city of Amritsar became a rallying cry and a focal point of nationalist resistance. As in Egypt, the British authorities sought to play on the divisions among Indians to retain their influence for a while longer, but they could not restore the illusion of imperial harmony and legitimacy that had surrounded the Delhi Durbar of 1911, held to mark the coronation of George V as the sovereign of India. When the Indian National Congress renounced the pursuit of Dominion status and adopted independence as its official goal in 1930, it brought to the center of politics a position that, until 1914, had been articulated only on the far margins of Indian political discourse.[34]

As Britain's imperial managers strained to restore order and contain cascading crises across their old domains, they also struggled to shape and control the new territories they had acquired as a result of the war, especially those detached from the defunct Ottoman Empire and awarded to the British Empire under the novel arrangement of the League of Nations mandate. The question of Palestine seemed—for the time being—relatively manageable, but efforts to reconcile the wartime commitments made to London's French and Arab allies and the concurrent need to find an instrument of control for the newly acquired, oil-rich mandate territory of Iraq, led to the ingenious idea of installing the Hijazi prince Faysal ibn Husayn, recently run out of his homeland by the rival House of Sa'ud and shortly thereafter out of Syria by the French, as monarch over Mesopotamia. That move, along with the brutal application of newly developed British airpower to suppress restive tribal revolts, managed to stabilize the situation in the mandate by the early 1920s, at least for a time.[35]

The French mandates proved even more troublesome in the interwar period, as did other parts of the French Empire: serious uprisings against French colonial rule in the interwar period included the Rif War (1925–6), the Syrian revolt (1925–30), the Kongo-Wara rebellion in French Equatorial Africa (1928–31), and the Yen Bay mutiny in Indochina (1930–1).[36] It is clear that the encounter of colonial workers and *troupes* with Europe's competing political, social, and economic ideologies (socialism, syndicalism, and communism among them) began to have an effect in many French colonies. Wilson's call for self-determination famously inspired Ho Chi Minh to enquire about the concept's applicability to colonial possessions outside Europe. In Africa, meanwhile, prominent political figures like Blaise Diagne exploited the rhetoric and ideals of French universalism and egalitarianism to carve out an enhanced role for non-white people within the French Empire, while French possessions in North Africa grew increasingly restive in the course of the 1920s.

---

[34] D. A. Low (ed.), *Congress and the Raj: Facets of the Indian Struggle, 1917–1947* (London: Heinemann, 1977).

[35] Priya Satia, "The Defense of Inhumanity: Air Control and the British Idea of Arabia," *American Historical Review*, 111 (2006), 16–51.

[36] See Martin Thomas, *The French Empire between the Wars: Imperialism, Politics and Society* (Manchester: Manchester University Press, 2005), 211–44.

Certainly, the vast majority of African veterans did not rise against their colonial masters.[37] But, if *troupes indigènes* did not provide a constituency for the organization of anti-colonial violence, it was not because these men were satisfied in the happy enjoyment of increasing rights and acceptance under a progressive and humanitarian French republican colonialism. First of all, there were practical obstacles to paramilitary mobilization. Once demobilized and thrust back into colonial societies, these men resumed their places in a social and political hierarchy that was profoundly more racist and rigid than that of the metropole or the army, and where the mechanisms of social and political control were more or less well developed and deployed by vigilant and suspicious colonial governments assiduous in the use of racial and legal controls to uphold white "prestige."[38] Where rebellions did occur, they invariably met a ruthless response. The French army and colonial authorities deployed overwhelming force against the four major rebellions of the interwar period, making use, like the British, of the latest military technology, such as air power, gas, and tanks, as well as superior numbers, firepower, communications, and logistics.

The British and French were not the only empires struggling to consolidate territorial gains and revive the legitimacy of imperial rule in the immediate post-war years. Japan's leaders fought successfully in Paris to retain their wartime gains of territory and other concessions in China, obtaining the recognition of the other Allied powers of their takeover of former German territories in Shandong Province. At the same time they brutally suppressed the widespread resistance associated with the March First Movement in their colony of Korea, a movement that erupted in the spring of 1919, inspired in part by Wilsonian rhetoric of self-determination. Despite Korean hopes for US support, however, Washington adopted a studied posture of neutrality on the question of Korea, whose status as a colony it considered a settled matter.[39]

The United States itself, of course, possessed several colonies in this period, territorial legacies of its victory in the Spanish–American War of 1898. Though Washington had already moved further than other colonial powers in allowing native self-government in in the Philippines and Puerto Rico, during the war years US forces occupied both Haiti and the Dominican Republic and also conducted several incursions into Mexican territory, even as Washington consolidated quasi-protectorates in Cuba, Nicaragua, and elsewhere in the Caribbean. As Christopher Capozzola shows in his chapter, though the United States did not recruit many colonial troops to fight in Europe, it did develop during those years an approach to policing its growing domains that would shape it relationships with colonies and quasi-colonies for decades to come. At the same time, Woodrow Wilson and

[37] Gregory Mann, *Native Sons: West African Veterans and France in the Twentieth Century* (Durham, NC: Duke University Press, 2006).

[38] Emmanuelle Saada, "The Empire of Law: Dignity, Prestige, and Domination in the 'Colonial Situation'," *French Politics, Culture and Society*, 20/2 (Summer 2002), 98–120. See also her *Empire's Children: Race, Filiation, and Citizenship in the French Colonies* (Chicago: University of Chicago Press, 2012).

[39] Manela, *The Wilsonian Moment*, 197–214.

his successors began to imagine a far more ambitious American imperium, a global imperium of nation states interlocked in a system of international organizations and governed by the principles of free trade. In this new order the United States would serve as first among equals, and within it US economic (and later, military) preponderance would sustain Washington's hegemony globally. Hence the US pursuit of a new order in East Asia, a goal at least temporarily achieved with the Washington Conference of 1922, which sought to stabilize the post-war order in the "Far East" in much the same way that Lausanne would do in the "Near East" the following year.

As Leonard Smith demonstrates in the final chapter of this book, empires constituted both problems and solutions at the Paris Peace Conference. The disintegration of the Habsburg Monarchy, Imperial Russia, and the Ottoman Empire created a vacuum of sovereignty in Central and Eastern Europe, and in the Middle East. The Wilsonian discursive framework accepted by the Great Powers at the time of the Armistice with Germany in November 1918 legitimized self-determined nation states as the successors to empire. As peacemaking continued beyond what had been the Western Front, the imperial Great Powers proved less and less able to control the peace being made. Imperial expansion through League of Nations mandates laid the foundations for restive successor states. By the time of the settlement in Anatolia in 1923, successor states sharply demarcated the limits of imperial authority.

Even the relationship between the white dominions and the British Empire had fundamentally changed. The dominions claimed a place at the conference in their own right and fought for their own interests.[40] Nonetheless the form of post-war nationalism in the settler dominions varied. For Canada and South Africa the pressing problem of appeasing large, disgruntled non-British ethnic communities, further embittered by the war, drove the mobilization of nationalist sentiment, as the ideological glue to keep these fragile polities together in the immediate post-war years. In both these dominions nationalism was articulated around a move away from the empire—more republican, self-sufficient, and grounded in a sense of cultural difference from the British.[41] In Australia and New Zealand post-war nationalism was equally strong, but in contrast oriented around the twin themes of national maturity and empire loyalty. Far from nationalism being the antithesis of empire, as in other settler dominions, in Australia and New Zealand nation and empire were inextricably linked.[42]

The geographical coverage of this volume reflects our ambition to restore the Great War's character as a *world* war, to give due attention to combatant empires

[40] See L. F. Fitzhardinge, "William Morris Hughes," in Bede Nairn and Geoffrey Serle (eds), *Australian Dictionary of Biography*, ix. *1891–1939* (Melbourne: Melbourne University Press, 1983), 393–400.

[41] M. S. Careless, *Canada: A Story of Challenge* (London: Cambridge University Press, 1953), 339–46.

[42] See, e.g., Stephen Garton, *The Cost of War: Australians Return* (Melbourne: Melbourne University Press, 1996), Joy Damousi, *The Labour of Loss: Mourning, Memory and Wartime Bereavement in Australia* (Melbourne: Melbourne University Press, 1999), and Marina Larrson, *Shattered Anzacs: Living with the Scars of War* (Seattle: University of Washington Press, 2009).

that usually receive little attention in general histories of the Great War, such as Portugal. As Filipe Ribeiro de Meneses argues, the young Portuguese republic held on tenuously to considerable imperial domains, which it was financially and economically unable to exploit. Even before the country entered the war, in March 1916, considerable fighting had already occurred in its principal African possessions, Angola and Mozambique, both with a number of local ethnicities and with the European-led garrisons of neighbouring German colonies. Once Portugal had become a belligerent, however, the situation worsened considerably: over two-thirds of Portugal's fatal war-related casualties were incurred in Africa, and the death toll among the indigenous population was incalculably higher. Serious questions were asked at the Paris Peace Conference about Portugal's suitability as a colonizer under the new Wilsonian dispensation. Nevertheless, the African campaigns were seen and commemorated in the metropole as part of the struggle against Germany and therefore as an essential component of Portugal's right to empire.

Italy is another important if often overlooked practitioner of imperial warfare in this period, as Richard Bosworth and Giuseppe Finaldi show in their chapter. Widely seen as the least of the Great Powers and yet compelled to measure itself against the imperial ghosts of ancient Rome, the "Third Italy" joined the race for empire when and where it could. Though the result was an empire of "rags and patches," the Italian invasion of Ottoman Libya in 1911 augured the road to war, and the Italian Empire was also represented in the war in Europe. African troops, enrolled in Eritrea and Italian Somalia, were part of the national military. From 1915 to 1918 the Italian military tried, often ineffectually and frequently brutally, to shore up their shaky rule in Libya, while all sensible tacticians demanded that the country focus its power in Europe. Once the European war had been won, Italy returned to its "pacification" of the "fourth shore," killing perhaps 100,000 indigenes under the Fascist dictatorship that took control in Rome in October 1922.

The Great War was a war of empires, fought primarily by empires and for the survival or expansion of empire. Ironically, perhaps, it delivered a debilitating blow to dynastic empires—for centuries the pre-eminent type of state organization—and to imperial expansion and acquisition as the main logic of relations between states in world affairs. None of the three dynastic empires on the side of the Central Powers survived the war in its pre-war form, and all of them (and their constituent parts, at least within Europe) were reorganized after the war into one republican form or another, even while sometimes preserving the territorial forms and usually some form of the oppressive practices of their imperial predecessors in new guises. The empires on the Allied side—with the notable and significant exception of Russia—managed to survive and even expanded their imperial territories. A war fought for the "rights of small nations", however, could not but undermine severely the legitimacy of imperial formations and strain the relations of imperial centers with even the most enthusiastic of imperial peripheries—namely the British Crown's "white dominions." It was not simply that equality in sacrifice implied equality in status and rights—after all, "peripheral" populations had been fighting for empires for millennia without expecting, or receiving, such a reward. It was that the logic of popular rule, which argued that political legitimacy derived not from divine sanction but from the people, had finally, after a long and arduous process, achieved near universal recognition. The argument from civilization, the imperial scoundrel's last redoubt, drowned in the ocean of blood that flowed in the battlefields, even—especially—in the empires' most "civilized" European provinces.

The post-war violence that wracked the territories of most of the participants, both winners and losers, was in part a struggle over the remnants of fallen empires. But it also reflected the crisis of imperial legitimacy ignited by the war and its aftermath. The spectacular appearance of President Wilson on the international stage, with his talk of self-determination and the rights of small nations, and the yet uncertain but growing specter of revolution in Russia and elsewhere in Eastern and Central Europe together made for a volatile mix of ideas, examples, and potential sources of support for the enemies of empire everywhere. The global movement of information and ideas, its pace quickened by the war and recent technological and institutional development, meant that the anti-imperial contagion spread quickly. By 1923, even as the United States retreated off the global stage for the moment, networks of communist organizers, emboldened by the support of the now consolidated regime in Moscow, set about establishing the organizational structure for revolution against empire across the colonial world. Meanwhile, the former European territories of the Habsburgs, in an often bloody and generally chaotic process whose general direction was nevertheless quite clear, were established as nation states. Across the world, the imperial state as a form of territorial governance was under attack and in retreat, while the nation state was on the rise. And, while it took another several decades and an even more destructive war between 1937 and 1945 to usher the process of imperial dissolution toward completion, the Greater War of 1911–23 was a crucial watershed in that process.

1

The Ottoman Empire

Mustafa Aksakal

'A LESS ABRUPT AND UNFORTUNATE END'

Was the Ottoman Empire in its final decade 'a largely successful experiment in multi-nationalism that was destroyed by the great powers in World War I'?[1] Or was it a failing state, one that took out loans it could not repay, oppressed its subjects, violated its non-Muslim populations, and stoked their desire for independence, thereby precipitating Great Power intervention and paving the empire's road to destruction? Or, as has been argued, had the Ottoman Empire, 'like the other multi-national, multi-religious empires', simply 'become an anachronism', an empire whose leaders embraced 'the inevitable' and decided 'to abandon the idea of empire and settle for a national republic'?[2] Perhaps, as has also been suggested, the empire's demise from 1850 on was an 'unavoidable failure' because of its comparative industrial disadvantage, its relatively small population (and hence military manpower), prized geostrategic location, and its multi-ethnicity in an age when political legitimacy depended on appeals to nationalism.[3] Halide Edib, the Ottoman novelist, feminist thinker, government official, and military officer, writing in 1928, reflected on the Ottomans' end, in terms that only hinted at the human catastrophe that had taken place:

[In October 1918,] I was conscious that the Ottoman Empire had fallen with a crash, and that it was not only the responsible Unionist leaders who were buried beneath the crushing weight of it. Though disintegration had begun nearly a century before, and though I firmly believe that, war or no war, the empire would have been doomed anyhow, yet with the aid of a far-sighted policy, there might have resulted a less abrupt and unfortunate end. But at that the absolute finality of the death of the empire was an unavoidable fact.[4]

---

[1] Donald Quataert, review of Kemal H. Karpat, *The Politicization of Islam: Reconstructing Identity, State, Faith, and Community in the Late Ottoman Empire* (New York: Oxford University Press, 2001), *American Historical Review*, 107 (October 2002), 1328.

[2] Feroz Ahmad, 'The Late Ottoman Empire', in Marian Kent (ed.), *The Great Powers and the End of the Ottoman Empire*, 2nd edn (London: Frank Cass, 1996), 5.

[3] Erik J. Zürcher, 'The Ottoman Empire 1850–1922: Unavoidable Failure?' in Zürcher, *The Young Turk Legacy and Nation-Building: From the Ottoman Empire to Atatürk's Turkey* (London: I. B. Tauris, 2010), 59–72.

[4] Halide Edib, *The Turkish Ordeal: Being the Further Memoirs of Halidé Edib* (New York: Century Co., 1928), 3.

The answers to all these questions depend on the sources one interrogates. Listening to largely European diplomatic accounts, historians might reach the conclusion that it was the empire's own mismanagement that assured its end. When Ottoman sources are privileged, a different picture tends to emerge, one in which the empire appears as a 'Victim of European Imperialism', always groaning under the predatory practices of the European Great Powers that sought its partition, in a game known as the 'Eastern Question', ever since Catherine the Great set her eyes on 'Tsargrad' (that is, Constantinople/Istanbul) and Napoleon Bonaparte declared that whoever possesses Constantinople could govern the world.

These opposite views of the empire were held by contemporary observers throughout the nineteenth century down to the First World War, and they have shaped assessments by historians since. This chapter is not the place to resolve this dichotomy, but I raise the issue here because it is implicit to any interpretation of the empire's final years. It should be noted briefly that neither the 'Ottoman failed state' nor the 'Victim of European Imperialism' paradigm can explain the empire's end. Even before the onset of European imperialism, between 1760 and 1830 the empire experienced a period of 'do-or-die' existence.[5] The appearance of ethnic nationalism in the Ottoman Empire, moreover, cannot be attributed to European intrigue alone; nationalism and the trend towards the nation state were global phenomena and not unique to the Ottoman Empire.[6] It is also beyond question, however, that European intervention on behalf of the empire's Christian populations politicized Muslim–Christian relations across the Ottoman lands in ways that fuelled ethnic and religious violence.

This chapter traces the empire's main developments without taking its final demise in 1923 as a foregone conclusion. It treats the empire's leaders and its peoples as actors on their own stage, operating under the conditions of war and, after 1915, total war. This chapter, in Halide Edib's Words, is about the empire's 'abrupt and unfortunate end'.

A CURIOUS EVENT THAT HAPPENED ON THE WAY TO TARSUS

As Archduke Franz Ferdinand prepared to visit Sarajevo in late June 1914, an unusual incident put the people of Tarsus, an Ottoman town over a thousand miles to the east, near Adana, into panic mode. Gendarmerie headquarters there had received a delivery of sealed mail from the imperial government in Istanbul. The accompanying instruction said the mailbag should be opened only at the time of mobilization. But the bag had been unfastened nonetheless, revealing mobilization orders to be sent to all surrounding villages. Not surprisingly, the inadvertent news

---

[5] Virginia H. Aksan, *Ottoman Wars, 1700–1870: An Empire Besieged* (New York: Pearson Longman, 2007), 7.

[6] Andreas Wimmer, *Waves of War: Nationalism, State Formation, and Ethnic Exclusion in the Modern World* (Cambridge: Cambridge University Press, 2013), 1–5.

flash unleashed confusion and rumours of impending conscription and war.[7] Why did Istanbul take measures for mobilization in late June 1914, days *before* a 19-year-old Bosnian Serb slayed the Habsburg archduke and his wife, and *before* it became apparent that the couple's murder would result in war between Austria–Hungary and Serbia, and perhaps a general, worldwide war? Was the Ottoman state predisposed to war, as reflected in the Tarsus authorities' premature announcement of the conscription orders? Or was this simply a bureaucratic lapse in a routine procedure to which no great significance should be ascribed?

When Austria–Hungary declared war on Serbia on 28 July 1914—and Germany on Russia, France, and Belgium within a week's time—the Ottomans' imperial foundations were still shaking from a series of major domestic and international crises, and three wars since 1911 alone. While the Ottoman dynasty survived until 1922, outlasting the ruling houses of the Habsburgs, Hohenzollerns, and Romanovs, millions of the Ottoman peoples, mostly civilians, did not. The House of Osman had ruled the Ottoman domains since about 1299. It had first established itself in the northern and western parts of Anatolia, before moving into south-eastern Europe in the fourteenth century and conquering the eastern Arab lands in the first quarter of the sixteenth. At that point the Ottoman sultan also arrogated to himself the title of caliph, the pinnacle of the world's Muslims. The last sultan of the House of Osman, Mehmed VI, was sent into exile in 1922, followed by the proclamation of the Turkish Republic on 29 October 1923—nine years to the day after the Ottoman Black Sea naval attack on Russia that thrust the empire into the world war. The caliphate was abolished in March 1924. Mehmed VI's burial in Damascus, outside the borders of Ataturk's republic, symbolized the new regime's efforts at excising the Ottoman past from the new Turkey.

The life story of Franz Ferdinand's assassin, Gavrilo Princip, intertwined with the empire's life story. Princip had been born in Ottoman Bosnia in 1894. He, and the organization for which he carried out the attack, *Young Bosnia*, was demanding Bosnia's union with Serbia, a state that had gained its formal independence from the Ottoman Empire in 1878, but without Princip's Bosnia. Instead, Bosnia, along with Herzegovina, had been first occupied in 1878, and then, in 1908, annexed, by the Habsburgs.

THE OTTOMAN SPRING AND THE WARS OF 1911–1913

The Ottoman constitutional revolution of July 1908 resulted in empire-wide elections and the first parliament since 1878, ushering in a brief Ottoman spring. 'The country at once sprang to life', reported a young Russian correspondent in *Pravda*, Leon Trotsky, in December 1908.[8] The 1908 'popular revolution from above'[9]

---

[7] BOA, DH.EUM.EMN 85/18, 12 Haziran 1330 (25 June 1914), and 15 Haziran 1330 (28 June 1914).

[8] Leon Trotsky, *The Balkan Wars, 1912–13: The War Correspondence of Leon Trotsky*, trans. Brian Pearce, ed. George Weissman and Duncan Williams (New York: Nonad Press, 1980), 4.

[9] Nader Sohrabi, *Revolution and Constitutionalism in the Ottoman Empire and Iran* (Cambridge: Cambridge University Press, 2011), 114.

initially looked a lot like a military coup, but the momentary opening demonstrated the potential of the empire's political viability.[10] Mass rallies and festivities
celebrated the event. Deputies elected to the parliament represented the various
parts of the empire. A multitude of new organizations, clubs, and newspapers advocated unity and conciliation among the empire's ethnic groups (Ottomanism),
and decentralization.[11] According to Fırka-i İbad, an Ottomanist political party,
'today the government of Turkey [*Türkiye hükümeti*] and the Ottoman nation con-
sists of Turkish, Arab, Albanian, Kurdish, Armenian, Greek Orthodox [*Rum*],
Jewish, Bulgarian, and other many different elements. All elements are in unity
and alliance with each other.'[12] However, those who launched the coup and forced
the proclamation of the constitution—the Committee of Union and Progress—
showed little commitment to democratic politics. Large-scale ethnic violence in
Adana and political assassinations, including those of journalists, belied the hopes
of 1908. By 1911, popular support for the new government headed by the Committee of Union and Progress had waned rapidly, and parliamentary strength
shifted towards the new Freedom and Entente Party.[13]

In September of that year, Italy attacked and occupied Ottoman Tripoli in
North Africa (Libya), with little cause other than a desire for empire, prompting
protests against the injustice across Ottoman lands and beyond.[14] To put down the
ensuing local resistance, Italian authorities publicly hanged fourteen of the agitators. In Izmir, an emotional play decried the Italian attack and galvanized popular
support.[15] In the hope to attract European diplomatic backing, Ottoman politicians
and scholars of international law pointed to the illegitimacy of the Italian action,
without much success.[16] A year later, in October 1912, while still at war with Italy,
Istanbul faced yet another military crisis. A combined army of Bulgarian, Greek,
Montenegrin, and Serbian troops seized the three Ottoman European provinces of
Kosovo, Manastır, and Salonica, amidst great atrocities committed against civilians

[10] Y. Doğan Cetinkaya, '1908 Devrimi ve Toplumsal Seferberlik', in Ferdan Ergut (ed.), *II. Meşrutiyet'i
Yeniden Düşünmek* (Istanbul: Tarih Vakfı, 2010), 13.

[11] Michelle U. Campos, *Ottoman Brothers: Muslims, Christians, and Jews in Early Twentieth-Century
Palestine* (Stanford: Stanford University Press, 2011); Ilham Khuri-Makdisi, *The Eastern Mediterranean
and the Making of Global Radicalism, 1860–1914* (Berkeley and Los Angeles: University of California
Press, 2010).

[12] Quoted in Gökhan Kaya, *II. Meşrutiyet Döneminin Demokratları: Osmanlı Demokrat Fırkası
(Fırka-i İbad)* (Istanbul: İletişim, 2011), 199.

[13] Ali Birinci, *Hürriyet ve İtilâf Fırkası: II. Meşrutiyet Devrinde İttihat ve Terakki'ye Karşı Çıkanlar*
(Istanbul: Dergâh Yayınları, 1990), 72.

[14] Timothy W. Childs, *Italo-Turkish Diplomacy and the War over Libya, 1911–1912* (New York: Brill,
1990), 36. For responses outside the empire, see Firoozeh Kashani-Sabet, *Frontier Fictions: Shaping the
Iranian Nation, 1804–1946* (Princeton: Princeton University Press, 1999), 144; Mohammad Hassan
Kavousi Araghi and Nasrollah Salehi (eds), *Jihadieh: The Holy War Fatwas of the Grand Ulama and
Mujtaheds in World War I* (Tehran: Unit for Documentary Publication, 1997).

[15] Mehmed Sezai, *Cihad-ı Mukaddes yahud Trablusgarb'da Osmanlı-İtalya Cengi* (İzmir: Keşişyan
Matbaası, 1327/1911); Günver Güneş, 'II. Meşrutiyet Döneminde İzmir'de Tiyatro Yaşamı,' *Ankara
Üniversitesi Osmanlı Tarihi Araştırma ve Uygulama Merkezi Dergisi*, 18 (2005), 151–71; Ö. Faruk
Huyugüzel, *İzmir Fikir ve Sanat Adamları (1850–1950)* (Ankara: Kültür Bakanlığı, 2000), 400–1.

[16] Hasan Sırrı, *Hukuk-u Düvvel Nokta-i Nazarında Osmanlı-İtalya Muharebesi* (Kostantiniye:
Matbaa-i Ebüzziya, 1330/1914).

by all sides.[17] In July 1913, during the Second Balkan War, Ottoman troops retook Edirne/Adrianople, a former imperial capital, against the Great Powers' strong admonition. But, despite Edirne's recapture, the empire had now lost territory it had held since the fourteenth century. The empire was also losing its Christian population. Estimates of the Ottoman population put the total (excluding Egypt) for 1872 at around twenty-nine million, with just over half residing in the empire's European territories. In 1872, almost one-half of the population was non-Muslim. By 1906, the population had shrunk to some twenty-one million, with non-Muslims accounting for roughly one-quarter of the total population.[18]

For some the defeat in the Balkan Wars proved beyond doubt the disloyalty of the empire's Christians. Christians had provided one-quarter of the Ottoman forces in the First Balkan War, and it was their performance that had caused defeat, some declared—and not the fact that the Ottoman armies faced vastly larger forces in most theatres.[19] The former Ottoman governor of Salonica—a prominent Ottoman urban centre now also lost—published an open letter, claiming that the empire's Orthodox Christians had not only failed in their military service but also refrained from joining the empire's Muslims in making financial donations to support the war effort.[20] Muslim-owned companies marketed their products in advertisements hostile towards non-Muslim subjects and businesses. After 1912 the designation 'Ottoman' in print advertisement stood 'exclusively' for 'Muslim/Turkish', as one author has argued.[21] In the countryside, townsmen and villagers encountered yet another generation of refugees. They heard first hand the reports of ethnic cleansing from the survivors themselves (see Fig. 1). According to official Ottoman records, 297,918 Muslim refugees arrived in the empire from the Balkans by 1915, a number that possibly rose to as high as 640,000 by 1920.[22]

The man atop the Ottoman military during the years of the First World War, War Minister Enver Pasha (1881–1922), cut his teeth in the guerrilla warfare of Libya and the bloody conflicts in the Balkans (and had been one of the revolutionary officers who overthrew Sultan Abdülhamid II in 1908–9). Enver ('bey' until January 1914, 'pasha' thereafter) and the men around him—many of whom themselves hailed from the Balkans—interpreted these conflicts as Christian

[17] *Report of the International Commission to Inquire into the Causes and Conduct of the Balkan Wars* (Washington: Carnegie Endowment for International Peace, 1914).
[18] Cem Behar, *Osmanlı İmparatorluğu'nun ve Türkiye'nin Nüfusu, 1500–1927* (Ankara: Devlet İstatistik Enstitüsü, 1996), 38, 55–8.
[19] Fikret Adanır, 'Non-Muslims in the Ottoman Army and the Ottoman Defeat in the Balkan War of 1912–1913', in Ronald Grigor Suny, Fatma Müge Göçek, Norman M. Naimark (eds), *A Question of Genocide: Armenians and Turks at the End of the Ottoman Empire* (Oxford: Oxford University Press, 2011), 120; Edward J. Erickson, *Defeat in Detail: The Ottoman Army in the Balkans, 1912–1913* (Westport: Praeger, 2003).
[20] Mustafa Aksakal, *The Ottoman Road to War in 1914: The Ottoman Empire and the First World War* (Cambridge: Cambridge University Press, 2008), 53.
[21] Yavuz Köse, 'Between Protest and Envy: Foreign Companies and Ottoman Muslim Society', in Eleni Gari, M. Erdem Kabadayı, and Christoph K. Neumann (eds), *Popular Protest and Political Participation*, Studies in Honor of Suraiya Faroqhi (Istanbul: Istanbul Bilgi University Press), 265.
[22] Behar, *Osmanlı İmparatorluğu'nun ve Türkiye'nin Nüfusu, 1500–1927*, 62; Onur Yıldırım, *Diplomacy and Displacement: Reconsidering the Turco-Greek Exchange of Populations, 1922–1934* (New York: Routledge, 2006), 89.

Fig. 1. Refugees in Thrace, *c.*1915. The upheaveal of 1911–23 turned millions into refugees and displaced people.

aggression.[23] All sides made use of religious language throughout these conflicts, with the Greek king, for example, claiming that his armies were fighting 'the holy struggle of justice and freedom for the oppressed peoples of the Orient'.[24]

These experiences of violence imbued Enver and large segments of society with a deep sense of victimhood.[25] As one paper put it, 'our honour and our people's dignity cannot be preserved by those old books of international law, but only by war'.[26] Violence, the paper claimed, could be overcome only with even greater violence. Between January and June 1914 some 200,000 Orthodox Christians were expelled from Anatolia's western coastal regions and Thrace.

To others, such as the members of the liberal Freedom and Entente Party, or important figures such as Amir Shakib Arslan and Sati' al-Husri (both of whom played leading roles in pan-Arab nationalism after the war), Ottomanism—the movement emphasizing coexistence of the Ottoman peoples of different religious and ethnic backgrounds within the imperial framework—continued to offer a viable path into the future.[27] In fact, Shakib Arslan, in early 1915, led a unit of

---

[23] M. Şükrü Hanioğlu (ed.), *Kendi Mektuplarında Enver Paşa* (İstanbul: Der Yayınları, 1989), 242.
[24] Quoted in Mark Biondich, *The Balkans: Revolution, War, and Political Violence since 1878* (Oxford: Oxford University Press, 2011), 75.
[25] Enver Pascha, *Um Tripolis* (Munich: Hugo Bruckmann, 1918).
[26] *Ahenk*, 13 October 1912, quoted in Zeki Arıkan, 'Balkan Savaşı ve Kamuoyu', in *Bildiriler: Dördüncü Askeri Tarih Semineri* (Ankara: Genelkurmay Basımevi, 1989), 176.
[27] Shakib Arslan, *Sīrah Dhātīyah* (Beirut: Dār Al-Talī'yah, 1969), 236–92.

Arab volunteers in support of Cemal Pasha's First Suez Canal Campaign against British-held Egypt. For some, Ottomanism still appeared as a viable imperial framework throughout, and even after, the First World War, but after 1912–13 it remained marginal.[28]

The notion that the empire's multi-ethnicity—in an age of nationalism and European imperialism—threatened the Ottoman Empire's very existence was, of course, not new in 1912. After the war with Russia in 1877–8, Sultan Abdülhamid II had declared it unacceptable that non-Muslims inhabited regions of strategic importance for the defence of the capital.[29] By 1908, some leaders of the Committee of Union Progress had already decided that there should be 'no nationalities' in the empire, that the empire should not 'become a new Austria', referring to the 1867 *Ausgleich* that converted the Habsburg Empire into a dual monarchy and more recent reforms. Their goal was the creation of 'a unified Turkish nation-state with Turkish schools, a Turkish administration, [and] a Turkish legal system'.[30] However, even though the Committee of Union and Progress had successfully launched the Revolution of 1908, within a couple of years it had lost much of its support and held on to political power through coercion and rigged elections. The Italian and the Balkan wars put the Unionists back in the driver's seat; without these wars, it is quite possible that the Committee of Union and Progress's decline might have continued and that not their vision but that of others might have become policy. The convergence of traumatic defeat, militarist leadership, and the First World War, however, proved catastrophic.

THE GREAT WAR AS GREAT OPPORTUNITY

The Committee of Union and Progress turned the military crises of 1911–13 to its advantage. A mix of young military officers and civilians, the organization's leaders believed in taking initiative. Influenced by an international discourse on the pseudo-science of Social Darwinism, the committee's supporters advocated bold action. This had been displayed already, as we have seen, by Enver Bey and his men in the 1908 constitutional revolution, the armed resistance against Italy, and the Second Balkan War that brought the return of Edirne. In January 1913, moreover, military officers had stormed the offices of the grand vezir, killed the war minister, and toppled the cabinet, replacing it with one dominated by the Committee. The new cabinet, backed by officers trained by the German General Colmar von der Goltz, arranged for a German military mission to reform the army. Arriving in

---

[28] For the evolution and residual persistence of Ottomanism, see Abigail Jacobson, *From Empire to Empire: Jerusalem between Ottoman and British Rule* (Syracuse: Syracuse University Press, 2011); see also Michael Provence, 'Ottoman Modernity, Colonialism, and Insurgency in the Arab Middle East', *International Journal of Middle East Studies*, 43 (2011), 205–25.

[29] Adanır, 'Non-Muslims in the Ottoman Army and the Ottoman Defeat in the Balkan War of 1912–1913', 115.

[30] Report of a conversation with Dr Nazım, quoted in M. Şükrü Hanioğlu, *Preparation for a Revolution: The Young Turks, 1902–1908* (Oxford: Oxford University Press, 2001), 260.

Istanbul in December 1913, the German military mission joined British naval officers and French gendarmerie officers already employed in the empire. As military reform proceeded, the government also sought international cover in the form of a military alliance. Rebuffed when he sought an alliance with London in 1913, Grand Vezir Said Halim opened talks with Berlin. An alliance with Germany, Said Halim and Enver hoped, would provide military security against attacks such as those from Italy and the Balkan states, and provide necessary cover for domestic development and industrialization. Germany itself, and Japan, offered successful models for this vision of rapid 'militarist modernization'.[31]

A military alliance would also give Istanbul a stronger hand in any diplomatic negotiations, such as those involving the Great Powers' demands for improving living conditions and personal security in the empire's eastern Anatolian provinces, home to largely Armenian and Kurdish populations. Large segments of the press, moreover, supported the aggressive tone and activist policies of the Committee of Union and Progress. 'Our entering the [First World] War was not the work of a single individual', a prominent officer later recalled, 'but the result of various complex factors', especially 'our press' and 'public opinion'.[32]

It was only the conjuncture of the July crisis that induced Berlin to agree to the signing of a military alliance on 2 August 1914. For the Ottoman leaders, the alliance treaty, good for seven years, was a major diplomatic achievement. The defeat of Germany—and the total war whose threshold they had just entered—was difficult to fathom from the vantage point of 1914. Having demanded and received gold, men, and materiel from Germany, and determined to preserve the alliance even at the cost of war, the Ottoman navy struck at Russia across the Black Sea on 29 October 1914.

The immediate military impact of the operation was slight but its consequences were enormous in terms of the destruction and devastation that followed. The European war had now spread deep into the eastern Mediterranean, and over the next four years it would incinerate the Ottoman Empire's social fabric. By stepping into the fire of war, the Ottoman leadership demonstrated commitment to its German allies. Berlin would have to honour Ottoman interests in any negotiated peace settlement—provided, of course that Berlin itself would be sitting at the negotiating table, either as victor or on equal terms with its adversaries. 'When I contemplate all that Russia has done for centuries to bring about our destruction, and all that Britain has done during these last few years,' declared Cemal Pasha, the navy minister, 'then I consider this new crisis that has emerged to be a blessing. I believe that it is the Turks' [*Türklerin*] ultimate duty either to live like an honourable nation or to exit the stage of history gloriously'.[33] Goltz Pasha expressed the event in similarly grandiose terms: 'Bravo, Old Turkey now has the opportunity

---

[31] Murat Belge, *Militarist Modernleşme: Almanya, Japonya ve Türkiye* (Istanbul: İletişim, 2011).
[32] Kâzım Karabekir, *Cihan Harbine Neden Girdik, Nasil Girdik, Nasil İdare Ettik*, ii (Istanbul: Tecelli, 1937), 32–86.
[33] Archive of the Turkish General Staff (ATASE), BDH, Klasör 87, Yeni Dosya 449, Fihrist 1–2 and 1–3, 2 November 1914.

[…] in one fell swoop, to lift herself up to the heights of her former glory. May she not miss this opportunity!'[34]

In the first five months of its participation in the war, Istanbul launched three additional campaigns—one ideological, two military. In November 1914, the Ottoman sultan declared the war to be a holy war, calling not only on the empire's own Muslim subjects but also on Muslims worldwide, residing in the empires of Britain, France, and Russia, to support the Ottoman war effort and that of its allies, the German and Habsburg empires. Kaiser Wilhelm II of Germany, in particular, had demanded such a declaration, and, while the Ottoman leadership was seemingly complying with the kaiser's wishes, Istanbul had its own, domestic agenda for the jihad proclamation. From the Ottoman perspective, the jihad declaration did not aim so much at mobilizing Muslim populations in the colonial empires of the Entente—in British India and Egypt, the Russian Caucasus and Central Asia, and French North Africa—but at mobilizing the Ottoman Empire's own Muslim populations behind Osman's banner.[35]

Next, Istanbul launched two offensive operations into former Ottoman territories. In late 1914, the Third Army crossed into territory lost to Russia in 1878. In early 1915, a force led by Cemal Pasha attempted to cross the Suez Canal into Egypt, occupied by Britain since 1882. Both campaigns failed, and neither operation succeeded in inspiring revolution among the Muslims of the Russian and British empires. Aimed at capturing the town of Sarıkamış, the campaign into Russia resulted in a military disaster. Fighting in freezing temperatures and already riddled by disease, the Ottoman Third Army lost tens of thousands of its men within a few days.[36] In the collective memory of the war in Turkey, the Sarıkamış fiasco has been a mirror image to the triumph of Gallipoli of 1915–16. And, while Sarıkamış became personified by Enver and stood for the empire's failures and decay, Gallipoli became personified by Mustafa Kemal and stood for the republic's defining triumph, the 'Turks' finest hour'. In its immediate aftermath, however, the defeat was pinned on the region's Armenian population and Armenian volunteer battalions that had joined the Russian side.

VIOLENCE AND VIABILITY

In 1909 the new parliament passed a law for mandatory military service that applied to all Ottomans of military age, Muslims and non-Muslims alike. In 1911, nearly one-quarter of all the youths entering military service were non-Muslim.

[34] Bundesarchiv-Militärarchiv, N 80-1, fo. 201, 9 November 1914.

[35] Mustafa Aksakal, '"Jihad Made in Germany?" The Ottoman Origins of the 1914 Jihad', *War in History*, 18 (April 2011), 184–99.

[36] There is a significant range for the casualty numbers of the Third Army at Sarıkamış, as well as its original strength. See Hikmet Özdemir, *The Ottoman Army, 1914–1918: Disease and Death on the Battlefield*, trans. Saban Kardaş (Salt Lake City: University of Utah Press, 2008), 50–67; Michael A. Reynolds, *Shattering Empires: The Clash and Collapse of the Ottoman Empires, 1908–1918* (Cambridge: Cambridge University Press, 2011), 125. Reynolds gives the strength of the Third Army as 95,000 men, Özdemir as 112,000.

The wars of 1911–13, however, and the strains they placed on Muslim–Christian relations inside the empire, undermined attempts at using the imperial army as a unifying 'school of the nation' (as Mustafa Kemal later described the Turkish military in the republic). With the declaration of mobilization in August 1914, the army conscripted all men between the ages of 20 and 45—some three million altogether by the war's end. While the majority of conscripts originated from Anatolia, perhaps over a quarter came from the empire's Arab lands.[37] Food and labour shortages among civilian populations set in immediately. Scores of soldiers succumbed to disease even before the empire had entered the war in late October 1914, while others deserted.

If imperial coexistence was still possible in August 1914, that possibility was destroyed over the course of the war. War in August 1914 immediately intensified accusations of non-Muslims' and non-Turks' alleged disloyalty to the empire. Armenians, and Kurds, were cast as potential allies of Russia; Jews as those of Britain; Arab Christians, of France; Arab Muslims (around Sharif Husayn of Mecca), of Britain; and Orthodox Christians, of Greece. A violent dynamic emerged, and grew stronger as the war continued: the state took pre-emptive measures against populations whose loyalty it suspected, while those steps in turn antagonized entire regions. The conflicts that resulted from these state policies together with wartime conditions of hunger, disease, and famine, over the course of four years, dissolved all remaining imperial sinews.

Armenian conscripts, in particular, were suspected of deserting to the Russian side as soon as the war began. Small movements among Armenians calling for independence had existed since the 1870s, but neither Armenian elites nor the patriarchy in Istanbul, nor the roughly 2.1 million Armenians, largely peasants, had supported revolutionary groups.[38] Already before the defeat at Sarıkamış had become apparent, however, Armenians in the ranks were being singled out as potential defectors to the Russian side. Some were being shot pre-emptively—'accidentally', as one soldier, Ali Rıza, reported.[39] These suspicions appeared confirmed when several volunteer battalions, consisting of Ottoman Armenians and led by a former deputy in the Ottoman parliament, formed alongside the Russian army.[40] Ali Rıza could not believe that Armenians and Turks could ever be 'brothers and fellow citizens' again, swearing that he would 'poison and kill 3 or 4 Armenians' when given the opportunity. The ties that had held together the empire's ethnic and religious groups were now rapidly being destroyed.[41]

---

[37] Beşikçi, *The Ottoman Mobilization of Manpower in the First World War*, 253.

[38] Richard G. Hovannisian, 'The Armenian Question in the Ottoman Empire, 1876–1914', in Richard G. Hovannisian (ed.), *Armenian People from Ancient to Modern Times* (New York: St Martin's Press, 2004), ii. 234–5; Dikran Mesrob Kaligian, *Armenian Organization and Ideology under Ottoman Rule, 1908–1914* (New Brunswick: Transaction Publishers, 2009), 227–36; M. Şükrü Hanioğlu, *A Brief History of the Late Ottoman Empire* (Princeton: Princeton University Press, 2008), 197–202.

[39] Ali Rıza Eti, *Bir Onbaşının Doğu Cephesi Günlüğü, 1914–1915* (2000; Istanbul: Türkiye İş Bankası, 2009), 104.

[40] G. Pasdermadjian, *Why Armenia Should Be Free: Armenia's Rôle in the Present War* (Boston: Hairenik Publishing Company, 1918).

[41] Eti, *Bir Onbaşının Doğu Cephesi Günlüğü*, 135.

Following the Sarıkamış disaster, on 25 February 1915, War Minister Enver issued an official order for all Armenians in uniform to be disarmed and placed in labour battalions, rendering them 'sitting ducks'.[42] With the bitter defeats at Sarıkamış and Suez behind them, and facing an Allied naval attack at the Straits, the Unionists by April 1915 declared Armenians to be in rebellion. On 24 April 1915, the government began arrests of Armenian political leaders, businessmen, and intellectuals, including those residing in Istanbul. On 27 May 1915, Interior Minister Talat issued orders for the deportation of Armenians on the grounds that they endangered Ottoman military operations. In July 1915, the army was assigning soldiers to labour in agriculture 'because all the Armenians have been deported and the Muslims have been conscripted'. If no soldiers were made available, the harvest would be jeopardized and 'dearth and famine' would seize the country, endangering 'the army's supplies' and thus opening the road to military 'disaster'.[43]

Dispossessed of their property and land, Armenians were marched southwards in a trail of tears during which many of the deported, especially women and children, starved to death, died of exhaustion, or were murdered. A tragically typical story is offered by Hagop Mıntzuri. Hagop had been born into an Armenian family near the city of Erzincan. Of military age, he was conscripted as a baker in August 1914. He would not see his wife, Voğida, or any of his four children, Nurhan aged 6, Maranik aged 4, Anahit aged 2, or baby Haço, ever again. They, along with Hagop's 55-year-old mother, Nanik, and his 80-year-old grandfather, Melkon, and all the other Christians of the village, were deported, never to be heard from again.[44]

Writing about the Armenian *Aghet* ('the Catastrophe') in 1921 from his hideout in Berlin, Talat claimed he first had opposed the deportation order because he knew that police and gendarmerie forces had been conscripted into the army and 'replaced by militias'. To task these irregular forces with the gathering of Armenian village populations and their deportation, 'I knew', said Talat, 'would have appalling consequences'.[45] If these hesitations were ever authentic, by early 1915 they had disappeared. The stated purpose behind the deportations was to prevent any subversion of Ottoman military operations in eastern Anatolia by locals. Similar to the earlier expulsion of western Anatolia's Greek Orthodox (Ottoman Turkish: *Rum*) in the spring 1914, the expulsion of Anatolia's Armenians aimed at eliminating all traces of any nationalist movement that could challenge Ottoman authority. When in May 1918 the government negotiated its eastern boundaries with Russia, Ottoman leaders opposed the creation of an Armenian state. Talat—since 1917 also grand vezir and hence 'pasha'—had been born in territory ceded to Bulgaria. An Armenian state, he posited, would

---

[42] Erik Jan Zürcher, 'Ottoman Labour Battalions in World War I', in Hans-Lukas Kieser and Dominik J. Schaller (eds), *Der Völkermord an den Armeniern und die Shoah* (Zurich: Chronos, 2002), 187, 193.

[43] BOA, DH SFR 54A/10, coded telegram, Interior Minister Talat to Commander of the Third Army, 2 Temmuz 1331 (15 July 1915). Talat expected 'a minimum of five thousand men'.

[44] Hagop Demirciyan Mıntzuri, *İstanbul Anıları, 1897–1940* (Istanbul: Tarih Vakfı, 1993), 133.

[45] Enver Bolayır (ed.), *Talât Paşa'nin Hâtıraları* (Istanbul: Güven Yayınevi, 1946), 64.

'become a "Bulgaria of the East"', a state intent on expansion at Ottoman expense, and therefore had to be avoided at all cost. The 'abscess must be removed
with its roots', he added.[46]

Arab and Kurdish leaders and populations whose loyalties the state questioned
were also put under surveillance and deported. In August 1914, even before Istanbul had entered the First World War, for example, the governor of Bekaa district, a fertile valley home to sizeable Maronite Catholic, Greek Catholic, and
Orthodox communities, expressed anxiety about the 'malicious population of
Mount Lebanon and especially the city of Zahla'. According to his report, the
newspapers of Zahla were displaying 'an excessive support for France', thereby
'wounding the hearts of the Muslim ummah'. This had been going on 'since the
Balkan wars'. By now Zahla's 'affection for France' had reached 'levels of worship'.
Such audacity, the governor insisted, was unacceptable. He recommended the
immediate dismissal of Zahla's military governor, Ibrahim Abu Hatir Efendi, who
was allowing 'such open' hostility to the Ottoman state, and the shuttering of the
local paper, *Zahla al-Fatat*.[47] Bekir Sami, Beirut's governor, described the prevailing dynamic in Mount Lebanon in absolute terms: 'Both the Maronites and
the Orthodox support France and Russia in their hearts and minds [*kalben ve
ruhen*].'[48] As to the Druze, they had previously leaned towards Britain, but now,
the governor surmised, 'because they are more or less related to Islam, in their
hearts they are leaning towards the Exalted Government of the sultan'. But, the
governor went on, the British consul 'is working day and night to win over the
Druze' to their side.

The empire had entered the First World War at a moment when its imperial
fabric, following the Balkan Wars, had already begun to fray. A tiny incident caused
Governor Bekir Sami to blow his top, illustrating this highly charged climate.
On 11 September 1914, a man by the name of Shoufani, in the village of Suq
al-Gharb, created a public spectacle by taking down 'an Ottoman flag flying over
one of the shops and trampled it under his feet'. The local police officer forced
Shoufani to return the flag, and left the matter at that. When Bekir Sami, Istanbul's man on the spot, heard about the incident, he became enraged and reported
the event back to the capital in the gravest possible terms. Shoufani's action, he
wrote, 'proved the overt and blatant hatred the people of Mount Lebanon harbour
against the government'. Unless strict measures were taken, the governor warned,
more 'incidents such as this one' would occur. 'I believe that the moment has come
to take necessary measures against the Mountain [*Cebel'e karşı tedabir-i lazıma
ittihazı zamanı geldiğine*].' He proposed that the government end Mount Lebanon's autonomous status, which had been in effect since 1861. By ruling Mount

---

[46] Akdes Nimet Kurat, *Türkiye ve Rusya: XVIII. Yüzyıl Sonundan Kurtuluş Savaşına Kadar Türk Rus
İlişkileri (1798–1919)* (Ankara: Ankara Üniversitesi Basımevi, 1970), 661–2, citing Talat to Halil Bey, 24
May 1918, Foreign Ministry Archives, File 124; also quoted in Reynolds, *Shattering Empires*, 210.
[47] BOA, DH EUM 4. Şube 1/4, Governorate of Syria to Interior Ministry, 13 Ağustos 1330
(26 August 1914).
[48] BOA, DH EUM 4. Şube 1/4, *Urgent* (Müstaceldir), Governor Bekir Sami to Interior Ministry,
20 Ağustos 1330 (2 September 1914).

Lebanon directly once again, Istanbul could tighten its grip on the region and exercise control over the population, Bekir Sami argued.[49]

Mount Lebanon was put under strict surveillance because it was suspected 'that with the influence of the [French] Consul in Beirut and the connivance of the railway company weapons would be smuggled inside Mount Lebanon'. Therefore, it was decided that 'each and every train departing Beirut' for Zahla 'must be placed under continuous and secret surveillance'.[50]

The region from Aleppo to Suez, the empire's Arabic-speaking lands, was placed under the military rule of Cemal Pasha, the Commander of the Fourth Army. Acute shortages of food raged in all parts of the empire, but nowhere was it as ghastly as in Syria, and especially in Mount Lebanon. Cemal's regime conscripted men into the army and labour battalions. It also raised special war taxes to finance the two attacks on the Suez Canal and Egypt. A plague of locusts, moreover, struck the region in 1915, eating up every green shoot. And an Anglo-French naval blockade prevented relief from arriving from outside. Shortages of trains, and their strict control by the military authorities, prevented the rapid dissemination of the food supply. The result was widespread starvation by December 1915. In Syria, one out of seven persons—over half a million people—had starved to death by war's end (see Fig. 2 for attempts to destroy locust eggs using flamethrowers).

Shakib Arslan, perhaps the most prominent Arab intellectual of the interwar period, acted as a critical liaison between Cemal Pasha and the Arab population under his rule. Shakib also knew well both Enver and Talat. In his account of his time as Cemal's assistant, Shakib reports that he tried at great lengths to change Cemal's mind about the arrests and deportations of Arab leaders. He especially opposed deportations and the public hangings of prominent Arabs in Beirut in August 1915 and in Damascus in May 1916. Shakib cautioned Cemal that the executions 'will be the reason for the separation of Arabs and Turks'.[51] One scholar has concluded that 'Cemal's actions in Syria were comparable in nature, if not in extent, to those policies pursued with respect to the Armenians in Eastern Anatolia. Both emanated from a fear that a nationalist uprising would come into being with encouragement from enemy powers.' In both cases, however, 'the threat was more perceived than real'.[52]

Further research will have to show whether the state used food as a weapon against the population of Mount Lebanon and Syria, as many charged at the time. What is clear, however, is that the deprivation brought by the war and the state's own policies enfeebled Ottoman legitimacy in the Arab lands. Ohannes Pasha, an Armenian Christian, assumed the post of governor of Mount Lebanon in 1913,

[49] BOA, DH EUM 4. Şube 1/4, *Coded Telegram* (Şifre), Governor Bekir Sami to Interior Ministry, 30 Ağustos 1330 (12 September 1914).
[50] BOA, DH EUM 4. Şube 1/4, Governorate of Syria to Interior Ministry, 19 Ağustos 1330 (1 September 1914).
[51] Shākib Arslān, al-Amīr, *Sīrah Zātiyyah* (Beirut: Dār al-Tāl'iyya lil'taba'a wa al-nashr, 1969), 171.
[52] Hasan Kayalı, *Arabs and Young Turks: Ottomanism, Arabism, and Islamism in the Ottoman Empire, 1908–1918* (Berkeley and Los Angeles: University of California Press, 1997), 197.

Fig. 2. Locust burning in Palestine, *c.*1915. In a single day, a swarm the size of Manhattan could consume roughly the equivalent amount of food consumed by forty-two million humans over the same period.

then still 'a true Ottomanist'. By war's end, his faith in the empire was dead.[53] In Lebanese collective memory, the Ottoman word for mobilization from this era even today is recalled with a shudder.[54] Private İhsan, a conscript in Jerusalem, echoed similar feelings, noting in his diary on 17 December 1915: 'If the government had any dignity, it would have saved wheat in its hangars for public distribution at a fixed price, or even have made it available from military supplies. If these conditions persist, the people will rebel and bring down this government.'[55] As

[53] Elizabeth F. Thompson, *Justice Interrupted: The Struggle for Constitutional Government in the Middle East* (Cambridge, MA: Harvard University Press, 2013), 118.

[54] Najwa al-Qattan, '*Safarbarlik*: Ottoman Syria and the Great War', in *From the Syrian Land to the States of Syria and Lebanon*, ed. by Thomas Philipp and Christoph Schumann (Beirut and Würzburg: Ergon, 2004), 163–73.

[55] Salim Tamari (ed.), *Year of the Locust: A Soldier's Diary and the Erasure of Palestine's Ottoman Past* (Berkeley and Los Angeles: University of California Press, 2011), 143.

Salim Tamari recently put it, 'four miserable years of tyranny', in the end, 'erased four centuries of a rich and complex Ottoman patrimony'.[56]

The Anglo-French naval blockade, parked off the Syrian coast, deepened the region's prevailing conditions of the hunger crisis. During 1913–14, the empire had imported a net amount of roughly 88,000 tons of grain cereals. The war put an end to imports, while military conscription and the confiscation of draft animals reduced the available agricultural labour force. The acreage of harvested land was cut in about half. All those outside the age of military conscription became subject to agricultural conscription, as schoolchildren, the elderly, and women transformed into field workers. As conscription expanded to press ever more men into military service, the War Ministry established a women's labour battalion that employed thousands of women.[57]

As Syria's famine was unfolding, the French consul in Cairo alerted his government to the fact that tens of thousands had starved to death and suggested providing relief through food aid. The British response, however, made clear that making conditions worse was the whole point of the blockade: 'His Majesty's Secretary of State for Foreign Affairs expresses his earnest hope that the French Government will not encourage any such scheme. [...] The Entente Allies are simply being blackmailed to remedy the shortage of supplies which it is the very intention of the blockade to produce.' The French concluded that their British allies 'consider the famine as an agent that will lead the Arabs to revolt'.[58]

Since his appointment in 1908 as the grand sharif of Mecca—the custodian of the holy cities of Mecca and Medina—Husayn ibn Ali sought to govern Arabia with as little interference from Istanbul as possible. In return for this semi-autonomous rule, Husayn promised to provide public order and ensure the region's stability. In August 1914, with war afoot in Europe, the local governor called for Husayn's immediate dismissal. If the war continued, the governor claimed, the sharif would undoubtedly join a foreign power.[59] Another imperial fissure threatened to burst under the weight of global and total war.

By the time Husayn rose against Istanbul, in June 1916, his position had become untenable. After an eight-month campaign, despite great human and material losses, the Entente had abandoned its mission to capture the Dardanelles and Constantinople. In its main operation in Iraq, a British army, including a large contingent of Indian troops, had moved up from Basra, captured Baghdad, but suffered defeat at Kut in April 1916. Led by General Charles Townshend, British intelligence had counted on the support of the Shia population, whose loyalty to the

[56] Tamari (ed.), *Year of the Locust*, 5.

[57] Zafer Toprak, *İttihad-Terakki ve Cihan Harbi: Savaş Ekonomisi ve Türkiye'de Devletçilik, 1914–1918* (Istanbul: Homer Kitabevi, 2003), 81–98; Yavuz Selim Karakışla, *Women, War and Work in the Ottoman Empire: Society for the Employment of Ottoman Muslim Women (1916–1923)* (Istanbul: Ottoman Bank and Research Center, 2005), and 'Osmanlı Ordusunda Kadın Askerler', *Tarih ve Toplum* (June 1999), 14–24.

[58] Elizabeth Thompson, *Colonial Citizens: Republican Rights, Paternal Privilege and Gender in French Syria and Lebanon*, The History and Society of the Modern Middle East (New York: Columbia University Press, 2000), 19–23; for quotations, see p. 22.

[59] Kayalı, *Arabs and Young Turks*, 184.

Ottoman Sunni state it considered weak. Under the circumstances, British pressure focused on the sharif. Stuck between Cemal Pasha's iron reign, on the one hand, and the threat of British military invasion across the Red Sea, on the other, Husayn took the British offer for an Arab state under his rule. Equipped with British money, materiel, and intelligence, several thousand Arabs took up arms against Ottoman forces. Entente hopes that Husayn's action would galvanize a general Arab revolt from Mecca to Damascus, however, were dashed. Crippled by famine, Syria proved to be tightly controlled by Cemal, as Husayn's uprising failed to generate any serious challenges to imperial authority there.

The Russian Revolution erupting in 1917 allowed the Ottomans to return to Erzurum and Trabzon, which the Russian army had previously occupied, and to garner additional territory in the Caucasus. As the war rolled on, however, the empire could not match the Entente's resources and numerical superiority in manpower. British troops captured Jerusalem in December 1917. By October 1918, British forces had reached Aleppo in northern Syria, and a second British army was moving towards the Ottoman capital after breaking through at Salonica. The Ottomans, like their allies, had been defeated. On 30 October 1918, a group of Ottoman representatives signed an armistice aboard a British battleship. A few days later, another group of Ottomans, including Cemal, Enver, and Talat, escaped Istanbul for Europe aboard another vessel, this time a German one.

CONCLUSION: THE SLOW END OF EMPIRE

In both the occupied Arab lands and the unoccupied Anatolian lands the process by which empire was replaced by the nation state was far from straightforward. With the armistice in place, the Ottoman government aimed at preserving whatever territory remained unoccupied. Nor did the fighting stop. In the first half of 1919, British and French forces occupied Istanbul, while Greek forces landed on the Aegean coast in the west and Italian forces in the south. In the east, independent Armenian and Kurdish states were poised to take shape.

In their own Wilsonian Moment, Ottoman officials and civic and political organizations evoked the US president's twelfth point, which advocated 'a secure sovereignty' to the 'Turkish portion of the present Ottoman Empire'. Flanked by posters displaying Wilson's twelfth point, Halide Edib and a host of speakers addressed a crowd of 200,000 in May 1919. With British and French forces occupying the sultan's government in Istanbul, local elites, former commanders, and demobilized soldiers formed resistance organizations. Initially these were relatively disjointed until they gained greater coordination in 1919. Eventually they became centralized under the command of Mustafa Kemal, the hero of Gallipoli and a former rival and political opponent of Enver Pasha. The ideology that undergirded this movement was based on religious rather than ethnic or national identity. In August 1920, the sultan's government in Istanbul agreed to the signing of a peace treaty in the French town of Sèvres. News of the treaty galvanized the resistance movement, which rejected it, secured Bolshevik aid, and defeated Armenian forces in the east before clashing repeatedly with Greek armies, culminating in the capture of Izmir amid great violence in September 1922. The Ankara assembly now abolished by vote the office of the sultanate, while retaining, however, the office of the caliphate for another two years. The Ottoman sultanate had come to an end. Ankara sent its representatives to Lausanne for peace negotiations. The resulting treaty, signed in July 1923, recognized the sovereignty of the Ankara government within the empire's remaining territory. After much destruction, Wilson's twelfth point, as far as the 'Turkish portions of the present Ottoman Empire' were concerned, had become reality. As for 'the other nationalities', a new regime of British and French mandates was set up, but certainly not one that afforded 'an absolutely unmolested opportunity of autonomous development', as Wilson had put it unproblematically.

The structural weaknesses that plagued the empire from the nineteenth century forward—its military insecurity, the unresolved questions of ethnic and religious plurality, wanting economic development—also defined, in varying degrees, the unstable regimes that replaced the Ottomans. The great number of casualties, displaced people, and forced migrations, moreover, produced long-term socio-economic consequences, as urban populations did not return to pre-war levels until the early 1950s. In Anatolia/Turkey, living standards dropped dramatically; GDP in the 1920s stood at about half of pre-war figures.[60] The population of Ottoman Anatolia hovered just under sixteen million in 1913; as late as 1927 it was still under fourteen million.[61] The war's transformative effects on Syria were no less profound, as it left behind an equally devastated landscape and a 'shattered social order'.[62]

War in the Ottoman Empire during 1911–22 generated conditions that destroyed the state's imperial fabric. Halide Edib's retrospective wish that there had been a 'far-sighted policy' is worth recalling. The history of the empire's final decade continues to be deeply politicized. The 'political tragedy' and 'cataclysm' David Stevenson recognizes in his history of Europe has an Ottoman version as well: here the tragedy is that the Ottoman leaders who were brought to power by the wars of 1911–13 were no longer able to see political solutions and instead opted for military ones. They did so because of the empire's experience since the nineteenth century. Having given up on diplomacy and institutions of the international system, they opted for refashioning the empire and its people into a 'nation in arms'. Not all of the empire's peoples would be willing or given the opportunity to serve in that 'nation in arms'. That new direction heralded the end of the empire.

[60] Michael Twomey, 'Economic Change', in Camron Michael Amin, Benjamin C. Fortna, and Elizabeth B. Frierson (eds), *The Modern Middle East: A Sourcebook for History* (Oxford: Oxford University Press), 528.
[61] These statistics are challengeable, but the general trends they indicate seem consistent across available sources. For these population figures, see Behar, *Osmanlı İmparatorluğu'nun ve Türkiye'nin Nüfusu*, 65.
[62] Thompson, *Colonial Citizens*, 19.

2

The Italian Empire

Richard Bosworth and Giuseppe Finaldi

In 1911 the Italian government sponsored many grandiose celebrations of the fiftieth anniversary of the foundation of its nation state in the Risorgimento. In patriotic rhetoric it was a moment to hail the achievements of the 'Third Italy'. The adjective implied an ownership of time and a tradition of empire, claims common across the self-consciously 'civilized' world to have 'history' inscribed on the side of nation-building and greatness in past and future written into national identity. But for Italy there were evident complications. The 'First Italy' had flourished in that classical era when Rome gave order to all Europe, Asia Minor, and North Africa, an imperium still cherished by the world's statesmen in the belle epoque, trained as they were in Latin and Greek. The 'Second Italy' was of vaguer political base but recalled the Renaissance, when citizens of the Italian states led the Western world in culture, learning, and the arts, helping civilization to be reborn after it had fallen under the yoke of 'barbarism'. Here had been a gentler, kindlier empire than that of the Caesars perhaps, but an empire indeed whose artefacts dominated every museum and gallery.

The title Third Italy implied a determination for the nation state, born again in the Risorgimento, to match these boasted and formidable ancestors. Yet, by every measure of power in the age of blood and iron, Italy was only the 'least of the Great Powers', with an economy lagging behind the product of both the First and Second Industrial Revolutions, a society whose masses were uneasily nationalized at best, and a military mainly recalled for the humiliating naval defeat by the Austrians at Lissa in 1866 and, worse, by the Ethiopians of Emperor Menelik thirty years later at Adowa.[1] Adding a further complication was the fact that Rome was the location of a (spiritual) empire on which the sun did not set, the Vatican, the administrative hub of the world-girdling Catholic Church. The overwhelming majority of Italians remained Catholics of some definition. But the battles of the Risorgimento had arrayed state against church in a conflict that would not be resolved until the Lateran Pacts signed by Pope Pius XI and Fascist dictator, Benito Mussolini, in 1929. Before the First World War, members of the Liberal elite were usually anti-clerical in their approach to the Papacy, their ideology reinforced through Freemasonry,

---

[1] For background detail, see Richard Bosworth, *Italy and the Approach of the First World War* (London: Macmillan, 1983), and *Italy and the Wider World 1860–1960* (London: Routledge, 1996).

still damned by the Church as devilry. In their turn, prelates were sardonic about the Liberal usurpers in Rome, with the Jesuit paper, *La Civiltà Cattolica*, mocking the celebrations of 1911, for example. At its heart the Vatican had not altogether surrendered its claims to 'temporal power' and, had Italy lost the First World War, it may well have sought somehow again to rule Rome.

In very many ways, then, the spectre of 'empire' hovered over the Italian nation state as it sought to find its place in the world. In particular, the Latin words *mare nostrum* became a habitual part of every political vocabulary well before Fascism boasted of its special commitment to *romanità* (the classical Roman spirit). The beat of the hoped-for empire's wings could be heard when a local member of the 'generation of 1914' like the Futurist Filippo Tommaso Marinetti urged the bombing to pieces of the historic centres of Rome, Venice, and Florence, maintaining that only thus could modern Italy shake itself free from the pernicious 'glories' of its past and forge a grand future imperial destiny. The current 'empire of rags and patches' in this or that East African desert was there when the English historian Arnold Toynbee, commencing his contemplation of 'the rise and fall of civilizations', wrote off current-day Italians as 'dagos' and 'parasites', even while he declared himself 'transported' by what he could find of the 'Ancients'.[2] The unfulfilled reckoning with the past was there yet again when, after Italy had entered the First World War nine months late on 24 May 1915, not quite a Great Power and not really a small, its most authoritative daily, *Il Corriere della Sera* in Milan, editorialized that the 'pinnacle of the Risorgimento' had been reached when Italy had 'drawn its sword and spoken in the Roman manner from the Campidoglio'.[3]

LIBYA

Italy's version of the First World War was to prove as imperial as that of the greater powers, but imperial in its own manner, fluctuating between the (weak) reality of boots on African ground and (hugely powerful) myth. After all, *alea jacta est*, a dice had been cast in 1911 (Caesar's phrase was commonly used by journalists at the time), when the celebration of fifty years of nationhood debouched readily into a naval and military (and indeed aerial; it was now that Italy pioneered bombing from above) campaign. On 29 September the Italian minister in Constantinople formally told the Ottomans that Italy was at war with them; troops were already sailing across the Mediterranean with the purpose of seizing the vilayets of Tripolitania and Cyrenaica, romantically renamed by their European invaders 'Libya', the title they had held under the Caesars. Nationalists summoned the information that the territory had once produced vast quantities of grain for Rome; the place, they said, in what pious Catholics might view as blasphemy, was 'our promised land'.[4]

---

[2] William H. McNeill, *Arnold J. Toynbee: A Life* (Oxford: Oxford University Press, 1989), 41–4.
[3] *Il Corriere della Sera*, 5 June 1915.
[4] See, e.g., Giuseppe Piazza, *La nostra terra promessa: Lettere dalla Tripolitani marzo-maggio 1911* (Rome: Lux, 1911).

A ditty, entitled 'Tripoli, bel suol d'amore' ('Tripoli, beautiful soil of love'), became the most popular song of the year and resounded cheerfully from many a band-stand in Italy's numerous beautiful and 'historic' squares. More practically, it was also put about that the conquest would provide an unlimited amount of fertile land for the peninsula's, especially its southern half's, poor peasants. It would thereby staunch the 'haemorrhage' of emigrant blood to the Americas (as Antonino Di San Giuliano, Foreign Minister 1911–14 had earlier put it); in 1913 more than 870,000 Italians left their country, ironically constructing, outside the nation state, an informal empire of the Italies, which was and would remain much more exten-sive as well as more economically and culturally productive than any conquered by Italy.[5]

Still more importantly as far as patriotic policymakers were concerned, a bright new colony across the Mediterranean would finally catapult Italy into the ranks of the truly Great Powers and wash away the disgraceful memory of Adowa. Among those notably attracted to imperial designs were members of the royal family, the Savoys, doubtless hoping that they might thereby lessen the sneers of the grander Great Power dynasties. In such hankering, they found implicit alliance in many of the bourgeoisie, who 'always wore sailor suits'[6] and read for pleasure and excite-ment the tales of Emilio Salgari, with their portrayal of derring-do in far-off places, where women's bodies enticingly were not as fully clothed as they were in Europe. For many 'respectable' Italians, dreams of empire were part of the recipe of being respectable.

Not everyone agreed. Empire could divide Italians as readily as it could unite them. Socialists, like the young Benito Mussolini, regarded the intrusion into Libya as a clumsy attempt to divert the working class from its proper struggle against the bosses. Some of the more cautious liberals and republicans worried that the moderate and rational nationalism of the Risorgimento was being subverted by the excessive and dangerous imperial rhetoric of lush poet, Gabriele D'Annunzio, or, from 1910, philosopher of the Nationalist Association, Enrico Corradini. Jour-nalist and historian, Gaetano Salvemini, voiced the fears of others who felt that Italy's limited resources would be squandered on conquering a 'big box of sand' when investment would be better directed at Italy's south, at infrastructure and modernization. Still others challenged the wisdom of seeking territory abroad when, on the country's very borders, Italians allegedly languished under 'foreign' Austrian oppression.[7] For such irredentists, the key to all Italian policy should lie in Europe and not be diverted into African chimeras. The nation must finally be composed of all Italian speakers and Italy should reach its natural borders on the Brenner, in the Carso above Trieste and along the Istrian and Dalmatian littoral. In

---

[5] For background, see R. J. B. Bosworth, *Italy: The Least of the Great Powers: Italian Foreign Policy before the First World War* (Cambridge: Cambridge University Press, 1979), and GianPaolo Ferraioli, *Politica e diplomazia in Italia tra XIX e XX secolo: Vita di Antonino di San Giuliano (1852–1914)* (Sove-ria Mannelli (CZ): Rubbettino, 2007).

[6] S. Agnelli, *We Always Wore Sailor Suits* (New York: Viking, 1975).

[7] Antonio Schavulli (ed.), *La guerra lirica, il dibattito dei letterati italiani sull'impresa di Libia (1911–12)* (Ravenna: Pozzi, 2009).

response, the pro-war journalist Giuseppe Bevione urged the country's political masters to believe in the 'virtues of our race' and trust it to be capable at last of a 'grand endeavour'.[8] After all, he added, moral qualms were inappropriate because the Arabs, Berbers, and Jews of Libya were waiting with baited breath for their hated Ottoman overlords to be routed by the stern but fair and heroic descendants of Roman legionaries.[9]

However, when Italian armies landed, a bitter surprise awaited: after the swift and easy occupation of the vilayets' main coastal towns, facilitated by their being situated within range of Italian naval artillery, the invasion stalled. Turkish forces made a tactical retreat and tenaciously resisted. More ominously, they were joined by most locals, apparently oblivious to centuries of Ottoman 'oppression'. Such resistance was soon given terrible proof. A fortnight after their landing the Italians had pushed out of Tripoli, holding a semi-circular perimeter with a 25-kilometre radius. On the morning of 23 October, Ottoman forces mounted a vigorous counter-attack and broke through at Sciara Sciat. At the same moment, indigenous forces rose in the Italian rear, and a bloodbath ensued. Captured Italians, it was later reported, were crucified on date palms, castrated, mutilated; a well was found choked with the bodies of prisoners whose hands and feet had been tied before they were thrown in alive.[10] The Italians, who only a few days before had been jocosely wondering how soon their African holiday would end, panicked and turned on the Arab 'traitors' with ferocity. Under the eyes of an appalled foreign press, days of savagery followed. The streets of the Libyan capital filled with corpses and gallows, dispelling any illusion that Italy was going to make of Tripoli a 'land of love'.[11]

Imperial war, the Italians were being forced to learn, was not a stroll in the park, nor could it reliably be separated from policy at home, where socialists had begun blocking troop trains and organizing stoppages at crucial ports. Worse, the Libyan war carried dangerous implications for Italy's uneasy international situation as the third member of the Triple Alliance with imperial Germany and possible irredentist target, Austria–Hungary, while remaining 'friends' with each of the Triple Entente, imperial Britain, imperial France (often an annoying 'Latin stepsister' with patronising claims to be a more doughty heir of Rome than the Italians were) and imperial Russia.[12]

But, for the moment, the military were ready to shut their eyes and think only of the nation. Unable to break out of the siege, in a desperate bid to force the Ottomans to concede defeat, the navy escalated the war to the Eastern Mediterranean: Beirut

[8] Giuseppe Bevione, *Come siamo andati a Tripoli* (Turin: Bocca, 1912), 178.

[9] Claudio Segrè, *Fourth Shore: The Italian Colonization of Libya* (Chicago: University of Chicago Press, 1974); Francesco Malgeri, *La Guerra Libica: (1911–1912)* (Rome: Edizioni di storia e letteratura, 1970); Edward Evans-Pritchard, *The Sanusi of Cyrenaica* (Oxford: Clarendon Press, 1949).

[10] Angelo Del Boca, *Gli italiani in Libia, Tripoli bel Suol d'Amore* (Milan: Mondadori, 1993), 110.

[11] William Stead, *Tripoli and the Treaties* (London: Bank Buildings, 1911), 59–81.

[12] For a patriotic account of Italian diplomacy throughout the war, see Luca Riccardi, *Alleati non amici: Le relazioni politiche tra l'Italia e l'Intesa durante la prima Guerra mondiale* (Brescia: Morcelliana, 1992).

was bombed in February 1912; in April various forts defending the Dardanelles were shelled and in May the Dodecanese islands in the Aegean, including Rhodes, Cos, and Patmos, were occupied. On the night of 19 July a brash ship's captain, Enrico Millo, 'forced' the Dardanelles, leading a flotilla of five torpedo boats twenty or so kilometres up the Straits in a daring but reckless raid, which the prime minister, Giovanni Giolitti, had not authorized, although the Liberal leader did firmly reject any suggestion from his allies and friends of a retreat from his peremptory declaration in October 1911 that Italy had annexed Libya.[13]

It was, however, not such élan that brought the Ottomans to the negotiating table but the brewing of the Balkan Wars in the autumn of 1912, although the financial lures of the Venetian entrepreneur Giuseppe Volpi, employed since the summer in ingratiating state-sponsored Italian business with the Young Turk leadership, may have been a useful aide. Whatever the case, overstretched, the Ottoman regime, whose own empire was threatening to dissolve, chose to deploy its forces in preserving what was left of its country's European territories and grudgingly conceded that its African possessions could no longer be defended. At Ouchy, a suburb of Lausanne, in October 1912, the peace treaty was signed confirming Italian annexation.

The relationship between what gentlemen agreed in the cosy surrounds of their Swiss hotel and what might actually happen in Tripolitania and Cyrenaica was by no means certain. The fact that among the Ottoman commanders fighting in Libya was Enver Bey, as well as the young Mustafa Kemal, demonstrates the calibre of Italy's opponents, suggesting it was unlikely that the loss of the provinces had yet been accepted as permanent should further disturbance—say, a world war—take place. Enver Bey, to be a member of the triumvirate that ruled the Ottoman Empire from 1914 to 1918 and instrumental in bringing the Empire onto Germany's side, was a committed 'Young Turk', pledged that the Ottoman Empire's feeble past yielding to European encroachment should be reversed. When Enver quit Libya to fight in the Balkans, he left behind weapons and men, and the Arab 'rebels' were assured that arms would continue to arrive from Istanbul while the locals continued to resist Italian rule. The Ottoman jurisdiction over Libya's religious affairs, guaranteed by the Ouchy treaty, became a channel through which covert funds, gleaned across the Muslim world, reached the anti-Italian *mujahidin*.[14] The running sore in Libya worsened after 1915, especially after Italy had belatedly declared war on the Ottoman Empire (15 August; it was not officially in combat with Germany until a year later). During the months between Ouchy and the Sarajevo assassination, Italy had sought to impose a rule that was its own but followed European standards of African empire. It met with limited success.

Since, although the Libyan campaign was over, battle continued, the more immediate issue was the Italians' minimal experience of colonial and desert warfare. There was a huge learning process to be undertaken and a dearth of expertise. The

[13] Del Boca, *Gli italiani in Libia*, 167–74.
[14] Rachel Simon, *Libya between Ottomanism and Nationalism* (Berlin: Klaus Schwarz, 1987), 105, 120–1.

Fig. 3. Italian soldiers dancing during time off in Tobruk, May 1914.

only positive discovery, from the Italian perspective, was how useful could be the deployment of Eritrean ascari. These mainly Muslim 'imperial' troops, recruited from Italy's 'first-born' colony on the Red Sea coast, became the core of military impetus over the next years. The various defeats of Italian forces, even though in private referred to by Ferdinando Martini, Minister of Colonies between 1914 and 1916 (he had been governor of Eritrea 1897–1907), as 'worse than Adowa',[15] could, under draconian censorship, be hidden from the press in Italy. Back in Rome, thousands of Eritrean ascari victims were ignored, while the sacrifice of Italian conscripts could also, as far as possible, be concealed; perhaps 10,000 died, almost double those lost at Adowa.[16]

A determined effort to impose Italian power beyond the coastal cities had, by July 1914, resulted in what, on paper at least, looked like a successful two years of campaigning. The Fezzan, south of Tripoli, as well as much of the Cyrenaican Gebel were in Italian hands, utilizing heavily armed mobile columns thrusting into the interior. 'Thrusting' might be something of an exaggeration, however, since it took Colonel Antonio Miani a year (August 1913 to August 1914) to march from Sirte on the Mediterranean to Ghat on the southern border with Algeria.[17] Nevertheless, by the summer of 1914 it looked feasible to establish Italian power in depth. It was, however, August 1914, and, as Angelo Del Boca, the pre-eminent

[15] For his philosophizing about empire in 'Affrica', which embraced genocide, see Ferdinando Martini, *Nell'Affrica italiana: Impressioni e ricordi* (rev. edn) (Milan: Treves, 1895).
[16] Nicola Labanca, *Oltremare* (Bologna: il Mulino, 2002), 121; Angelo del Boca, *A un passo dalla forca* (Milan: Baldini Castoli Dalai, 2007), 80.
[17] Angelo Del Boca, *La disfatta di Gasr Bu Hàdi* (Milan: Mondadori, 2004), 43–67.

Italian historian of empire of his generation, put it, the war 'suddenly reshuffled all the cards'.[18]

The card that came out on top of the deck was 'the Great Arab Revolt', a direct response to the Ottoman Sultan's proclamation of holy war in November 1914. Italy, being neutral, was not Turkey's prime enemy, but Britain was, and an attempt to conquer Egypt became the fulcrum of a German–Ottoman plan to break British power in the entire Middle East. The Senussi Islamic order, whose two million members were spread across Egypt's western borderland, the Libyan Desert, and on to French West Africa, became a valuable asset in the planned invasion of Egypt concocted by the Germans and Enver Bey. Suddenly the demoralized Libyan *mujahidin*, abandoned in 1912, were proclaimed to be the holy warriors of Allah in a renewed and titanic struggle against the infidel. In the Fezzan, Ahmad al-Sharif led renewed Senussi rebellion, and, with Italy loath to invest resources for empire there as it prepared to intervene for the nation in the Alps, the edifice of Italian power in the colony slowly disintegrated.

In April 1915 at Gasr Bu Hadi south of Misrata a column of Italian troops was annihilated, leaving more than a thousand dead and hundreds in the hands of the Arab insurgents. The fleeing Italians abandoned to the enemy an arsenal of rifles, millions of rounds of ammunition, machine guns, and field cannons.[19] At Tarhuna in June the Italian column evacuating the besieged city was set upon; every Eritrean who had been garrisoning the town was slaughtered, perhaps in revenge for a massacre carried out at Sirte the year before. More than 2,000 died on the Italian side and almost 400 were taken prisoners by the insurgents. One after another the territories occupied up to 1914 fell to the rebels, while German submarines began furnishing the local resistance with arms and other material support through the port of Gasar Hamad near Misrata.[20]

For Italy the issue had become simple: did empire matter or should it concentrate on its irredentist ambitions in Trento and Trieste? Should it pour more resources into the colony to recover what had been lost in 1914–15 or withdraw to the positions attained at the beginning of the invasion in 1911—that is, areas within range of naval artillery? Unsurprisingly, the latter choice predominated: even for the grander empires, during the 'world war', 'Europe' mattered more than 'Africa'. It is difficult to determine how far this abdication was due to the strength of the mujahidin or to Italian weakness. In reality what had happened was that the outbreak of war in Europe had already shifted the attention of the nation's elite 'public opinion' away from Libya, a focus that in any case had become steadily blurrier since 'victory' had been proclaimed in October 1912. The likes of D'Annunzio and Corradini (now joined by Mussolini and even Salvemini) had turned their pens from imperial debates to 'reclaiming' lands across the north-eastern border and so to Roman-style battle and victory there. Suddenly,

---

[18] Del Boca, *Gli italiani in Libia*, 261.
[19] Del Boca, *Gli italiani in Libia*, 273–83.
[20] Ali Abdullatif Ahmida, *The Making of Modern Libya* (New York: State University of New York Press, 1994), 121.

the nation's wordsmiths concentrated on heroism in the 'Fourth War of the Risorgimento' in Europe rather than hailing legionary advance in North Africa.[21]

This urgent re-evocation of the spirit of Garibaldi and Mazzini, however, did
not mean that empire had been forgotten. Rather Prime Minister (1914–16)
Antonio Salandra, Foreign Minister Sidney Sonnino (1914–19), and especially
Gaspare Colosimo, Martini's successor at the colonial ministry, 1916–19, as well
as a host of lesser commentators, saw the European war as building a case for colonial gain once the winners should gather for the post-war settlement.[22] Ambition
in the wider world grew with fighting in Europe. Assuming that victory must complete the nation's European destiny in Trento and Trieste, by 1916 Colosimo had
drafted a list of additional imperial gains extending Italian rule over not just Libya
and the Horn of Africa but swathes of Asia Minor (assuming the final collapse of
the Ottoman Empire), Dalmatia (replacing Habsburg rule in territories which, it
was widely emphasized, had once been beneficently ruled by the empire of the
Venetian Republic, another grand historical ghost that rhetoricians could add to
the spirit of Rome in backing the expansion of the Third Italy), and even the officially forgotten but nonetheless still remembered Ethiopia. There was even a plan,
brought to fruition in 1919, to grab the Austrian relic of a 'concession' in China to
that at Tientsin (Tianjin), which Italy had been granted by the greater powers after
its (lacklustre) participation in the suppression of the Boxer rebellion in 1901.

Victory, however embattled and 'mutilated' (D'Annunzio's querulous adjective),
expanded ambition across the national elite. A congress hastily convened by the
Italian Colonial Institute, a colonialist pressure group founded in 1905,[23] attuned
itself to the new spirit. 'We offer no opposition to France's and England's pre-eminence
as far as colonies are concerned,' one speaker at the conference affirmed politely in
January 1919. We can even accept 'that they round off their already dominant position with more. But in either case Italy must attain territorial equality overseas,' he
added truculently.[24] Francesco Caroselli, a functionary destined for a long career
in administering Italy's colonies, published his own thoughts on Italy's newly acquired status as the war reached its victorious conclusion: 'From now onwards,' he
pronounced, 'renewed by the war, the contribution that our Fatherland will give to
civilization and to the world's shared progress will not be inferior, materially or
morally, to that of any other Great Power'.[25]

In German historiography in the 1960s, Fritz Fischer caused consternation
when he suggested that Bethmann Hollweg's dreams of *Mitteleuropa* and *Drang
nach Osten* bore parallels with Nazi empire to come. Italian historians, blithely patriotic in the view that the First World War was 'the greatest triumph' in national

---

[21] Mario Isnenghi, *Dieci lezioni sull'Italia contemporanea*, (Rome: Donzelli, 2011), 156.

[22] Robert L. Hess, 'Italy and Africa: Colonial Ambitions in the First World War', *Journal of African History*, 4 (1963), 105–26.

[23] Bosworth, *Italy, the Least of the Great Powers*, 57–67.

[24] Istituto Coloniale Italiano, *Atti del convegno nazionale coloniale per il dopo guerra delle colonie, Roma, 15–21 Gennaio 1919* (Rome: Tipografia dell'Unione, 1920), 83.

[25] Francesco Caroselli, *L'Africa nella guerra e nella pace d'Europa* (Milan: Treves, 1918), 395.

history,[26] have scarcely asked whether Colosimo's targets and the hopes of all those members of the national elite who paid their dues to the Istituto Coloniale exceeded those of any later Fascist in their imagining of Italian rule over the *mare nostrum* and beyond.

In regard to this lustful dreaming, it might be conceded that there was little Italy could do in Africa itself for its post-war claims to be bolstered. All Italy's colonies bordered Allied rather than German or Turkish territory, so the opportunity of expansion into other empires—with the understanding that what was held during the war would be rendered permanent afterwards—was not open to Italy (except for their naval outposts in the Dodecanese islands, where an Italian presence annoyed the British, who half feared a potential threat to their cherished 'route to India'). Hanging on and making what was already possessed as least burdensome as possible while the conflict in Europe lasted became the keystone of wartime policy. Luigi Cadorna, Italian chief of staff, a Piedmontese whose background made him naturally Euro-centric, was in any case opposed to wasting precious assets fighting tribesmen in Africa. He had been assigned the job of getting the Italian army ready for a major European war in July 1914 and was already aghast at finding how much money, men, and materiel had been deployed in Libya.[27] It was, therefore, all but automatic that, in July 1915, Cadorna gave the order to abandon the Fezzan and Tripolitania, reducing Italian territory to Tripoli itself and to the port of Homs. After the Italian collapse at Caporetto in 1917, he even considered relocating the Italian troops (a not inconsiderable 40,000) left in Libya to the breach on the north-eastern front. The Italian commander was flatly refused by Colosimo, who warned that any further withdrawal would lead to Libya immediately becoming a 'Turko-Austro-German province', eliminating thereby any residual feeling among the British that Italy was doing its bit for the Allied cause in Africa.[28]

The good news from the Italian perspective was that Cyrenaica was not entirely lost, even if not because of Italian military prowess. In this region, a withdrawal to the coast had already taken place in 1915. More importantly, the Senussi leader, Ahmad al-Sharif, had been convinced by the Turks to attack Egypt as part of that Turko-German dream of drowning the British protectorate with an irresistible Islamic flood. Only a negligible number of Egyptians responded to the Ottoman *fatwa*. Al-Sharif soon discovered that his easy victories over the Italians could not be replicated against the British: his forces were routed at Agagia in February 1916. The belligerent Senussi leader was hustled into retirement and his cousin, Mohamed Idris al-Senussi, amenable to the British, took over as leader of the brotherhood. Italy was thus provided with a way out of its embarrassingly weak position in Libya's eastern territories. Britain agreed to include the Italians in a negotiated

---

[26] For historiographical background, see R. J. B. Bosworth, *The Italian Dictatorship: Problems and Perspectives in the Interpretation of Mussolini and Fascism* (London: Arnold, 1998), 99.

[27] Luigi Cadorna, *La Guerra alla fronte italiana*, i (Milan: Treves, 1921), 7–8.

[28] Vanni Clodomiro (ed.), *Il diario di Gaspare Colosimo (1916–1919)* (Rome: Istituto Storico Italiano, 2012), 320.

settlement over the fate of Cyrenaica. In exchange for Italy's recognition of the Islamic brotherhood as the de facto government in the region, Italy was permitted to
preserve direct rule over a sliver of territory in the north. The Acroma accords,
signed between Italy and Idris al-Senussi in April 1917, left each of the two parties
claiming a vague preponderance throughout Cyrenaica. Somewhere between the
lines, it was understood that a modus vivendi granted effective independence to
the Senussi in all territories beyond a coastal strip (never more than 40 kilometres
wide) where Italy predominated. Although after 1918 this agreement was couched
in Wilsonian terms as a sign of the benevolent new spirit pervading international
and colonial relations, it proved to be, as pioneer British anthropologist Edward
Evans-Pritchard put it, a 'truce rather than a treaty' when (Fascist) Italy was ready
again to don the mantle of empire-building.[29]

But trouble lay not far below the surface already in 1918. The Senussi's religious
connection with Constantinople had been broken at the cost of the Order assuming
a 'national' rather than an Islamic guise. In other words, the political solution
reached was good for the short-term aim of winning the war with Turkey, but less
ideal for the long-term prospects of uncontested Italian colonial rule. Yet, the situation could have been worse. If Al-Sharif had not attacked the British, what basis
could any Italian legitimacy have retained in Cyrenaica? As things stood, Italy had
saved a glimmer of imperial authority only because, for the British, 'obligations to
Italy [as an ally] proved stronger than [the] cynicism' that Italy's performance in
battle, whether in Africa or Europe, with its reinforcement, notably at Caporetto, of
ancient clichés that 'Italians could not (or would not) fight', was engendering.[30]

When victory in Europe neared, even Tripoli and its surrounding oasis, the last
redoubt of North African imperial glory, were reduced to a state of siege. Defended
by trenches, forts, machine gun turrets, artillery stations, and electric fences,[31] the
Italians inside were frightened, vicious, and recriminatory. Every Arab was a potential assassin and every stray dog barking, every mewling cat or palm frond blowing
in the wind at night, according to Gherardo Pantano, an officer stationed in the
beleaguered city, resulted in strafes of panicked machine-gun fire to no purpose
except momentary relief in the darkness. During the day, conversation in the city's
cafés and messes centred around the 'gallows, shootings and destruction necessary
to conquer Tripolitania in a proper and final way'. Such talk, for the time being,
resulted only in the venting of racist rage on those unfortunate 'natives' who had
remained within the fortified perimeter, most, according to Pantano, ruing that
they had missed their chance to join the rebels.[32] 'Roman (re-)conquest', rendered
more brutal by a Fascist gloss once Mussolini had marched on Rome in October
1922, was to come after.[33] But it had been planted in the minds of the frustrated
occupiers well before.

---

[29] Evans-Pritchard, *The Sanusi*, 145.
[30] Hew Strachan, *The First World War*, i. *To Arms* (Oxford: Oxford University Press, 2003), 751.
[31] Del Boca, *Gli italiani in Libia*, 299.
[32] Gherardo Pantano, *Ventitre anni di vita africana* (Florence: Casa Editrice Militare, 1932),
323–4.
[33] For Fascist evocation, see Rodolfo Graziani, *Pace romana in Libia* (Milan: Mondadori, 1937).

EAST AFRICA

Eritrea (or what assumed that name in 1890 from a classical Greek term for 'red land' that had not possessed any political meaning until European conquest) had been acquired by Italy in the 1880s through bargaining with local chieftains and edging out anaemic Ottoman suzerainty. Eritrea's most evident purpose as a stepping stone to further expansion in Ethiopia and a wider East African empire had been abruptly arrested at Adowa in 1896. Paradoxically, after that loss, Italian rule in the colony became more determined, if scarcely at the centre of national power politics. No longer a mere appetizer for the future Ethiopian banquet, Eritrea, under the ten-year governorship of Ferdinando Martini, slipped into a relatively peaceful existence in which the foundations of a permanent if sleepy national colony were laid, one where a tiny handful of Italians of often doubtful definition lived. Martini may have gone out of his way to build neo-Renaissance colonnades in his up-country capital, Asmara. But, ironically, not even in the wildest colonialist imagining could it equal the 'Little Italies' spreading in New York or Buenos Aires.

Nonetheless, relations with Ethiopia were mostly cordial. A treaty in 1902 demarcated the borders between the Italian colony and the highland empire, and in 1906 the tripartite 'agreement' between Britain, France, and Italy virtuously guaranteed Ethiopia's integrity, although Italy foreshadowed its preponderance (and indeed a united East African empire) should events precipitate after the death of Menelik, as quite a few of the Italian diplomatic establishment in their secret hearts assumed they would. Part of the motivation behind the 1906 'agreement' was that a legation, promising that Germany's new *Weltpolitik* would stretch to Addis Ababa, was on its way to Menelik's court from Berlin.[34] There was even talk of Japanese 'penetration' of Ethiopia. But such chatter scarcely preoccupied Italian decision-makers before 1914.

The outbreak of what after all was world war set off some tremors in Eritrea, mainly as a result of the fluctuating politics of the Ethiopian empire next door. Unlike in Libya, throughout the conflict there was no inkling of rebellion in this colony. Somewhat to the surprise of the governor, Giuseppe Salvago Raggi, Muslims and Christians, thrown together in the Eritrean militias, for example, some of whom were dispatched to fight and die in the hinterland of Tripoli, remained loyal subjects of Rome.[35]

But, across the border, there was trouble and, between 1914 and 1916, it threatened to spill into Eritrea. In December 1913 Menelik died, still a celebrated conqueror but with the unity of his empire by no means secure. Power passed to his young grandson Lij Iyasu. His short reign (1913–16) still divides opinion in Ethiopia.[36] For some commentators, he is seen as a modernizer aiming to transcend

[34] Edward Keefer, 'Great Britain, France, and the Ethiopian Tripartite Treaty of 1906', *Albion*, 13 (1981), 374.
[35] Giuseppe Salvago Raggi, 'Memorie dell'ambasciatore Giuseppe Salvago Raggi', in Glauco Licata, *Notabili della Terza Italia* (Rome: 5 Lune, 1968), 487–8.
[36] Cf. Bahru Zewde, *A History of Modern Ethiopia 1855–1974* (London: James Currey, 1991), 121.

religious difference in favour of a fuller Ethiopian national identity, the potential inventor, in other words, of a new history, a nationalizer of the masses.[37] For more critical analysts, he was an apostate determined to destroy the time-honoured place of traditional Orthodox, Coptic, Christianity in restructuring Ethiopian society under an insincerely egalitarian Islam, a heretical foe of 'real' national history. His contemporary detractors, chief of whom was future emperor, the long-lived Tafari Makonnen (who took the name Haile Selassie on his ascent to the throne in 1930), accused Iyasu of betrayal of his religion and country. This spiritual and national apostasy was allegedly symbolized by Iyasu's gift to the Turkish consul in Harrar Mahazar Bey in 1914 of an Ethiopian flag where the usual Ge'ez inscription 'The Lion of the Tribe of Judah has prevailed' had been overlain with the Arabic 'There is no God but Allah and Muhammad is the messenger of Allah'.[38]

Such gestures, apocryphal or not, were of slight interest outside Ethiopia had the year not been 1914 and the recipient of Iyasu's standard the Turkish consul. Iyasu's dalliance with Islam meant that the German and Turkish 'global strategy' delineating itself in the early months of the war was finding fertile soil even in the Ethiopian high lands.[39] Convinced by the German legation that it was only a matter of time before the Central Powers were victorious in Europe, Iyasu and his friends and backers abandoned their traditional deference to Britain and France. What German and Turkish agents suggested in the military sphere was an Ethiopian attack on the Sudan that could accelerate the collapse of British power in Egypt. Victory attained, Iyasu at his leisure could add to his territories Eritrea, parts of Kenya, as well as all Somalia.[40] In other words the dream consisted of a vast Islamic empire, of which he (in 1914 still a boy of 19) would be the head, with an Islamized Ethiopia at its centre. Abandoning the Christian elite in Addis Ababa, Iyasu made Muslim Harrar his base, from where he established relations with Mohammed Abdullah Hassan, known derogatorily in Europe as the 'Mad Mullah',[41] who, for more than a decade, had been the fulcrum of Islamic resistance to British and Italian colonialism in Somalia. A more reliable ally was Iyasu's father, Ras Mikael, himself a convert from Islam to Christianity, who could command 80,000 men in the Wollo province bordering southern Eritrea.

Although Italy was as yet neutral in the European conflict, Ethiopia's new direction alarmed Italian diplomats and policymakers. In a military parade the young wearer of the crown had promised his men he would be anointed emperor only after he had 'occupied Asmara and watered his horses in Massauwa', Eritrea's chief port.[42] In early 1915 Salvago Raggi found himself confronting five agents from

---

[37] Harold Marcus, *A History of Ethiopia* (Berkeley and Los Angeles: University of California Press, 1994), 114.

[38] Haile Selassie, *My Life and Ethiopia's Progress, 1892–1937: The Autobiography of Emperor Haile Sellassie I* (Oxford: Oxford University Press, 1976), ch. 7.

[39] Caroselli, *L'Africa nella Guerra*, 209–10.

[40] Strachan, *The First World War*, i. 747.

[41] Douglas Jardine, *The Mad Mullah of Somaliland* (London: Jenkins, 1923), 246.

[42] Emilio Bellavita, *La battaglia di Adua* (Genoa: Fratelli Melita, 1931), 498.

Germany who arrived in Eritrea with the request to travel into Ethiopia. The German party included eminent professor of African archaeology Leo Frobenius, who was suspected of supplementing the scholarly study of Sudanese rock art with international intrigue.[43] Frobenius was prevented from going further, but he did succeed in getting some pamphlets in Arabic and Amharic smuggled across the border, where they reached Lij Iyasu, stoking his already considerable fantasies.[44]

After Italy had entered the war on the Entente's side, the situation looked likely to precipitate, but in reality Eritrea had gained the protection of the two African superpowers, Britain and France. Lij Iyasu's German-sponsored Islamic empire proved fleeting. In September 1916 young Ras Tafari and the Christian old guard staged a coup proclaiming Menelik's daughter, Zewditu, empress, with her cousin, Tafari, regent. Iyasu was deposed on grounds of apostasy. After the war, he was put under allegedly luxurious house arrest to die conveniently in November 1935, just after Fascist Italy had begun its invasion of Ethiopia with its propaganda mentioning the possible restoration of a rightful monarch. Back in 1916, it had been the Italian minister in Addis Ababa, Giuseppe Colli di Felizzano, who had provided the 'proof' that Iyasu had converted to Islam,[45] although the machine guns promised by the French might also have stimulated Tafari's boldness.[46] Ethiopia descended into a civil war that looked much like the dynastic strife that in the past had frequently plagued the country after the death of a monarch, but this time there was a First World War veneer to the bloodshed. When, in early 1917, Zewditu was crowned, the British, French, and Italians sent representatives to the ceremony, but the Germans and Turks did not. Iyasu's fall meant that, in Massauwa and Asmara, colonial rule could return to its customary lethargy. Apart from this short-lived scare, as Salvago Raggi recalled on a visit to Italy, he had been led to understand that, thereafter, 'the colony would not be called to play any part whatsoever in the war'.[47]

If Eritrea was an oasis of peace (of a kind), Somalia remained even more on the periphery of the global conflict. Italian power there had been imposed, again more through dealings with local chiefs than military action, in the 1890s. The coastal towns were leased from the Sultan of Zanzibar with British backing and passed in concession to a chartered company whose enterprising managing director, Eugenio Filonardi, spent the decade travelling along the Somali coast getting natives to place their towns and villages under Italian 'protection'. Usually small amounts of money or a few cannon shots from Filonardi's ship stationed out at sea were sufficiently convincing for the signature to be marked along the dotted line. Through such rough-and-ready methods supplemented by a substantial payment to the rulers of two large sultanates in the north bordering British Somaliland, the Mijjertein and Obbia, the protectorate took shape, at least on European maps.

[43] Salvago Raggi, 'Memorie dell'ambasciatore Salvago Raggi', 500–1.
[44] Strachan, *The First World War*, i. 747.
[45] Bellavita, *La battaglia di Adua*, 499.
[46] See Harold Marcus, 'The Embargo on Arms Sales to Ethiopia, 1916–1930,' *International Journal of African Historical Studies*, 16 (1983), 263–79.
[47] Salvago Raggi, 'Memorie dell'ambasciatore Salvago Raggi', 500.

Somali society was sundered along tribal lines, with slavery the pillar of its economy. Somali pastoralists lorded it over the Bantu farmers in a brutal but time-honoured division of labour that Muslim law sanctioned according to minutely defined rules and regulations.[48] Italy's attempts to suppress slavery were sporadic and half-hearted, the resources required to contain such a radical transformation of the Somali economy and replace it with something more 'modern' being unavailable. In 1903, sixteen Italians lived in the protectorate, mostly as British-style 'residents' or pseudo 'district commissioners', an even smaller tally than in Eritrea. They preened themselves with their authority over dingy satrapies and, under armed escort, sought to milk what they could for themselves during their brief tenures.[49] After a series of well-publicized corruption scandals, in 1905 the chartered experiment, not quite a latter-day East India Company, was shut down, and Somalia became a colony proper.

There had been revolts against Italian rule. The Bimal tribe, for example, rose in response to Italian attempts to suppress slavery,[50] and some areas of even the coastal towns were no-go areas for whites.[51] Italy was prepared to forgo jurisdiction over entire regions, as happened in 1904, when, to avoid fighting, the 'Mad Mullah', Mohammed Abdullah Hassan, was given the Nogal valley to rule as he pleased. Nevertheless, the colony in the years up to 1914 was relatively quiet, partly because the Somali, unlike the Libyans and Ethiopians, did not have easy access to European weapons.

During the First World War the only issue perturbing the colony, apart from the dearth of news arriving from Europe,[52] was a series of potential threats that, as in Eritrea, never consolidated into actual ones. A few locally recruited Ascari sufficed to police Somalia's coastal towns. As has been described above, the consequences of an Ethiopian shift from acquiescence in the European-dominated order in East Africa to belligerence under the rule of Lij Iyasu were as potentially disquieting in Somalia as in Eritrea. However, the eventual Italian declaration of war on the Ottoman Empire and the consequent adding of Italy to the list of Christian states against which jihad was proclaimed 'passed unnoticed in Somalia'.[53]

Nonetheless, Sayed Mohammed Abdullah Hassan, whose Dervishes had been conducting guerrilla warfare against both Italian and British authority in northern Somalia since the 1890s, certainly knew of the *fatwa* and responded positively to overtures for an aggressive alliance with Iyasu. In 1917, the Mullah was nominated the 'Emir of the Somali' by the Ottomans, although, since the official letter informing him of this honour was seized by Italian agents in Aden, news of his appointment

---

[48] Enrico Cerulli, *Somalia, scritti vari editi e inediti*, ii (Rome: Istituto Poligrafico dello Stato, 1959), 19–29.

[49] Angelo Del Boca, *Gli italiani in Africa Orientale I: Dall'Unità alla marcia su Roma* (Milan: Mondadori, 1992), 782.

[50] Lee Cassanelli, 'The Ending of Slavery in Italian Somalia: Liberty and the Control of Labour, 1890–1935', in Susan Miers and Richard Roberts (eds), *The End of Slavery in Africa* (Madison: University of Wisconsin Press, 1988), 312–13.

[51] Gustavo Chiesi, *La colonizzazione europea nell'est Africa* (Turin: UTET, 1909), 427–8.

[52] Robert Hess, *Italian Colonialism in Somalia* (Chicago: University of Chicago Press, 1966), 116.

[53] Hess, *Italian Colonialism*, 116.

may never have reached him.[54] As to Germany stoking the Mullah into leading an Islamic uprising, the only agent who got through was a mechanic called Emil Kirsche. Wandering across Ethiopia—he had sought refuge there in order to escape internment in French Djibouti at the war's outbreak—he was sent by Lij Iyasu to the Mullah's court at Taleh, where, on pain of a flogging, he was expected to perform miracles with the latter's motley collection of broken firearms. Any illusion that Mohammed Abdullah Hassan had thereby joined Christian Germany in a united front against the British and Italians may have been dispelled by the fact that, whenever the Mullah was in the presence of the unfortunate Kirsche, he would stop up his nose and cover his mouth with a cloth in order 'that he might not breath the same air as the white infidel'.[55]

From the Italian perspective, in world war, as had been true before 1914, Sayed Mohammed Abdullah Hassan could be left to his own devices in a distant part of northern Somalia spanning the border with British Somaliland and policed by the newly formed British Camel Corps. Similarly, the hemming-in of his Dervishes fell not to the Italian armed forces directly but to the Italian 'protected' sultans of Obbia and the Mijjertein, who proved effective in curbing the area under the Mullah's command. Throughout the war the Mullah essentially ran his own Dervish kingdom on the Ethiopian marches of the British and Italian possessions, but offered little inconvenience to European power along the coast, where it mattered most in what was therefore a curious East African version of the 'live and let live policy' that sometimes quietened the trenches of Flanders. The dreamed-of alliance of the Mullah, Ethiopia, Germany, and the Ottoman Empire, lost any traction after Iyasu's ousting in 1916. As in Libya, the Italians kept as much of the coast as possible and postponed full-scale occupation of the territory and any 'modern' imperial control over the majority of the population until the war in Europe had been won. Repressed little King Victor Emmanuel was not a man to leave behind many quotable quotes in his obsessively 'factual' diary, but a historian might conclude that he and the rest of the Liberal establishment were agreed that, at least while battle continued on the Isonzo and Piave or above Monte Grappa, all of Africa was not worth the bones of a single Piedmontese or even Neapolitan grenadier.

CONCLUSIONS

During the Great War Italy did nothing to consolidate its power in Africa. It abandoned most of Libya and added very little to what had already been achieved in Eritrea and not achieved in Somalia. Yet, incongruously, while, on that continent, Italian power waned, in ministries in Rome and among writers looking to the post-war new world order and hoping they could win a major place in it, plans were being drawn up for the acquisition of imperial territory. Among these men

---

[54] Francesco Caroselli, *Ferro e fuoco in Somalia* (Rome: Sindacato Italiano Arti Grafiche, 1931), 244.
[55] Jardine, *The Mad Mullah*, 247.

Fig. 4. Italian residents in Eritrea give thanks for Italy's victory in the European war, Asmara, 7 November 1918.

such ambition was warranted because Italy had been correct in choosing, and decisive in contributing to, the winning side in the First World War. Readily the national motivation of the 'Fourth War of the Risorgimento' was expanded to urge an empire that would match those of the greater powers, and the 'history' of Rome and Venice lay conveniently around to make it seem that the Third Italy would thereby restore an imperium rather than behave with outlandish novelty. It did not matter that in Libya Italian rule was precarious and in East Africa tenuous; the time had come for Eritrea and Somalia to be united in a huge African protectorate embracing Ethiopia and French Djibouti. Libya's countless square kilometres could be supplemented in Chad and on Egypt's borders. Italy's small islands in the Eastern Mediterranean could be stepping stones to large sections of Anatolia and, perhaps, spheres of interest still further east.[56]

The story of the Dodecanese islands was typical. Conquered at first as bargaining counters to speed Ottoman acquiescence to Italy's annexation of Libya, the islands remained in Italian possession until defeat in the Second World War. Between 1912 and 1914, the excuse that the war in Libya was not really over allowed Italy to declare that it was not obliged by the Ouchy peace treaty to give them back.[57]

[56] Giuseppe Piazza, 'Le noste rivendicazioni coloniali nell'Oriente africano', *Nuova Antologia*, 188 (1917), 179; Savino Acquaviva, *L'avvenire coloniale d'Italia e la guerra* (Rome: Atheneum, 1917); Hess, 'Italy and Africa'.

[57] P. Carabott, 'The Temporary Italian Occupation of the Dodecanese: A Prelude to Permanency', *Diplomacy & Statecraft*, 4/2 (1993), 285–312.

When the First World War broke out, the chances of their being returned to Turkey evaporated for good, but Greece, on grounds of national self-determination, could claim them and did so in Paris at the war's end. Italy appeared to be prepared to cede the islands if Greece supported its claims on south-western Anatolia, but Greece's own ambitions in Turkey and its eventual defeat at the hands of Kemal's republic in 1922 dashed Italian ambitions in Asia Minor. The Dodecanese, acquired as bargaining chips, kept as stepping stones, now appeared as little more than an accident of recent history. Still, by 1923 there were no longer any obstacles to their permanent annexation, although reasons to do so, beyond the patriotic principle of never giving up territory once conquered and their value as symbols of a purported new Italian influence in the Eastern Mediterranean, were unclear. Were the islands to be 'colonies'? The official term used was 'Italian Possessions in the Aegean'.[58] Like so much of the Italian 'empire', the islands were kept in the hope of some opportunity for further gain presenting itself in the future. Perhaps, too, there was some pleasure in finding ways around what had at first been insistent British demands, inspired by half fears of hostile naval bases athwart the route to India, that the islands go to Greece

While these manifold dreams were being sketched on paper or in Italian minds, the colonial foothold survived in Tripoli, while, outside the city, the indigenous inhabitants reorganized their society without so much as a nod in the direction of their supposed colonial masters. There was even talk, which came to fruition in 1918, of creating a 'Tripolitanian Republic', whereby this remarkable and autochthonous political innovation, like the Senussi Order in Cyrenaica, became the de facto ruler of the entire territory outside Italy's coastal redoubts.[59] In the immediate post war, the Tripolitanian 'Republic' and Idris al-Senussi's 'monarchy' were recognized as the interlocutors with Italian officialdom in Rome, who sometimes talked as though they now approved a 'liberal Wilsonian' approach to colonization. In reality, however, negotiation on any terms was the only policy available in the circumstances, a sign of Italian political and economic weakness, in retrospect feeble evidence that Liberal Italy was a benign colonizer compared with its Fascist successor.

Benito Mussolini did become prime minister in October 1922 and dictator of a 'totalitarian' state in January 1925. Fascism was pledged to reinforce national claims that Italy was a Great Power, backed by loud boasts of an empire to be forged, notably in the *mare nostrum*. In practice, such *romanità* was scarcely possible, although the regime did brutally reoccupy Libya and then essay the conquest of Ethiopia (where Caesar's legions had never trod) in 1935–6. In 1939, it also seized Albania, establishing a curiously imperial regime there, very different from German annexation, with worthy pledges to train Albanians in Fascism.

Such matters lay ahead. But a neat example of the continuity in imperial dreams and purpose between the Liberal and Fascist systems is given in the career of

---

[58] Labanca, *Oltremare*, 181. For a study of the complex reaction of the islanders to Italian rule, see Nick Doumanis, *Myth and Memory in the Mediterranean: Remembering Fascism's Empire* (London: Macmillan, 1997).
[59] Ahmida, *The Making*, 106.

Giuseppe Volpi, the sometime artificer of peace in 1912, as well as the rich businessman who, in 1917, persuaded the national government to finance industrial development at Marghera so that his native (and once imperial) Venice could become great 'again'. This was the man for all seasons who, in July 1921, was nominated governor of Tripolitania by Giovanni Amendola, Minister of Colonies, a liberal democrat destined to die in 1926 after a brutal Fascist beating. But Volpi remained in Tripoli until July 1925, cheerfully accepting instruction from the Mussolini government to press on with reconquest. Indeed, it was Volpi, glowingly defined as 'the faithful friend of his friends, who also knew how to be the friend of the enemies of his friends in order to realize arrangements that would not cause discontent to anyone', who launched the career of then colonel, Rodolfo Graziani.[60] This, the most vicious of Fascist generals, would soon boast of implementing 'Roman peace' in the colony at the sacrifice of perhaps 100,000 Libyan dead. Such 'pacification' lay in the future. However, in 1925, when Volpi returned triumphant from his imperial duties to assume the richer post of Minister of Finance, he was elevated by King Victor Emmanuel to be Count of 'Misurata' (Misrata), a euphonious title that his son, who still lives in Venice, bears to this day.

After all, far and away the greatest practical reason for Italy to possess Libya (no oil was discovered under Italian rule), or its other desperately poor colonies, was to plant colonists in them. The gap between this theory and reality weighed heavily on the entire Italian imperial project. Coming to terms with Italy's colonial subjects, granting them autonomy and a share in a notional 'greater Italy' in either the French or the British manner, was never seriously envisaged (except, belatedly, in Albania). What Italy expected of empire was not Italophone natives running their own affairs, with a 'district commissioner' here and there overseeing taxes and law and order, but land. Italy wanted an Australia or an Argentina not an India. The events of the Great War had done nothing to jolt this perceived need; rather, in the post war, the empire of the Third Italy was a still more blatant failure in its fundamental purpose. In 1921, not counting military personnel, 656 Italians resided in Somalia, 3,635 in Eritrea, and 27,495 in Libya.[61] Of the last, most were labourers, artisans, shopkeepers, or office workers in Tripoli, a large proportion of whom would in likelihood have been there had Libya never become an Italian colony. After all, a far larger number of Italians had settled themselves from 'the Italies' to find a life in Tunis, Algeria, or Alexandria and construct their own *mare nostrum*, beyond the national state. There they mended shoes, built houses, baked bread, ran cafés, or, like the Ferrero family, which moved to Algiers in 1907, ended up exporting couscous and Tunisian Harissa chilli sauce to the world. As for the mass of rural poor tilling abundant land in a far-flung empire, by 1921 four decades of rhetoric and of killing had resulted in the settlement there of as many peasants as would have fitted comfortably into a single rural hamlet within Italy.[62] The Third Italy never did more than construct an empire of illusions.

---

[60] G. Tomasin, 'Giuseppe Volpi', *Ateneo Veneto*, 184 (1997), 132.
[61] Del Boca, *Gli italiani in Africa*, 867.
[62] Del Boca, *Gli italiani in Libia*, 453.

3

The German Empire

Heather Jones

INTRODUCTION

Germany's relationship with empire was a particularly complex one, which challenges traditional chronological and spatial understandings of imperialism in the Great War. Its pre-war manifestations have long been the focus of historiographical study. It is a perennial historical argument, and a staple of undergraduate essays the world over, that German imperialism was a factor in causing the First World War. Otto von Bismarck's reluctant acceptance of the acquisition of a handful of German overseas colonies in the late nineteenth century and Bernhard von Bülow's advocacy of *Weltpolitik* are frequently cited as the fatal turns on a road that led inevitably to clashes with other empires, in particular, as Germany sought to build a navy to match its growing colonial aspirations and rival those of the imperial state it most longed to copy—Great Britain.[1]

To this debate on the role of German imperialism in causing the First World War has more recently been added a wave of new work, on the nature of the pre-First World War German colonial project in Africa, which emphasizes its violent, at times genocidal, repression of native uprisings, by the Herero, Nama, and Maji-Maji peoples. This has resulted in a historiographical discussion as to the singularity or similarity of the German colonial project in Africa to that of other empires and its long-term possible legacy for Nazism.[2]

Both of these debates about the pre-war German Empire ultimately force us to engage with more fluid chronological boundaries regarding Germany's Great War. First, the debate on the role of German imperialism in the origins of the war increasingly points to 1911 and the Second Moroccan Crisis as the key rehearsal for 1914, when French fears of German violent aggression radicalized dramatically, leading France further to embrace the Russian military alliance. The same year, the Italian invasion of Ottoman Libya triggered debates in Germany about a potential

---

[1] On the war origins debates, see William Mulligan, *The Origins of the First World War* (Cambridge, 2010); Holger Afflerbach and David Stevenson (eds), *An Improbable War? The Outbreak of World War I and European Political Culture before 1914* (Oxford, 2007).

[2] See, on these debates, Jürgen Zimmerer, *Von Windhuk nach Auschwitz? Beiträge zum Verhältnis von Kolonialismus und Holocaust* (Münster, 2010); Robert Gerwarth and Stephan Malinowski, 'Hannah Arendt's Ghosts: Reflections on the Disputable Path from Windhoek to Auschwitz', *Central European History*, 42/2 (2009), 279–300.

future war between empires. In 1911 Europe saw the birth of forms of war culture, particularly in the press, that would feed directly into cultural mobilization in 1914. Second, the historian Isabel Hull has argued that German military radicalization in Europe after 1914 followed the template of the 'battle of annihilation' utilized in the German repression of the Herero, Nama, and Maji-Maji. In this interpretation, Germany's Great War violence originates in part in the colonies, as early as 1904.[3]

If examining Germany in terms of an empire rather than a nation state thus suggests that certain forms of Great War violences began in imperial practices before 1914, it also raises the idea that this overlap continued later than previously thought, into the period 1918–23. The new Polish state, which incorporated territory, particularly in Posen and Silesia, that had formerly been part of the 1871 Wilhelmine Reich, saw violent clashes, which often revealed elements of a decolonization paradigm, between German irredentists who viewed ethnically Polish parts of the 1871 Reich as legitimate German imperial territory and Polish secessionists who sought to join the new Poland, exemplified by the Silesian Uprising.[4]

Of central importance here is to understand the full complexity of what the idea of 'empire' actually meant for the German state by the time of the First World War. The German case certainly fulfilled Charles Maier's definition of Empire as a supranational entity, characterized 'by ethnic hierarchization', but it was also more complex, with decentralized federal internal structures within the Reich, as well as diversifying overseas soft and formal colonial power.[5] In other words, the term 'German Empire' encompassed multiple imperial functions of the German state. Moreover, during the war, the term 'German Empire' in fact referred to several overlapping imperial components that made up the *Kaiserreich*—first, the term 'German Empire' referred to what might be defined as the 'internal' empire, the territory within the pre-1914 boundaries of the Reich that had been designated as an empire at its foundation in 1871; second, the term referred to the wartime vision of Germany as a European continental empire, ruling over annexed territories as well as satellite states, brought into Germany's sphere of control as a result of the conflict; and, third, the term referred to Germany as a global empire, invoking the pre-war colonial empire that Germany had built up overseas in Africa, Asia, and the Pacific. Examining to what extent Germany envisaged the war in 'imperial' terms thus necessitates considering each of these three components of the German Empire, as well as how they overlapped. The German Empire at war, in other words, should not be seen as a set of separate military fronts, but rather as an interconnected series of imperial assumptions that grounded military and foreign policy decision-making across its different combat and occupation zones, which stretched

[3] Isabel Hull, *Absolute Destruction: Military Culture and the Practices of War in Imperial Germany* (Ithaca, NY, 2004).
[4] Timothy Wilson, *Frontiers of Violence: Conflict and Identity in Ulster and Upper Silesia, 1918–1922* (New York and Oxford, 2010).
[5] See the discussion on the definition of empire in the Introduction to this volume, p. 3.

from Shandong in China to Zanzibar in Africa and Samoa in the Pacific to Cour-
land in the Baltics.

This chapter will look at each of the three components of the German Empire,
in turn, to explore how ideas of empire shaped Germany's war effort and experience and how the different territorial components of Germany's empire related to
each other at war. With the recent shift to re-examining the global nature of the
First World War in the historiography, such an exploration is timely. Significantly,
it will also help us to draw some conclusions regarding the accuracy—or not—of
the British wartime claim, which figured prominently in Allied propaganda, that
the German state in the First World War was an empire waging a war of imperial
colonial conquest—a somewhat ironic accusation given that elements in the
British government and establishment used the guise of coming to the defence of
Belgium as a means to wage a war aimed at imperial strategic territorial acquisition, particularly in the Middle East.[6]

THE 1871 GERMAN EMPIRE

It is important to emphasize here the fundamental nature of the German state,
which illustrates the first component of the German Empire that was at play
during the First World War—the German state within its borders of 1871 as an
imperial state. The *Kaiserreich* was understood at the time as being simultaneously
both a nation state and an empire. The ambition to 'empire' was present from the
very outset of the foundation of the state in 1871, when Germany laid claim to
imperial status in the use of the term *Reich*, intended as a revival of an older idea
of 'the Holy Roman Empire of the German Nation', which had ceased to exist in
1806 when Napoleon dissolved it as a legal entity.[7] This new state was emphatic-
ally not designed to be a kingdom like Prussia; it was instead an imperial federation. The new German Empire thus laid claim to the status and complexity of an
imperium, yet it was, initially, an empire without colonial overseas territories. It
formed them instead in what might be termed its internal borderlands: in both
its policy and discourse towards non-German minorities it created colonial spaces
to be conquered within the frontiers of the state.[8] The most important internal
components in this were the non-ethnically German regions of the Reich, in
particular, Alsace-Lorraine, obtained as a result of the Treaty of Frankfurt at the
end of the Franco-Prussian War and the eastern ethnically Polish areas.[9] To quote
Sebastian Conrad, during the period between 1871 and 1914: ' "Poland" increasingly took on the role of an ersatz colony—in fact almost an actual colony—for

---

[6] See Sir Valentine Chirol's preface to the British propaganda translation of Colonel H. Frobenius's
book *The German Empire's Hour of Destiny* (London, 1914).

[7] Fritz-Konrad Krüger, *Government and Politics of the German Empire* (London, 1915), 13.

[8] Kristin Kopp, 'Gray Zones: On the Inclusion of "Poland" in the Study of German Colonialism',
in Michael Perraudin and Jürgen Zimmerer (eds), *German Colonialism and National Identity* (New
York and London, 2011); Robert Lewis Koehl, 'Colonialism inside Germany: 1886–1918', *Journal of
Modern History*, 25/3 (1953), 255–72.

[9] Ernest Barker, *The Submerged Nationalities of the German Empire* (Oxford, 1915).

the German empire.'[10] The Polish areas of Posen and West Prussia saw particular discrimination: 'the German colonisation programme pursued by the government from 1886 increased tension in both provinces, especially once legislation was passed in 1908 permitting the expropriation of Polish-owned land for resettlement with Germans.'[11] As Philipp Ther has pointed out: 'In ethno-linguistic terms, the empire of 1871 was not as German as the confederation of 1815. Millions of Poles and Polish-speaking people were included.'[12]

It was initially this *primary* level of Empire—represented by the boundaries of the Reich itself—that most Germans mobilized to defend in 1914, in particular, supporters of the Social Democrats, since 1912 the largest party in the Reichstag. The popular view of the war in Germany in August 1914 was that at the outset it was seen as a defensive conflict, waged to defend the borders of the 1871 Reich against encirclement and against Russian belligerence.[13] Yet among the responses to what was perceived as an attack on the Reich by Russia and France were those who argued that the best way to defend the Reich was to expand it—by creating a new colonial periphery under German control. Bethmann-Hollweg stated as much when he referred to: 'securing our frontiers against every danger, blocking the invasion-gates of Belgium and Poland.'[14] It is this drive for security that explains the annexationist imperial ambitions of Bethmann-Hollweg's 1914 September Programme, revealed by Fritz Fischer in *Germany's Aims in the First World War* (1967).[15] This programme envisaged a number of German expansionist gains in the event of victory, including that Luxembourg would become a German federal state, Belgium would lose territory to Germany in annexations and become a vassal state, a *Mitteleuropa* economic unit would be created that favoured Germany, the borders of Russia would be 'thrust back as far as possible from Germany's eastern frontier', and Germany would also seek to create a 'continuous central African colonial Empire'.[16] Such expansionist ideas gained ground as the war continued, ultimately dividing German public and political opinion by 1917, exemplified by the Reichstag Peace Resolution that year, when those parties who opposed the idea of German annexations of conquered territories to the Reich clashed with right-wing voices who supported expansion.

How to consolidate the empire of 1871 and protect it was fundamental, in other words, to German wartime mobilization—this is also very clear in the fears

---

[10] Sebastian Conrad, *Globalisation and the Nation in Imperial Germany* (Cambridge, 2010), 25. See also Kristin Kopp, 'Contesting Borders: German Colonial Discourse and the Polish Eastern Territories', Ph.D. Dissertation, University of California, Berkeley, 2001.

[11] Alexander Watson, 'Fighting for Another Fatherland: The Polish Minority in the German Army, 1914–1918', *English Historical Review*, 126/522 (2011), 1137–66, at p. 1140.

[12] Philipp Ther, 'Beyond the Nation: The Relational Basis of a Comparative History of Germany and Europe', *Central European History*, 31/1 (2003), 45–73, at p. 54.

[13] See Jeffrey Verhey, *The Spirit of 1914: Militarism, Myth and Mobilization in Germany* (Cambridge, 2000); Gerhard Hirschfeld, ' "The Spirit of 1914": A Critical Examination of War Enthusiasm in German Society', in Lothar Kettenacker and Torsten Riotte (eds), *The Legacies of Two World Wars: European Societies in the Twentieth Century* (Oxford and New York, 2011).

[14] Fritz Fischer, *Germany's Aims in the First World War* (London, 1967), 98.

[15] Fischer, *Germany's Aims*, 101–4.

[16] Fischer, *Germany's Aims*, 103–4.

regarding Germany's internal non-German population of about 3.5 million Poles and 1.8 million Alsace-Lorrainers, who were seen in terms of imperial subjects, not culturally recognized as full German citizens, potentially disloyal and secessionist and thus discriminated against.[17] There was relief when Polish conscripts obeyed the 1914 call-up.[18] On mobilization in Posen, the description used for these men was 'Prussian subjects with the annotation "mother tongue: Polish"' ('subjects' rather than 'citizens'), and few Poles served as officers.[19] Alsace-Lorrainers from March 1915 were subject to scrutiny and if deemed unreliable were sent to fight on the Eastern Front; Poles were dispersed across reliable German-speaking majority units from November 1915.[20] The debates regarding how to mobilize these non-German groups within the 1871 empire, and the restrictions that the army placed upon where they could be deployed to fight, followed closely the lines of pre-1914 concerns regarding implementing policies to 'Germanize' these groups and consolidate Polish-speaking and French-speaking areas into the overall Reich—an internal, if small-scale, project of imperialism. These issues can be described as 'local' imperial fears, regarding the internal minorities within the Reich.

Yet such local imperial fears fused with broader transnational ones during the war. The clearest example of this is the constant trope in German wartime propaganda that the 1871 Reich faced defending its border against a 'world of enemies'.[21] This drew closely upon German fears of the British and French *empires* rather than their metropole states—and, in particular, upon fears of British and French non-white colonial subjects. This appears to have been linked closely to earlier discourses stemming from how the Herero uprising and its ruthless repression had been portrayed to the German population within the borders of the 1871 Reich.[22] Germany's own poor treatment of its colonial subjects, and their rebellion, was now projected onto British and French colonial subjects who were being used to fight against the Reich both on the Western Front, where Britain used Indian troops and France, which had been debating the use of African troops to compensate for French demographic decline since General Mangin's book *La Force noire* in 1910, used black African and Arab units, and overseas. Germany accused these colonial troops of not waging war according to European customs and norms. The fusion of local imperial fears and overseas colonial anxieties is also visible in the cultural mobilization of white German settlers in Germany's African colonies.

[17] For the figures on population, see Ernest Barker, *The Submerged Nationalities of the German Empire* (Oxford, 1915), 7. Germany also had a population of 150,000 Danes in North Schleswig. On discrimination, see Watson, 'Fighting for Another Fatherland'; Alan Kramer, 'Wackes at War: Alsace-Lorraine and the Failure of German National Mobilization, 1914–1918', in John Horne (ed.), *State, Society and Mobilization in Europe during the First World War* (Cambridge, 1997), 110–21.

[18] Watson, 'Fighting for Another Fatherland', 1142.

[19] Watson, 'Fighting for Another Fatherland', 1144, 1145.

[20] Watson, 'Fighting for Another Fatherland', 1156, 1158.

[21] See, for an example of this language, Emil Zimmermann, *Die Bedeutung Afrikas für die deutsche Weltpolitik* (Berlin, 1917); also Wilhelm Doegen, *Kriegsgefangene Völker*, i. *Der Kriegsgefangenen Haltung und Schicksal in Deutschland* (Berlin 1919 [1921]).

[22] David Ciarlo, 'Picturing Genocide in German Consumer Culture, 1904–1910', in Perraudin and Zimmerer (eds), *German Colonialism and National Identity*.

As Daniel Steinbach has shown, settlers projected a German concept of *Heimat*, the idea of a German homeland that Germans were honour bound to defend, a concept widely present in the cultural mobilization within Germany in 1914–15, onto the African landscape—for example, likening Mount Kilimanjaro to the Bavarian Alps—in order to inspire settlers to fight to defend the colony.[23] Thus settlers tried to define the colonial space within a national language of *Heimat* while, inside the German metropole, imperialist phrases were often used to define the interaction with non-German regions—national and imperial ideas were not segregated between the internal and overseas empire.

Indeed, as Sebastian Conrad has shown, the *Kaiserreich* was part of a globalizing world, and saw itself as the metropole of a German Empire that had both overseas and internal imperial components.[24] Since the 1880s, influential German lobby groups, such as the Colonial League, the Navy League, and the Pan-German League, had craved overseas colonies to turn the German Empire of 1871 into a more contemporary model of nation-state imperium, as pioneered by Britain and France, and ultimately this public pressure forced Bismarck to shift policy and the German Empire to acquire overseas colonies.[25] Here it is important to emphasize that in 1914 there was no sharp opposition between 'empire' and 'nation state' *per se*. The two were generally not seen as diametrically opposed; the radicalization and spread of the idea that they were usually in opposition was itself largely a consequence of the Great War.[26] For many Europeans, the most economically advanced form of state was one in which the core was a nation state with multiple colonial satellite territories, either neighbouring, as in the case of the European continental land-based empires such as Russia, or overseas, as in the case of Britain and France.[27] The pinnacle of modernity at the time, and indeed into the interwar period, was seen as statehood constructed along the British or French model, which was seen as successfully combining nation state and imperium. This belief that a nation-state imperium was the most modern and economically advanced form of state helps to explain much regarding German imperial wartime ambitions. Germany was seen as *both* a nation state and an empire before and during the First World War, without this being viewed as a contradiction, and imperial fantasies infused much of German culture in a similar way to what had occurred in Britain and France.[28]

---

[23] Daniel Rouven Steinbach, 'Defending the "Heimat": The Germans in South West Africa and East Africa during the First World War', in Heather Jones, Jennifer O'Brien, and Christoph Schmidt-Supprian (eds), *Untold War: New Perspectives in First World War Studies* (Boston and Leiden, 2008), 196.

[24] Conrad, *Globalisation and the Nation in Imperial Germany*.

[25] Roger Chickering, *We Men Who Feel Most German: A Cultural Study of the Pan-German League, 1886–1914* (London, 1984).

[26] On this post-war clash between Empire and nationalism, see Niall Ferguson, *The War of the World: History's Age of Hatred* (London, 2006); Mark Cornwall, *The Undermining of Austria-Hungary: The Battle for Hearts and Minds* (Basingstoke, 2000).

[27] See, e.g., the discussion in Krüger, *Government and Politics*, 260–3.

[28] Lora Wildenthal, *German Women for Empire, 1884–1945* (Durham, NC, and London, 2001); Jeff Bowersox, *Raising Germans in the Age of Empire: Youth and Colonial Culture, 1871–1914* (Oxford, 2013).

THE WARTIME CONTINENTAL GERMAN EMPIRE

It is in this interwoven understanding of the relationship between empire, nation state, and modernity that the broader context is to be found for the second component of German Empire during the war: Germany's development of war aims that envisaged it becoming a major European land-based continental empire. This resulted from the rapid German military conquest of large amounts of continental European territory, particularly in the East, which gave rise to new ideas of a German continental empire. In many ways what occurred here was a contingent dynamic, similar to that described by Robinson and Gallagher in their theory of imperial expansion with regard to the British Empire, whereby a lack of security at the periphery drove imperial expansion to protect existing territory: satellite states and annexations, used as part of a process of colonizing the East, were now seen as a valid way to protect the 1871 Reich boundaries from any future Russian aggression.[29] As Friedrich von Schwerin, the President of Frankfurt/Oder and a member of the Pan-German League, wrote in a memorandum in March 1915 for the chancellor's office, the war marked 'an opportunity—perhaps for the last time in world history—for Germany to reengage its imperial mission in the East' (see Fig. 5).[30]

Fig. 5. Carving out an Eastern Empire: Wilhelm II presenting medals in Warsaw, September 1915.

[29] John Gallagher and Ronald Robinson, with Alice Denny, *Africa and the Victorians: The Official Mind of Imperialism* (London, 1961). William Roger Louis (ed.), *Imperialism: The Robinson and Gallagher Controversy* (New York, 1976).
[30] Cited in Annemarie H. Sammartino, *The Impossible Border: Germany and the East, 1914–1922* (Ithaca, NY, 2010), 31.

This continental wartime empire differed from the other two levels of German Empire—the internal and the global—in several ways. First, it was entirely a consequence of the conflict and the superiority of the German army that had allowed it to gain control of vast swathes of land and several major cities, mostly in Eastern Europe, although also including parts of northern France and Belgium in the west. It was thus temporary, contingent on wartime occupation, and had to be rapidly consolidated under immense pressure owing to the blockade and Germany's need for wartime resources and also within a wartime climate of radicalizing expectations. Second, it embraced the idea of annexations as a means of acquiring and sustaining empire—the language of annexation framed the vision of how this continental empire would be developed, often disregarding international law. In this light, the German Fatherland Party, which rapidly gained a million members following its foundation in 1917, saw the east as a site of future German Empire by dint of conquest rights. In Andrew Donson's analysis of wartime youth literature, such imperial voices were all too present: '"I see tomorrow a great future brought to Germany," a boy in a wartime story for youth dreamed, "I see my Fatherland at the height of its power as the Empire of Europe–a goal we can all be happy to die for."'[31] Third, this was partly a diaspora-driven Empire—based on pre-1914 dreams of uniting ethnic German populations scattered across Eastern Europe into a greater German 'Imperium' which would also encompass practices familiar to other empires of the time—population resettlement and hierarchies of control over economic resources.[32] As Annemarie Sammartino has convincingly argued: 'German successes on the Eastern Front encouraged wide-ranging fantasizes [*sic*] about territorial expansion and population displacement in the occupied territories. The *Auslandsdeutsche* provided both the excuse for these plans and the proof of their potential success.'[33] In this way, the wartime German continental empire merged existing ideas regarding how European states controlled their overseas possessions with how a future German land-based continental empire would operate. This was fundamentally new and radical: applying ideas of racial hierarchy and colonial understandings of the limited rights of natives to self-determination to newly occupied white European cultures came as a shock to international public opinion. In this attempt to conflate overseas colonialism and older notions of European imperium, Germany was breaking new ground. For example, the head of the German police force in Ober Ost, the German occupation regime in the Baltic region, was General Rochus Schmidt, an 'old East African' who had served in Germany's African colony; Schmidt's 'untrained gendarmes notoriously abused their power over native populations' in Eastern Europe, just as his earlier police had in Africa.[34]

With regard to Eastern Europe, the idea of a continental German Empire had long been a dream of expansionist minded military, right-wing radicals and state

[31] Andrew Donson, 'Models for Young Nationalists and Militarists: German Youth Literature in the First World War', *German Studies Review*, 27/3 (2004), 579–98, at p. 588.

[32] Sammartino, *The Impossible Border*, 18–44.

[33] Sammartino, *The Impossible Border*, 29.

[34] Vejas Gabriel Liulevicius, *War Land on the Eastern Front: Culture, National Identity and German Occupation in World War I* (Cambridge, 2000), 78.

bureaucrats charged with dealing with the Reich's internal Polish question—of how to turn 'Poles into Germans', a process that mimicked some elements of the French Third Republic's activities at the time.[35] It was thus a project closely linked to the internal empire within the Reich's pre-1914 borders, as it was integrally connected to earlier understandings of how to assimilate the Reich's internal Polish population. The wartime dream of a German continental European empire in the East thus had old roots.[36] It was a pre-1914 rhetorical discourse that actualized unexpectedly during the conflict.

New work, examining the nature and cultural attitudes of German occupation regimes in Eastern Europe, charged with building this new German continental empire, substantially supports Fritz Fischer's argument—that the First World War was an imperial war for Germany, which aimed to defend, consolidate, and expand the German Empire, developing territorial designs, during the conflict, upon the Baltic region, the Ukraine, Romania, and much of what had been Russian Poland.[37] As Vejas Gabriel Liulevicius has revealed, Germany's war in the East was being waged as a war of colonial conquest, with local inhabitants increasingly viewed as 'natives', and conquered lands targeted for ruthless exploitation, particularly Ober Ost, where 'in the streets, natives were required to make way for German officials, saluting and bowing. Violence became increasingly routine [...] Brutality toward natives went unchecked from above, due to the imperative of presenting a unified front.'[38] Ober Ost law was applicable only to natives, while Germans were to be judged by German law—a classic colonial division of legal norms within contemporary empires, which usually distinguished between the rights of a citizen and those of an imperial subject.[39] Colonial settlement of these newly conquered areas by Germans was also envisaged, something that had been promoted by nationalist groups in the pre-war period who advocated German migration to the East, as well as the order such settlement would bring to the region.[40] Here there were also clear overlaps with pre-war rhetoric regarding German settlement in Africa and its 'civilizing mission'.[41]

THE GLOBAL GERMAN EMPIRE AT WAR

As suggested above, these colonial dimensions to Germany's war effort in Eastern Europe did not occur in isolation—by 1914 Germany had a well-established overseas

---

[35] Sammartino, *The Impossible Border*, 19–21; Eugen Weber, *Peasants into Frenchmen: The Modernization of Rural France 1870–1914* (Stanford, 1976).

[36] Gregor Thum, 'Mythische Landschaften: Das Bild vom deutschen Osten und die Zäsuren des 20. Jahrhunderts', in Gregor Thum (ed.), *Traumland Osten: Deutsche Bilder vom östlichen Europa im 20. Jahrhundert* (Göttingen, 2006).

[37] Liulevicius, *War Land on the Eastern Front*; Christian Westerhoff, *Zwangsarbeit im Ersten Weltkrieg: Deutsche Arbeitskräftepolitik im besetzten Polen und Litauen 1914–1918* (Paderborn, 2011).

[38] Liulevicius, *War Land on the Eastern Front*, 63.

[39] Liulevicius, *War Land on the Eastern Front*, 76.

[40] Liulevicius, *War Land on the Eastern Front*, 71.

[41] Wildenthal, *German Women for Empire*.

global empire, which was central to how it perceived and imagined its war effort as a whole, encompassing, in Africa, German South-West Africa, German East Africa, Cameroon (Kamerun), and Togoland; in Asia, its leased territory in the bay of Jiaozhou in the North Chinese province of Shandong, obtained on a ninety-nine-year lease in 1898, where a small German colony was established at Qingdao (Tsingtao); and in the Pacific, Samoa, German New Guinea, Kaiserwilhelmsland, and the Bismarck Archipelago, counting the Marshall, Caroline, and Mariana islands among its possessions.

Germany was also gaining ground at establishing an extensive German informal empire as well. This was particularly effectively developed through military missions and trade, with a focus on using 'soft-power' approaches to establish German informal imperial influence in North Africa, particularly Morocco, and the Ottoman Empire, where German General Liman von Sanders was sent to act as a military adviser.[42]

In other words, by 1914 Germany was becoming a serious imperial player. Some recent historiography has claimed that the German overseas empire was not very important, due to its size and its low economic value to the Reich, which had significantly to subsidize it, with the exception of Togo.[43] However, this assumption is largely because the focus has been upon the economic value of Germany's overseas colonies for the *Kaiserreich*'s home economy. In contrast, if we consider empire in strategic and symbolic terms, Germany's imperial overseas acquisitions had far greater impact owing to their location. By 1914 the German Empire was on the rise in a series of geographically sensitive regions for Britain and France—Morocco, the Ottoman Empire, and the neighbourhood of Britain's new South African colony following the tumult of the divisive Boer War. Germany was gaining serious leverage in these areas. This did not always set it at loggerheads with Britain, which often chose, pre-1914, to collaborate with Germany's imperial ambitions—for example, providing trade supplies via South Africa during the German ruthless crushing of the Herero people in German South-West Africa in 1904–7.[44] However, German soft power began increasingly to come into competition with British and French imperial designs before 1914. Moreover, it was envisaged very much in terms of creating substantial military links in the event of war; this was precisely what occurred in the case of the Ottoman Empire, where General Liman von Sanders, initially head of the German military mission, played a significant role in the Ottoman Empire's war effort, commanding the Turkish first army and later the Turkish fifth army at Gallipoli before ending the war commanding a force made up of Ottoman and German troops on the Palestine front. In the case of the Ottoman Empire, pre-war imperial soft power morphed into a close wartime military alliance.

---

[42] Liman von Sanders, *Five Years in Turkey* (Annapolis, 1927), 13.

[43] Krüger, *Government and Politics*, 274.

[44] Ulrike Lindner, 'Transnational Movements between Colonial Empires: Migrant Workers from the British Cape Colony in the German Diamond Town of Lüderitzbucht', *European Review of History: Revue européenne d'histoire*, 16/5 (2009), 679–95. Hew Strachan also argues that Britain and Germany largely cooperated in pre-war colonization in Africa: Hew Strachan, *The First World War in Africa* (Oxford, 2004), 2.

Germany's aim for its global empire at the outbreak of war in 1914 encompassed two main strategies: first, to 'open the war up' to divert British forces from the war in Europe to defend imperial outposts.[45] Second, to foment revolution within the British, French, and Russian empires, particularly among Muslim subjects through promoting the call to Jihad, issued on 12 November 1914, by Germany's ally the Ottoman Sultan, a policy promoted to the Kaiser by Max von Oppenheim.[46]

The German wartime 'programmes for revolution' are revealing of Germany's overall imperial ambitions. They were not isolated events but a supplementary imperial strategy to conventional warfare, directed by the German Foreign Office in conjunction with the Political Section of the Reserve General Staff, encompassing the Islamic world, Russia, the Caucasus, North Africa, and the Near East, as well as Ireland.[47] Dissident groups were targeted for German financial support with the intention of promoting revolutionary subversives into power, with the expectation that their subsequent regime would welcome German influence, thereby extending soft German imperial power and creating effective buffer states to protect Germany's borders: discussions took place in Berlin in 1918 with Finnish, Georgian, Persian, and Indian revolutionaries; the Irish nationalist Roger Casement was assisted in his attempt to create a force to fight Britain in Ireland from among Irish prisoners of war in German camps.[48] The German government promoted separatist movements in areas Germany had occupied, as well as further afield, in Flanders and among Russia's oppressed border nationalities—in particular, in the Ukraine—and in what had been Russian Poland.[49] Oskar von Niedermayer led a German mission to promote subversion in Afghanistan, while Werner Otto von Hentig and Mahendra Pratap travelled to Afghanistan with the aim of contacting political revolutionaries in India.[50] This process was profoundly transnational, based on 'the vision of Germany's economic expansion into Mitteleuropa, the Near East, the Caspian basin, into Central Asia and across the borderlands of the English and Russian Empires, as well as the targeted mobilization of dissident groups of all kinds as agents in the service of German empire', who exchanged ideas: 'the Persian Committee, for example, paid particular attention to the situation of the Ukrainian nationalists in 1918 and were in contact with Indian nationalists throughout the war.'[51]

However, Germany's two initial global wartime strategies for its empire were unsuccessful. Germany's overseas colonies fell rapidly at the start of the war, failing substantially to divert British or French forces from Europe, and Germany's

---

[45] Strachan, *The First World War in Africa*, p. vi.

[46] Sean McMeekin, *The Berlin-Baghdad Express: The Ottoman Empire and Germany's Bid for World Power, 1898–1918* (London and New York, 2010).

[47] Jennifer Jenkins, 'Fritz Fischer's "Programme for Revolution": Implications for a Global History of Germany in the First World War,' *Journal of Contemporary History*, 48, 2 (2013), 397–417, p. 401.

[48] Jenkins, 'Fritz Fischer's "Programme for Revolution" ', 403.

[49] Jenkins, 'Fritz Fischer's "Programme for Revolution" ', 402–3.

[50] Jenkins, 'Fritz Fischer's "Programme for Revolution" ', 409.

[51] Jenkins, 'Fritz Fischer's "Programme for Revolution" ', 399.

revolution programme saw little success—with the one, important exception, of the Bolshevik Revolution in Russia.

Germany's enclave at Qingdao in China was among the first to be lost, swiftly conquered by Japan, an Entente ally, which had long coveted it. On 7 August, Britain requested Japan's help in controlling the German navy in East Asian waters, and Japan used this as a pretext to demand that Germany hand over control of Qingdao. When Germany refused, Japan responded by declaring war. Germany immediately requested that all adult male Germans in China travel to Qingdao to defend it; approximately 2,500 did so, joining 2,500 German soldiers already stationed in the city.[52] Qingdao fell on 7 November 1914, following a brief Japanese siege, involving 28,000 Japanese troops; casualties were an estimated 224 Germans but approximately 4,000 Japanese.[53] Some 5,000 German soldiers and civilians became prisoners of the Japanese, who generally treated them well. Japan also conquered the islands of German Micronesia. Germany's colonies of Western Samoa, New Guinea, and the Bismarck Archipelago were captured between August and November 1914 by Australian and New Zealand forces upon British request. All these colonies were mandated to the captor states after the war, with the exception of Qingdao, returned to China in 1922.

In Africa, Togo was the first German colony to fall, lightly defended when the Allies attacked to capture its radio communication posts. Here, on 12 August 1914, Sergeant-Major Alhaji Grunshi of the British West African Frontier Force 'became the first soldier in British service to fire a round in the Great War'; within thirteen days, on 25 August, the German governor of Togo surrendered.[54] Of the remaining German African colonies, South-West Africa surrendered on 9 July 1915, largely conquered by South African troops allied with Britain. The South African Prime Minister Louis Botha and Minister for War Jan Smuts had wanted to invade South-West Africa in response to a British request, coveting its territory for a 'greater South Africa'. But Boer soldiers in the South African army rebelled against assisting the British, whom they had fought bitterly in the Boer War, just over a decade before. However, the rebellion failed. On 13 May 1915, Windhoek, the capital of German South-West Africa, fell. A total of 1,300 German *Schutztruppen* died defending South-West Africa; their South African opposition lost only 250 men. The third German African possession to surrender was Cameroon. Douala was captured in September 1914, and the remainder of the colony was conquered by 20 February 1916. Fighting in extremely difficult conditions, the forces defending Germany's African colonies faced high losses owing to disease and required large numbers of African porters: in Cameroon, the Germans estimated between two and three porters for each soldier; in total, Germany employed as many as 40,000 porters in the campaign.[55]

Thus the new possibilities for a German continental land-based empire within Europe that Germany's military success opened up ironically came into being at

---

[52] Klaus Mühlhahn, 'Prisoners of War and Internees (East Asia)', 14–18-Online (forthcoming).
[53] Mühlhahn, 'Prisoners of War and Internees (East Asia)'.
[54] Strachan, *The First World War in Africa*, 1.
[55] Strachan, *The First World War in Africa*, 5.

precisely the moment when Germany was faced with losing the third dimension of its 'German Empire', its overseas colonies, of which only German East Africa remained unconquered by the end of 1916. There, a guerrilla-style force led by Paul von Lettow-Vorbeck continued to fight Allied forces, largely by eluding them. The leader of a German colonial *Schutztruppe* force of approximately 218 Europeans and 2,542 black soldiers in German East Africa at the start of the war, Lettow-Vorbeck, pursued a mobile campaign, initially aided by naval raids by the *Königsberg*, a German battleship that evaded the Allies until 11 July 1915. However, by the second half of the war Lettow-Vorbeck's forces were greatly diminished and ultimately had to retreat into the Portuguese colony of Mozambique in order to continue fighting. They did not surrender until 25 November 1918 at Abercorn—the war in Africa outlasted the war in Europe.

Lettow-Vorbeck's exploits had considerable influence on German metropole culture.[56] He and his men were honoured with a parade through Berlin upon their return in 1919. The praise heaped upon Lettow-Vorbeck's plucky resistance within Germany during and after the war set up a legitimizing discourse for borderland guerrilla campaigning under an independent, autonomous, charismatic military leader—something that bore similarities to the discourses that emerged in the Baltic Freikorps campaigns in 1918–19. Similarly, during the war, the 'heroic' war in the colonies was used as a source for patriotic stories aimed at mobilizing German youth: in particular, the case of the *Emden*, the German cruiser torpedoed in the Indian Ocean in 1914 after it had sunk sixteen British ships, and the exploits of its landing crew who were captured by the British but later escaped, was the subject of wartime adventure stories.[57] Discourses of colonial military valour long outlasted the reality of German control of its overseas colonial possessions.

Above all, the war in Africa challenged pre-war white cultural unity in pursuing the colonization project. This had obvious implications for German, British, and French settlers, many of whom, in 1914, initially hoped that the war would not spread to the African colonies and that white unity would be preserved. This was the case in German East Africa; in contrast, there was a degree of war enthusiasm in 1914 in German South-West Africa.[58] The settlers' main fear was that, if Africa's white population took sides against each other in the war, these divisions might be exploited by the natives to gain power. Seeing whites fighting among themselves would undermine the idea of white civilization as superior; worse, if the colonial authorities opted to use black troops in the war in the colonies against enemy white populations, this would undermine the racial hierarchy on which white rule rested—and might encourage blacks to rebel against the colonial racial order.[59] This was the reason why, after Lettow-Vorbeck's surrender, the British were careful

[56] Michael Pesek, 'Colonial Heroes: German Colonial Identities in Wartime, 1914–1918', in Perraudin and Zimmerer (eds), *German Colonialism and National Identity*.
[57] Donson, 'Models for Young Nationalists and Militarists', 587.
[58] Steinbach, 'Defending the "Heimat"', 188–90.
[59] Strachan, *The First World War in Africa*, 2.

not to disarm his white troops in the presence of black natives, as this was seen as something that would humiliate all whites in black eyes.[60]

Thus the spread of war to the colonies in Africa in 1914 destroyed the idea of a homogenous, shared white colonial project; one corollary of this was that it also further empowered developing anthropological ideas that there were 'different' white races, which, in turn, interacted with notions in Europe of racial hierarchies among European peoples. Perhaps the clearest transnational vector here for such ideas were anthropologists who, before the war, had worked overseas, investigating 'native' peoples.[61] With the outbreak of the conflict such travel became impossible, so Germany's anthropological imperialism came 'home'—anthropologists continued their work on classifying racial difference and cultural behaviour by studying prisoners of war in German camps.[62] This included classification not only of black or Asian racial groups but also of white 'races' of Europe, including Tartar, Slav, Norman, or Celtic, for example, further contributing to ideas of racial hierarchies within Europe and lending them scientific respectability.

The war thus had a major impact on the relationship between discourses of race and German imperialism—which had ramifications across the three imperial components of the German Empire. Perhaps the most important element of this was the way that the war changed the construction of how race determined what constituted 'legitimate' and 'illegitimate' violence. Before the war, it was culturally accepted that certain kinds of violent practices were not permitted in war among the 'civilized' nations but that these limitations did not apply in wars against colonized indigenous peoples overseas, where greater extremes of violence were permissible before 1914, although it is important not to assume that no limits at all applied: Germany's genocidal extremes in repressing the Herero in 1904–7 provoked angry responses from large segments of European society, particularly the socialists, and led to criticism from other colonial powers, who rebuked Germany for poor colonial management. However, overall, before the First World War, violence perpetrated by whites upon blacks, in particular, could be culturally legitimized in ways that were not possible with regard to violence between white groups or by blacks upon whites. This legitimization was heavily based on the common idea in Europe at the time, infused with contemporary racism, that black populations used extreme forms of violence in war, such as mutilation of corpses, cannibalism, killing of prisoners, and torture.

During the First World War, this relationship between race and legitimate forms of imperial violence—and the debate that surrounded it—moved physically to Europe when the British used Indian units, and the French used black African and North African Arab units, on the Western Front (see Fig. 6). Many

---

[60] The National Archives, Kew, WO 158/907, General von Lettow's force: treatment of troops as prisoners of war, December 1918.

[61] Andrew D. Evans, *Anthropology at War: World War I and the Science of Race in Germany* (Chicago, 2010).

[62] Heather Jones, 'Imperial Captivities: Colonial Prisoners of War in Germany and the Ottoman Empire, 1914–1918', in Santanu Das (ed.), *Race, Empire and First World War Writing* (Cambridge, 2011), 175–93.

Fig. 6. Imperial PoWs: Captured black and white French troops at Fort Douaumont.

Germans believed that colonial troops brought their extreme, barbaric violent practices from the colonies to Europe and argued that the use of non-white troops on European battlefields was a war crime; this was partly also an argument of political expediency, as Germany did not have access to the numbers of trained colonial troops that Britain and France had.[63] In turn, German violence against the Herero in 1904–7 was made into a central tenet of British wartime propaganda, accusing Germany of colonial misrule. At the same time, in Eastern Europe, Germany and Austria–Hungary used forms of arbitrary violence, such as the indiscriminate execution of partisans, that had previously been associated with colonial warfare. If race was the key factor that determined whether a particular kind of violence could be used legitimately or illegitimately in the overseas component of the German Empire, before 1914, the war in Europe saw this spreading to Germany's wartime territorial acquisitions in Eastern Europe, where ethnic groups were increasingly classified and perceived in racialized terms, and these classifications legitimized their exploitation and, often violent, oppression. A blurring of the distinction between the overseas colonial sphere and the German Empire's European war fronts was clearly occurring, as debates raged between the belligerents about what constituted the legitimate imperial use of violence, by Germany

[63] Christian Koller, '*Von Wilden aller Rassen niedergemetzelt': die Diskussion um die Verwendung von Kolonialtruppen in Europa zwischen Rassismus, Kolonial- und Militärpolitik (1914–1930)* (Stuttgart, 2001); Jones, 'Imperial Captivities'; Auswärtiges Amt, *Völkerrechtswidrige Verwendung farbiger Truppen auf dem europäischen Kriegsschauplatz durch England und Frankreich* (Berlin, 1915); *Liste über Fälle, die sich auf planmäßige Ermordung und Mißhandlung einer größeren Zahl von deutschen Kriegsgefangenen durch farbige Truppen beziehen* (Berlin, 1919).

as an occupier or colonizer, and France and Britain as colonial masters, on both Eastern and Western fronts.

There were clearly transnational links and influences between the overseas and continental European components of Germany's wartime imperialism, particularly in terms of imperial governance, anthropology, and in the idea of a specifically German imperial 'civilizing mission'. Moreover, the language applied to the war in Europe—barbarism, tribal hatreds, atrocity—borrowed heavily from descriptive frameworks that had been used for war in the colonies before 1914. The rumours regarding German troops cutting off Belgian children's hands had close links to the pre-war reporting of actual such mutilations of black workers in King Leopold's Congo colony. Debates about race and violence invoked not only fears about how tribal warfare practices might be imported to Europe but also deeper fears that Europe itself was in fact no different from Africa—one of the validations for white European superiority globally was the belief that whites exercised self-restraint with regard to violence. Freud, and many others, likened the war violence to the primitive in Europeans emerging. In this conflict, European civilization suddenly appeared as a constructive veneer—the war in Europe became 'African', ironically while combat in Africa in 1914–18 was increasingly constructed as romantic, framed in the language of adventure, heroic leadership, and exploration.

Nowhere is this more evident than in the paradox that, while Germany decried the use of blacks, Indians, and Arabs on the European battlefield because they were believed to use unacceptable primitive, barbaric forms of violence, it also lauded the fighting behaviour of its own black soldiers, the Askari, in the German colonies.[64] In particular, those black troops who fought with Lettow-Vorbeck in East Africa were idealized. His black Askari increasingly came to be portrayed as 'civilized' and romanticized, while the war in Europe was increasingly depicted as primitive and barbaric. This portrayal of the Askari was largely a myth: as Michelle Moyd has pointed out, 'nearly 3000 askari (of about 12,000)' deserted Germany's East African *Schutztruppe* forces during the war.[65] Yet the depiction of the Askari was one of loyalty to Germany, typified by the following description from Lettow-Vorbeck's memoirs:

All our troops, native as well as Europeans, had always held the conviction that Germany could not be beaten in this war, and were resolved to fight on to the last [...] whenever I discussed this topic with one of my orderlies he always assured me: 'I will always stick by you and fight on till I fall.'[66]

In a complete reversal of pre-1914 norms, war in the colonies now appeared less extreme, less violent, more limited, and more gentlemanly, than war in Europe, partly because industrial warfare did not take place in the overseas sphere, partly because it was so difficult to get information about what was really happening in the colonies back to Germany during the war, owing to Allied success in controlling

[64] Michelle Moyd, ' "We Don't Want to Die for Nothing": *Askari* at War in German East Africa, 1914–1918', in Das (ed.), *Race, Empire and First World War Writing*, 90–107.
[65] Moyd, ' "We Don't Want to Die for Nothing" ', 100.
[66] General von Lettow-Vorbeck, *My Reminiscences of East Africa* (London, 1920), 318.

the sea routes and radio transmission stations, and, most importantly of all, because the war in most of Germany's colonies was over by 1916.[67] This was further fuelled after the war by the gallant behaviour of the former colonial antagonists towards each other: Lettow-Vorbeck became a friend of Jan Smuts, his erstwhile opponent. On one occasion in 1929, Lettow-Vorbeck was a guest at a banquet of British East African veterans, where Smuts proposed a toast to him.[68]

This depiction of a chivalric colonial contest in Africa in the First World War was, of course, an illusion: the war devastated large swathes of African agriculture and cost the lives of 'upwards of 200,000' Africans serving as soldiers or labourers in Africa, the majority succumbing to disease rather than enemy bullets.[69] It was also a myth that was confined to the depiction of combat: German propaganda accused the French of interning German settlers, including women and children, from French-controlled areas, in terrible conditions in Dahomey. Likewise, Germany accused France of mistreating German prisoners of war, who were captured on the Western Front but sent to prisoner-of-war camps in North Africa. One of the major accusations was that France had placed black and Arab troops in charge of guarding these prisoners.[70] German propaganda claimed this exposed these men to torture and primitive colonial violence by these guards; in reality, the protests were as much because keeping German prisoners of war in North Africa, particularly Morocco, was a deliberate humiliation by France of Germany's pre-war imperial ambitions in the region. In contrast, Britain evacuated many of its German prisoners of war from Africa to Egypt and also to Ahmednagar in India; however, little polemic emerged regarding these transfers.[71]

In reality, the region where German imperialist ambitions touched most closely upon extreme violence during the war was the Ottoman Empire, which was part of the German Empire's informal soft-power sphere, through German trade projects and Germany's role in advising the Ottomans militarily, rather than an actual component of Germany's empire. Here, historiographical debate continues as to what extent Germany was complicit in the Ottoman genocide of the Armenians, particularly at the local level, given German failure to protect Armenians working on the Berlin–Baghdad railway—a construction project under German control. German intervention to prevent the Armenian genocide was never likely; its overriding imperative was to retain its soft-power influence upon its vital wartime ally, particularly as the Ottoman Empire's evident weakness meant that such influence was likely to enable Germany to gain access to Middle Eastern markets and trading routes in the future.

[67] *Der Heldenkampf unserer Kolonien, Nach den amtlichen Mitteilungen des ReichsKolonialAmts zusammengestellt* (Berlin, 1915). See also Pesek, 'Colonial Heroes: German Colonial Identities in Wartime, 1914–1918'.
[68] Bundesarchiv Berlin R 72/1188 13.6.1935, *Deutsche Allgemeine Zeitung*, 'Deutsche Frontkämpfer in London. Eine Erinnerung'.
[69] Strachan, *The First World War in Africa*, 3.
[70] Jones, 'Imperial Captivities'.
[71] I am grateful to Mahon Murphy for this information: Mahon Murphy, 'The Geography of Internment', unpublished chapter.

Indeed, the loss of Germany's entire overseas empire, with the exception of German East Africa, by 1917 meant that German imperialist ambitions were now increasingly forced to focus on Eastern Europe and the Middle East. On the one hand, this emboldened Pan-Germanist and other radical right-wing voices, who saw the opportunity for annexations of territory and growing imperial influence; on the other, it provoked major opposition from those who had entered the war believing it to be a purely defensive conflict, such as the SPD and the Centre Party. During the First World War there was never a consensus around what Germany's imperial future should be—public opinion was divided on this question, and powerful groups within Germany such as the SPD, who had opposed empire in the pre-war period, continued to do so in wartime. They initially lost ground during the euphoria at Germany's territorial gains in the first half of the war in 1914–16, but regained it by 1917 as war weariness grew among German workers. But, by that point, German imperialism had also gained a wide swathe of motivated supporters who mobilized in the Fatherland Party and viewed new forms of 'empire' as the only acceptable reward for the huge costs of the war, although they differed as to which components of empire should be prioritized in the event of a German victory. In other words, what was often described as a 'national' German war effort could only be redeemed by 'imperial' rewards: the situation in Germany's overseas empire and in Europe thus interacted closely.

British propaganda clearly portrayed Germany's war effort as one of imperial expansion. Edwyn Bevan, writing in February 1918, warned his readers of Germany annexing the Flanders coast and the French mining districts of Briey and Longwy, creating a *Mittel-Europa* of 'a closer union, political, military and economic, between the German Empire and its Allies—Austria-Hungary, Bulgaria and Turkey—in such wise that there is a continuous belt of German power from Hamburg to the Persian Gulf, a great Central European realm capable of defying the world' and establishing a great German Empire in tropical Africa, 'extending right across the Continent from the Atlantic to the Indian Ocean'.[72] This British belief—that Germany's war aims intended global imperial domination—was a major impediment to any negotiated peace during the war.

Such imperial interpretations of what was at stake in the First World War were common. As Jennifer Jenkins points out: 'More than one diplomat had visions of zeppelins carrying German goods over the Causcasus to the Persian Gulf' in a new imperial sphere where German trade dominated, created by the war.[73] Moreover, as the war continued, the weakness of Austria–Hungary led increasingly to it too being viewed as a German satellite state. With the Treaty of Brest-Litovsk in spring 1918 it became clear which tendency within Germany had won out: the annexationist expansionist vision in the East had delivered spectacular results, and Brest-Litovsk, had it survived, would have marked the foundation of a new continental land-based German Empire. Only a few short months later, all would be

---

[72] Edwyn Bevan, 'Introduction', to Emil Zimmermann, *The German Empire of Central Africa as the Basis of a New German World-Policy* (London, 1918), pp. vii–viii.
[73] Jenkins, 'Fritz Fischer's "Programme for Revolution"', 416.

reversed with defeat on the Western Front, which meant Germany never regained its overseas empire, lost its continental European territorial wartime acquisitions, including those set out in the Treaty of Brest-Litovsk, and lost large elements of the 1871 empire with the return of Alsace-Lorraine to France and the territorial losses to the new Poland. All three of the original imperial components of the German Empire at war in 1914–18 were no more.

CONCLUSION

The German Empire at war in 1914–18 was both an imperial state and an imperial project in progress. Its three imperial components, the Reich of 1871, the wartime continental empire of occupation, and the overseas colonies, overlapped and interacted in ways that still remain to be explored by historians. Germany, as an empire, was a major player in pre-1914 globalization, free trade, and civilizing mission ideology—pre-1914 globalization went hand in hand with imperialism. It is not possible to understand the loss of status experienced by the German state with the November 1918 Armistice and Treaty of Versailles without recognizing the scale and complexity of the German Empire that fought the war, and its dismantlement in its aftermath. Indeed, without recognizing the sheer scale and complexity of the imperial dimensions and aspirations of the *Kaiserreich*, it is not possible fully to understand the reasons why Weimar appeared such a mutilated state to German nationalists in the interwar period: well into the 1920s, German right-wing groups protested vigorously at Germany's loss of colonies and Eastern territory in the wake of the Treaty of Versailles. Figures such as the former colonialist Heinrich Schnee were instrumental in campaigning for the return of Germany's African colonies; others, such as the head of the Reichswehr, Hans von Seeckt, focused on the lands lost to the new state of Poland.[74] A central aspect of interwar Germany's instability was caused by the difficulty of transitioning from empire to republic—a difficulty epitomized by the title of Weimar's constitution, which still used the old term *Reich*, 'die Verfassung des deutschen Reiches', for a new republican state.

This brings us to the question posed at the outset: to what extent should we see Germany in the First World War as an empire waging a war of imperial colonial conquest? It is clear from this chapter that German imperial visions during the Great War were multifaceted and complex. The German case differed from the British and French in that its aspiration to a continental land-based European empire during the war incorporated a diaspora dynamic; its recourse to colonial forms of coercion against white populations in Europe was also new and radical. Yet, the aspiration to global empire in itself was not that different from the British and French: with regard to both the Middle East and Africa, Britain, France, and Germany all nursed similar imperial ambitions. Likewise, the structure of the 1871 *Kaiserreich*, as both empire and nation state, can be compared with the United Kingdom, which was both the

---

[74] Heinrich Schnee, *German Colonization Past and Future: The Truth about the German Colonies* (New York, 1926).

metropole of a global empire and a 'British' nation state and also sought to assimilate the ethnically distinct entity of Ireland. The British Empire also distinguished between British citizens and British subjects—a legal hierarchy that ensured that all were not equal before the law. Both Britain and Germany waged their war under the leadership of a King–Emperor. Ultimately, in many regards, the German Empire at war was not so different from its enemies. For contemporaries, there was no distinct opposition between nation state and empire: the modernity of the British and French nation-state–empire model was what Germany aspired to.

Overall, Germany was also subject to broader trends. The post-war collapse of internal, land-based European empires, and their imperial ideologies regarding the control of neighbouring subject European ethnicities, radicalized violence in ways that, while far from identical, did bear some similarities to post-colonial violences in overseas colonies. It is surely not too great a step to see the German Freikorps in the East, small units of paid, professional fighters, including war veterans, engaged in forms of warlordism, largely beyond metropole control and often recruited from the German diaspora living beyond the Reich's borders or in its borderlands, as having some commonalities with a remnant colonial settler force, radicalizing in response to imperial collapse and withdrawal, such as would occur, later in the century, in the Rhodesian case, to name but one potential comparison. The brutality of the Freikorps' fighting practices in the Baltics appears to have had a colonial dimension—as a radical response to German imperial overstretch and retreat.

More broadly, the wave of violence in Eastern Europe after 1918 stemmed from imperial vacuum and disputed borders among nation states that succeeded empires in the region—both classic traits of post-colonial conflict later in the century—as was the common attempt across this zone to impose radicalized national identities upon peasantries that had hitherto often largely identified overwhelmingly with local or imperial–dynastic ones. The legacy of Germany's empire in the East—both the Reich Empire of 1871 and the wartime expansionist temporary empire of occupation—was part of this fraught semi-decolonization process: German imperial withdrawal from the area was contested well into the interwar years by the German right, while the new Polish state radicalized its imposition of nationalism in order to break culturally with its previous imperial rulers—Russia and Germany. Its border wars with the Ukraine, Soviet Russia, and Lithuania, its attempts to incorporate experienced veterans who had fought in the imperial German forces into a new Polish national army, and its scapegoating of minority populations as ethnically 'other' were all symptomatic of fears stemming from the former imperial powers' refusal to accept that they had lost all rights to interfere in those territories that now belonged to the new Poland.

Prior to the First World War, globalization had been driven by empire. In its wake, this relationship was much more fraught. For the Weimar Republic, exclusion in Europe was matched by exclusion from British and French imperial markets. Flows of people and goods within the British Empire partly cushioned the UK economy from the turbulence of the interwar period. Weimar had no such global protection. Instead Weimar struggled with the problematic legacy of

German wartime imperialism. The language of 'empire' now focused upon the 'lost territories' of the 1871 Reich, to Poland, in particular, destabilizing the republic. The imperial hierarchical distinction between German citizen and subject also arguably turned inwards and can be seen in the interwar debates that raged over who could be considered a German citizen and whether Jews, Communists, or Eastern European migrants should be excluded. The ideology of *Lebensraum* became cumulative heir to all the various migration policies that had once been envisaged for the three components that made up the German wartime empire. Ironically, it was with the loss of empire and the foundation of the Weimar Republic that Germany faced adopting a purely nation-state model for the first time, something German nationalists found ultimately impossible to come to terms with. This sense of loss of an imperial 'Reich' identity was something the Nazis recognized as a source of resentment during Weimar—it was no accident that they won over support with a rhetoric based on establishing a 'third Reich'. Ultimately, the Nazis were able to remobilize elements of the deeply complex earlier German relationship with the idea of the 'imperial', in support of their notion of a 'racial empire', with appalling consequences.

4

Austria–Hungary

Peter Haslinger

INTRODUCTION: THE HABSBURG MONARCHY BEFORE 1914

Before the First World War, the Habsburg Monarchy seemed an anachronistic element of European politics to some observers. With a population of fifty-one million, Austria–Hungary was the third most populous state structure in Europe in 1910 (after the Russian and the German empires). Nevertheless, it was less and less capable to cope with the challenges of a new era that was to be based on the principle of the nationalizing state, political mobilization, and mass communication. The well-functioning bureaucracy in the western territories notwithstanding, the complex fabric of the Habsburg Monarchy resembled the old principle of a composite dynastic structure, and the concept of rule still rested upon an old universalistic self-understanding and the idea of solidarity among the peoples of the monarchy. The decisive aspect in this respect was that the population of Austria–Hungary was comparatively diverse as regards its spoken language.[1] As a consequence, dynastic patriotism and loyalties were designed to work as complementary to ethnic feelings and thus allow for the integration of the distinct national groups under the ruler and his administration.[2] Accordingly, Habsburg rulers had obtained political legitimacy from balancing between ten and twelve 'tribes' (*Volksstämme* or ethnolinguistic communities) within the political system of the monarchy since the end of the eighteenth century. Also for that reason, the political system of the Habsburg Monarchy oscillated between autocratic rule with militaristic features and restricted parliamentary democracy. Helmut Rumpler holds that it was this combination that 'fit the necessities

---

[1] According to the official figures of the Austrian and Hungarian censuses of 1910, 23.36% spoke German, 19.57% Hungarian, 16.37% Czech or Slovak, 9.68% Polish, 8.52% Serbian, Croatian, or Bosnian, 7.78% Ukrainian, 6.27% Romanian, 2.44% Slovene, and 1.5% Italian; the remaining 2.3 million spoke a variety of other languages. Robert A. Kann, *Geschichte des Habsburgerreiches 1526 bis 1918* (Vienna and Cologne: Böhlau, 1990), 581.

[2] Lawrence Cole and Daniel Unowsky (eds), *Limits of Loyalty: Imperial Symbolism, Popular Allegiances, and State Patriotism in the Late Habsburg Monarchy* (New York and Oxford: Berghahn Books, 2007).

of the nationally, culturally, and economically highly heterogeneous community of lands'.[3]

After the unity of the monarchy was threatened by the revolutions and wars of independence in 1848–9, the new emperor Francis Joseph designed a divide-and-rule policy hoping to prove that national groups could coexist within his multilingual empire, despite the fact that nationalizing tendencies increased again during the 1860s. The most momentous step in this respect was the Austro-Hungarian compromise (*Ausgleich*) of 1867, after which Hungary, now a sovereign kingdom, began to pursue interests and a nationalizing agenda of its own. The Hungarian example evoked fantasies and political desires on practically all sides (especially among Czech, Polish, and Croatian[4] elites). Ideas that had emerged since the early nineteenth century and that noted that territories of compact linguistic settlement that existed across crown land boundaries were entitled to have a say in political decision-making grew ever more popular. Because of constant Hungarian opposition, however, the now ageing emperor and king Francis Joseph deliberately prevented the creation of further proto-national territories.

After the 1897 Czech–German dispute over the use of languages in regional administration had seriously challenged the whole political system, Francis Joseph increasingly began to apply emergency legislation within the Austrian state and to approve of initiatives at the regional and local level that transformed political life based on the proportional representation of ethnic groups (like the so-called small compromises in Moravia 1905–6 or Bukowina 1910, as well as local arrangements as in Budweis/České Budějovice in 1913). In other crown lands and cities of the Austrian state (such as Vienna, Prague, or Ljubljana/Laibach), however, national activists were quite free to implement their nationalist agendas—even if they aimed at the linguistic assimilation of local minorities within the limits of state legislation. In the Austrian state, no linguistic group formed the target of a systematic policy of discrimination from the centre. Although the political system of Austria–Hungary did not satisfy any of the national movements entirely, including the dominant German and Hungarian ones, Francis Joseph's policy enjoyed some success by creating a political framework for negotiation. Therefore, on the eve of the First World War, national compromise seemed possible even in Bohemia, the most developed crown land, which had become practically ungovernable by 1913 owing to national strife between Czech and German political representatives.[5]

With no serious colonial ambitions to gain positions overseas, military circles still cherished expansionist fantasies in the direction of the Balkans. These had been fuelled by the integration of Bosnia and Hercegovina into the Habsburg

---

[3] Helmut Rumpler, 'Grenzen der Demokratie im Vielvölkerstaat', in Helmut Rumpler and Peter Urbanitsch (eds), *Die Habsburgermonarchie 1948–1918*, vii/1 (Vienna: Verlag der Österreichischen Akademie der Wissenschaften, 2000), 1–10, at p. 1.

[4] In 1868, Croatio–Slavonia reached a status of autonomy within Hungary; soon, however, Hungarian governments tried to erode this position.

[5] E. Drašarová, R. Horký, J. Šouša, and L. Velek (eds), *Promarněná šance: Edice dokumentů k česko-německému vyrovnání před prdní světovou válkou. Korespondence a protokoly 1911–1912*, 2 vols (Praha: Národní archiv, 2008); Peter Haslinger, *Nation und Territorium im tschechischen politischen Diskurs 1880–1938* (Munich: Oldenbourg, 2010), 197–207.

Monarchy. The two provinces were occupied by the Austro-Hungarian monarchy after the Congress of Berlin in 1878, and, although internationally Bosnia remained part of the Ottoman Empire up to its annexation in 1908, it was integrated into the economic system of the Habsburg Monarchy, and all important issues were decided upon exclusively in Vienna. On the local level, however, Ottoman structures and legal norms were kept or adjusted to serve Austro-Hungarian interests. As a consequence, the confessional–national communities played a defined role within the political system of Bosnia-Hercegovina from the beginning of Habsburg rule. The Catholics (or Croats), the Orthodox (Serbs), and the Muslims (Bosnjaks as they were called by the Viennese administration) had proportional political representation in bodies that had a say in strictly cultural and local affairs only.[6]

From the point of view of Emperor Francis Joseph, Bosnia-Hercegovina was the only territory acquired and not lost during his reign, and the Muslims of Bosnia represented the newest and most exotic stone in the imperial mosaic of ethnic and confessional plurality. In the 1880s, a whole series of publications from military circles described Bosnia-Hercegovina as a region full of vital natural resources such as ore or timber, but also as a region untouched by modern civilization and therefore as a target for 'cultural development' (*Kulturarbeit*) by a European great power.[7] The Bosnian Muslims were envisaged either as a people unable to follow the paths of modern European development or as noble savages whose successful integration into the empire could serve as an example that the imperial idea was an integrative force bridging cultural hierarchies. For some authors close to the imperial administration, Bosnia also seemed to provide opportunities for further expansion into the Balkans, where the Ottoman system proved less and less capable of fostering loyalty and safety. In contrast to all other European powers and their selfish interests, so these publications suggested, the Habsburg Monarchy was be the only state experienced enough to handle carefully the different ethno-linguistic and ethno-confessional cleavages while at the same time fulfilling the civilizing mission necessary to bring peace and prosperity to a neglected region of Europe.[8]

If the ever-worsening German–Czech relationship formed the Gordian knot of the nationality question in Austria, the question of South Slavs was an issue of major concern in terms of foreign politics, first of all in the direction of the Balkans and Russia. In order to prepare alternatives to the dualistic structure, the successor to the Habsburg throne, Archduke Franz Ferdinand, contemplated the transformation of Austria–Hungary into a trialistic monarchy with a South Slav state beside

[6] Robin Okey, *Taming Balkan Nationalism: The Habsburg 'Civilising Mission' in Bosnia, 1878–1914* (Oxford: Oxford University Press, 2007).

[7] Emerich Bogović, *Zur bosnischen Frage: Eine Studie* (Zagreb: Leopold Hartman, 1880), 61. Cf. also Josef Neupauer, *Wie könnte die europäische Cultur nach Bosnien verpflanzt werden?* (Vienna: Selbstverlag, 1884).

[8] Examples for this discourse can be found in Johann von Asbóth, *Bosnien und die Herzegowina: Reisebilder und Studie* (Vienna: Hölder, 1888); J. M. Baernreither, *Bosnische Eindrücke: Eine politische Studie* (Vienna: Hölder, 1908); Moritz Graf Attems, *Bosnien einst und jetzt* (Vienna: Seidel, 1913).

Austria and Hungary. In 1905, the Dalmatian Croat Franjo Supilo organized a congress in Fiume (Rijeka) to foster collaboration between Serbs and Croats within Austria–Hungary. A major irritation to Russia and Serbia, however, was the annexation of Bosnia-Hercegovina proclaimed on 3 October 1908, and it added to the pre-war tension between the great European powers. Despite the transformation of the political system of Bosnia-Hercegovina in 1910 that introduced a regional parliament with some authority, the province remained politically unstable because of the radicalization of a younger generation that saw limited prospects for advancement. All south Slav subgroups formed new associations that adopted a different approach towards the Habsburg Monarchy. According to Ivo Lederer, *Slovenski Jug* (Slovene Youth), *Mlada Bosna* (Young Bosnia), *Ujedinjenje ili smrt* (Unification or Death) and many others

shared two points in common: hatred of Austria–Hungary and the vision of an eventually united Yugoslav state. [...] By 1911, spurred by pro-Yugoslav currents in Croatia, Slovenia, Montenegro, and particularily in Dalmatia, Belgrade, with the blessing of Saint Petersburg, set out to realize earlier Serbian dreams of a Balkan concert. The new alliance produced dramatic results, and the triumph of Serbian arms in 1912–13 lent credence to Serbia's mission as the Piedmont of the South Slavs.[9]

THE WAR THEATRE IN THE EAST AND THE HABSBURG MONARCHY

The results of the two Balkan Wars (8 October 1912–21 July 1913) were not only a serious setback to Austria–Hungary's strategy of soft imperialism in the Balkans. The wars also made it clear to any observer that Austria–Hungary had lost ground on the Balkan peninsula vis-à-vis its principal rival in the region, the Russian Empire. Not only had the Habsburg Monarchy little influence on the territorial expansion of Serbia and Montenegro. Even the only success of Austro-Hungarian foreign policy in the region, the founding of an Albanian state, resulted in new tension in the international arena.[10] The end of Ottoman rule in most of Europe stimulated expansionist ideas in Vienna, as articulated by the Austro-Hungarian foreign minister, Count Leopold Berchtold, who considered launching a war against Serbia.[11]

In the summer of 1914, the strategy of diverting public opinion from increasing interior conflicts through a localized war gained popularity among the political elites of Austria–Hungary.[12] Enthusiasm for war against Serbia was widespread in the

---

[9] Ivo J. Lederer, 'Nationalism and the Yugoslavs', in Peter Sugar and Ivo Lederer (eds), *Nationalism in Eastern Europe* (Seattle: University of Washington Press, 1969), 396–438, at p. 428.
[10] Aleš Skřivan, *Deutschland und Österreich-Ungarn in der europäischen Politik der Jahre 1906–1914* (Hamburg: Döllinger und Galitz Verlag, 1999), 314–21.
[11] Graydon A. Tunstall, 'Austria–Hungary', in Richard F. Hamilton and Holger H. Herwig (eds), *The Origins of World War I* (Cambridge: Cambridge University Press, 2003), 112–49, at p. 117.
[12] Manfried Rauchensteiner, *Der Tod des Doppeladlers: Österreich-Ungarn und der Erste Weltkrieg* (Graz and Vienna/Cologne: Styria, 1993), 59.

streets of major cities of the Habsburg Monarchy, and all in all dynastic loyalty was still unquestioned. As Martin Zückert argues, 'a long established "traditional" obligation to the empire dating back to the sixteenth century became clearly recognizable'.[13] Nevertheless, Austria–Hungary entered the First World War with a whole landscape of national–political friction. The outbreak of the war soon began to upset a delicate balance that had been functioning until 1914—by an increasingly complex system of regional compromises and an overall strategy of imperial divide and rule. The assassination of Franz Ferdinand in Sarajevo on 28 June 1914 thus triggered a chain of events that not only altered the basic elements of Habsburg politics but also opened windows of opportunity for alternative future scenarios that would render the complicated and partly dysfunctional political system unnecessary.

First, for the imperial and military circles the war opened prospects for territorial expansion. When the imperial council of ministers behind closed doors decided to declare war on 19 July 1914, it first refrained from annexing Serbia and expressed its intention to reduce its territory only through border adjustments of mainly strategic character. As the war continued, however, Austrian government and military circles and the foreign office came forward with concepts for farther reaching territorial expansions, even if this implied creating a third state-like entity beside Austria and Hungary within Habsburg territory. Although the influential Hungarian prime minister István Tisza successfully opposed any concrete step in that direction, these considerations made it clear to any observer that the dualistic structure of the Habsburg Monarchy was not to be preserved at any cost, even in the case of a victory. Moreover, it became clear as well that the Austro-Hungarian positions in terms of its war aims were highly dependent on considerations within German foreign policy, and therefore also influenced indirectly by the War Aims Movement and the Pan-German League.[14]

For the transformation of the dual structure of Austria–Hungary into a trialistic monarchy, there were three options that shifted in importance and priority during the war. Most frequent and known to the public were references to the so-called Austro-Polish solution that first materialized in concepts developed by Foreign Minister Berchtold and in debates within the imperial council in August 1914 (where plans for issuing a corresponding declaration were dropped only after the forceful intervention by Tisza). Even after the manifesto of Wilhelm II and Francis Joseph declaring a self-governing and independent Kingdom of Poland on 5 November 1916—saying that the Central Powers established a Polish kingdom out of former Russian territory—this option remained on the Habsburg agenda. Piotr Wandycz, however, reminds us of one side effect of that joint declaration that further limited chances for the Austrian concept to materialize: 'While the manifesto was a statement of intentions rather than a political arrangement it

---

[13] Martin Zückert, 'Imperial War in the Age of Nationalism: The Habsburg Monarchy and the First World War', in Jörn Leonhard and Ulrike von Hirschhausen (eds), *Comparing Empires: Encounters and Transfers in the Long Nineteenth Century* (Göttingen: Vandenhoek & Ruprecht, 2011), 500–17, at p. 502.

[14] Ian F. W. Beckett, *The Great War 1914–1918* (Harlow: Longman, 2001), 137–8.

internationalized the Polish question to a point of no return. What is more it placed the Poles in a position of being courted by both belligerent camps.'[15]

The second set of considerations reminds us of Franz Ferdinand's idea to create a South Slav state within the Habsburg Monarchy; under circumstances of war, however, this concept implied an expansionist element: this third state under Habsburg rule was thought to contain vast parts of Serbia and Montenegro, sometimes even Northern Albania. In the joint council of ministers on 7 January 1916, it was Tisza again who strongly opposed the integration of Serb territory and more Slav population, and the decision was postponed.[16] The third and less common option foresaw the attachment of Romania or at least part of its western territories to the Habsburg Monarchy. Behind all these options, however, there was no overall strategy, so that preferences shifted with the continuation of the war and became at the same time more and more dependent on German considerations.[17] Even when, after the death of Francis Joseph I, his successor Charles initiated a discussion over the war aims in the imperial council on 12 January 1917, territorial expansion to the north-east (Poland) and south-east (Serbia, Montenegro, Romania) was highlighted as a war aim. The minimum objective was to preserve the territorial integrity of the Habsburg Monarchy.

But also in terms of considerations by the Allied powers for a post-war European settlement, the Habsburg Monarchy was forced onto the defensive by the continuation of the war. First, in order to stop potential allies of the Central Powers from entering the war to fight the Entente, French, British, and Russian policymakers offered considerable territorial gains to Italy and Romania in the secret treaties of London (April 1915) and Bucharest (August 1916). Russia, Serbia, and Montenegro were also to expand westwards into what was then Austro-Hungarian territory after the victory of the Entente.[18] Aside from these considerations and secret diplomacy, however, there was yet another important element that began to shape French and British foreign policy's perspectives. Exile circles from the Habsburg Monarchy, first of all of Czech(oslovak) and South Slav background, soon began to seek contact with British and French experts on Central Europe, like Henry Wickham Steed, Robert W. Seton-Watson, or Ernest Denis (the activities of Tomáš

---

[15] Piotr Wandycz, *The Polish Question* (Berkeley: University of California Working Papers), 4.

[16] Wolfdieter Biehl, *Der Erste Weltkrieg: 1914–1918* (Vienna, Cologne, and Weimar: Böhlau, 2010), 135.

[17] After the United States had entered the war on 6 April 1917 and the distribution of military power had shifted in favour of the Entente, the two main Central Powers secretly met in Bad Kreuznach on 23 April and 17–18 May 1917 jointly to define Germany's and Austria–Hungary's war aims. Accordingly, Germany would have acquired the Baltic territories and Poland, while, in exchange, Eastern Galicia would have been handed over to Russia in an attempt to neutralize it. For that loss of territory, Austria–Hungary would have been recompensed with parts of Romania and a South Slav state that included Serbia, Montenegro, and Northern Albania. By 5–6 November the same year, however, at the Berlin war aims conference, the tendency had shifted towards the Austro-Polish solution, while the Baltic territories and Romania would have been under German control. Biehl, *Der Erste Weltkrieg*, 159, 163.

[18] In regard of the Russian perspective, Foreign Minister Sazonov suggested that the Habsburg Monarchy assigned Galicia to Russia, both Bosnia-Hercegovina and Dalmacia to Serbia, and eventually Transilvania to Romania, while the remaining territory should be divided into an Austrian empire and a Hungarian as well as a Czech kingdom that should also include Slovakia.

Garrigue Masaryk and Edvard Beneš, later president and foreign minister of the first Czechoslovak republic, were the most important). Although until spring 1918 Entente decision-makers were reluctant to embrace the concept of the 'New Europe' that advocated for the multinational empires to be replaced by nation states, the possibility of doing so if there were no other options found growing acceptence in the middle stratum of the British and French foreign offices. So, even if Entente plans for the post-war future of the Habsburg Monarchy rather implied the transformation of the political system and the interior constitutional composition without questioning its very existence, alternative options began to be chanelled into the foreign-policy administrations and planning circles as early as 1915.

Moreover, the military machinery of Austria–Hungary soon proved to be ill pre-pared for the conditions of mechanized war and mass mobilization. Inappropriate preparation, less-developed infrastructures, and the inappropriate use of ser-vicemen and supplies were factors that confined the ability of the Habsburg Empire to cope with the challenges that armies faced in the First World War. Insufficient troop stands, obsolete artillery, an insufficient railroad network, an industrial base too deficient to fight a total war, and a poorly functioning supply system placed the Habsburg army at a major disadvantage.[19] This general picture has been demon-strated in great detail by Graydon Tunstall in his work on the Winter War in the Carpathians, which in 1914–15 left one million killed or injured on both sides of the Russian–Austro-Hungarian front: 'The Carpathian theatre lacked the [...] communication lines, and other important resources necessary for maneuvering mass armies. [...] Mountain warfare as characterized by the Carpathian winter of-fensives produced a combat experience vastly different from the trench warfare of the west.'[20]

For a long time, it has been taken for granted that on the Western Front the First World War produced overall mobilization of societies and the establishment of war cultures in all spheres of everyday life.[21] Thus technical and infrastructural innov-ation resulted in the mass experience of anonymous death. As Dennis Showalter has stated, the 'net result of all this flexibility and adaptability was the loss of millions of men, the expenditure of millions of shells, and the consumption of millions of tons of resources for nothing remotely resembling proportionate achievements'.[22] This kind of overall mobilization and the establishment of war cultures, however, were much less characteristic for the war theatres in the East. In contrast to the 'culture of competence' and bureaucratization in the West,[23] the

[19] Graydon A. Tunstall, *Blood on the Snow: The Carpathian Winter War of 1915* (Lawrence: Univer-sity Press of Kansas, 2010), 209.
[20] Tunstall, *Blood on the* Snow, 1, 4–5.
[21] Horst Bauerkämper and Elise Julien, 'Einleitung: Durchhalten! Kriegskulturen und Hand-lungspraktiken im Ersten Weltkrieg', in Horst Bauerkämper and Elise Julien (eds), *Durchhalten! Krieg und Gesellschaft im Vergleich 1914–1918* (Göttingen: Vandenhoeck & Ruprecht, 2010), 7–28, at p. 7.
[22] Dennis E. Showalter, 'Mass Warfare and the Impact of Technology', in Roger Chickering and Stig Förster (eds), *Great War, Total War: Combat and Mobilization on the Western Front, 1914–1918* (Cambridge: Cambridge University Press, 2000), 73–93, at p. 82.
[23] Showalter, 'Mass Warfare and the Impact of Technology', 81.

social and infrastructural systems proved less capable to adapt to the new character war had now acquired, and because of its more mobile operations the involvement of the civilian population into warfare was also greater.[24] What also made a profound difference to the front in the West were the dynamics of 'disintegrative mobilization'. Dietrich Beyrau and Pavel Shcherbinin have argued that the empires situated in the centre or the eastern half of Europe proved less capable in creating political consensus over war aims. Rather, they were destabilized from within by lack of political legitimacy and complex interethnic relations that got thrown off balance in the course of the war.[25]

Besides the mounting difficulties in supply that plagued other belligerent states as well, there are three aspects that should be mentioned here for the case of Austria–Hungary: first, the war not only encouraged expansionist fantasies at the imperial level but also fostered initiatives to substitute the complex political fabric the dual monarchy had acquired in the past decades with a clear structure of quasi-national states that were based on the predominance for Germans and Hungarians within this renewed system. Until the outbreak of the First World War, Francis Joseph I had respected the complex constitutional arrangements and discretely encouraged constitutional experiments to balance competing national movements. Now, under the influence of high military circles, the Austrian emperor and Hungarian king soon began to abandon this policy of integrative flexibility. First, in 1915 the Austro-Hungarian relationship was redefined towards further recognition of Hungarian souvereignty in exchange for fixing the conditions of a joint foreign trade policy and shares in financing the military, the so-called *Ausgleich*, for twenty years and not only for ten years as usual. Secondly, in March and April 1916 German national circles from within Austria and a group of their leading politicians approached Francis Joseph and high military circles with two memoranda laying out their plan finally to introduce a centralized system in the Austrian state and legally to codify German dominance within.

In the course of the war, geopolitical thinking, however, became accepted also by the less dominant nations—not only by their representatives in exile but also by those who remained politically active within the borders of Austria–Hungary. These approaches developed under the conditions of censorship until early 1917—if necessary by the creative adaptation of the Central Powers' logic of war propaganda. Until then, alternatives to the integrity of the Habsburg Empire remained clandestine and often highly contested messages. Their common aim was to secure the existence of the nation under any circumstances in the future. This is interconnected with yet another factor that has to be taken into consideration when explaining how the composite monarchy of Austria–Hungary transformed into a de-composite political system: the extent of retaliation that applied not only along the front but also in the hinterland against groups that had been singled out

---

[24] Hew Strachan, 'War and Society in the 1920s and 1930s', in Roger Chickering and Stig Förster (eds), *The Shadows of Total War: Europe, East Asia, and the United States, 1919–1939* (Cambridge and New York: Cambridge University Press, 2003), 35–54, at pp. 35, 54.

[25] Dietrich Beyrau and Pavel P. Shcherbinin, 'Alles für die Front: Russland im Krieg 1914–1922', in Bauerkämper and Julien (eds), *Durchhalten!*, 151–77, at p. 175.

for closer observation. Especially counterproductive were administrative and judicial measures that introduced collective suspicion and ethnic labelling as a *Leitmotiv* of Austro-Hungarian political culture. Various forms of pre-emptive repression alienated groups that had cherished a critical loyalty towards the Habsburg dynasty thus far and still had hopes for a reform of the empire that in the long run would support their wish for national emancipation. Most of these repressive measures applied against South Slavs, Ukrainians, and Jews. They culminated not only in atrocities carried out against the civil population in Serbia proper (as in Šabac on 17 August 1914 or in Lješnica two days later), but also against Austrian or Hungarian citizens in the Vojvodina and Bosnia-Hercegovina as well as in the execution of approximately 30,000 locals (including women) in Galicia for suspicion of spying for the Tsarist army and enabling its advance westwards. Preventive repression also included the internment of some 10,000 Serbs, Ukrainians, and Italians as well as military trials against some 1,000 Czechs, Ukranians, Serbs, Slovenes, and Italians, many of whom were sentenced to death and executed.[26]

NATIONAL MOBILIZATION AND IMPERIAL DESINTEGRATION

When Francis Joseph I died on 21 November 1916, he had symbolized the unity of nations and the territorial integrity of the monarchy for almost fifty-eight years. For his successor Charles I (Charles IV as Hungarian king), the economic situation within Austria–Hungary was already barely manageable. The introduction of state control over the distribution of grain in 1915 had been followed by first hunger riots on 16 May 1916 in Vienna and a drop of harvest figures in the fall of 1916 to half of the pre-war level. In 1917, within the Austrian state 9 million self-supporters who were still independent of state supply stood against 16.5 million who depended on food aid.[27] In order to save his empire, Charles therefore decided to redefine the political guidelines and to mobilize all national groups behind the Habsburg agenda again. He announced an amnesty for political prisoners on 2 July 1917 and ordered the release of, among others, 1,000 Czechs, including the national democrat Karel Kramář, who had been tried and sentenced to death for high treason for his contacts with Tsar Nicholas II in 1914. By this step, Charles I almost automatically reactivated pre-war demands for the federalization of Austria–Hungary. Now, under circumstances of war, general exhaustion, and desperation, an issue that had been part of everyday politics before 1914 soon acquired new mobilizing as well as antagonizing dynamics. When the Austrian parliament

---

[26] Jürgen Angelow, 'Der Erste Weltkrieg auf dem Balkan: Neue Fragestellungen und Erklärungen', in Bauerkämper and Julien (eds), *Durchhalten!*, 178–94, at p. 183. See also Alfred Eisfeld, Guido Hausmann, and Dietmar Neutatz (eds), *Besetzt, interniert, deportiert: Der Erste Weltkrieg und die deutsche, jüdische, polnische und ukrainische Zivilbevölkerung im östlichen Europa* (Essen: Klartext, 2013); Anton Holzer, *Das Lächeln der Henker: Der unbekannte Krieg gegen die Zivilbevölkerung 1914–1918* (Darmstadt: Primus Verlag, 2008).

[27] In Hungary the ratio was slightly better: 10.5 to 6.5. Biehl, *Der Erste Weltkrieg*, 124, 154.

reopened still under the impression of revolutionary events in Russia on 30 May 1917, representatives of several national movements openly voiced their discontent with repression and censorship and insisted on the implementation of historical rights for their regions and peoples in accordance with their specific national agendas.[28] Only a few weeks later, with the Corfu declaration signed on 20 July 1917, the Serbian government in exile and Habsburg South Slav politicians that were active against the Habsburg Monarchy agreed to create a Yugoslav state after the end of the war.[29]

Charles I was certainly full of good intentions, but 'the gap between the narrative of Habsburg legitimacy based on the notion of the state as the executor of the benevolent will of the emperor and the reality of the dislocation caused by war became too great'.[30] In the months that followed, debates over concepts of autonomy and self-determination were based on the new kind of geopolitical thinking that increasingly mobilized non-German and non-Hungarian political elites and academic circles. By that time, a whole market for publications had developed that aimed to draw the attention of their readers to the dangers threatening the nation if it did not to stand up against those who were defined as a potential threat to its future existence.

In this heated atmosphere, growing mass desertions added fuel to the fire. Many of these deserters were recruited in legions and functioned as symbolic combat units on the side of the Allied forces—only some of them, like the Czechoslovak Legion, were to play a decisive role in the fightings later on. As a consequence, ethnic German politicians raised accusations of Czech illoyalty, separatism, and chauvinism in national and local newspapers, and German representatives launched an attack on their Czech counterparts in the Viennese parliament in December 1917, accusing them of having harboured subversive feelings against Austria–Hungary long before the war. In the course of events, they published a book of more than 400 pages that documented their allegations.[31] In reaction, on 6 January 1918 the Czech representatives issued a declaration that made direct reference to the slogan of self-determination that would give the Czechoslovaks the right to create an independent state and to participate at the future peace conference. By including the Slovaks in their national territorial agenda, the document openly questioned the dualistic constitutional system and challenged German–Hungarian hegemony.[32]

[28] Jan Galandauer, 'Prohlášení českého svazu z 30. května 1917: Zapomenutá programová revoluce', *Český časopis historický*, 91 (1993), 582–92, at p. 587. See also H. L. Rees, *The Czechs during World War I: The Path to Independence* (Boulder: East European Monographs, 1992).

[29] Mark Cornwall, *The Undermining of Austria–Hungary: The Battle for Hearts and Minds* (Houndmills and London: Macmillan Press, 2000), 118.

[30] Daniel Unowski, 'Dynastic Symbolism and Popular Patriotism—Monarchy and Dynasty in Late Imperial Austria', in Jörn Leonhard and Ulrike von Hirschhausen (eds), *Comparing Empires: Encounters and Transfers in the Long Nineteenth Century* (Göttingen: Vandenhoeck & Ruprecht, 2011), 237–65, at p. 265.

[31] Deutschnationale Geschäftsstelle (ed.), *Das Verhalten der Tschechen im Weltkrieg* (Vienna: H. Schürff, 1918); Richard Lein, *Pflichterfüllung oder Hochverrat? Die tschechischen Soldaten Österreich-Ungarns im Ersten Weltkrieg* (Münster, Vienna, and Berlin: LIT, 2011), 9.

[32] *Vznik Československa 1918* (Praha: Ústav mezinárodních vztahů, 1994), 32, 36–7.

This vicious circle of verbal escalation was, of course, closely connected with two documents that were highly influencial for shaping discourses in Austria–Hungary. The first is the declaration of the Rights of the Peoples of Russia, issued by the Bolshevik government on 15 November 1917, which declared the right of peoples of Russia to self-determination, including secession and formation of a separate state.[33] This not only encouraged Moldova, Finland, and Lithuania to take that step by the end of that year; in general, the 'immediate impact of the Russian revolution was immense in Central and Eastern Europe'.[34] The second document that is highly relevant here is Wilson's Fourteen Points, which he made public in a joint session of Congress on 8 January 1918, where the famous tenth point reads as follows: 'The peoples of Austria-Hungary, whose place among the nations we wish to see safeguarded and assured, should be accorded the freest opportunity to autonomous development.' In the same statement, however, the territorial integrity of the Habsburg Empire had already been questioned by the demand to readjust the frontiers with Italy 'along clearly recognizable lines of nationality' and the creation of an independent Polish state that 'should include the territories inhabited by indisputably Polish populations'.[35]

In January 1918 strikes paralysed the economy of Austria–Hungary, and for the whole year local riots, plundering, and mutinies were widespread and frequent. Because of the unrest and lack of assistance from the Austrian central government in Vienna, the regional administrations in the different crown lands acquired more and more responsibilities in the field of social politics. One fact that has often been neglected in this respect is that, with few exceptions, local and municipal administration as well as one segment of the crown land bureaucracy were not part of the Austrian administrational system. Therefore, these structures—together with their personnel—functioned as a zone of retreat for national movements under the condition of war and led to a regionalization of power constellations in many parts of the Austrian state (not so much in Hungary). In an atmosphere of increasing tension, any attempt to consolidate the position of the Habsburg Monarchy internationally led to irritations, distrust, and resistance by at least one of the national groups involved. Such difficulties resulted, for example, from the peace treaty with Ukraine in Brest Litovsk on 9 February 1918. Hoping to secure substantial grain imports, Austria–Hungary agreed that the region of Chelmo/Chełm was to be ceded to Ukraine, and in a secret protocol that was signed on 8 February the monarchy promised to create a Ukrainian crown land in Eastern Galicia and Bukowina.[36] As soon as news about this deal began to spread, the Polish press of

---

[33] Walter John Raymond, *Dictionary of Politics: Selected American and Foreign Political and Legal Terms* (Lawrenceville: Brunswick, 1992), 120.

[34] Ivan T. Berend, *Decades of Crisis: Central and Eastern Europe before World War II* (Berkeley and Los Angeles, and London: University of California Press, 1998), 123.

[35] <http://wwi.lib.byu.edu/index.php/President_Wilson%27s_Fourteen_Points> (accessed 10 July 2013).

[36] Wolfram Dornik and Peter Lieb, 'Die Ukrinepolitik der Mittelmächte während des Ersten Weltkrieges', in Wolfram Dornik et al., *Die Ukraine zwischen Selbstbestimmung und Fremdherrschaft 1917–1922* (Graz: Leykam, 2011), 91–128.

Fig. 7. Embattled imperial borderlands I: Austro-Hungarian trenches in the formerly West Russian province of Volhynia, 1917.

Fig. 8. Embattled imperial borderlands II: the destroyed market square of the city of Ostrołęka, formerly part of the Russian Empire, in May 1916.

Galicia raised accusations that Austria–Hungary had betrayed the interests of her Polish citizens.[37]

Between 8 and 11 April 1918 the congress for suppressed nationalities was held in Rome, with representatives of Czechs, Slovaks, South Slavs, Italians, Poles, and Romanians claiming complete independence and the right to the territory inhabited by the respective nations. More important, however, was a decisive blow to hopes on some sides for a separate peace with the Habsburg Monarchy. The so-called Sixtus affair of 12 April 1918[38] made it perfectly clear that for France a separate arrangement for the Habsburg Monarchy was not a viable option any more, and months after that a series of declarations followed that sealed the partition of Austria–Hungary into national states. On 9 August 1918 the British government recognized Czechoslovakia as a belligerent power that stood on the side of the Entente and, after some hesitation, the United States followed suit with a de facto recognition on 3 September 1918. As soon as last hopes for a separate peace with Austria–Hungary had 'faded from the diplomatic agenda in the spring of 1918 [...] the three major powers opted for the nationalist solution'.[39]

In August and September 1918, representatives of all national communities were already active in designing a strategy for securing maximum influence on decision-making processes. The leading circles of all national movements of post-war Austria–Hungary were absorbed by merging the different concepts for a future independent state, be it within Austria–Hungary or from the exile. By that time, the war had created a dynamic that had already reached the point of no return in the summer of 1918. The last signal necessary was the collapse of the Balkan front in mid-September 1918. On 6 October 1918, seventy-three South Slav representatives from the imperial council and the crown land diets founded the national council of Slovenes, Croats, and Serbs, and, on 14 October, the installation of an interim Czechoslovak government was announced in Paris. When Emperor Charles summoned Anton Korošec, a Slovene politician, president of the Yugoslav Club in the Austrian parliament and an influential politician in interwar Yugoslavia, to his court on 11 October to tell him that the Habsburg Empire could be transformed in the way the South Slavs had desired, Korošec simply responded: 'What has happened already is enough to make us distrust you.'[40] As this episode

---

[37] Biehl, *Der Erste Weltkrieg*, 214.

[38] Between January and May 1917, Charles initiated secret negotiations with France via two brothers of his wife Zita, Sixtus of Bourbon-Parma and Franz Xaver of Bourbon-Parma, offering Alsace-Lorraine to France. The secret mission was made public by Clemenceau on 12 April 1918, causing major irritation on the side of the German ally of Austria–Hungary. Tamara Griesser-Pecar, *Die Mission Sixtus: Österreichs Friedensversuch im Ersten Weltkrieg* (Vienna and Munich: Amalthea, 1988); Manfried Rauchensteiner, ' "Ich habe erfahren, dass mein Kaiser lügt": Die Sixtus-Affäre 1917/18', in Michael Gehler and Hubert Sickinger (eds), *Politische Affären und Skandale in Österreich: Von Mayerling bis Waldheim* (Thaur, Vienna, and Munich: Kulturverlag, 1995).

[39] Zara S. Steiner, *The Light that Failed: European International History 1919–1933* (Oxford: Oxford University Press, 2007), 80, 82.

[40] Janko Pleterski, 'The Southern Slav Question', in Mark Cornwall (ed.), *The Last Years of Austria-Hungary. A Multi-National Experiment in Early Tenteeth-Century Europe* (Exeter: University of Exeter Press, 2002), 119–48, at p. 145.

clearly shows, concepts of sovereignty and self-determination for national collect-ives had finally become incompatible with dynastic loyalties inherited from the past. When Charles I tried to initiate an overall reform of the constitutional system on 16 October with the aim of encouraging the creation of national states that would still unite under the Habsburg rule, the preparations for the various revolu-tions, and the creation of independent nation states were already in full swing.

HABSBURG SUCCESSOR STATES—NEIGHBOURS OR COMPETITORS?

Although, in October and November 1918, a series of revolutions finalized the end of the Habsburg Monarchy, we can say that this was only the last step in a process of gradual dissolution by mobilization. This process, however, did not end in No-vember 1918. According to Mark Hatlie, the First World War in Eastern Europe was ambivalent insofar as it did not have a clear end.[41] The gradual disintegration of the imperial orders, the socio-revolutionary atmosphere, the national euphoria, and the competition of the successor states over certain territories created an overall context of anxiety and uncertainty. In addition, those prisoners of war who re-turned from captivity in Russia were, not without justification, thought to be al-ready under the influence of Bolshevism. As Ivan T. Berend suggests:

the war generation could not escape the shocking effects of the war, and social discontent was increasingly linked to disappointment and disillusionment. [...] The Great War pre-pared the soil: it mobilized and armed the people and provided an opportunity for the en-tire adult male population to organize, train itself, and launch armed attacks against its enemies in the name of national aspirations. Goals that before the war had seemed impos-sible to achieve suddenly became reality at the end of the war.[42]

It was, therefore, in the very interest of the elites of the new national states to transform the emerging social revolution into a national one. The overall radical-ization that followed the end of the war opened windows of opportunity on two levels: on the local level, for retaliation against war profiteers and representatives of competing groups (which also resulted in inter-ethnic violence and pogroms), and on the level of the elites of the emerging states, which sought to secure the best positions possible for the forthcoming peace conference, to avoid the breakdown of order and supply during the winter of 1918–19, and to curb radicalisms on the left and right. When we take up Robert Gerwarth's and John Horne's question, 'how military violence became subsumed into politics following the First World War',[43] it is important to refer to the complete plasticity of the situation. Given the Allied war aims and the provisions of the secret treaties with Italy, Serbia,

---

[41] Mark R. Hatlie, 'Riga und der Erste Weltkrieg. Eine Exkursion', *Nordost-Archiv. Zeitschrift für Regionalgeschichte*, NS 17 (2008), 13–33, at p. 13.
[42] Berend, *Decades of Crisis*, 115, 146.
[43] Robert Gerwarth and John Horne, 'The Great War and Paramilitarism in Europe, 1917–23', *Contemporary European History*, 19 (2010), 267–73, at p. 269.

Montenegro, and Romania that had been published by the Bolsheviks in the daily *Izvestija* in November 1917 in order to discredit the old diplomatic order before the eyes of the world, a new quality of mobilization resulted from the territorial competition that rapidly emerged between the new national neighbour states. As a consequence of wartime geopolitical planning as well as the ethnically mixed settlement structures of many border zones within the Habsburg Monarchy, new points of reference emerged. The incompatibility of concepts and imagined national territories created considerable potential for further escalation—and encouraged various groups to continue military activities against representatives of competing territorial concepts.

In many regions of Austria–Hungary the transition from the imperial administration to that of the emerging national states was comparatively smooth and accompanied only by vandalism against symbols of the old order. Where in October–November 1918 autonomous crown land administrations were already in the hand of one nation, the representatives of the imperial or central state level normally just passed administrative responsibilities to their regional counterparts or to various national councils or civil guards. In mixed or contested areas, however, where the future location of borders was disputed, measures for self-defence soon merged with preventative action in anticipation of steps by competitors to define the sovereignty of a nation state. At this point, distrust was not directed exclusively against representatives of the fading monarchical–imperial order. National antagonism over the location of borders also perpetuated wartime inter-ethnic rivalries and discord over the future form of state. Under these circumstances, conflicts of interests and wartime forms of political mobilization such as mass meetings, memoranda, or symbolic politics transformed easily into violent confrontation between rival groups and included the intimidation of elites or other social segments. Sometimes, local populations were severely affected by the consequences of war only after November 1918 because inter-ethnic conflicts now appeared in areas where there had not been much violence before—either because of the presence of paramilitary forces or as a result of the threatening perspective that future state boundaries would separate local communities.[44]

As a result, we can identify several regions that were characterized by cultures of violence: Austrian Silesia, Southern Carinthia, Western Hungary, Eastern Galicia, or South-Eastern Slovakia are telling examples of how contact zones of ethnic and religious groups transformed into spaces demarked by 'frontiers of violence'.[45] Here, the spiral of violence was initiated less by the war than by the dynamics of the post-war period. The example of Lemberg (Lwów/Lviv) demonstrates the complexity of this period, as Austrian imperial authorities and Polish and Ukrainian

---

[44] For paramilitary violence in East Central Europe in general, see Robert Gerwarth, 'The Central European Counter-Revolution: Paramilitary Violence in Germany, Austria and Hungary after the Great War', *Past and Present*, 200 (2008), 175–209; Julia Eichenberg, 'The Dark Side of Independence: Paramilitary Violence in Ireland and Poland after the First World War', *Contemporary European History*, 19 (2010), 231–48.

[45] K. T. Wilson, *Frontiers of Violence: Conflict and Identity in Ulster and Upper Silesia, 1918–1922* (Oxford: Oxford University Press, 2010). See also Annemarie H. Sammartino, *The Impossible Border: Germany and the East, 1914–1922* (Ithaca, NY, and London: Cornell University Press, 2010).

national movements competed for influence, with the Jewish community—which suffered immensely during the pogroms of November 1918—being victimized by both national movements.[46] From a more general perspective, James Diehl points to the extent of militarization of political mentalities: 'The massive mobilization of societies for the First World War brought previously passive or marginalized groups into the national economy and political arena. Postwar empowerment of previously disenfranchised groups made mass politics a reality. Wartime sacrifice combined with postwar economic difficulties created widespread disillusionment', especially among the successor states of the former Central Powers, as the example of Hungary clearly shows.[47] As post-war economic difficulties mounted, the

wartime practice of dividing the world into friends and foes and demonizing enemies was carried over into peacetime and furthered by the increasingly ideological nature of politics. [...] Social and political opponents were seen as an existential threat and delegitimized. Compromise was ruled out. Total destruction of one's enemies was sought. Domestic politics became infused with the attitudes and tactics associated with total war.

Moreover, the ending war had made the hardware for taking action available.

Arms were ubiquitous, and some states lost their monopoly on the means of violence. In addition to military hardware, there was a form of social war surplus that facilitated the militarization of politics: veterans. [...] As a result, every belligerent nation was host to a substantial postwar army of men unable to psychologically demobilize. In dealing with this problem the established democracies had an advantage.[48]

The new quality of mobilization resulted from the territorial competition that rapidly emerged as a consequence of wartime geopolitical planning. Even now, after the war had officially ended, the leading representatives of national communities tried to secure direct communication channels with Paris, London, and Washington and started producing and presenting brochures and maps that should attune the leading Allied powers, first of all France, to the future location of certain borders. They also offered the use of national troops under Allied command in order to be physically present in places that were of strategic interest.

The 'extensive, unlimited violence [that] characterized the secession states of Eastern Europe', and that Alan Kramer refers to, was not so widespread in the Habsburg Monarchy as in its Russian and Ottoman counterparts, since in many regions of Austria–Hungary the transition from the imperial administration to that of the emerging national states was comparatively smooth and accompanied

---

[46] Christoph Mick, *Kriegserfahrung in einer multiethnischen Stadt. Lemberg, 1914–1947* (Wiesbaden: Harassowitz, 2010), 247.

[47] For example, Hungary faced two waves of terror conducted by representatives of the Republic of Councils between March and August 1919 ('Red terror') and immediately after that by right-wing paramilitary squadrons ('White terror'). But, also in Austria, the new government was 'confronting revolutionary turmoil in the streets of Vienna, a near-total collapse of the agricultural and industrial economies and near-mental breakdown from the trauma of defeat' in 1919. Günter Bischof, Fritz Plasser, and Peter Berger (eds), *From Empire to Republic: Post-World War I Austria* (New Orleans: University of New Orleans Press, 2010), 5.

[48] James M. Diehl, 'No More Peace: The Militarization of Politics', in Roger Chickering and Stig Förster (eds), *The Shadows of Total War: Europe, East Asia, and the United States, 1919–1939* (Cambridge and New York: Cambridge University Press, 2003), 97–112, at pp. 97–8.

only by vandalism against symbols of the old order. It created a serious issue, however, in those contested areas, 'where power was weak and regions changed hands several times'.[49]

Economic and infrastructural exhaustion and worsening health conditions—intensified by the Spanish influenza that hit populations exhausted by four years of warfare[50]—fuelled group conflict on the local level and stimulated geostrategical competition over the location of future boundaries among decision-makers as well as in radical circles that were willing to engage in preventive military action. This resulted either in the so-called small wars—that is, military conflicts that were regionally definable and were fought over the location of borders (as between Czechoslovakia and Poland over the Dutchy of Teschen), or civil wars (as in Finland) or in a dynamics where one radicalization was followed by another (as in Hungary or Bulgaria). In some areas or military campaigns, as in the Baltic countries or during the Soviet–Russian war, several factors were intertwined with each other. In this context the national mission statements did not only acquire elements of cultural and social liberation, emancipation, and participation, including promises for agrarian reform, social security for workers, and the introduction of women's suffrage. They also included negative messages that classified groups within the population of one's future state territory as being foreign or too dominant in the political and economic sphere and had therefore prevented the national collective from prospering in the past.

CONCLUSIONS

Many contemporary observers could not help but notice the long-lasting legacy of all these dynamics. For example, in 1921, Italian prime minister Francesco S. Nitti voiced his scepticism about the stability of the new geopolitical order in Europe:

The recent treaties which regulate, or are supposed to regulate, the relations among peoples are, as a matter of fact, nothing but a terrible regress, the denial of all those principles which had been regarded as an unalienable conquest of public right. President Wilson, by his League of Nations, has been the most responsible factor in setting up barriers between nations.[51]

The long-lasting effects of war and mass mobilization were especially visible in the case of all successor states of the Habsburg Monarchy. Here the momentum of mobilization and demobilization was not only determined by the war itself. It very much depended on pre-war structures and political attitudes that transformed during the war. Because of the political shift towards repressive measures that were

[49] Alan Kramer, *Dynamic of Destruction: Culture and Mass Killing in the First World War* (Oxford: Oxford University Press, 2007), 279, 292.

[50] The number of worldwide deaths of this pandemic that started in March 1918 is estimated to be twenty-seven million. Colin Nicolson, *The First World War: Europe 1914–1918* (Harlow: Longman, 2001), 248.

[51] Francesco S. Nitti, *Peaceless Europe* (London: Cassell and Company, 1922), p. vii.

motivated by ethnic labelling, the war automatically encouraged territorial fantasies that were directed at implementing alternative political scenarios.

As soon as imperial loyalties began to fade and the dismemberment of the Habsburg Empire gained momentum, these geopolitical and ideological concepts emphasized the friction resulting from the multinational and multireligious composition of the population. The dismantling of the imperial administrations and the disintegration of a common sense of public order and personal safety opened a window of opportunity for settling old scores and trying to enforce radical revolutionary agendas. The fact that this open situation also offered opportunities to implement utopian concepts for one's national society further accelerated the use of violence at the micro level.

In these contested regions, the First World War was only a first step towards the mobilization of minds and resources. Often, its populations were most severely affected by the consequences of war after November 1918—because of either the presence of regular or paramilitary forces battling against each other or the threatening perspective that a new state boundary would separate local communities. The change of the political system from the dynastic Austro-Hungarian to those of the various nation states made political life much more democratic and enabled political participation of parts of the population that had had no say in politics until then. The dissolution of the multinational monarchy, however, solved hardly any of the problems that came from the conflict of interest of competing national groups. The creation of new mid- or small-sized states that either were multinational, contained substantial percentages of minority population, or were forced to digest the loss not only of territory but also of conationals to neighbouring states duplicated rather than solved the main problem the Habsburg Monarchy was struggling with before the war. It goes without saying that this geopolitical scenario had severe consequences for the future stability of almost all successor states during the interwar period.

5

The Russian Empire

Joshua Sanborn

INTRODUCTION: NATIONALISM AND EMPIRE ON THE EVE OF THE WAR

The Russian Empire well deserved its place at the table of Great Powers. Though Muscovy was only a modest East European principality in the fifteenth and early sixteenth centuries, it expanded in size and influence throughout the modern age. The famous tsars (Caesars)—Ivan the Terrible, Peter the Great, Catherine the Great—were all ambitious imperial conquerors. Ivan seized the Volga River and opened the pathways to Asia. Peter slogged his way to victory in the north and founded a new capital on the edge of the Baltic. Catherine annexed half of Poland and firmly established Russian power on the northern coast of the Black Sea. Their successors consolidated and continued to expand: into Transcaucasia, Central Asia, northern China, and to the edge of the Balkan Peninsula. By the end of the nineteenth century, Russia was the largest empire in the world, covering one-sixth of the dry land on earth. And, despite the access to waterways that military conquest had opened up, Russia was very much a dry land empire. Attempts to develop naval power had certain modest local successes (as against Sweden in the Great Northern War), and certain notable failures as well (as against Japan in the Russo-Japanese War). But, in the end, naval weakness and the slow pace at which Russia developed rapid transportation systems meant that Russia's capacity to project force and power beyond its borders was mostly limited to how far its soldiers could walk.

In a sense, then, Russia was a very large man with very short arms and slow feet: impossible to ignore, very dangerous at close range, but able to be neutralized if one maintained a respectful and wary distance. We should not assume that such a man was clumsy, however. To the contrary, when it came to establishing and maintaining imperial control, the government frequently showed considerable dexterity. The history of the building of the Russian Empire is a history of accommodation as well as a history of force. The grip of our imperial man was reliable: firm when under pressure, relaxed when it suited him. The consolidation of Russian power in conquered regions normally happened by means of extensive co-optation and a resort to arms only when necessary. Indigenous elites retained power in local administrations and courts, and many were brought into the imperial noble class.[1] The Russian Empire, in other words, fit Charles Maier's definition of an empire as "a regime that centralized power, but enlist[ed] diverse social and/or ethnic elite in its management."[2] This was an empire that succeeded through de facto decentralization and the creation of personal networks of power. Local governors and governors general were responsible for the populations and territories under their control. They maintained bureaucracies, sometimes quite bulky ones, but they derived their authority from the person of the tsar who had appointed them. It was a hierarchical structure of status and authority that ran from the emperor through his nobility to the serfs, townsmen, and other corporate groups within society such as religious and ethnic minorities in Russia's borderlands.

In the second half of the nineteenth century, however, several developments made the continuation of this very successful pattern impossible. The fundamental changes brought about by the emancipation of the serfs in 1861 and the ensuing "Great Reforms" opened the door to modern mass politics in Russia. Nationalism was a key mechanism by which mass politics developed over the next fifty years. If most nationalist movements in Eastern Europe were quite small and limited in the first half of the nineteenth century, they began to expand rapidly in the latter half.[3] The Polish Rebellion of 1863 and a wave of Ukrainian activism in the 1870s frightened the imperial elite, and when Alexander III took the throne in 1881, he took the dangerous decision to launch a disruptive program of forced assimilation known as "Russification."[4] Russification was a failure that led to a significant and angry backlash. It did more to increase ethnic awareness among the masses in the imperial periphery than the diligent work of indigenous ethnographers or political agitators ever had.

The 1890s saw significant political developments. Both in the borderlands and in the center, illegal political parties formed: Polish nationalist parties on the left and right, the Jewish Bund, and the Russian Social Democratic Labour Party to name just a few. In addition, imperial foreign policy changed. The building of the Trans-Siberian Railway allowed politicians and economic elites in St Petersburg to engage in aggressive fantasies about East Asia. In the very first years of the new century, Russia joined the anti-Boxer coalition, pursued a sphere of influence in Manchuria and on the Liaodong peninsula, and made forays into the Japanese sphere of influence in northern Korea. The resulting disastrous war between Russia and Japan (1904–5) sparked an imperial crisis not only internationally, but domestically as well. Russification, the emergence (and suppression) of mass

[1] Andreas Kappeler, *The Russian Empire: A Multiethnic History*, trans. Alfred Clayton (Harlow: Pearson/Longman, 2001), 129.

[2] Charles S Maier, *Among Empires: America's Ascendancy and its Predecessors* (Cambridge, MA: Harvard University Press, 2006), 31.

[3] Kappeler, *The Russian Empire*, 220–35; Miroslav Hroch, *Social Preconditions of National Revival in Europe: A Comparative Analysis of the Social Composition of Patriotic Grounds among the Smaller European Nations* (Cambridge: Cambridge University Press, 1985).

[4] See Edward C. Thaden, "Russification in Tsarist Russia," in Edward C. Thaden, *Interpreting History: Collective Essays on Russia's Relations with Europe* (Boulder: Social Science Monographs, 1990), 211–20.

political institutions, and the social ferment typical of a phase of rapid industrial-ization all produced a very combustible situation, which exploded in the early months of 1905. A serious revolution ensued, one that consumed the entire em-pire and threatened to topple the tsar. Russian liberal political activists successfully pressed for civil liberties and political freedoms for everyone in the empire, but they focused their attention on "Russian" concerns, such as the creation of a new parliament. Nationalists and socialists also had political aims, but these were not met quite so easily. Right-wing nationalists turned their frustrations on the Jewish populations of Ukraine and Poland, while left-wing nationalists fumed at the injustices of the new "constitutional" imperial regime.

Nevertheless, the genie of political participation and ethnic party mobilization had been released from the bottle, and the years between 1905 and 1914 were filled with complicated political battles regarding ethnicity and the imperial state. Local nationalists sparred with newly invigorated Russian nationalists on issues large and small, most notably regarding the extension of elected local governments (*zemstvos*) into the western borderlands.[5] In no case, however, was separatist na-tionalism a real danger for the integrity of the empire. The government had not bowed to nationalists at the moment of crisis in 1905, and it would not do so after the revolutionary wave had passed. If anything, the government insisted even more provocatively on its own imperial prerogatives, as the prime minister Petr Stolypin embraced Russian nationalism as a novel and necessary governing strategy for a modern empire. He was assassinated in the borderlands, at the Kiev Opera House, in 1911.

WAR IN A COLONIZED SPACE, 1914–1916

For the entire course of the Great War on the Eastern Front, the imperial belliger-ents fought with multi-ethnic armies in colonized spaces. In August 1914, Russia conducted a general mobilization, calling to the colors reservists who had finished their peacetime tours of duty years earlier to join the cadre army in the west. The composition of the army was thus determined by the recruitment choices it had made over the forty years since the adoption of "universal" conscription in 1874. Since the budget was too small to support a truly universal conscription at any time prior to the war, the state had the capacity to make decisions about which imperial subjects would serve. The exemption regime was a conscious one. Draft lottery numbers were far less important than the draft category a particular young man fell into. Some of these selection criteria were individualized: the medical exam, for instance, was an important moment of filtration. Some of them were incentive based, as with the exemptions or special treatment for particular professions. But many of them were ethnopolitical in nature. Finns were exempt from the draft, a point ratified and made clear after a botched attempt to implement

[5] Theodore R. Weeks, *Nation and State in Late Imperial Russia: Nationalism and Russification on the Western Frontier, 1863–1914* (DeKalb, IL: Northern Illinois University Press, 1996), 131–51.

conscription in 1901. Many peoples in the Caucasus and Transcaucasus were exempt, thanks to fears that arming recently hostile warrior peoples might be unwise. And most ethnic groups in Russian Asia, most notably the recently conquered Kazakhs, Kyrgyz, and Uzbeks in Central Asia, were exempted because of doubts as to whether they were sufficiently advanced "civilizationally" to discharge their military duties honorably and forcefully. At the same time, many other ethnic groups— Poles, Ukrainians, Belorussians, Latvians, and so on—were drafted on an equal basis with those in central Russia. Fears of nationalism sometimes led to policies to deploy potentially restive ethnicities on fronts far from their homes, to limit the percentage of them in a given military unit, or to restrict admission to the officer corps, but all of these groups were part and parcel of the imperial Russian army. Jews, as always, were a special case. They were drafted, but they were frequently abused, and they were prohibited from positions of leadership in the army. Many young Jewish men responded by trying to evade the draft, but most served under oppressive conditions both in war and at peace.[6]

Ethnic issues in the military would play a large role in the accelerating collapse of the empire in 1916 and 1917, but, for the first two years of the war, the imperial issue of greatest importance had to do with civilians. It was a fact of tremendous consequence that the combat zones and deep rears of the fighting armies were all located in colonized spaces. None of the major battles of the Eastern Front occurred in modern-day Russia, Germany, Austria, or Hungary, and only a handful lie in contemporary Turkey. Most took place in what are now Poland, Lithuania, Latvia, Belarus, and Ukraine. The result of this colonial battleground is that the Russian army was, in important ways, an army of occupation even when it was fighting on its own side of the 1914 border. This dynamic of military occupation was made more intense by the decision in the first days of the war to declare all of the deep combat zones under martial law. The old system of imperial governance was superseded by military rule in a zone larger in area than Germany, commanded by men with no experience whatsoever with civilian administration.

As a result, the state began to fail. It was this transformation in the state and in governance that had the most impact on the collapse of the empire. War, not nationalist activism, crippled the empire. The rise of separatist nationalism that we will discuss below filled a vacuum created by the failure of the imperial state. That failure was not complete until 1917, but we can see the early stages of it occurring just days into the war. Imperial administrators in the borderlands, some of them experienced, were pushed out of the way. Martial law meant that they had to report to Stavka (General Headquarters) in addition to their civilian ministries in Petrograd. This confusion of authority, combined with the danger of capture by German forces, led many to flee even before major combat operations started. The ones who stayed faced perilous situations. The case of State Councillor Agafonov, the chief of the Polish border district of Nieszawa, was common. He did his best

---

[6] These issues are discussed at length in Joshua A. Sanborn, *Drafting the Russian Nation: Military Conscription, Total War, and Mass Politics, 1905–1925* (DeKalb, IL: Northern Illinois University Press, 2003).

to perform his duties during mobilization, ensuring that men and horses went to the collection point in Kutno a bit under 100 kilometres away, and then organized a mass prayer service on the town square of Nieszawa on 5 August 1914. A German detachment of 200–50 men traipsing the Vistula River landed around the town during the service, surrounding it and sending the population into a panic. Agafonov was held hostage by the Germans, forced to announce various decrees, and threatened repeatedly. When the Germans retreated a couple of weeks later, he fled Nieszawa, first to Kutno, and then to Warsaw.[7] In Warsaw, he joined many other shaken civilian officials, most of whom had fled earlier in order to avoid his fate or worse.

With imperial administrators stripped away, only two possible sources of governance remained: military authorities or local authorities who remained in their homes. These two groups—one of them heavily armed, largely Russian, and imperial; the other composed of unarmed local elites, many of them with nationalist sympathies—would have an uneasy relationship. Somewhat surprisingly, the locals did most of the governing. Stavka had no civilian administration office at the start of the war, and it took them weeks to get even a bare-bones operation off the ground. With no personnel and little idea of what they were doing, they were ineffective. Combat troops on the ground intersected with local civilians, but in haphazard ways. The opportunity arose for local elites, especially in Poland, to govern, and they took advantage of it up and down the border zone.[8] If we can identify a moment when the institutional seedlings of new independent states were first planted on the territory of the Russian Empire, it was here in the first days of the war.

This is not to say that the army played no role in local civilian life. To the contrary, it was enormously important, but often in ways that undermined state power and social stability, and thus the imperial system as well. There were two major areas that the army meddled in with pernicious results: the economy and ethnopolitical relationships in the borderlands. The transformation of the imperial economy at war is a large (and understudied) topic. I will touch here only upon the issue that was most evident and important to civilians and statesmen alike: inflation. Everyone in a position of power knew that the emergency situation created by the war could lead to rising prices. Unfortunately, very few of them understood the deep and inexorable reasons for inflation. Supply shrank as international trade evaporated, workers were mobilized into the army, and violent extraction made trade dangerous. Demand increased, especially on the part of the massive army now living in the borderlands. So too did the fiscal situation require the Ministry of Finance to pursue inflationary policies in order to facilitate the feeding and

---

[7] "Dokladnaia zapiska Nachal'nika Neshavskago uezda Statskogo Sovetnika Agafonova," n.d. (but after 16/29 August 1914), Gosudarstvennyi arkhiv Rossiiskoi Federatsii (GARF), fond (f.) 217, opis (op.) 1, delo (d.) 304, listy (ll.) 213–15ob.

[8] These developments are treated in further depth in Joshua Sanborn, "Military Occupation and Social Unrest: Daily Life in Russian Poland at the Start of World War I," in Golfo Alexopolous, Julie Hessler, and Kiril Tomoff (eds) *Writing the Stalin Era: Sheila Fitzpatrick and Soviet Historiography* (New York: Palgrave Macmillan, 2011), 43–58.

equipping of the military. Nevertheless, the consensus in the military, the civilian realm, and a surprisingly large sector of the tsar's administration was that the core reason for wartime inflation was price gouging by irresponsible speculators. Thus, some of the first edicts issued by civilian authorities like Agafonov and later military commanders were commands to tradespeople to keep their prices fixed. Officials issued extensive lists indicating the maximum prices that merchants could charge and promised dire consequences if those prices were raised. Fear of speculation also led them to arrest any merchants they found warehousing goods, as they suspected that they were saving them only to create artificial shortages that would justify higher prices. These policies gutted the borderland economy, as they made it increasingly difficult for trade to occur. Many merchants fled or went out of business. New entrepreneurs tended to work the now flowering black market. The response by the government was to double down on their policies, not only in the borderlands, but also deep within the empire, where the ravages of inflation soon spread.

This anti-trading sentiment, in the context of both historical anti-Semitism and the more modern brand that had matured in the last decade before the war, was bound to be inextricably tied to a campaign against the Jews of the western borderland. Again, this was deeply influenced by the new conditions of the war. The campaign was spearheaded by the Russian army, especially General Ianushkevich, the Chief of Staff at Stavka. As Eric Lohr has pointed out, the army was involved in "nearly every pogrom" in 1915.[9] Jews were threatened, persecuted, beaten, arrested, murdered, and deported in large numbers, and local officials and civilians frequently took part in the assaults.[10] When civilians took a major role, economic frustrations rooted in inflation were often central to the conflict.[11] But this campaign was only the most evident sign of a larger shift in ethnopolitics. The imperial government had rightly been wary of mobilizing ethnicities prior to the war, looking anxiously even at the activities of Russian nationalist groups that supported the monarchy. That restraint disappeared virtually the moment that war was declared. A massive campaign to expropriate ethnic German property developed over the course of the war. "Ruthenians" in Galicia were encouraged to embrace their non-Austrian identities. Polish, Georgian, and Armenian volunteers were allowed to form ethnic military units after years in which such a step was forbidden. Prisoner-of-war camps were combed through and sorted by ethnic group, and Slavic prisoners from the Austro-Hungarian armies were placed in better conditions and urged to unite to support the cause of the Entente.

If this was the situation in territories on the Russian side of the border, the situation in the occupied zones of Austrian Galicia was even more problematic.

---

[9] Eric Lohr, "1915 and the War Pogrom Paradigm in the Russian Empire," in Jonathan Dekel-Chen, David Gaunt, Natan M. Meir, and Israel Bartal (eds), *Anti-Jewish Violence: Rethinking the Pogrom in East European History* (Bloomington: Indiana University Press, 2011), 41.

[10] The most extensive descriptions of the atrocities were recorded by a Jewish aid worker at the time. S. Ansky, *The Enemy at his Pleasure: A Journey through the Jewish Pale of Settlement during World War I* (New York: Henry Holt, 2002),

[11] Lohr, "1915 and the War Pogrom Paradigm in the Russian Empire," 47.

Price control policies were identical on both sides of the border, but the army's administrators wreaked even more havoc by instituting unreasonable exchange rates between Russian and Austrian currencies. In addition, the third economy of looting and requisitions was much more pronounced in foreign occupied territories than it was on the Russian side of the border. By the end of 1914, much of the local population, even the Slavic portion of the population, lived in fear and resentment of Russian troops.[12] The ethnopolitical situation became more pronounced there too, as military extremists and various other religious and political fanatics swarmed into Galicia in an attempt to remake it in their own image. With no countervailing institutions to slow them down, the only brake on their behavior was the troubled new governor general of the occupied territories, Count Georgii Bobrinskii. Bobrinskii was no liberal, but he was alarmed by extremism. In the end, he too lost control of the situation and ended up blamed for many of the policies he had resisted. The occupation was a total disaster, alienating potential friends and weakening Russian power in significant ways.[13]

All of this came crashing down in 1915. The Austro-German offensive that began along the Gorlice–Tarnów line under General Mackensen in the spring of 1915 was wildly successful, driving Russian troops and occupying forces not only out of the Galician territories they had conquered in 1914, but deep into the Russian Empire as well. By the end of the summer, Russia had lost all of its Polish territories and big chunks of contemporary Ukraine. The army had been pushed back into the Lake Narach area of Belarus and to the gates of Riga in Latvia. The old Russian Empire would never return to Poland (though it would, briefly, to parts of Austrian Galicia), but the experience of ethnic mobilization, local governance, and finally military organization would become tremendously important for nationalist elites in the years to come.

In the imperial metropole, the military defeats of 1915 deeply undermined the legitimacy of the tsarist regime and tore at the fabric of Russian society. The political opposition, which had decided in a burst of patriotic spirit in 1914 to support the tsarist regime, changed course in 1915. It faulted the government not only for the shoddy leadership that helped lead to the military disasters, but also for its handling of civilian affairs. The stream of refugees and deportees that flowed to central Russia and Siberia in 1914 turned into a torrent over the course of the summer of 1915. They joined the tens of thousands of Armenian refugees who had fled to Russian territory for protection during the Turkish-sponsored genocide of that same year. Of the six million displaced persons, more than half had been driven away between April and September 1915. Local authorities and civilian ministers alike worried that these migrants would spread disease, put a burden on the economy, and bring the chaos of the front lines tangibly home. In many ways,

---

[12] Peter Holquist, "The Role of Personality in the First (1914–1915) Russian Occupation of Galicia and Bukovina," in Dekel-Chen et al. (eds), *Anti-Jewish Violence*, 54.

[13] Holquist, "The Role of Personality"; Mark von Hagen, *War in a European Borderland: Occupations and Occupation Plans in Galicia and Ukraine, 1914–1918* (Seattle: University of Washington Press, 2007); A. Iu. Bakhturina, *Politika Rossiiskoi imperii v vostochnoi Galitsii v gody pervoi mirovoi voiny* (Moscow: AIRO-XX, 2000).

they were not mistaken. But there were other unexpected effects as well. Most of the refugees, being civilians from the borderlands, were not ethnically Russian. As they arrived into the foreign territory of the Russian central provinces, impoverished and endangered, they turned to one another and their own political elites for help. As a result, refugeedom quickly became a nationalizing experience, as Polish, Latvian, Armenian, Jewish, and other ethnic aid societies took on the main tasks of organizing relief.[14] The "refugee question" was just one of the troubled political issues that highlighted the imperial dimension of the war to Russian politicians and public activists. The disaster of the Galician occupation, the Armenian genocide, the raising of ethnic military units, the attempts to undermine enemy empires through nationalist recruitment in prisoner-of-war camps (and through intelligence operations): all these were key features of the growing political crisis. That crisis now had to be fully understood not simply as a question of autocratic legitimacy, but as an imperial crisis full blown.

That crisis was temporarily eased between the fall of 1915 and the summer of 1916. The army proved able not only to stop the enemy advance into its territory, but even to engage in significant conquest of its own. The major gains came against the Ottomans to the south. In late 1915 and early 1916, increased German and Ottoman activity in Persia spooked the British and Russian authorities who had placed the weakened country under their joint sphere of influence in 1907. The British asked the Russians to send troops into Northern Persia to fend off the threat, and the Russian command acquiesced. General Baratov led a successful expedition that occupied Hamadan and Qom in December 1915 and made plain the nature of Russian military and political pre-eminence in the area. That dominance was weakened after an ill-advised effort to relieve British forces besieged at Kut-al-Amara in April 1916 ended in wastage from disease and an Ottoman counter-offensive, but the Russian Empire was still clearly alive and kicking in the Middle East. This was even more apparent during the successful invasion of Eastern Anatolia, when General Iudenich proved able to capture the major strategic locations of Erzerum and Trabzon in early 1916. Russian forces gained ground in Europe as well, when a spring offensive led by General Brusilov on the South-Western Front allowed Russian forces to move back into much of the occupied zone they had conquered and then fled over the previous year. Once more, questions of Galician occupation came to the forefront, though this time chastened administrators moved more cautiously than they had in the first year of the war.

STATE COLLAPSE AND DECOLONIZATION, 1916–1918

The rally of Russian arms in 1916 could not save the old regime. In the first place, the military victories were uneven and indecisive. Conquering Northern Persia, Eastern Anatolia, and Eastern Galicia was impressive, but it would not end the

[14] The best work on refugees during the war is Peter Gatrell, *A Whole Empire Walking: Refugees in Russia during World War I* (Bloomington: Indiana University Press, 1999).

war. Not only did the Germans remain firmly entrenched along the northern sector of the line, but the Russians also did not knock the weakened Ottomans and Austrians out of the war. In the second place, the military commanders who found success (mostly Iudenich and Brusilov) did so by pioneering departures from the status quo, not by reaffirming it. Indeed, Brusilov was forced to engage in fierce battles with other front commanders and his own superiors to be allowed to try a new tactical and strategic direction, and, even when he demonstrated his effectiveness, they refused either to change their own ways or even to support his offensive in substantial ways.

Most importantly, though, the Russian victories could not fix what was broken politically and socially in the empire. Soon enough, those problems emerged in ever more deadly forms. The first to break was the economic system, particularly in terms of labor. Thanks to the massive mobilization of men into the armed forces, the Russian Empire suffered from labor shortages throughout the war in virtually every sector of the economy. As in other combatant countries, the labor force changed to adjust to the new circumstances. Women moved into many roles previously unavailable to them, not only in the industrial economy, but in the countryside too, where they were forced to do the "men's work" around the village in addition to their own taxing pre-war duties. But even this was not sufficient. As a result, the state turned to forced labor. The most obvious supply of this labor was the prisoner-of-war population, which reached two million strong and which was widely deployed in rural and urban areas alike. But from the very start of the war, army commanders had commandeered local labor to perform crucial infrastructure work too. The need for this labor grew increasingly acute. Even before the territorial gains over the spring and summer, generals were desperately pleading for more labor. They soon learned that the pool of prisoners of war had run dry, and they already knew that no more local labor was available. So many had fled as refugees that there was no surplus at all. As a result, in May and June of 1916, the Council of Ministers put together a plan to draft ethnic minorities exempt from military service into forced labor brigades. The bulk of these workers were to come from the areas of Central Asia that had been annexed in the latter half of the nineteenth century. Nicholas II ordered the draft in an imperial rescript on 25 June 1916.[15]

If we were to pinpoint a moment when imperial rule moved from a crisis situation into a revolutionary situation, it would be here, in the summer of 1916 in Uzbekistan and Kazakhstan. All the pathologies of Russian imperial control were on display in 1916: lack of foresight, bungled implementation, corruption, and brutality. Since they had not planned to draft these men, they had no registration lists. With no registration, officials turned to co-opted local elites to tell them who was eligible for the draft. Many of these drew up lists of their enemies rather than of the young men in their districts and excluded those who had paid them off.

---

[15] For more on this labor crisis, see Joshua A. Sanborn, "Unsettling the Empire: Violent Migrations and Social Disaster in Russia during World War I," *Journal of Modern History*, 77 (June 2005), 290–324.

Fig. 9. Kazakh laborers at the Eastern Front.

Conscription began on 2 July, and riots began just two days later, in Khojent. They spread rapidly, and Turkestan had to be placed on martial law on 17 July. In August, disorder erupted in Syr Daria, where detachments of rebels thousands strong attacked the major Russian rail lines. By September, the whole steppe was consumed. Rebel violence, which had originally been targeted at local elites, and then at imperial officials and institutions, was now increasingly directed at Russian settlers. The homesteads of 9,000 Russian families were destroyed, and more than 3,500 colonists died. An openly anti-colonial civil war was under way. The Russians drafted 110,000 Uzbeks, Kazakhs, and Kyrgyz, but tens of thousands of these men died, fled, or were incapacitated. Semirechie alone lost 20 percent of its population and 50 percent of its livestock (see Fig. 9).[16]

As 1917 dawned, then, the empire was very different from how it had been two and a half years earlier. The western borderlands were under either foreign occupation or the increasingly coercive military regime. Nationalists were quietly gaining influence as the failing state created an ever larger political vacuum. In the Middle East, the empire was expanding, but only within the context of ever more evident ethnic war in the region.[17] In Central Asia, rebellion had torn apart local societies and led to vicious colonial reprisals. Still, the Romanov dynasty remained, and

[16] See here Edward Dennis Sokol, _The Revolt of 1916 in Russian Central Asia_ (Baltimore: Johns Hopkins University Press, 1953); G. Sapargaliev, _Karatel'naia politika tsarizma v Kazakhstane (1905–1917)_ (Alma-Ata: Nauka, 1966); Marco Buttino, _Revoliutsiia naoborot: Sredniaia Aziia mezhdu padeniem tsarskoi imperii i obrazovaniem SSSR_, trans. Nikolai Okhotin (Moscow: Zven'ia, 2007).

[17] Michael A. Reynolds, _Shattering Empires: The Clash and Collapse of the Ottoman and Russian Empires, 1908–1918_ (Cambridge: Cambridge University Press, 2011), esp. 134–65.

with it the more than 300 years of personal and institutional authority that organized political life across the entire expanse of the empire. While the monarch remained, so too did imperial control.

It was thus the February Revolution that marked the beginning of the end. The demonstrations and riots that brought the capital to its knees were little concerned with empire as such. The protests began with complaints about food shortages and soon expanded to include criticisms of the war effort and the competence of the government. Within days, they were demanding an end to the autocracy. With no domestic political support, even amongst the military high command, the tsar was forced to abdicate. His departure left a huge symbolic and institutional hole in the middle of the political system, a fact that even concerned some of the most ardent critics of the monarch. The bodies that replaced the autocracy—the revived Soviets of urban workers and soldiers and the Provisional Government headed by liberals from the parliament and from the major war aid agencies—shared a basic platform of civic equality and national self-determination. What future would the empire have in such conditions? This was a question that all minority nationalists had to ask over the course of 1917, but it was one insufficiently appreciated by the liberal politicians who accepted ministerial appointments in the new government. Those men envisioned a future in which Russian chauvinism and national supremacy would come to an end, allowing for a multi-ethnic state based on the ideals of equality and mutual respect. But they also assumed that this state would retain its sites of power in central Russia, would use Russian as its language of state, and would remain within its current boundaries. Moreover, they continued to envision Russia as a charter member of the imperial club of Great Powers.

These tacit assumptions constituted a major blind spot for liberals, and they ruined many a political career over the course of the revolutionary year of 1917. The first such casualty was Pavel Miliukov, the leader of the Constitutional Democratic (Kadet) Party. Miliukov was completely undone by imperial issues. One of Miliukov's first acts as the new Minister of Foreign Affairs was to affirm that Russia would continue to meet its alliance obligations and would continue to fight the war against "Prussian militarism." His uncompromising stance alienated many on the left, and he almost immediately had to walk it back. He reassured the allies that Russia would stay in the war, but he also promised that the government would "open a way to the expression of the popular will" regarding the continuation of hostilities. He continued to insist on imperial war aims as well, most notably that Russia would take control of the Straits upon the successful conclusion of the conflict. This opened a political space to attack Russia's liberal leadership as more committed to imperial gain than to the welfare of its own soldiers and citizens. Socialist politicians immediately took their opportunity. Moderates like Irakli Tsereteli articulated a policy of revolutionary defensism in which the army would continue to fight, but only to preserve the revolutionary democracy and the homeland. They would seek a peace based on the slogan of "no annexations or indemnities." When Miliukov balked, the newly returned Vladimir Lenin took the opportunity to push the discourse in a more radical direction, proclaiming in the very first of his famous April Theses that the Great War was an "unconditionally predatory imperialist war." The conflict soon moved to the streets, where crowds of protesters railed against "Miliukov-Dardanelleski" and demanded his removal. Days later, both Miliukov and the Minister of War Aleksandr Guchkov resigned rather than cede control over Russian foreign policy to the Soviet.[18]

If liberals had difficulty coming to terms with the imperial character of their foreign policy, the same was true with their domestic policy as well. The end of the dynasty gave hope to nationalists in the borderlands that the political situation would change dramatically. Nationalists in Finland, Ukraine, Georgia, and elsewhere began dreaming up new ideas, new programs, and new institutions. In Ukraine, for instance, just four days after Kiev had learned of the success of the revolution in Petrograd, Ukrainian politicians established the Central Rada (Parliament) as the hub of the nationalist movement, with the famous historian and cultural figure Mykhailo Hrushevsky as its chairman. The Rada "presided over the impressive revival of Ukrainian political and cultural life."[19] Banned newspapers reappeared, ethnic military units were formed, and a dialogue between new political parties was established. Still, gestures towards independence were made cautiously and infrequently. The Rada declared only autonomy, not independence, when it took its first major constitutional step in June of 1917, a pattern that would be repeated in Finland. Even autonomy was too much for Russian liberals (not even to speak of those on the Russian right). The Provisional Government reacted with suspicion towards the emergence of national ideals, especially on the eve of a major military offensive in Ukraine, and it negotiated with the Rada only under great duress and at the cost of the resignation of most of the Kadets in the government.[20]

With the imperial consensus fraying and snapping in the metropole, the peripheries of the empire descended into violent disorder. Once again, combat played an important role. The Russian army, still convulsing with Revolution, launched a desperate offensive in Galicia in June. The offensive succeeded briefly, but, when the Central Powers counter-attacked, the Russian lines broke, this time for good. Units disappeared, fought each other, ransacked towns, burned manor houses, and dispersed violently toward their homes. The late summer of 1917 was a period of open anarchy in Ukraine, with not just imperial control but state control as such evaporating into an orgy of violence. In August, the city of Riga, which had held firm as the northern tip of the front in Latvia, surrendered to German forces. In Petrograd and Moscow, the position of old regime imperialism became less and less tenable. The Soviets not only became more powerful, but increasingly fell under Bolshevik dominance. Instead of hunger, they promised food; instead of class dominance, they promised land; instead of war, they promised peace; and, instead of empire, they promised national

---

[18] These details and quotes come from Bruce Lincoln's cogent (and aptly titled) chapter "New Men and Old Policies," in W. Bruce Lincoln, *Passage through Armageddon: The Russians in War and Revolution* (New York: Simon and Schuster, 1986), 346–71.

[19] Serhy Yekelchyk, *Ukraine: Birth of a Modern Nation* (Oxford: Oxford University Press, 2007), 69.

[20] Lincoln, *Passage through Armageddon*, 390–1; Richard Pipes, *The Formation of the Soviet Union: Communism and Nationalism, 1917–1923* (Cambridge, MA: Harvard University Press, 1964), 58–9.

Fig. 10. Soldiers recruited from German POW camps training as the new 1st Division of the Ukrainian Army, 1918.

self-determination. In October, they seized the capital, arrested the ministers of the Provisional Government, and proclaimed that all power in Russia had passed to the Soviets.

If the February Revolution had been the signal to nationalists to press for autonomy, the October Revolution was the sign to secede. Not only had the Bolsheviks used self-determination as a slogan, but they were also plainly going to have a difficult time surviving even in their Central Russian urban strongholds. Prior to the Bolshevik seizure of power, Russia had been shorn of Poland, Lithuania, and much of Latvia. Soon after the coup, forces hostile to the Bolsheviks holed up in Estonia, close to the capital. Finland achieved its independence through negotiations with Lenin and the Council of People's Commissars over the New Year's holiday. Ukraine began fighting a civil war in earnest, especially after the Rada signed a separate peace with Germany in order to fend off the Red threat (see Fig. 10). For nationalists in Finland, Latvia, Lithuania, Poland, and Ukraine, "independence" now meant dependence on the ambitious German Empire, a condition that became even more acute in March 1918, when the Bolsheviks ceded nearly all of these borderlands to German suzerainty in the Treaty of Brest-Litovsk.

In the Caucasus, nationalists were pinned between the collapsing Russian Empire and the barely more healthy Ottoman state. The Ottomans sought to press their advantage immediately after Brest-Litovsk. Chafing at the large-scale repopulation of Eastern Anatolia by Armenian refugees under Russian protection, they sponsored assaults by Kurdish paramilitary groups as a way of reducing Armenian power and stoking the violent discord between the two groups. Just as importantly, the Young Turks changed their views on the desirability of creating an independent state in the Transcaucasus. Enver Pasha now viewed such a state favorably as a potential buffer against the Russian disorder and a means of restraining Armenian sentiment by diluting it in a multi-ethnic state.[21] It turned out, however, that many nationalists in the region were also committed socialists, and they at first wanted to throw their lot in with "Russian democracy." The fragile young Transcaucasian Seim (Parliament) called for war with advancing Ottoman forces in April 1918 rather than give up on the Revolution, but its resistance lasted only a short time. On 22 April 1918, the Seim declared independence at the point of Ottoman bayonets.

Less than a month later, the empire unraveled still further. The revolt of the Czech Legion along the route of the Trans-Siberian Railway in May 1918 opened the possibility for anti-Bolshevik forces to form their own government in Russian Asia, which they promptly did. The "Committee of Members of the Constituent Assembly," or Komuch, spread its power along the Volga River in the wake of the Czech Uprising in the summer of 1918 and then moved further east. Bolshevik power was dwindling. In August, the Komuch and the Czechs took Kazan', the city on the Volga that had served as Ivan the Terrible's first imperial conquest in 1552. Its western borderlands under German control, its Caucasian territories pressed in by the Ottomans, and wide swathes of the south and east under the command of various statelets and warlords, Russia under Bolshevik rule was reduced to the borders of old Muscovy. The story of the Russian Empire in the Great War was one of complete and total collapse.

CONCLUSION: THE DEATH AND REBIRTH OF EMPIRE IN THE RUSSIAN CIVIL WAR

Somewhat surprisingly, the utter imperial collapse did not spell the end of imperialism, even of the open and acquisitive sort. All across the former borderlands in 1918 and 1919, avowed Russian imperialists fleeing Bolshevik rule rubbed shoulders with nationalists seeking autonomy or independence. These "White" Russians had learned no substantive political lessons from the previous years of turmoil. Many insisted, as they had throughout 1917, that fundamental changes to the state and territorial order had to await resolution through the Constituent Assembly. That body, long promised during 1917, had met just once in 1918 before being dispersed by Bolshevik soldiers. Elites on the periphery, even had they possessed the limitless patience required to place their hopes upon the Assembly, had little interest in its restoration. The events of 1917 had demonstrated to anyone paying attention that Russian politicians across the spectrum from moderate socialist to arch-conservative envisioned a large and indivisible Russian state that would retain its imperial conquests.

---

[21] Reynolds, *Shattering Empires*, 195.

The behavior of White generals and politicians confirmed their basic chauvinism and willful political blindness on a daily basis. It was obvious that the Revolution had weakened the power of the center and had allowed for political and military entrepreneurs on the periphery to establish regimes of local and regional control. Indeed, the White armies and political cells were themselves manifestations of this fundamental decentralization of power and violence. White warlords emerged early and constituted a major anti-Bolshevik force in many regions, most notably in Siberia.[22] General Denikin's "Volunteer Army" in South Russia and General Iudenich's Northwestern White Army in Estonia were also very much local in scope, even if they had grander political goals. Yet, these White leaders seemed both mystified and offended by other regional political and military actors, even those that promised support for the anti-Bolshevik crusade. Denikin, for example, huffed angrily at the pretensions to autonomy expressed by the Cossack governments that hosted his men along the Don and Kuban rivers. He also haughtily rejected the desperate pleas of Hetman Skoropadskii for assistance in Ukraine, despite the fact that Skoropadskii was the best Ukrainian politician he could hope for, saying that "the Volunteer Army did not recognize as legal authority in Little Russia the authority of Hetman Skoropadskii, who had used forces which were hostile to Russia [i.e. Germany] for the purpose of creating an independent Ukrainian state."[23] Similarly, Denikin rebuffed attempts by the Georgian government to seek mutual protection from the threat of the Red Army. Instead, he sought reparations for "Russian" property lost when Georgia had declared independence. In the end, the Whites chose to attack Georgian troops militarily (at Sochi) rather than to seek a marriage of convenience.[24] Similar tales could be told regarding Iudenich's behavior in Estonia and Admiral Kolchak's government in Siberia. Unreconstructed imperialism was one of the main reasons that the anti-Bolshevik forces were unable to coordinate their efforts in the Russian Civil War.

Ethnopolitics were also evident in the policy of White armies toward civilian populations. Most notably, 1919 became a year of White terror against the Jewish population of Ukraine. Many different anti-Bolshevik groups participated in the slaughter. The troops of Symon Petliura and the Ukrainian Directory were most prominent, accounting for 40 percent of the violent incidents, but units of the Volunteer Army also participated, promising to destroy the "diabolical force that lives in the hearts of Jew-Communists." The assaults began in January in Volynsk and soon spread to the rest of Ukraine. The scale of depredation was much larger than that encountered in pre-war pogroms and even exceeded the violence surrounding the mass deportations of Jews during the Great War. In some cities, as many as one in three Jews was murdered. The violence was marked by humiliation, rape, and torture. More than 1,500 pogroms took place. Estimates of the number

---

[22] Jamie Bisher, *White Terror: Cossack Warlords of the Trans-Siberian* (London and New York: Routledge, 2005).

[23] Peter Kenez, *Civil War in South Russia, 1918: The First Year of the Volunteer Army* (Berkeley and Los Angeles: University of California Press, 1971), 236.

[24] Kenez, *Civil War*, 247–50.

of murdered Jews vary widely, from a low of 50,000 to a high of 200,000. Hundreds of thousands more were wounded or crippled.[25]

White anti-Jewish terror was just one aspect of the kaleidescope of violence that descended upon the former empire between 1918 and 1921. As state control evaporated and the economy collapsed entirely, criminal violence increased. Hordes of people crisscrossing the territory also brought violence in their wake: POWs from the Central Powers returned home by foot, urban residents fled starving cities and sought food in the countryside, and political refugees hopped trains, rode horses, and walked to find regimes that would welcome them. Disease also ran rampant in these conditions. Then there was the warfare itself. In the Civil War, every town, every village, was a potential battleground. Some of the fighting was low-level skirmishing between intruding platoons or food requisition forces and hastily organized self-defense forces. Some took place between larger formations, as in the battles in Siberia and South Russia between the largest White and Red Armies. Finally, there were large-scale revolts and incidents of political violence. In July 1918, the left wing of the Socialist Revolutionary Party, which had made common cause with the Bolsheviks after the October Revolution, broke free in a demonstrative rebellion. They assassinated the German Ambassador, briefly took hostage the head of the Cheka (the Soviet political police), and fomented a large uprising in the city of Iaroslavl under Mikhail Murav'ev, a defector from the Red Army. The Bolsheviks proved able to counter the military threat through a bloody invasion and terror campaign in Iaroslavl and beyond. Just as importantly, though, the defeat of the Left SRs, who had fought for decentralization and a loose confederation of socialist governments, left the way clear for Bolshevik centralizers to reimagine the formation of a new centralized state on the lands of the former empire. On 10 July 1918, they did just that, creating a draft constitution at the Fifth All-Russian Congress of Soviets that ensured centralized party control at all levels of the government.[26]

This brings us to the issue of Red imperialism. Lenin had long advocated for a centralized and disciplined party, and the entire leadership believed that a dictatorship was necessary to consolidate and develop the Revolution. He was not, to say the least, a principled advocate for decentralization. Nor, of course, did he believe that the Revolution should be limited only to the Great Russian ethnic heartland. The Revolution and its revolutionaries were always multinational. Where territories were able to be contested, the Red Army would be sent to conquer, regardless of pre-war borders or patterns of ethnic settlement. To Lenin's credit, he recognized that it would be easy for colonized peoples to see Red troops not as liberators but as a renewed wave of Muscovite power. This was particularly problematic because the pre-war pattern of colonization had created ethnically Russian working classes in urban conclaves in the imperial borderlands. Thus, a "dictatorship of the

[25] O. V. Budnitskii, *Rossiiskie evrei mezhdu krasnymi i belymi* (Moscow: ROSSPEN, 2006), 275–6; W. Bruce Lincoln, *Red Victory: A History of the Russian Civil War* (New York: Simon and Schuster, 1989), 321; Serhy Yekelchyk, *Ukraine: Birth of a Modern Nation* (Oxford: Oxford University Press, 2007), 81.

[26] Lincoln, *Red Victory*, 129.

proletariat" that relied upon urban soviets as its local political base would run a serious risk of tainting the communist project with the stain of chauvinistic colonialism. In certain places, such as the regions in Central Asia that had seen the ethnic bloodbath of 1916–17, this outcome was particularly likely and dangerous. These fears were fully borne out. Central Asia became a vicious arena of ethnic exploitation in which indigenous people were excluded not only from political power but also from access to needed resources. A terrible famine devastated the region. Unsurprisingly, violent rebellion soon followed as groups of desperate and discontented men joined together to protect their lives and cultures from the new batch of Slavic oppressors.[27] These uprisings in the borderlands were more than annoyances. They threatened Soviet rule as such. The Bolsheviks could start the process of re-creating the state through conquest, but if they failed to come to accommodation with non-Russian peoples, their rule would be permanently jeopardized.

Thus, the Bolshevik leadership cast about for solutions to the imperial dilemma in ways that neither their predecessors in the tsarist nor Provisional governments had contemplated and in ways that their White opponents steadfastly refused to countenance. Lenin's solution was both pragmatic and ideological. The Bolsheviks acknowledged the recent revolutionary history of empire and nation (and their own slogans in 1917) by affirming the rights of nations to "self-determination" and by establishing a long-desired federal system in the state apparatus. At the same time, they pursued their own vision of revolutionary politics by insisting upon dictatorial control for a single party—their own—that was centralized and strictly hierarchical. Just as, in Stalin's famous phrase, the party would pursue a policy that was "national in form, socialist in content," so too did it plan for a somewhat Potemkin federalism, one federal in principle but Bolshevik in practice. It was not meaningful devolution or decentralization in any real way.[28]

In reality, the process of state and empire building in the Civil War was far more messy. It had to be. The economy was in free fall, vicious fighting was taking place everywhere, some of the land was occupied by foreign armies, and much of the rest was taken from time to time by anti-Bolshevik movements and by garden-variety warlords. It was difficult to transmit timely instructions to local officials from Moscow, and, even when those directives were received, they were often ignored. Just as importantly, the correlation of forces varied widely. What worked in Minsk could very well be destructive in Tashkent. Still, a certain pattern emerged, especially over the course of 1919: the Red Army and Cheka would enter a territory bubbling with conflict and defeat the forces that opposed them, killing the recalcitrant and seeking leverage with important groups and figures who wavered politically. This group of wavering borderland actors often included indigenous elites. Local Bolsheviks would attempt to punish and exclude these nationalists, while Moscow would insist on attempting to co-opt them.[29] The outcome of these conflicts and negotiations again depended on the time and place, but by the end of the

---

[27] See Buttino, *Revoliutsiia naoborot.*

[28] Terry Martin, *The Affirmative Action Empire: Nations and Nationalism in the Soviet Union, 1923–1939* (Ithaca, NY: Cornell University Press, 2001), 13.

[29] For more details on this process, see Pipes, *The Formation of the Soviet Union.*

war a new imperial space had been created with its center in the Kremlin. By 1921, the Bolsheviks had retaken much of the territory that the tsars had controlled. Finland, Estonia, Latvia, Lithuania, and Poland had become independent states, but Ukraine, Georgia, Armenia, Azerbaijan, and all of Russian Central Asia were incorporated into the new communist federation. Conquered by the Red Army and governed by the Party, local societies and elites lived under no illusion that they enjoyed self-rule. Nevertheless, it was just as obvious that this was a different kind of empire: Russian chauvinism was publicly denounced (if not always weakened in practice), the Red leaders rejected the term "empire" itself, and the traditional structures of power had been forever disrupted. A new "affirmative action empire" was created as the top leadership sought to create a new political elite in the borderlands that would ensure Bolshevik hegemony at the same time as it reassured locals that the communist project was their own. That project, too, would run aground, but not before creating lasting political and social effects in the Soviet political space.[30]

---

[30] Martin, *The Affirmative Action Empire.*

6

The French Empire

Richard S. Fogarty

In 1923, the chronological endpoint of this volume's consideration of the histories of empire during the First World War, Albert Sarraut published *La Mise en valeur des colonies françaises*. Sarraut, who was then Minister of the Colonies and had formerly been Governor General of Indochina (later in the 1930s he twice served as Prime Minister), argued that France had to make better material use of its empire, and this "mise en valeur," or rational economic exploitation, became the watchword of overall French colonial policy between the wars. That France not only should but could embark on this ambitious project to make empire really pay was clear, Sarraut claimed, from the experience of the Great War: "The colonies were thus no longer simply these faraway lands where the dreams and fantasies of novelists played out! They were lands overflowing with intense life, rich in men, rich in natural resources, which demonstrated their vitality at the hour of greatest danger. By these positive results, the 'colonial enterprise' showed that it 'paid.'"[1] The two pillars upon which France had then stood, and would stand in any future war, he made clear, were the economic aid the colonies could offer and their manpower reserves.

Long before Sarraut wrote these lines, the French Empire played a critical role in the events leading up to the formal beginning of war in 1914, and these highlight the imperative of expanding the chronological lens through which we view the Great War, as this volume seeks to do. From the 1890s, the French government was deeply concerned over imperial rivalries with Germany, successfully discouraging, for instance, French investors from helping to finance the Kaiser's planned Berlin–Baghdad railway line. Any account of the road to war in Europe must run through Morocco, where Franco-German imperial rivalries were even more acute. In 1905, and again in 1911, tensions seemed to point toward war, even a general European war given the alliance system that governed interstate relations in the region, when German demands for influence in a territory that was increasingly falling under French control provoked intense diplomatic crises. Violence was not absent from these events: not only did the Kaiser signal German designs on Morocco by sending a gunboat to the port of Agadir in 1911, only to see his plans foiled by Entente unity and Austrian indifference; France was actively engaged in

---

[1] Albert Sarraut, *La Mise en valeur des colonies françaises* (Paris: Payot, 1923), 51.

military operations in Morocco up to and even after 1912, when the territory became part of the colonial empire as a protectorate.

The effects of French imperial ambitions continued to reverberate, inside and outside the empire. In the autumn of 1912, inspired by the recognition of France's colonial claims on Morocco, Italy went to war with the Ottoman Empire and moved into Libya and Tripolitania.[2] That same year, in order to address an increasingly dangerous international security situation, the French army started official conscription among the indigenous populations for the first time in both French West Africa and Algeria. French army officer Charles Mangin had argued strenuously in his 1910 book *La Force noire* that France's European and global security depended upon colonial reservoirs of men available to serve as soldiers.[3] In part as a result of these pre-war impulses, the French army would recruit extensively among the indigenous populations of the empire during the war. And long after the Armistice, Mangin and others would seek to highlight the value of empire and reassure a France in relative decline with similar arguments about "100 million Frenchmen" safeguarding the defense of the metropole and colonies alike.

The French colonial empire, then, is a key part of the wider chronological and global story of the Great War. The colonies also played a crucial role in the French wartime and post-war imagination, and that was because the empire played a notable role in helping France to conduct a total war between 1914 and 1918. And the war's effects continued to shape events in the colonies after 1918 precisely because of the empire's prominent role in France's war effort. In a very real way, the Great War did not merely involve France as one of the principle combatants, but "La plus grande France," or "Greater France," as the combined entity of the nation and its overseas possessions was known, went to war in 1914. This Greater France was a classic example of the kind of polity Charles Maier had in mind when he offered the definition of empire that serves as the organizing principle of this volume on empires at war: its territory was extensive, dispersed globally, in fact; its organization was multi-ethnic, hierarchical, and centralized; and its existence depended on the cooperation of colonized elites (as well as others it raised to more or less elite status).[4] The imperial center in Europe was tightly bound to the colonies, in political, economic, and cultural terms.[5] This meant that the stresses and strains of war did not just act on the metropole, but reached into the spaces and lives of the far-flung empire in profound and far-reaching ways. This is, of course, unsurprising given the status of the Great War overall as a world war, but it is important to remember that the huge extent of the French colonial empire at the time—then the world's second largest and stretching from North and West Africa, to Madagascar, Indochina, the Pacific, and the Caribbean—helped ensure that the

    [2] James Joll, *The Origins of the First World War*, 2nd edn (London: Longman, 1992), 59.

    [3] Charles Mangin, *La Force noire* (Paris: Hachette, 1910).

    [4] Charles S. Maier, *Among Empires: America's Ascendancy and its Predecessors* (Cambridge, MA: Harvard University Press, 2006), 31.

    [5] Hence the by now axiomatic treatment, by historians of the French and other empires, of metropole and colonies in a "single analytic field." See Frederick Cooper and Ann Laura Stoler, "Between Metropole and Colony: Rethinking a Research Agenda," in their *Tensions of Empire: Colonial Cultures in a Bourgeois World* (Berkeley and Los Angeles: University of California Press, 1997), 1–56.

war was truly global.[6] The participation of more than 500,000 non-European colonial subjects as soldiers, and another 200,000 as workers, in the war effort in Europe stands as the most vivid, if not the only, illustration of the integral role of empire in France's war.

The global reach of the Great War had consequences felt throughout Greater France. True, the war did not fatally weaken France's grip on the colonies, by provoking moves toward independence in the colonies, for instance. But there were signs that the confidence in the stability and profitability of empire on display in works like Sarraut's, and in events like the celebratory International Colonial Exposition in Paris of 1931 (which provided concrete, spectacular manifestations of Sarraut's textual celebration of the utility of empire and its contributions to French grandeur) papered over very real cracks and fissures in the imperial edifice.[7] It would be the Second World War that would have the most direct destabilizing influence upon French rule in the colonies, but the first global, total war began a process that culminated after the second.[8] And this process originated in part in response to the pressures France put on its empire in exploiting the two areas Sarraut identified as the greatest sources of colonial support: economic aid and manpower.

MISE EN VALEUR

The empire helped lay the foundation for this first modern, industrialized war, in which the race to mobilize and deploy physical resources in depth and over the long term played a, perhaps the, critical role. Sarraut calculated that the French territories under the authority of the Ministry of the Colonies—West and Equatorial Africa, Indochina, and Madagascar, as well as those smaller possessions dotting other parts of Africa, the Indian and Pacific Oceans, the Caribbean, and various other parts of the world—contributed almost 650 million francs to the

[6] Some in Germany described the war from the beginning as *Der Weltkrieg*. Hew Strachan, "The First World War as a Global War," *First World War Studies*, 1/1 (2010), 3–14, argues conclusively and concisely for the view of the war as both global and imperial. See also his *The First World War* (New York: Viking, 2003), and *The First World War*, i. *To Arms* (Oxford: Oxford University Press, 2001); John H. Morrow, Jr, *The Great War: An Imperial History* (New York: Routledge, 2004); Michael S. Neiberg, *Fighting the Great War: A Global History* (Cambridge MA: Harvard University Press, 2006); William Kelleher Storey, *The First World War: A Concise Global History* (New York: Rowman & Littlefield, 2010); Lawrence Sondhaus, *World War One: The Global Revolution* (Cambridge: Cambridge University Press, 2011), and Andrew Tait Jarboe and Richard S. Fogarty (eds), *Empires in World War I: Shifting Frontiers and Imperial Dynamics in a Global Conflict* (London: I. B. Tauris, 2014).

[7] On the reassuring self-image that the 1931 Colonial Exposition offered up to the French public, see Herman Lebovics, *True France: The Wars over Cultural Identity, 1900–1945* (Ithaca, NY: Cornell University Press, 1992), 51–97.

[8] Martin Thomas, *The French Empire between the Wars* (Manchester: Manchester University Press, 2005), shows clearly the structural weaknesses that plagued the French Empire after the First World War. On the effects of the Second World War on the empire, see his *The French Empire at War, 1940–45* (Manchester: Manchester University Press, 1998). Fredrik Logevall, *Embers of War: The Fall of an Empire and the Making of America's Vietnam* (New York: Random House, 2012), argues more forcefully for the preponderant role of the Second World War in fatally weakening French colonial control in Indochina.

cost of the war through war loans and charitable donations, and shipped about 2.5 million tons of various materials to France between 1914 and 1918.[9] French territories in North Africa—Tunisia, Algeria, and Morocco—classified for various reasons as separate from the rest of the empire, added nearly a billion francs in war loan subscriptions and some three million tons of war-related materials.[10] This was not insignificant, but one must remember that the French government raised some 100 billion francs domestically in bonds during the war, so the colonial contribution was less than 2 per cent, and that France was spending 34 billion francs a year on the war by 1918.[11] Moreover, the amount of war-related materials imported to France from elsewhere dwarfed the colonial contribution, and the colonies served mainly as sources of foodstuffs and not of materials like coal and oil that fed the heavy industries of war, nor of manufactured goods.[12]

Yet French efforts to make the empire pay during this time of existential threat and urgent need had effects that were felt widely in the colonies. The French state intervened more directly than ever in colonial economies, setting priorities and determining both the production and allocation of resources, though there were of course regional and temporal variations across the empire and over the four years of the war. The colonies that made up the vast federation of French West Africa (l'Afrique Occidentale Française (AOF)) illustrate the point vividly. The first two years of the war saw little direct intervention by the state in the economy of the AOF, leaving the major French import and export companies operating in the area free to carry on their business as they saw fit. By 1916, however, the colonial administration began moving toward interventionism in response to demands from the metropole. Under the activist governor general Joost Van Vollenhoven in 1917, the state increasingly directed economic activity, particularly in the production of palm and peanut oils, the AOF's main exports. This intervention included directing the efforts of the native population toward increased production and transport of these products, redirecting and disrupting local economies. By the end of the war, the effort to contribute to France's war economy left "deep imprints nearly everywhere in the AOF," outside the more remote and undeveloped territories of Mauritania and Niger.[13] Discontent and labor unrest echoed well after 1918.

[9] Sarraut, *Mise en valeur*, 45, 50–1.
[10] Pierre Varet, *Du concours apporté à la France par ses colonies et pays de protectorat au cours de la guerre de 1914* (Paris: Presses modernes, 1927). See also Jacques Frémeaux, *Les Colonies dans la Grande Guerre: Combats et épreuves des peuples d'Outre-Mer* (Paris: 14–18 Editions, 2006). Tunisia and Morocco were officially protectorates, in which the French state recognized the de jure authority of the indigenous rulers (the Bey of Tunis and the Sultan of Morocco), but exercised de facto colonial control via the Foreign Ministry. Algeria was heavily populated with French settlers and administratively absorbed into metropolitan France, divided into three départements analogous to metropolitan départements, and governed under the authority of the Minster of the Interior.
[11] Leonard V. Smith, Stéphane Audoin-Rouzeau, and Annette Becker, *France and the Great War* (Cambridge: Cambridge University Press, 2003), 65.
[12] Frémeaux, *Les Colonies dans la Grande Guerre*, 87–8.
[13] Marc Michel, *L'Appel à l'Afrique: Contributions et réactions à l'effort de guerre en A.O.F, 1914–1919* (Paris: Publications de la Sorbonne, 1982), 450. The work as a whole traces this story in exhaustive detail. A shorter version was recently published: *Les Africains et la Grande Guerre: L'Appel à l'Afrique (1914–1918)* (Paris: Karthala, 2003). All references in this chapter are to the original, 1982 version.

Throughout the empire, wartime requisitioning meant that the state fixed the prices at which it obtained colonial resources, and so colonial producers obtained less than market value for their products. Transportation difficulties, particularly acute for more distant possessions in Indochina and Madagascar, and those Caribbean colonies whose products had to cross an Atlantic Ocean patrolled by German U-boats, sometimes blunted the economic aid the empire could provide, while also making imports to the colonies scarce and driving inflation. Even in colonies or sectors where wartime demands from the metropole stimulated growth and increased profits—such as Algeria, which had large, European-owned farms that provided a great deal of grain, wine, and mutton, and Morocco, which as a protectorate was sheltered from the some of the most direct kinds of French state intervention—the price of being enmeshed in an imperial economy was more apparent than ever to the colonized.[14] In some parts of the empire, like Madagascar, which saw a dramatic increase in its exports to the metropole, wartime pressures and domestic events combined to threaten a real "economic and monetary debacle."[15]

The mention of the monetary situation in Madagascar is indicative of the financial contribution that the metropole called on the colonies to make, in addition to shipping tons of goods at reduced prices. If it is true that the colonial contribution here was also a small percentage of the overall total raised, the vast majority of which came from domestic bond purchases and foreign loans, the amounts were not negligible in the colonial context. Here was empire "paying," as Sarraut put it in his post-war encomium to the role of the colonies, in a very literal sense. The federation of Indochina made the most important financial contribution to the war effort of all the colonies outside of North Africa. The 367 million francs in war bonds raised in Indochina accounted for well over half the total raised in all of the colonies. The colony also accounted for almost half of all the empire's contributions to charitable associations doing war-related work, while localities in Indochina were particularly active in "adopting" French villages destroyed by the war.[16] This is not surprising, since Indochina was one of the richest colonies in the French Empire, and much of this aid came from the wealthier planters and other European settlers. Nonetheless, as much as one-third of the total raised for war loans in Indochina came from the pockets of the indigenous population. The same proportion held for the larger contribution of Algeria, so the indigenous populations of the empire were fairly heavily invested in the French war effort.[17]

The example of Indochina serves as a reminder that this colonial contribution carried a cost to the indigenous economy and population, as well as to the stability of French rule. Beyond its financial contribution, Indochina exported to France more tonnage of war-related goods than any other colony save French West Africa,

---

[14] On Algeria's experience during the war, see Gilbert Meynier, *L'Algérie révélée: La Guerre de 1914–1918 et le premier quart du XXe siècle* (Geneva: Droz, 1981), and on Morroco's, see Mohammed Bekraoui, *Le Maroc et la première guerre mondiale 1914–1920* (Lille: ANRT, 1987).

[15] Maurice Gontard, *Madagascar pendant la première guerre mondiale* (Tananarive: Editions Universitaires, 1969), 90.

[16] Sarraut, *Mise en valeur*, 45–8.

[17] Frémeaux, *Les Colonies dans la Grande Guerre*, 86; Meynier, *L'Algérie révélée*, 602.

which was quite an achievement given the difficulties in transporting materials over the vast distance between south-east Asia and the metropole.[18] Yet the disruptions of the war caused a significant reduction in overall trade between colony and metropole, as merchants in Indochina had to sell on Asian markets when they could not reach France, and the disruption in the economic relationship caused economic difficulties into the post-war period.[19] And it is important to remember that, even if the Banque de l'Indochine continued to grow ever wealthier and the colonial budget of Indochina actually showed a surplus during the war years, suffering and discontent were evident in some areas. Rural Tonkin suffered through famine, while reduced colonial garrisons faced periodic menaces from pirates, nationalist insurgents, and even mutinying *tirailleurs indochinois* (indigenous soldiers) in 1917.[20] None of this seriously threatened French rule at the time, but was a reminder that the war, however distant its main combats, affected all areas of the French colonial empire and posed potential problems for future stability. Even a balance of payments that began to favor the colonies by the end of the war came at a price: the reduction of French imports meant that in some ways material standards of living declined, and the colonial exports that expanded were only those metropolitan authorities judged essential to the war effort, and so other sectors saw real declines and distortions of supply. Ultimately, as one historian has put it, "colonial commerce contracted everywhere."[21]

So the colonial contribution to the war effort is more apparent in some of its effects on the colonies rather than when measured as a percentage of total war materials shipped or money raised. The economic and financial contribution is also more apparent when one considers the place of empire in France's wartime culture. As historian Jacques Frémeaux notes, if it is true that it "would be entirely utopian to expect considerable aid from lands with limited resources when viewed in comparison with the norms of industrialized societies," it is also true that the colonies' "contribution is, in spite of everything, much more sizeable than one could have hoped."[22] And this was the sentiment, and the hope, underlying Sarraut's and others' enthusiasm for the colonial contribution to victory in 1918. Modern, industrial war consumed vast quantities of both money and resources, and the state hoped to find both in the colonies. In fact, when considering the economic and financial role of empire over the longer term in nineteenth- and twentieth-century history, one must keep in mind not just the hard facts found on balance sheets, but the place of the colonies in the economic imagination of the era. The French Empire's total receipts, its real payoff, never exceeded its costs.[23] But this did not mean that many political and business leaders did not expect the colonies to pay

---

[18] Sarraut, *Mise en valeur*, 50.

[19] Frémeaux, *Les Colonies dans la Grande Guerre*, 80–3.

[20] Frémeaux, *Les Colonies dans la Grande Guerre*, 91–2, 257–61. "Tirailleur," literally meaning "skirmisher" or "rifleman," was a term the French applied to all colonial infantrymen, adding "indochinois" for Indochinese in French uniform, "algérien" for Algerians, "sénégalais" for West Africans, and so on.

[21] Jacques Thobie, Gilbert Meynier, Catherine Coquery-Vidrovitch, and Charles-Robert Ageron, *Histoire de la France coloniale, 1914–1990* (Paris: Armand Colin, 1990), 75.

[22] Frémeaux, *Les Colonies dans la Grande Guerre*, 89, 93.

[23] See the pioneering, and very thorough, research of Jacques Marseille, in his *Empire colonial et capitalisme français: Histoire d'un divorce* (Pairs: Albin Michel, 1984). David S. Landes comes to the

real, worthwhile dividends. In short, if the empire was in fact a millstone around the neck of French capitalism and economic development, many were not only unaware of this fact, but believed the opposite.

It is perhaps this cultural phenomenon of belief in the economic utility of empire that continues to fuel contemporary thinking that runs along the lines first laid down by Marx, Hobson, and Lenin. In the case of France and the French Empire, Sarraut provides the best evidence of the economic faith in and boosterism of empire, often tied very closely to the experiences of the Great War. "Thus," he wrote, "these colonies, long regarded with insouciance as a burdensome luxury, yet indispensable to the international prestige of a great nation, showed in striking fashion, during perilous times, that they could deliver an effective support to the defense of the metropole."[24] In this respect, the colonies played a crucial role in what historians point to as so important in France's war: cultural mobilization.[25] In short, the empire was, for many, clearly even more important psychologically than materially, though dreams of the material basis of imperial wealth and strength fed the psychological vision.

One can see vividly what one historian has called the "official exaltation" over the potential economic contribution of the colonies to the French war effort, and the role of empire in cultural mobilization, in posters that advertised war loans.[26] For instance, two 1920 posters advertising bonds sold by the Crédit Foncier de l'Algérie et de Tunisie to help with post-war reconstruction emphasized the material aid the colonies offered to the metropole. These depicted busy ports during the war, symbols of France's ability to make its empire pay and the same ports from which flowed the millions of tons of materials exalted by Sarraut and others. The ports bustle with activity, native Algerians moving the produce of empire destined to enrich the war-devastated metropole. In one smoke rises from the smokestacks of factories turning the raw materials of the colonies into finished goods (see Fig. 11).[27] Such images conveyed a clear message: the raw materials and labor of the colonies help feed an economy geared for the first time toward fueling, and recovering from, modern industrialized war.

This and other posters demonstrate the place of colonial economies in the French cultural imagination during the war. They reminded the French public, in

same conclusions about the unprofitability of European empires more generally, in his *The Wealth and Poverty of Nations: Why Some Are So Rich and Some So Poor* (New York: W. W. Norton, 1998).

[24] Sarraut, *Mise en valeur*, 51.

[25] The historians affiliated with the Historial at Péronne are most associated with this approach. Smith, Audoin-Rouzeau, and Becker, *France and the Great War*, provides a good overview. See also Antoine Prost, "Les limites de la brutalisation: Tuer sur la front occidental, 1914–1918," *Vingtième siècle*, 1/81 (2004), 5–20; Jay Winter, "P vs C: The Still Burning Anger when the French Talk of the First World War," *Times Literary Supplement*, 16 June 2006; Leonard V. Smith, "The 'Culture de guerre' and French Historiography of the Great War of 1914–1918," *History Compass* 5/6 (2007), 1967–1979; and Pierre Purseigle, "Back from the Trenches," *La Vie des idées.fr* (23 April 2009) <www.booksandideas.net/Back-from-the-Trenches.html?lang=fr> (accessed 20 April 2013).

[26] Thobie et al., *Histoire de la France coloniale*, 75.

[27] Hoover Institution Archives poster collection FR 894: C. Boiry, "Crédit Foncier d'Algérie et de Tunisie, Emprunt national 6% 1920" (Paris: Devambez, 1920?). For a fuller discussion of these and other images, see Richard S. Fogarty, "Race and Empire in French Posters of the Great War," in Pearl James (ed.), *Picture This: World War I Posters and Visual Culture* (Lincoln, NB: University of Nebraska Press, 2009), 172–206.

Fig. 11. A poster advertising a 1920 war loan, to help pay war reconstruction costs. The colonies could provide economic aid for post-war rebuilding, just as they had aided the metropole in prosecuting the war.

the colonies and in the metropole, that France could count on its empire to work to its advantage in the existential struggle with Germany, that "la grande France [...] cannot lose."[28] These sentiments echoed into the post-war period, and not just in advertisements for reconstruction loans. Even the biggest boosters of the colonial empire before 1914 recognized that it was, as one historian has described it, a "patchwork."[29] After 1918, Sarraut was just one of many voices citing the war as proof that France could get more out of its empire with a more systematic approach. One of his predecessors as Minister of the Colonies, Henry Simon, called in 1919 for an end to the "caprice" and haphazardness that had marked the building of the empire, and the inauguration of a "regular plan" for colonial economic development and exploitation, the need for which was the "first lesson of the war."[30] Throughout the interwar period, the *mise en valeur* that appeared so tantalizingly during the war would drive French colonial policy toward greater efforts to exploit the empire.[31]

RESERVOIRS OF MEN

In 1915, an advertisement distinctive to the wartime environment appeared, one that would be tremendously successful and continue to appear widely and echo loudly in French culture for many decades after the end of the war. A smiling African, in the immediately recognizable uniform of a *tirailleur sénégalais*, one of some 134,000 who came to France to fight on the Western Front, appeared on posters and packaging for the hot breakfast drink Banania, rapidly becoming one of the most recognizable icons in the history of French advertising. The Banania image exploited the popularity of the soldiers among the French public, as did similar images of these soldiers used by many other advertisers, but it also made clear that this popularity was shot through with racialized assumptions about the nature of black Africans, and these assumptions helped distance colonial subjects, even those in French uniform, from the nation for which they fought. The overdrawn smile reflected the standard view of black Africans as good-natured and simplistic, and the overall effect was overtly paternalistic and racist. Reacting to the continued use of these images long after the war, Léopold Sédar Senghor, the great African poet and first president of an independent Senegal, wished he could tear posters featuring the insulting visage of the tirailleur from the walls of Paris.[32]

---

[28] Marie-Pascale Presvost-Bault, "Les Collections de l'Historial," in Weill, et al., *Les Affiches de la Grande Guerre* (Péronne, Somme: Martelle; Historial de la Grande Guerre, 1998), 24.

[29] Thobie et al., *Histoire de la France coloniale*, 59.

[30] Stephen H. Roberts, *The History of French Colonial Policy, 1870–1925* (1929; repr. Hamden, CT: Archon, 1963), 606.

[31] For a full and detailed examination of the history of the notion of *mise en valeur* in French colonial policy, see Alice L. Conklin, *A Mission to Civilize: France and West Africa, 1895–1930* (Stanford: Stanford University Press, 1997).

[32] For Senghor's reaction and more on Banania and images of the *tirailleurs*, see Anne Donadey, "'Y'a bon Banania': Ethics and Cultural Criticism in the Colonial Context," *French Cultural Studies*, 11 (2000), 9–29. See also Jean Garrigues, *Banania: Histoire d'une passion française* (Paris: du May, 1991); John Mendenhall, *French Trademarks: The Art Deco Era* (San Francisco: Chronicle, 1991);

The bodily human contributions of the colonies to the war effort were, in fact, far more famous than the importation of the kinds of materials that made "exotic" products like Banania possible. This is true whether measured by cultural impact in the metropole at the time or by the imprint left into the years after 1918, and in the historiography to this day. France recruited, and imported, both soldiers and workers. Nearly 200,000 colonial subjects came to France to work in war industries between 1914 and 1918. Most came from North Africa (and most of these from Algeria) and Indochina, along with a few thousand from Madagascar. (Though not colonial subjects, some 37,000 Chinese workers also added to the non-European workforce in France.) The French state closely monitored and controlled colonial workers in France, subjecting them to strict surveillance and segregation whenever possible, and generally discriminated against them in the workplace. One historian has characterized their situation as essentially one of "forced labour," which is no surprise given that one of his sources, a North African Muslim, wrote: "The infidels have taken me by force [...] I work like a condemned man."[33] Moreover, resentment, discrimination, and even racially motivated violence were common reactions among the French civilian population to the presence of these men on French soil and in French workplaces.[34]

Yet, if colonial workers were an important and visible aspect of the participation of Greater France in the war, the participation of soldiers like the *tirailleur sénégalais* pictured in the Banania advertisement loomed much larger, both numerically and culturally. Some 500,000 colonial subjects entered the French army and came to the metropole to serve on the Western Front. It is no accident that Sarraut's work lauding the imperial contribution to the war effort and recommending a more systematic post-war *mise en valeur* devoted a great deal of space to documenting and discussing the human capital the empire lent to the war effort—more space, in fact, than he devoted to chronicling the empire's economic and financial contributions. This was much easier to add up (in sheer numbers of men), and the presence of workers in factories and other work sites in France and of soldiers on the battlefield had made a striking impression. Soldiers attracted the most attention, since they were more numerous and their contribution to the war effort appeared more direct and entailed, potentially, the ultimate sacrifice. They would pay what French officials often referred to as the "blood tax." The soldiers stood for

Anne-Claude Lelieur and Bernard Mirabel, *Negripub: L'Image des Noirs dans la publicité depuis un siècle* (Paris: Société des Amis de la Bilbliothèque Forney, 1987). Dana S. Hale, "French Images of Race on Product Trademarks during the Third Republic," and Leora Auslander and Thomas C. Holt, "Sambo in Paris: Race and Racism in the Iconography of the Everyday," both in Sue Peabody and Tyler Stovall (eds), *The Color of Liberty: Histories of Race in France* (Durham, NC: Duke University Press, 2003), 131–46, 147–84, discuss the Banania figure and how it fits into the larger context of advertising imagery of the day.

[33] Tyler Stovall, "Colour-Blind France? Colonial Workers during the First World War," *Race & Class*, 35/2 (1993), 37, 47.

[34] Tyler Stovall, "The Color Line behind the Lines: Racial Violence in France during the Great War," *American Historical Review*, 103/3 (1998), 737–69. On colonial labor in wartime France, see also Bertrand Nogaro and Lucien Weil, *La Main d'œuvre étrangère et coloniale pendant la guerre* (Paris: Presses Universitaires de France, 1926), and John Horne, "Immigrant Workers in France during World War I," *French Historical Studies*, 14/1 (1985), 57–88.

many as spectacular confirmation of the genius and efficacy of France's generous civilizing mission in its empire, and the colonized owed this blood tax precisely because they allegedly benefited so much from France's tutelage.

France had made use of colonial subjects in its army in the colonies for many decades, and the immediate years before 1914 saw increasing agitation for expanding this use, both to police the empire and even to contribute to domestic national defense. Mangin's 1910 work advocating recruitment in West Africa, *La Force noire*, was a key contribution to this discourse. Adolphe Messimy (later Minister of the Colonies and, in 1914, Minister of War) supported Mangin's ideas with a blunt reference to the blood tax: "Africa has cost us heaps of gold, thousands of soldiers, and streams of blood. We do not dream of demanding the gold from her. But the men and the blood, she must repay them with interest."[35] By 1912, France had embarked upon conscription in two of its most important purported "reservoirs of men," Algeria and West Africa. In this way, the manpower resources of Greater France were clearly implicated in an overall push to expand France's army and capacity for national defense—in 1913, a controversial measure increased the term of universal obligatory military service for French men from two years to three—in a Europe and world that appeared increasingly threatened by German ambitions and militarism.[36]

When war began in 1914, France already had at its disposal almost 90,000 colonial subjects, known as *troupes indigènes* (or indigenous troops), in the army.[37] French casualties in the hundreds of thousands in only the first months of the war soon prompted further and intensified recruiting efforts in the colonies. By the end of 1914, after only five months of fighting, the French army had lost over 300,000 men killed. By the end of 1915, France had lost at least half of the over 1.3 million men who would be killed before the war ended, and more than half of the over 3 million wounded received their wounds by that same date.[38] The manpower crisis, then, combined with a sense of entitlement provided by the ideology of the civilizing mission, led authorities to turn to the empire as a source of soldiers.

It is no accident that the first moves toward an intensive recruitment in the empire began during the war's second terrible year. The following year saw still more intensive efforts. After difficulties with transport and local circumstances in the colonies had led to a slowing of recruitment in 1917, 1918 saw a renewed push to exploit imperial manpower resources under the reign of France's new and

[35] Quoted in Michel, *L'Appel*, 7.

[36] Eugen Weber, *The Nationalist Revival in France, 1905–1914* (Berkeley and Los Angeles: University of California Press, 1968); Gerd Krumeich, *Armaments and Politics in France on the Eve of the First World War: The Introduction of Three-Year Conscription, 1913–1914* (Dover, NH: Berg, 1984).

[37] Jean-Charles Jauffret, "Les Armes de 'la plus grande France,'" in Guy Pedroncini (ed.), *Histoire militaire de la France*, iii. *De 1871 à 1940* (Paris: Presses Universitaires de France, 1992), 61. The French army used the term *troupes indigènes* to designate colonial subjects in the army, even though, once outside their colonies of origin, these men were no longer technically "indigenous."

[38] Louis Marin, "Rapport sur le Bilan des Pertes en Morts et en Blessés des Nations belligérentes," *Journal Officiel, Documents Parlementaires*, annexe no. 633 (1920); *Données et Statistiques relatives à la Guerre 1914–1918* (Paris: Imperimerie Nationale, 1922).

implacable Prime Minister and Minister of War, Georges Clemenceau. The last year of the war yielded more colonial recruits overall than any of the previous four, though Indochina and Madagascar actually provided fewer soldiers that year than they had previously because of political and logistical problems specific to those colonies. In all, West Africa provided some 166,000 recruits during the war; Algeria, 140,000; Indochina, 50,000; Tunisia, 47,000; Madagascar, 46,000; and Morocco, 24,000.[39] Not all of these men served in Europe, but a large majority did, and joined the 90,000 *troupes indigènes* already under arms in 1914. So of the more than eight million Frenchmen who were mobilized for war to defend their nation between 1914 and 1918, half a million were not citizens at all, but colonial subjects.

The history of recruitment is long and complicated, but in general it proceeded by both voluntary enlistment and conscription. There were differences among colonies—so, for instance, enlistment was exclusively voluntary in Morocco, and only by conscription in Tunisia, with a mix of methods in Algeria, West Africa, Indochina, and Madagascar.[40] But it is important to keep in mind that, though there were no doubt many men who enlisted essentially voluntarily (for money, status, adventure, or opportunity), even many so-called volunteers had been more or less subject to coercive pressure. If colonial officials often reassured themselves that voluntary enlistments and expressions of devotion to and enthusiasm for the French cause in the war among indigenous elites demonstrated the strength of attachment to the empire among its subjects, one must keep in mind that this "empire loyalty" was more apparent than real. It did not often survive the initial months of the war, and was most in evidence among those with something to gain by proving their loyalty to the French administration. For others, compulsion was necessary to defend France and its empire.

In West Africa, for instance, coercion was an integral part of French methods, often channeled through regional colonial administrators and African intermedi-

---

[39] Exact figures are extremely difficult to determine, and these represent the best estimates drawn from numerous archival and published sources. Sarraut's figures (see *Mise en valeur*, 38–44) are precise, but not entirely accurate. For the French army's own early estimates, see Service Historique de l'Armée de Terre (SHAT) 7N440: Note au sujet de la situation actuelle des effectifs en indigènes coloniaux, 11 septembre 1918.

[40] Richard S. Fogarty, *Race and War in France: Colonial Subjects in the French Army, 1914–1918* (Baltimore: Johns Hopkins University Press, 2008), tells this story in general. For more detailed and comprehensive treatments of particular colonies, see: Michel, *L'Appel*; Joe Lunn, *Memoirs of the Mael-strom: A Senegalese Oral History of the First World War* (Portsmouth: Heinemann, 1999); Gilbert Meynier, *L'Algérie révélée: La Guerre de 1914–1918 et le premier quart du XXᵉ siècle* (Geneva: Droz, 1981); Driss Maghraoui, "Moroccan Colonial troops: History, Memory and the Culture of French Colonialism" (Ph.D. dissertation, University of California, Santa Cruz, 2000); Mohammed Bekraoui, *Les Marocains dans la Grande Guerre 1914–1919* (Rabat: Publications de la Commission Marocaine d'Histoire Militaire, 2009); Chantal Valensky, *Le Soldat occulté: Les Malgaches de l'Armée française, 1884–1920* (Paris: L'Harmattan, 1995); Jacques Razafindranaly, *Les Soldats de la grande île: D'une guerre à l'autre, 1895–1918* (Paris: L'Harmattan, 2000); Mireille Favre-Le Van Ho, "Un milieu porteur de modernisation: Travailleurs et tirailleurs vietnamiens en France pendant la première guerre mondiale," 2 vols (Thèse de doctorat, École nationale des chartes, 1986); Henri Eckert, "Les Militaires indochinois au service de la France (1859–1939)," 2 vols (Thèse de doctorat, Université de Paris IV, 1998); and Kimloan Hill, "A Westward Journey, An Enlightened Path: Vietnamese Linh Tho, 1915–30" (Ph.D. dissertation, University of Oregon, 2001).

aries at the local level by the use of a quota system administered by local indigenous auxiliaries. One way for notables to meet the recruitment quotas set by the
colonial administration with minimal social disruption was to "volunteer" men
who were dispensable within the community, and sometimes those unlikely to
pass physical evaluations: the poor, the sick, slaves, orphans, outcasts, younger
sons.[41] Colonial officials fined or imprisoned reluctant chiefs, and even took hostage the parents or other relatives of potential recruits. As one Senegalese veteran
recalled:

> Many of the young men fled [...] but they used to arrest their fathers. [...] Often mothers
> used to say to their sons: "You know your name has been written down and you ran away.
> And now your father has been arrested and he will be taken to prison. So go and enter the
> army." And often they used to go and enter the army, so that their fathers would be
> released.[42]

Whole villages might suffer collective punishment, such as the destruction of
crops, livestock, and other property, for noncompliance.[43] Such practices were well
known enough to be ridiculed in the satirical French weekly, the *Canard enchaîné*,
which noted that recruiters obtained allegedly voluntary enlistments by stretching
ropes across either end of a village and labeling all those between as volunteers and
"presumptive heroes."[44]

In Indochina enlistments were supposed to be voluntary, but forms of coercion,
both subtle and unsubtle, similarly called into question the enthusiasm of the indigenous population to defend the metropole. Local community leaders coerced
men, mostly poor peasants, into joining the war effort so that these notables could
prove their loyalty, and thus worth, to the French administration.[45] Even more
authentic voluntarism often stemmed from a desire to escape poverty and want,
rather than devotion to France.[46] In Madagascar, the payment of bounties to
agents for each recruit increased opportunities for corruption and called into serious question the voluntary nature of enlistments.[47]

Despite this, resistance to recruitment was not as great as one might perhaps
expect, and even the most serious rebellions of the war years often stemmed from
causes beyond the wartime demands of the colonial state. Two of the most serious
threats to French colonial rule during the war—an uprising by the court of Emperor Duy Tan of Annam, in Indochina, and resistance in Madagascar by the secret
anti-colonial society VVS, both occurring in 1916—were rooted in pre-war
grievances and circumstances. The war merely provided a convenient opportunity
to act while authorities were preoccupied with events in the metropole, but

---

[41] Michel, *L'Appel*, 44–54.
[42] Lunn, *Memoirs*, 40.
[43] Lunn, *Memoirs*, 40–1.
[44] Allen Douglas, *War, Memory, and the Politics of Humor: The* Canard Enchaîné *and World War I* (Berkeley: University of California Press, 2002), 169–70.
[45] Favre-Le Van Ho, "Un milieu porteur de modernisation," 1: 241–51.
[46] Favre-Le Van Ho, "Un milieu porteur de modernisation," 1: 232; Hill, "Westward Journey," 33–4.
[47] Gontard, *Madagascar*, 66–8; Valensky, *Le soldat occulté*, 299.

the French brutally and decisively suppressed both movements. Resistance to specifically wartime demands did occur, though, and intensive recruitment of both soldiers and workers exacerbated tensions that sometimes came out into the open. In the federation of Indochina, popular discontent and lack of cooperation significantly reduced the contributions of both Cambodia and Cochinchina. The Minister of War was not surprised, since Cambodians were, he argued, "absolutely devoid of the sentiments and mentality necessary for a patriotic *élan*."[48] Some Madagascans also refused to cooperate, and one group of men from the Comoros islands declared: "If the whites need us as *tirailleurs*, they will have to take us by force."[49] In West Africa, some men also demonstrated the reverse of the hoped-for patriotism, resisting recruitment via methods ranging from the intentional presentation of candidates unfit for service, to flight into the bush or neighboring areas not controlled by the French, to desertion, and even to outright armed revolt. Serious violence was infrequent, and usually had roots in longer-standing and broader resentment of French colonial policies, but intensified recruitment could raise levels of discontent from simmering to boiling.[50] Resistance to recruitment itself is not surprising, given that many Africans considered enlistment in the French army to entail "the certain death of their sons."[51] Or husbands—one widow regretted her husband's cooperation with the recruiters: he "died because he didn't want to run away."[52]

In Algeria, long-standing discontent with colonial rule also mixed with immediate concerns over recruitment. Conscription in 1914 led to a few "surprises," as French military euphemism characterized them.[53] In October in the commune of Mascara in Oran, a crowd violently attacked officials attempting to register Algerians for the draft, capturing, killing, and mutilating two indigenous Algerian soldiers serving the French.[54] This and other incidents did not prevent officials from maintaining order overall and obtaining recruits through both conscription and voluntary enlistments, but they did indicate the strains that wartime demands for the bodies, and perhaps lives, of the colonized placed on both the French and their colonial subjects, and the relationships between them. And French authorities were well aware that favoritism and injustice in the administration of the draft at the local level added to overall resentment of the demands.[55] An expanded and early draft in 1916, not coincidentally the crisis year of the Battle of Verdun, and more aggressive recruiting of volunteers in the colony created an "explosive

[48] Quoted in Favre-Le Van Ho, "Un milieu porteur de modernisation," 1: 208.
[49] Gontard, *Madagascar*, 89.
[50] Michel, *L'Appel*, 50–7, 85–8; Lunn, *Memoirs*, 44, 51 n. 15. On the more serious revolts, see Michel, *L'Appel*, 100–16; Conklin, *Mission*, 148–9; Luc Garcia, "Les Mouvements de résistance au Dahomey, 1914–1917," *Cahiers d'études africaines*, 10/1 (1971), 144–78; Hélène d'Almeida-Topor, "Les Populations dahoméens et le recrutement militaire pendant la première guerre mondiale," *Revue française d'histoire d'outre-mer*, 60/2 (1973), 196–241.
[51] Michel, *L'Appel*, 49.
[52] Lunn, *Memoirs*, 43.
[53] SHAT 7N2081: SA, "Bulletin Politique, mois d'octobre 1914."
[54] SHAT 7N443: Lutaud to PC, MG, and MI, telegrams of 5, 6, and 9 octobre 1914.
[55] SHAT 7N2081: SA, "Bulletin Politique, mois d'octobre 1914."

situation" among the Algerian population.[56] Revolts in the *département* of Constantine in the autumn were clearly the result of recruitment pressures.[57] Algerian soldiers and workers already in France took note, as postal censorship revealed.[58] Lamenting the forced recruitment of his three brothers, one Algerian placed his own family's troubles in a larger context, one that indicted French rule in Algeria generally: "Our entire country is in great misfortune because of conscription. May God change this unfortunate situation for Muslims into a better situation: Amen!"[59]

It is clear that recruitment caused some problems across the French Empire, and these incidents and broader discontents introduced at least some instability into colonial rule and relations between metropole and colony, colonizer and colonized. But this did not prevent France from recruiting hundreds of thousands of *troupes indigènes*, nor did it prevent these men from being very popular among many in France as symbols of the nation's success both in carrying out its civilizing mission and in waging total war to save the *patrie*. This popularity did not mean, however, that France's embrace of its colonial subjects was unambiguous. The army relegated many colonial subjects to labor rather than combat duty, since many officers doubted their martial value in a modern war against a European enemy. And military officials often viewed those *troupes indigènes* who did fight through a haze of stereotypes. West Africans, the conventional wisdom held, were fierce warriors because of their savage, primitive natures, and firm command by white officers was essential to channel this savagery productively. If some indigenous soldiers could in fact become officers, given France's commitment to at least some egalitarianism and meritocracy in the army (a commitment that stood out in contrast to British and American attitudes about race in the ranks), non-white colonial subjects could rise only to the lower levels of the hierarchy, and then only with great difficulty. The Muslim faith of North African soldiers caused many to doubt that these men could be reliable in a struggle against an alliance that included the Ottoman Empire. And Islam, particularly in the case of Algerians, turned out to pose an insuperable barrier to offering liberally the reward of citizenship to the men who fought to defend a *patrie* that would, evidently, never truly be theirs. Race and culture were sufficient barriers to prevent the naturalization of soldiers from other colonies as well.

That these were not barriers to many French women who became intimate with colonial workers or soldiers, some even marrying and starting families during and after the war, demonstrated that not everyone in France sought to exclude colonial subjects from the nation they were serving in its time of need. As one Indochinese sergeant wrote in a letter: "On Sundays, we go strolling with [French] women, as

[56] Meynier, *L'Algérie révélée*, 399.

[57] SHAT 7N2081: SA, "Bulletin de Renseignements sur les Questions Musulmanes," 12 novembre 1916; 7N2081 and 17N491: "Bulletins de Renseignements sur les Questions Musulmanes," novembre 1916–février 1917; Meynier, *L'Algérie révélée*, 591–8.

[58] SHAT 7N1001: Rapport sur les opérations de la commission militaire de contrôle postal de Tunis, pendant le mois de décembre 1916.

[59] SHAT 7N2107: Commission Militaire de Contrôle Postal, Tunis, Rapport sur les opérations de la commission pendant le mois de mars 1917.

we would do in Indochina, with our own women at home."[60] A Madagascan soldier was even more (love)struck: "What to tell you of white women? Down there
[in Madagascar], we fear them. Here they come to us and solicit us by the attraction of their charm....What delights in their smooches...I am forgetting about
Madagascar because of them."[61] Yet these liaisons caused a great deal of anxiety
among some officials and even soldiers at the front.[62] One unit of the French army
that mutinied in 1917 included in its list of demands: "We don't want the blacks
in Paris and in other regions mistreating our wives."[63]

This ambiguity in France's wartime embrace of its empire's inhabitants extended
to another issue of great importance to *troupes indigènes* and those who commanded them, and one of great importance in French culture generally: language.
The famous advertisement for Banania featuring the smiling *tirailleur sénégalais*, a
cultural artifact that stands as one of the most lasting and famous testaments to the
popularity of these soldiers, also exemplifies perfectly the ambiguity characterizing
attitudes about language and race. For it was not merely the image of the *tirailleur*
that carried a racist message. The slogan "Y'a bon!" that accompanied the ad campaign, and that became intimately bound to Banania even after the image of the
tirailleur disappeared in the late twentieth century, was inspired by the distinctive
pidgin French spoken by the West African troops.[64] French military officials did
nothing to discourage this and other ungrammatical expressions, and in fact they
encouraged their use by institutionalizing pidgin French as the preferred language
of training and command in West African units. This stemmed not only from expediency—the need to train quickly soldiers who spoke little or no French—but
also from the idea that learning proper French was too taxing for the simplistic
mentality of the *tirailleurs*.[65] One *tirailleur* condemned this impoverished language as "words found by the Europeans to make asses of the Senegalese."[66] This
poor French did indeed reinforce the view many in France held of black Africans
as primitive and unintelligent, and the Banania slogan gave the image wide cur-
rency in French society.

The characterization of West Africans as primitive savages produced a dual
vision of the *tirailleurs sénégalais*. On the one hand, their limited intelligence, combined with a childlike simplicity and innocence, bred in them a fierce loyalty to

---

[60] SHAT 7N995: Commission de Contrôle Postal de Marseille, "Annamites en France," 2 janvier
1917.
[61] SHAT 7N997: Contrôle Postal Malgache, Rapport du mois de Septembre 1917.
[62] Fogarty, *Race and War in France*, addresses all of these issues in detail. See also Tyler Stovall,
"Love, Labor, and Race: Colonial Men and White Women in France during the Great War," in Tyler
Stovall and Georges Van den Abeele (eds), *French Civilization and its Discontents: Nationalism, Colonialism, Race* (Lanham, MD: Lexington Books, 2003), 297–321.
[63] Smith, Audoin-Rouzeau, and Becker, *France and the Great War*, 124.
[64] Difficult to translate into English, "Y'a bon!" could be rendered literally as, "There's good!" Perhaps a more accurate way to think of the phrase in English is to imagine someone saying, "Is good!"
with a heavy foreign accent.
[65] See, e.g., *Le Français tel que le parlent nos tirailleurs sénégalais* (Paris: L. Fournier, 1916), a manual
for training French officers to use this pidgin French with West Africans under their command. See
also Gabriel Manessy, *Le Français en Afrique noire: Mythe, stratégie, pratiques* (Paris: L'Harmattan,
1994), and Fogarty, *Race and War in France*.
[66] Lucie Cousturier, *Des inconnus chez moi* (Paris: Editions de la Sirène, 1920), 105.

their French protectors. On the other hand, West Africans were ferocious warriors, even if ill-suited to some aspects of modern combat. *Tirailleurs sénégalais* found that French people they encountered often treated them like small children, while at the same time expecting them to wield the savagery inherent in their race on behalf of France at the front. Upon the arrival of his unit in France, one West African soldier heard people in the crowds lining the streets shouting: "Cut off the Germans' heads!"[67]

As with the economic role of empire, one can see in propaganda posters the place of *troupes indigènes* in the French wartime imagination and the nation's cultural mobilization. West Africans were the most well-known and popular troops among all of those who came from the empire to fight in France, in large part because of their reputation for primitive ferocity. But, although many images celebrated their courage, "they charge 'with fury' or demonstrate an 'infernal fierceness,' in a way that betrays their fearsome savagery."[68] And the same is true of depictions of troops from other areas of the empire, such as North Africa. In other words, these images made clear the distance that separated the intended viewer from the image, the native white French person from the exotic, savage, colonial other fighting on behalf of France.

Georges Clairin's 1918 poster advertising a war loan for the Crédit Foncier d'Algérie et de Tunisie is a good example of this exoticizing gaze (see Fig. 12).[69] The scene features North African soldiers, almost certainly Algerians, although they are not specifically named. These were the most numerous of any of the contingents from the colonies, and, as was the case with West African soldiers, many regarded them as fierce and primitive warriors best used as "shock troops." This attitude pre-dated the war, and stemmed in large part from visions of warfare France had encountered, and waged, in the period of colonial conquest in Algeria.[70] In this image, the horrors of the Western Front are completely sublimated in favor of a romantic, exotic vision of war waged on the open *bled* of North Africa. Algerians charge on horseback, a style of war thoroughly destroyed in reality on the Western Front by 1918, led by a dramatic figure on a magnificent, ornately caparisoned mount. The French tricolor flag waves in the background, reassuring viewers that all of this aggression is directed at a common enemy outside the frame of the picture, even though the central figure rides into battle under the green

[67] Bakary Diallo, *Force-Bonté* (Paris: F. Reider, 1926), 113.

[68] Laurent Gervereau, "La Propagande par l'image en France, 1914–1918: Thèmes et modes de représentation," in Laurent Gervereau and Christophe Prochasson (eds), *Images de 1917* (Paris: BDIC, 1987), 124.

[69] Library of Congress, POS-Fr. C53, no.2: Georges Clairin, "Pour la patrie: Souscrivez á l'Emprunt: Crédit Foncier d'Algérie et de Tunisie" (Paris: Devambez, 1918).

[70] On French views of Algerians, see Patricia Lorcin, *Imperial Identities: Stereotyping, Prejudice and Race in Colonial Algeria* (London: I. B. Taurus, 1995), 17–34. On the violence of conquest and rule in the colony, see Benjamin Claude Brower, *A Desert Named Peace: The Violence of France's Empire in the Algerian Sahara, 1844–1902* (New York: Columbia University Press, 2009), Jennifer E. Sessions, *By Sword and Plow: France and the Conquest of Algeria* (Ithaca, NY: Cornell University Press, 2011), and William Gallois, "Dahra and the History of Colonial Violence in Algeria," in Martin Thomas (ed.), *The French Colonial Mind*, ii. *Violence, Military Encounters, and Colonialism* (Lincoln, NE: University of Nebraska Press, 2011).

Fig. 12. A 1918 poster advertising a war loan. The martial ardor depicted celebrates the contribution of North African soldiers to the war effort, while the evident exoticism of the imagery suggests that such soldiers remain outside the imagined community of European France.

standard of the Prophet. The dangers of Islam have been tamed here, brought into the service of France. The exoticism is essentially otherworldly, as the host of Arab warriors in flowing white robes seems to rise ghostlike from under the ground. As usual, the message is dual. Such martial ardor will bring victory to a France bolstered by the manpower resources of its empire, but these men remain different, culturally and essentially outside the nation.

APOTHEOSIS OR TWILIGHT OF EMPIRE?

The French Empire played an important role in France's war effort between 1914 and 1918. If the contribution in men and materiel was relatively small in the context of the huge effort by one of the major combatants to wage the world's first industrialized war, the colonies still loomed large in certain respects in France's cultural mobilization and in the post-war vision of what the empire meant in national defense and national life. Formal demobilization was relatively simple and rapid from the French point of view, as colonial economies were reoriented toward normal activity and the French army shipped *troupes indigènes* home as quickly as possible. From colonial subjects' point of view, economic dislocation and the disruptions of recruitment were not so easy to forget or overcome. And cultural demobilization, in the metropole and in the colonies, was not so simple either.[71] As we have seen, the effects upon many French people were to enhance an awareness of the value of the empire, and to revivify efforts to make empire "pay," but a greater awareness of a different sort was also dawning in the empire and among its peoples. The real effects on post-war colonial stability were located in the realms of politics, culture, and memory, in the ways both native French people and *indigènes* of the colonies became more conscious than ever of the exploitative relationships and racism at the heart of empire and the gulf that separated colonizers and colonized.

Despite being welcomed as defenders of the nation in a time of great peril, colonial subjects did not gain appreciable relief from the racist, hierarchical social order that regulated their lives in the colonies and shaped visions of their activities in France. They certainly did not receive a warm welcome as equals into the national community. In that sense, the war merely reinforced French imperial control and the ideas and relationships that constituted it. To some, like Albert Sarraut, this validated the utility and proved the solidity of empire, and confirmed the genius of French colonialism and its civilizing mission. Viewed from other angles, though, the situation was less clear. Even a dramatic expansion of the empire at the end of the war, certainly the apogee of the empire's territorial extent, betrayed crucial weaknesses and insecurities at the heart of the French colonial enterprise.

At the 1920 San Remo conference, France and Great Britain settled their long simmering differences over colonial designs in former Ottoman territories of the Middle East, with France taking control over League of Nations mandates in Syria and Lebanon. Absorbing these, along with former German territories in Africa, added a great deal of territory and population to France's already extensive empire. The war, it seemed, had only expanded empire, strengthening French imperialism and colonial control. Yet, upon closer inspection, all was not for the best. Some French leaders desired and even expected a peaceful transition to French control in Syria, and the French boosters of empire known as the Syrian party argued that French influence in the region was already so strong and of such long standing that the population would easily accept French mandatory rule. But King Faisal, who set up Hashemite rule of the region in Damascus in 1918, was determined to maintain local control and opposed French moves to take over. It turned out that France had to fight for Syria, and, though it won the military conflict decisively at the July 1920 Battle of Maysalun, continued resistance demonstrated that many in Syria were not happy to be ruled by the French. The only way to retain effective control was to divide the territory into several small states, giving up on the

[71] On the concept of "cultural demobilization," see John Horne (ed.), "Démobilisations culturelles après la Grande Guerre," special issue of *14–18 Aujourd'hui-Heute-Today*, 5 (2002); and his "Kulturelle Demobilmachung 1919–1939: Ein sinnvoller historischer Begriff?," in Wolfgang Hardtwig (ed.), *Politische Kulturgeschichte der Zwischenkriegszeit 1919–1939* (Göttingen: Vandenhoeck & Ruprecht, 2005), 129–50; and "Demobilizing the Mind: France and the Legacy of the Great War, 1919–1939," *French History and Civilization: Papers from the George Rudé Seminar*, 2 (2009), 101–19 http://www.h-france.net/rude/rudeTOC2009.html (accessed 7 June 2013).

long-held French dream of "la Syrié intégrale."[72] During the entire mandate period, until 1946, France could maintain control over the restive population only by constant resort to violence, both overtly via military and police action on the ground and from the air, and more subtly, through urban planning and political initiatives aimed at undermining resistance.[73] Even ambitious attempts to deploy cultural enterprises—education, language, art, propaganda, youth movements, and more—to strengthen ties to France and buttress French influence and political control failed to do so, before the French bombing of Damascus in 1945 showed once and for all how a weak colonial regime had only violence at its disposal.[74] And even that could not prevent Syria from exiting the French Empire the following year.

The Middle East was not the only area where the effects and lessons of the Great War were not quite what French imperialists had hoped. In the realms of politics and culture, the hypocrisy of the French civilizing mission, the naked violence, injustice, and discrimination of colonialism, were what stood out most from the war and its aftermath. For many colonial subjects, the events of the war years became vivid, shorthand references for the larger injustices of French colonialism. For instance, on 1 August 1922, Nguyen Ai Quoc, later known as Ho Chi Minh, published an open letter in *La Paria*, a Parisian anti-colonial newspaper. Addressed to Minister of the Colonies Albert Sarraut, who would just the next year hold up the war experience as proof that the French empire "paid," Quoc's letter dripped with irony:

> Under your proconsulate the Annamese people have known true prosperity and real happiness, the happiness of seeing their country dotted all over with an increasing number of spirit and opium shops which, together with firing squads, prisons, "democracy" and all the improved apparatus of modern civilization, are combining to make the Annamese the most advanced of the Asians and the happiest of mortals.

Among other aspects of France's so-called civilizing mission, Quoc pointed specifically to events associated with the war, during part of which Sarraut had been governor general in Indochina (1917–19): "acts of benevolence [...] such as enforced recruitment and loans, bloody repressions, the dethronement and exile of kings, profanation of sacred places, etc.," and the close surveillance under which the French state had put politically active Indochinese living in France, such as Quoc, after the war.[75] In fact, the war provided the essential context for Quoc's letter, as it would for the political formation of Ho Chi Minh. And, although

---

[72] See Christopher M. Andrew and A. S. Kanya Forstner, *France Overseas: The Great War and the Climax of French Imperial Expansion* (London: Thames and Hudson, 1981).

[73] Daniel Neep, *Occupying Syria under the French Mandate: Insurgency, Space and State Formation* (Cambridge: Cambridge University Press, 2012).

[74] Jennifer M. Dueck, *The Claims of Culture at Empire's End: Syria and Lebanon under French Rule* (Oxford: Oxford University Press, 2010).

[75] Ho Chi Minh, "An Open Letter to M. Albert Sarraut, Minister of Colonies," in *Selected Works of Ho Chi Minh*, i (Hanoi: Foreign Languages Publishing House, 1960). Sarraut and Quoc would actually meet several times to discuss their differences. See William J. Duiker, *Ho Chi Minh: A Life* (New York: Hyperion, 2000), and Sophie Quinn-Judge, *Ho Chi Minh: The Missing Years, 1919–1941* (Berkeley and Los Angeles: University of California Press, 2002).

anti-colonialism in Indochina and Vietnamese nationalism had deeper and other roots than those that developed during and as a cause of the Great War, the experience of the region between 1914 and 1918 added crucial fuel to Quoc's critique and Ho's later independence movement.

Beyond grievances provoked by specific French actions during the war, the war may have contributed to a growing awareness of the immutability of a colonial order undergirded by racism, though this is difficult and perhaps impossible to quantify precisely. Another leader in the struggle against French colonialism, this time in Africa, Léopold Sédar Senghor, later evoked this aspect of the colonial war experience. The Banania posters featuring the smiling *tirailleur sénégalais* that he saw in Paris during the interwar period incensed him, and of course the connection of this image with the war was inescapable. He would later describe the intellectual and spiritual journey toward independence he and others made, noting that eventually the realization dawned: "Assimilation was a failure; we could assimilate mathematics or the French language, but we could never strip off our black skins or root out black souls. And so we set out on a fervent quest for the 'holy grail': our collective soul. And we came upon it."[76] That quest may well have begun before 1914, and it was not complete until after 1945, but the Great War's reverberations in the colonies and in colonial relationships certainly helped accelerate the journey.

---

[76] Léopold Sédar Senghor, "What is Negritude?" a speech delivered at Oxford University, October 1961, in Paul E. Sigmund (ed.), *The Ideologies of the Developing Nations*, rev. edn (New York: Praeger, 1967), 248.

7

British Imperial Africa

Bill Nasson

INTRODUCTION: SELF-DELUSIONS OF LOCAL NEUTRALITY

Reflecting in March 2013 on the tenth anniversary of British involvement in the controversial war in Iraq, the London daily the *Independent* concluded of that troubled invasion and the accompanying quagmire in Afghanistan that they had decisively 'ended the notion that Britain can conduct wars simultaneously on two fronts'.[1] Just over a century earlier, the reach of its imperial power had enabled it to do not only that, but more besides. However improvised, messy, and leaky the British Empire—or 'the British world-system'[2]—may have come to be seen by influential historians today, between 1914 and 1918 the British were able not only to sustain war 'on three fronts—in Europe, at sea and in the Middle East—to defend their empire'.[3] In addition, London's declaration of war against Berlin was open season for several lesser, essentially colonial campaigns, to capture scattered German territories in the Pacific and, the subject of this chapter, in Africa. The continent provides as striking an illustration as any that, for Britain, this conflict was to be a war with a long imperial reach, in which colonial British territories containing colonial British subjects of varied ethnic origins and political status would be activated to defend metropolitan interests. The responses, roles, and experiences of the imperial subjects enlisted to defend the needs of that European core would be highly differentiated, too. Thrust into a Herculean contest between global empires, the populations of British Africa would be enlisted not in a national war of defence, but in a multinational war of imperial expansion. For inhabitants of the vulnerable enemy imperial territories in its path, the First World War would mean enlistment in a war of imperial survival.

[1] *Independent*, 19 March 2013.
[2] In John Darwin's phrase: see his *The Empire Project: The Rise and Fall of the British World-System, 1830–1970* (Cambridge: Cambridge University Press, 2009).
[3] John Darwin, *Unfinished Empire: The Global Expansion of Britain* (London: Allen Lane, 2012), 330.

Initially, though, that course of events did not necessarily appear to be inevitable and clear-cut. Here, as in the Pacific case of German New Guinea and German Samoa, it is easy to follow the obvious argument that Britain did not go to war with Germany 'to get more colonies'.[4] On the other hand, its settled African colonial empire may have provided much for *Germany* to savour, a straining European state disgruntled by its imperial deficit. Equally, in 1914 African territorial gains were beyond its grasp, for Germany's local power had no hope of matching those of Britain or, for that matter, France. As for Britain, its war to preserve the global status quo against a German challenge did not necessarily entail any pressing need to add more colonial territory and subjects to its already populous African empire of over thirty-five million inhabitants. In any event, beyond some strategic considerations, there was, after all, 'little to tempt her' in Germany's West African colonies of Kamerun and Togo, in South West Africa and in East Africa, although this last possession was potentially agriculturally productive.

Overall, these four territories 'had not made money since they became German colonies, and did not look like doing so'. Nonetheless, 'the occasion of the war'[5] presented an irresistible opportunity for the British to get their hands on more of Africa, rather than just to mark garrison time there while the survival and future of their enormous colonial empire was resolved in France.

On that score, preserving the security of Britain's African soil would certainly come to weigh more heavily on the scales, but not until very late into the European theatre of the conflict. At that final stage, it is worth noting the impact on imperial nerves of the massive last-gasp German offensive in 1918, which knocked both the French and the British back on their heels. Facing the dismaying prospect of France and also Italy possibly abandoning the war, in June of that year Lloyd George's War Cabinet peered into an imperial abyss. With the French and the Italians disposed of, the rejuvenated Germans might toughen ties with the Ottomans, resulting in the entire Middle East falling into their lap. For an apprehensive Lord Milner, Lloyd George's Cabinet director of strategy, 'the whole world' of 'these islands' might then find itself imperilled. The remaining fight would then have to be 'above all, for Africa', into which 'the bridgehead of Palestine'[6] could well furnish an open door for the enemy. It was, though, but a fleeting nightmare.

Initially, being so far from the centre or the forcing house of 1914 hostilities, Britain's African colonial position seemed to suggest more inertia than any climactic confrontation with an imperial adversary. Certainly, in their own right, Africa's colonial territorial issues had not looked even remotely likely to prompt any Anglo-German showdown. We should not forget the opinion of Britain's Foreign Secretary, Sir Edward Grey, aired as recently as 1911, that it mattered little to the British whether their colonial neighbour was France or Germany. Indeed, if it came to that, Grey was even open to some agreeable arrangement whereby

[4] Bernard Porter, *The Lion's Share: A Short History of British Imperialism, 1850–2004* (Harlow: Pearson Longman, 2004), 228.

[5] Porter, *Lion's Share*, 228.

[6] Bodleian Library, Oxford, Milner MSS (Add.) c696: Milner to Lloyd George, 9 June 1918.

Portuguese African colonies, dismissed as 'derelict', could be divided up between a mutually consenting London and Berlin, and parcelled out 'in a pro-German spirit'.[7] However durable the long-established Anglo-Portuguese alliance, Lisbon's rickety African empire was regarded as small fry by the contemptuous London mandarins of the Colonial Office. Belgium was viewed with similar derision. In their African colonial governance they were bracketed together as not only the most inept, but also as 'the most cruel and inhumane of the colonial powers'.[8]

Equally, from a wider colonial vantage point, subterranean continental rivalries did not mean that there was much by way of local difficulty, in the sense that pre-war conditions in one colony were a serious nuisance to another. Where peasant or urban labour restiveness continued to throb through 1912 and 1913 in the aftermath of the recent Scramble for Africa and its wholesale partition by jockeying European powers, confrontations between disaffected subjects and colonial authorities were territorially bounded. Highly localized pockets and often virtually subterranean, they did not lap over the external frontiers of European colonies. Thus, British East Africa (Kenya) was not infected by the anti-colonial Maji-Maji rising of 1905–7 in German East Africa (Tanganyika). Similarly, the genocidal German–Herero war of 1904–7 in German South West Africa was a punitive German affair. Across the colonial border, the British dominion of South Africa slumbered on, barring some disquiet in more liberal English newspapers like the *Cape Argus* that Herero and Nama prisoners were being maltreated in German concentration camps 'just across its border'.[9]

Having been incapable of hammering together a serious territorial presence, Germany remained very thin on the ground. For Britain it was, of course, France and its more intermingled welter of north, central, and west African colonies that constituted the only other major imperial power. Although the surface area of the British colonial empire was smaller and less amalgamated, its more widely spread holdings in the south and south-central regions, in the east and west, and in the north, including a tongue of coastal territory on the Horn of Africa, made up the real continental core of European imperialism. Nor was it all show. Britain's empire held a far larger number of African subjects, a far more populous white settler minority, and much deeper pockets of mining, other industrial, and commercial agricultural production.

All the same, before the war Britain's military imprint was merely that of a shallow routine colonial commitment. Where it had established African colonial armies under a light peppering of white officers, these were tiny. For instance, Britain's central African territory of Nyasaland was held by no more than 100 Indian troops and a couple of white officers.[10] While such colonial forces were kept busy maintaining internal order and enforcing the new tribute demands of

---

[7] Quoted in Niall Ferguson, *The Pity of War, 1914–1918* (London: Penguin, 1999), 68.

[8] David Olusoga and Casper W. Erichsen, *The Kaiser's Holocaust: Germany's Forgotten Genocide and the Colonial Roots of Nazism* (London: Faber and Faber, 2010), 261.

[9] Olusoga and Erichsen, *Kaiser's Holocaust*, 262.

[10] Richard J. Reid, *A History of Modern Africa: 1800 to the Present* (Oxford: Blackwell, 2009), 187.

colonial civil administration, such as tax collection, they scarcely amounted to a serious concentration of military power. In particular, with no envisaged role in external offensives or in frontier defence, they were anything but a springboard for launching war operations. Indeed, the odds on Africa being able to escape being dragged into a global conflagration may at first have looked at least even.

In fact, the basic urge to sit out the war was visible at many levels. In West Africa, the governor of the British Gold Coast (Ghana), Sir Hugh Clifford, was implored by Major Kurt von Doering, the acting governor of the adjacent tiny German colony of Togo, to agree to a regional armistice that would preserve the territory's neutrality. A shared view was that the alternative of battle would expose African colonial subjects to the troubling spectacle of European men fighting each other. Who knew how calamitous the consequences for white prestige and authority might be? On the opposite coast, Sir Henry Conway Belfield, the governor of Britain's East African Protectorate (Kenya), had little stomach for hostilities and announced that 'the present war was of no interest to British East Africa'.[11] His neighbouring German counterpart, Dr Heinrich Schnee, was of like mind, all for regional neutrality and waving an olive branch with an attempt to have the capital of Dar es Salaam and the port of Tanga declared open free towns.

Immediately north-west of Britain's newest self-governing white settler state, the Union of South Africa, founded in 1910, lay German South West Africa. Criss-crossed by trade, kinship, and other fraternal ties between anti-British northern Cape Afrikaners and nearby German colonists, the border zone was highly porous. There, the governor, Theodor Seitz, and his senior officials stood on watch, but rattled no sabres, so as not to provoke South Africa. The colony would be defended against any enemy aggression, but the preferred duty would be to mark time until Berlin was able to secure its place in the sun through 'victory in Europe'.[12]

This studied early distancing from hostilities was voiced in other British imperial quarters. In industrializing South Africa, fringe bodies of the radical white working class, such as the Social Democratic Federation and the South African Industrial Federation, fluttered their anti-war manifestos ahead of Britain's war declaration. For left-wing militants disheartened by the sight of a British labour movement falling in behind an imperialist war effort, at least 'the war seemed to open up new opportunities in South Africa'.[13] If British workers at home were deaf, in more fluid colonial circumstances they might yet prick up their ears. So, carrying the European contraband of anti-imperialist war convictions, visiting labour militants or dissident British migrants egged on resistance to war.

It was not only the skinny white left in Africa in 1914 that feared what a wholesale war would bring. For commercial settler agriculture and merchant interests, it

[11] Bill Nasson, *Springboks on the Somme: South Africa in the Great War, 1914–1918* (Johannesburg: Penguin, 2007), 90.
[12] David Killingray, 'The War in Africa', in John Horne (ed.), *A Companion to World War 1* (London: Blackwell, 2012), 118.
[13] Jonathan Hyslop, *The Notorious Syndicalist: J. T. Bain: A Scottish Rebel in Colonial South Africa* (Johannesburg: Jacana, 2004), 264.

looked self-evident that hostilities would be bad for business. East African sisal planters, South African ostrich farmers, and Southern Rhodesian beef producers lost no time in voicing their worries. Major war would pose a risk to rural prosperity, as domestic markets as well as empire and wider world trade channels were likely to be endangered. No less daunting was the prospect of severe shortages if vital shipping routes from Britain became undermined. These concerns were over the flow not merely of industrial equipment and manufactures such as bicycles, blankets, and biscuits, but also, as an agitated white reader of Rhodesia's *Bulawayo Chronicle* pointed out early in July 1914, of the 'basic necessaries' of Pringle knitwear and Jaeger coats.[14]

CRUCIAL ASSETS AND SOME MIXED EXPERIENCES

Given the anticipated hazards of wartime shipping, there was a heavy focus on subtropical Africa's most valuable and most indispensable commodity, gold bullion. Strategically vital for the British, gold was the glistening lynchpin of the entire imperial coupling between South Africa, the world's leading gold producer, and London, with the Witwatersrand mines stocking the Bank of England with over two-thirds of its precious metal reserves in 1914. The outbreak of war would turn the security of gold supplies, the financial bedrock of Britain's global sterling system, into what the Johannesburg Chamber of Mines called 'a very complex question'.[15] It was certainly not one that could be left hanging. Although the costs of resolving it would later become a thorny issue between the Bank of England and Johannesburg's mining capitalists, London sealed an agreement whereby bullion would be protected from the hazards of German sea raiders through storage in an impregnable South Africa, while the City of London would provide credit cover for its purchase price until it was safe to resume shipments. Wartime troubles or not, the possession of Dominion gold from Africa remained the yardstick by which the financial power of The City would continue to be judged.

At the same time, the wartime shortages, which came with the contraction of overseas trade, were not quite the disaster that more gloomy observers had imagined. For southern Africa, with its over one million white settlers and ample economic assets, fledgling and still sluggish pre-war industrial development was boosted dramatically by the need for import substitution. By 1915, Union consumers short of textiles from Manchester and footwear from Northampton could get garments from local Cape Town factories and boots and shoes from workshops in Port Elizabeth. In a self-consciously national celebration of such productive independence, at the end of hostilities the *Agricultural Journal of South Africa* thanked a war boom for having enabled domestic commercial farmers to feed Britain's 'vast armies in the field', not only in the north of the continent and in the Middle East,

---

[14] *Bulawayo Chronicle*, 29 June 1914.
[15] Duncan Innes, *Anglo-American and the Rise of Modern South Africa* (Johannesburg: Ravan, 1984), 78.

but in France too, creating rosy conditions in which 'we in South Africa have a glorious opportunity of producing more'.[16]

The war that Britain got underway in its parts of Africa was, clearly, a chapter in the story of its 'utilizing the resources of its empire to allow it to act as a major power in a way unprecedented in its history'.[17] Here it was a war of parts, wrapped up swiftly along the continent's left flank, and shuddering on for the entire length of the world conflict in the eastern portion of the continent. And it was also an inglorious war. Low on morale-boosting triumphs on the battlefield, it left its pro-empire white volunteers to shed their blood in Europe to fertilize legends of heroism and sacrifice, as in the case of the South African Overseas Expeditionary Force, which, once nearly decimated on the Somme in 1916, became a symbol of Anglo-Afrikaner nationhood, 'hands joined for the British Commonwealth against a common foe'.[18]

No less significant to any understanding of the place of the war in the life of the most deeply remote and unconnected rural communities of, say, the heartlands of Nigeria or the far south of Southern Rhodesia was that it simply passed over the heads of inhabitants, its existence barely felt. Shortages and higher prices were the customary perennial burdens, given the instabilities of local ecological and pro-ductive systems. For that matter, too, the nature of Britain's colonial presence and control there by 1918 was more or less unchanged from what it had been in 1913. Indeed, for those unaffected Africans who had little idea that they were living under the British Crown, or that they belonged to a British South Africa Company charter colony, the war was, perhaps, no more than a time of listless loitering.

Where the inhabitants of British Africa were unable to turn the other cheek was where its maritime lifelines pressed. Although sea power undoubtedly played 'a relatively limited role in the Great War', compared to its major importance in both the French Revolutionary wars and the Second World War,[19] Africa was a strategic terminus for Britain's strategic global waterways. Its Atlantic and Indian Ocean waters were, in their way, the outer reaches of the English Channel, set to remain under the patrolling dominance of the Royal Navy from its harbours at Simons-town in the Cape and its West Africa Squadron base of Freetown. However limited the actual threat of local German commerce raiding to the sea lanes of the southern, western, and eastern reaches of Africa, it was still a menace to 'the links that would enable Britain to tap the resources of both its empire and its neutral trading part-ners'.[20] In that sense, although Britain's African conflict was over colonies, it was less a war about the land and far more a war about the sea.

---

[16] *The Agricultural Journal of South Africa* (February 1919), 6.

[17] Philip Murphy, 'Britain as a Global Power in the Twentieth Century', in Andrew Thompson (ed.), *Britain's Experience of Empire in the Twentieth Century* (Oxford: Oxford University Press, 2012), 40.

[18] Sir Herbert Baker, *Architecture and Personalities* (London: Hodder & Stoughton, 1946), 90.

[19] Paul Kennedy, 'The War at Sea', in Jay Winter (ed.), *The Cambridge History of the First World War*, i (New York: Cambridge University Press, 2014).

[20] Hew Strachan, *The First World War* (London: Simon & Schuster, 2006), 71.

RESTIVENESS BENEATH WARTIME BURDENS

For some of those on the land who were caught up by it, the war was associated—
to one or other level of intensity—with a minor string of lightning-flash risings
and rebellions against its most harsh impositions—notably mass labour conscription for the protracted campaign in East Africa. At the same time, the conflict that
erupted was also in one sense the architect of a general intensification of established grievances over colonial exactions, involving such things as enforced tax
tribute, requisitioning, and the impressment of labour levies. Thus, pre-war prick-
liness over the heavier hand of colonial pacification was aggravated by the war,
tipping groups in places like British Nyasaland into what amounted to a claustro-
phobic 'crisis'.[21] There, where wholesale conscription had arrived early and where
losses of labouring auxiliaries in early campaigning against German forces had
been high, resentments soon boiled over. They threw up the distinctively dignified
figure of John Chilembwe, a towering evangelical Baptist preacher who flitted
about denouncing the war and, during 1915, whipping up a fleeting utopian rising
to 'strike a blow and die'.[22]

Along the south-eastern coast, meanwhile, the more excitable among dispossessed Zulu communities hankered after a British defeat and accorded Germany
special status: even beer awaited the arrival of its High Seas fleet at the Natal coast.
For they assumed that, once Natal had been taken, their 'land shortage' might be
remedied by a more charitable European power.[23] At the same time, the withdrawal of garrisons from Transkeian districts for offensive service elsewhere also
encouraged such daydreaming among disaffected peasant inhabitants. Being tuned
psychologically to the existence of Germans and of Germany's distant doings and
advances against 'the English' and 'the King' became 'a kind of metaphor of
resistance'.[24]

Coursing alongside such partial exhibitionism were other, more general repudi-
ations of an unwelcome European war. Thus, both the Gold Coast and Nigeria
witnessed the sprouting of independent African Christian movements that brought
out their fed-up followings in witness against the claims of an incomprehensible
war that ought to have remained a business between Europeans overseas. Moving
towards defensive withdrawal, a form of spiritually psychic secession from a de-
tested wartime world, these marginal religious formations could also take on a
millenarian hue, invoking a coming apocalyptic moment. For a crop of local religious leaders from Northern Rhodesia across and up to the Gold Coast, it remained

---

[21] Timothy Stapleton, 'The Impact of the First World War on African People', in John Laband
(ed.), *Daily Lives of Civilians in Wartime Africa: From Slavery Days to Rwandan Genocide* (Pietermaritz-
burg: University of Kwazulu-Natal Press, 2007), 129.
[22] Ian Linden and Jane Linden, 'John Chilembwe and the New Jerusalem', *Journal of African History*, 12/4 (1971), 631.
[23] Albert Grundlingh, *Fighting their Own War: South African Blacks and the First World War* (Johannesburg: Ravan, 1987), 16.
[24] William Beinart and Colin Bundy, *Hidden Struggles in Rural South Africa: Politics and Popular
Movements in the Transkei and Eastern Cape, 1890–1930* (Johannesburg: Ravan, 1987), 201.

only for Africans to ready themselves to embrace the imminent end of a sinful world. For, as the plague of war-ridden European rule receded, what lay ahead was the second coming of Christ. More ironic than messianic was the view from South Africa of the Xhosa Christian educationist D. D. T. Jabavu. African people 'were taken by surprise', he remarked sardonically in September 1914, 'that the European nations who led in education and Christianity should find no other means than the sword and accumulated destructive weapons to settle their diplomatic differences'.[25]

MOBILIZING A MIXED BAG OF MEN

The recruitment or conscription of African participants in the settlement of those differences was hardly straightforward for British command. There was, to be sure, service experience in units such as the King's African Rifles or the West African Frontier Force. Beyond their barracks there were other men. For unskilled young men in the countryside who were itching to escape the frequently suffocating patriarchal authority of overbearing village elders, army service offered the enticements of flight, including travel and comparatively reasonably paid employment. Others who enlisted did so because a return to military life represented an opportunity to regain a tough warrior identity, which had been confiscated after the conclusion of colonial conquest.

Even among those who enlisted for lowly, back-bending service overseas in France in the South African Native Labour Contingent, there were recruits who clung to an imaginatively loose sense of an empire citizenship and a 'civilized' belonging. As 'Christians' and 'not heathens' of 'the King's country', declared one contingent recruit in 1917, their 'great duty' lay with 'King and Union'.[26] On that score, few were more ardent than the purring Coloured leader of the Cape-based African People's Organization. Abdullah Abdurahman was fond of lecturing his audiences on the peril of any slackening in support of the British cause, for, 'if the British Empire fell, they would all go with it'.[27]

Probably far more common were less lofty—or more elastic—motives for soldiering enlistment. For many ordinary colonial recruits, the war was an additional rhythm to that most mundane of human activities, work, and from 1914 served as an alternative for southern and central African labour migrants who might otherwise have headed for the gold mines of Johannesburg. A wily personal business, employment in Britain's widespread African war at times involved a rich tapestry of inventiveness and fabrication. In Nyasaland, for instance, British ethnic recruitment preferences for the Yao, feted as soldiers of the finest 'martial spirit', quickly gripped the calculating imagination of volunteers for the local battalions of the King's African Rifles (KAR). Relishing in the cultivation of a strutting military aesthetic, a motley

---

[25] *Imvo Zabantsundu*, 8 September 1914.
[26] *Tsala ea Batho*, 16 September 1914.
[27] *APO*, 22 August 1914.

assortment of would-be soldiers laid claim to the pristine character of a Yao masculinity, known to be 'much sought after by KAR recruiting officers'.[28]

Nor was this the only subversion by common African fighters not famous for any real ideological or political attachment to the imperial cause to which they were harnessed. For, once they were in the ranks, loyalties could turn out to be almost gossamer thin. Therefore, in the course of the lengthy East African struggle, there were British African soldiers who served on the German side, at times brazenly switching back and forth. In fact, they were merely doing what some of the Yao of Nyasaland had done in pre-war years, discharging themselves from the KAR to join Germany's East African garrisons. With pay and service perks there better than anything available in British colonial ranks, some men from territories such as Northern Rhodesia and Nyasaland viewed bouts of *askari* service as the sensibly more remunerative option. It was not for nothing that the Germans in East Africa often resorted to English terms of command, drill routines, and bugle notes. Nor, for that matter, was it altogether unusual for language to be reversed, with British officers resorting to German parade ground address.[29]

As with eastern Africa from 1914 onwards, regional migrant labour channels in central and southern Africa as well as in the Gold Coast, Nigeria, and elsewhere in British West Africa became enmeshed in military enlistment drives for troop volunteers. In these sweeps, the needs of the war sought to capture local migrants in order to press into khaki men who customarily combined peasant production with stints of wage labour. But, in making their way within established labour routes, British army recruiters had still to make do and could not afford to be too discriminating. One striking consequence is that a hefty proportion of soldiers in the Gold Coast Regiment came not from British Africa but from French West Africa, as men fled across into British colonial territory to save themselves from virtually enslaving conscription by hungry French recruiters. Another remarkable impact of such wartime mobility was that up to '70 percent' of First World War soldiers in the Rhodesia Native Regiment were drawn from neither southern nor northern British South Africa Company colonies, but 'originated from other territories'.[30] For those in charge of imperial forces, there was much they did not know or were unable to know about who many of the Africans they commanded were, and even less of why they were under British arms.

HOSTILITIES

Africans placed under arms were confined to African soil, as it was British policy to restrict them to service on the continent. What, then, of the military engagements into which they were fed? The first of those represented the opening British shots of

---

[28] Risto Marjomaa, 'The Martial Spirit: Yao Soldiers in British Service in Nyasaland (Malawi), 1895–1939', *Journal of African History*, 44/3 (2003), 422.

[29] Marjomaa, 'Martial Spirit', 425.

[30] Stapleton, 'Extra-Territorial African Police and Soldiers in Southern Rhodesia (Zimbabwe), 1897–1965', *Scientia Militaria*, 38/1 (2010), 106.

the First World War and came from Gold Coast forces in August 1914, which had been mobilized there in July in anticipation of the outbreak of European hostilities.

Coordinating with France, Britain moved swiftly to pocket Germany's weakly defended West African colonies of Togoland and Kamerun. In effect the opening round of the world war, this minor campaign of imperial conquest was undertaken by Gold Coast Regiment battalions and accompanying colonial levies and by soldiers from Dahomey and other neighbouring French colonies. Boxed in by enemy territory, the Germans in Togo had only one card they could try to play, that of peace, so they pleaded with the Allies to hold off so that West Africa could be spared through some negotiated regional armistice. Rapid invasion by Britain from the west and France from the east dashed any lingering diplomatic illusions.

The primary British objective was, of course, strategic—the quick seizure of Togo's port capital and the destruction of German wireless station facilities, something that was easily achieved after a thin line of local paramilitary *Schutztruppen*, had been brushed aside before the end of August. While sharing a brief and effective improvised campaign, competitive instincts remained in a corner of imperial minds, with lukewarm coordination between Britain and France a consequence of 'both powers being eager to control the German colony'.[31]

Unlike Togoland, little more than an Atlantic coastal strip, German Kamerun proved a rather harder nut to crack, with its mountainous interior and dense forest approaches providing a hardy defence screen for German forces, which confronted an invading British West African Frontier Force, which tramped across from neighbouring Nigeria. Again, Britain linked up with France, which thrust in troops from their West and Equatorial African possessions. And here, again, what the British had foremost in their sights was seizure of the ports to scupper German vessels and wrecking of the wireless station to disable enemy communications. Predictable, too, was the stuttering nature of Anglo-French coordination, with poor communications across a field of deeply divided military command and slack liaison between London and Paris over overall policy. The independent—and generally unwanted—intrusion of Belgium, which had failed to keep the Congo neutral, further complicated matters for Britain.

In what soon became a slithering fight for control of Kamerun, Britain's invading forces did not have an easy run, and by 1915 its mostly Nigerian infantry was having to be reinforced by Asian troops in the shape of an Indian battalion. Ending up floundering in West African rivers and swamps, it contributed little to the eventual success of imperial arms. At times, the British were even knocked back right on their heels by impudent German strikes into Nigeria, causing panic across its eastern border and even scattering the local ruler, the Emir of Yola. The beleaguered Germans were able to hold on until February 1916, when the last of the last-ditch defenders in the north either surrendered or fled for the sanctuary of the neutral Spanish enclave of Rio Muni. It left Britain on top at the end of a campaign that had mostly 'stuttered' along to its end.[32]

---

[31] Killingray, 'Africa', 116.
[32] Gisela Graichen and Horst Grunder, *Deutsche Kolonien: Traum und Trauma* (Hamburg: Ullstein Verlag, 2007), 323.

In its move against Berlin's southernmost colony, German South West Africa, London was wholly free of having Paris to cloud the campaign picture and needed to take scant if any account of Lisbon's nearby colonial presence in Portuguese West Africa (Angola) immediately to the north. All that was required was a push from its satellite Dominion. Early in August, the Union of South Africa, constitutionally at war alongside the other self-governing Dominions, was requested by the Colonial Secretary, Lewis Harcourt, to render Britain what he termed, in a memorable phrase, 'a great and pressing imperial service'.[33] This was to mount a snap expeditionary force, which, aided by the Royal Navy, would overrun German South West Africa to do what had become most necessary and most urgent, taking the major harbours and snuffing out the key wireless stations to check enemy communications and movement in the South Atlantic ocean.

This huge colony had massively exposed land and sea frontiers that were virtually impossible to plug. And the German defences that Britain faced were puny. Established for the guarding of settlers and to douse any prospective further African unrest following the Herero rising of the earlier 1900s, they were not up to seeing off any external assault, least of all that which now loomed, a combined land and amphibious invasion by a strong and well-armed neighbouring adversary.

The South West Africa expeditionary force comprised only white combatants and a few Cape Coloured artillerymen because of Pretoria's racial bar on the arming of Africans, in contrast with Britain's other campaigns. which were carried essentially by colonial African soldiers, backed at times by Indian and small units of other empire troops. It made this theatre of hostilities the closest example of a 'white man's war' in the course of imperial war in Africa. The Union thrust in what, in comparative terms, was a massive force of around 45,000 combatants by the beginning of 1915, serviced by about 33,000 unarmed African and Coloured servicemen.

Pretoria launched its local offensive in mid-September 1914 with Britain at its elbow. Conditions for a coastal landing were secured by the Royal Navy, which had by then eliminated any threat of German naval interference by destroying Vice-Admiral Maximilian Graf von Spee's East Asiatic Squadron. Its guns then shelled the wireless installations and harbour facilities at the key German ports of Swakopmund and Luderitz. Britain's navy also deposited an armoured car unit and aircraft to equip a recently formed South African Aviation Corps. At the end of 1914, the Royal Flying Corps switched a handful of its pilots from France to south-western Africa to expand the air strength of South Africa's forces. Their portly commander, General Louis Botha, had once been a republican Boer commando warrior venerated for surging about on horseback (see Fig. 13). Now, in the German colony he was busily overrunning, Botha made a fuss of taking to the desert air in a Royal Flying Corps Henry Farman biplane. For Britain's African empire, there could scarcely be a more perfect transition from colonial war adversary to imperial war collaborator, nor from nineteenth-century saddle to twentieth-century cockpit.

---

[33] Gerald L'Ange, *Urgent Imperial Service: South African Forces in German South-West Africa, 1914–1915* (Johannesburg: Ashanti, 1991).

Fig. 13. An adaptable Afrikaner who had earlier fought against the British Empire but now relished fighting for it: General Louis Botha, prime minister of the Union of South Africa.

With immensely greater military strength, superior transport, and ample supplies and equipment, the Union's combined amphibious and land incursion overwhelmed its German opponents in just a few months. Unable to fall back any longer and any further, Governor Seitz surrendered his colony in July 1915. That represented the first British imperial victory of the war, and the first binding armistice, one of magnanimous terms. London's strategic objective of eliminating Germany's ports and radio communications had been attained in a fairly cheap fringe action that had cost a combined death toll of just over 200 soldiers.

Uncontested, the vital sea lane 'around the Cape of Good Hope' could now be assured of 'its former importance'[34] to British imperial defence, given the risk to the Suez Canal routing to India and Australia from the Ottoman alliance with the Germans. For the Colonial Secretary, 'instead of South Africa falling away from the British Empire', as might have been feared fewer than two decades previously, its loyal forces had 'won a notable victory in the cause of that Empire'. Elsewhere, Dominion capitals were taken by the spectacle of Afrikaner commandos, chameleon

---

[34] Antony Lentin, *Jan Smuts: Man of Courage and Vision* (Johannesburg: Jonathan Ball, 2010), 30–1.

colonials turned empire loyalist, now trotting into the colony's capital, Windhoek, in support of King George V. Underlying all of this was the calculating reality of Louis Botha's and Jan Smuts's own expansionist, sub-imperial agenda. In the eyes of its government, South Africa's conquest of South West Africa had, first, laid to rest the anti-British, Boer republican ghosts of the turn of the century. For the Union, the time had come, and it was one ripe for 'entering the prestigious adult world of colonial power'.[35]

At bottom, its own colonial reach to incorporate a former German South West Africa into its future was a territorial assimilation that far exceeded Britain's war-time grasp at more limited imperial strategic objectives. That said, having enabled the British to lock German shipping out of the South Atlantic, South Africa was left to the run of what was now a spacious backyard. The mild terms of Union military occupation from 1915 were aimed at fostering German compliance and stable white minority collaboration, as rural Afrikaners were encouraged to settle alongside German settlers in the territory. By 1917, a satisfied Jan Smuts was tell-ing one of his admiring London audiences that 'we have started to create a new white base in South Africa, and to-day we are in a position to move forward to-wards the North and the civilization of the African continent'.[36] While still far from slipping the leash of London, 'from its beginning' the military campaign to absorb German colonial lands north of the Orange River had been 'conceptualized as a long-term territorial expansion'. Resolving the strategic problem of a couple of Atlantic ports and long-range transmitters ended up by ushering in a new colonial overlordship, as South West Africa 'moved from being the flagship colonial posses-sion of a distant European metropole, the German motherland, to becoming the hinterland of an emerging imperial power beyond its southern border'.[37] Watered by Britain's wartime need, the 1910 Anglo-Afrikaner vision of a wider Union began to mushroom. Sporadic resistance by Baster people and other indigenous inhabitants to the more unwelcome administrative impositions of that wider Union in the early-to mid-1920s was quelled by punitive paramilitary policing with 'militant' displays of force, aided by 'the advent of the aeroplane'.[38]

HOSTILITIES—HARDER GOING

Lasting as long as the hostilities in Europe, the campaign in East Africa was most bitter and unrelenting, and the consequences of local economic dislocation were most severe. What emerged there was an African version of a war of attrition—its mode that of mobility while bleeding all the while. In fact, it even outlasted the

---

[35] Marion Wallace, *A History of Namibia from the Beginning to 1990* (Johannesburg: Jacana, 2011), 216.
[36] J. C. Smuts, *War-Time Speeches* (London: Hodder & Stoughton, 1917), 85.
[37] Giorgio Meschier, 'Arteries of Empire: On the Geographical Imagination of South Africa's Railway War, 1914/1915', *Kronos: Southern African Histories*, 38 (2012), 46.
[38] Andries M. Fokkens, 'The Suppression of Internal Unrest in South West Africa (Namibia), 1921–1933', *Scientia Militaria*, 40/3 (2012), 113, 140.

war, which had otherwise been concluded in November 1918. In the last recorded hostilities on 12 November, German *askaris* (local East African soldiers) ambushed an enemy motorcyclist in the bush. Among his scattered despatches were notification and details of the previous day's Armistice.

By then drained of strength, isolated and cornered, the still undefeated German force of around 150 *Schutztruppen* and colonial officials and almost 4,500 *askaris* with accompanying camp followers now discovered that their war had been ended for them elsewhere. So it was that, on 25 November 1918, British forces under the command of a South African general, Jaap van Deventer, accepted the surrender of Germany's last column at Abercorn in Northern Rhodesia. This at last terminated the great violence, waste, and brutality of the snaking campaign that had preceded this, squeezing across the region between British East Africa and Portuguese East Africa (Mozambique) and thrusting across and down into North-Eastern Rhodesian territory and British Nyasaland.

At its outset, it was again Germany's East African ports and wireless stations that mostly filled British sights. Striking early at an enemy colony that was roughly the size of France, the Royal Navy shelled Dar es Salaam and made a grab for the rail bridgehead port of Tanga, landing an Indian Expeditionary Force ashore at the beginning of November 1914. The plan was to combine this with a ground invasion from Kenya, with a view to taking control of the railway to sever the spine of the Germans' communications capacity.

But this knock-out blow connected poorly. Despite being outnumbered by British invaders, the pugnacious commander of Germany's East African forces, Paul Emil von Lettow-Vorbeck, not only saw off the coastal threat but also turned to raiding British territory, slicing into Kenya and hitting the strategically important Uganda railway. By the time action in this subsidiary African theatre had finally ended, the overall death toll among all British imperial fighting forces and support units 'exceeded the total of American dead in the Great War'.[39]

Still, early on there were any number of British observers, among them highly regarded army commanders like Brigadier-General Reginald Hoskins, for whom East Africa appeared an unlikely arena to sustain warfare for any length of time. Blanketed by fetid swamplands, debilitating parasitic diseases such as malaria and typhoid, gouging scrub and dense bush, scorching heat, and stifling humidity, its operational environment looked impossibly extreme. But by the end of 1915, by which time the British had been having to contend with the Belgians wriggling in alongside in pursuit of their own expansionist colonial ambitions, East African campaigning was in full flow against German forces that were up to the challenge.

Although by then Britain's troop strength was only slightly greater than that of its enemy, its faltering East Africa command now reached for another card in an attempt to break the Germans with a decisive offensive in 1916. That was a 25,000-strong South African expeditionary contingent under the personal

---

[39] Edward Paice, *Tip and Run: The Untold Story of the Great War in Africa* (London: Weidenfeld & Nicholson, 2007), 3.

command of Jan Smuts, a vain soldier–politician never to be deterred by his lack of experience of large and complex command. For the Union's pro-war press, with existing Anglo-Indian forces wallowing and unable to make headway, the ease with which the Union's 'hardy commandos' had recently mopped up Germany made a compelling case for sending in 'the right stock of Europeans'.[40] Tenacious white Springboks would clear Britain's East African quagmire and restore sagging empire morale.

However welcome the Union reinforcements, the shipping-in of a South African troop contingent raised eyebrows at the War Office, given British military policy to employ colonial Africans to do the job of overcoming the Germans in East Africa. Any white troops from settler societies in South Africa and Southern Rhodesia were meant to be used to strengthen British forces in their major European campaigning. Equally, in this particular case, figures outside the War Office had set their eyes on a larger political prize further to secure the basis of British Africa. Both Harcourt and the Union's governor-general, Lord Buxton, had concluded in 1915 that a contribution to the imperial campaign in East Africa was a natural and tactically desirable next step for South Africa, given the continuing wartime split in its white electorate. It would, it was optimistically imagined, have an 'entirely positive effect in South Africa by allowing Boers, loyal to Britain, to take part in the war without having to fight openly alongside the British in Europe for what could be interpreted as British interests'.[41] This was, if not tortured, then at least dubious reasoning—apparently it would be more palatable to anti-imperialist Afrikaners for the springbok to lie down with the lion at the foothills of Kilimanjaro than for them to do so near the river Somme.

After all, warring imperial Britain's interests in Africa were indissoluble from those in Europe. And this time, it again had geo-political implications for the Union. For a perpetually scheming Smuts, the political dividend from a conquest of German East Africa primarily by Union Defence Forces troops would be an opportunity for territorial horse-trading with both London and Lisbon. With the German colony under its hooves and Britain appreciative in its recognition of South Africa's military ascendancy, the Union could grant Portugal the southern part of the colonial territory it had commandeered, in a swop for its plum east coast port of Delagoa Bay in Mozambique.

However, Britain's empire in East Africa was not about to be opened up to an over-ambitious local Dominion. In German South West Africa, Pretoria had been given its head, with only a distant squint from Whitehall. By contrast, in East Africa, General Smuts had a big fly in his ointment. It was close War Office oversight of a campaign that, once Smuts had inveigled himself into replacing General Sir Horace Smith-Dorrien as overall commander of British forces in February 1916, became a South African expedition. Or, as *The Great War* proclaimed in January 1917, the empire's effort against Lettow-Vorbeck was 'General Smuts'

---

[40] *Rand Daily Mail*, 28 November 1915.

[41] Anne Sansom, *Britain, South Africa, and the East African Campaign, 1914–1918* (London: I. B. Tauris, 2006), 95.

Great Campaign in German East Africa'.[42] Yet, for all that, Pretoria was unable to use the military initiative it had been given to lever a conquered colony into its lap.

That military initiative was, in any event, fated to slip from Smuts's hand. Hampered by his own inexperience in running a large imperial command of over 50,000 soldiers of varying nationality, culture, and language, and out of his depth in unfamiliar and unremittingly harsh field conditions, he ended up nowhere near achieving his over-blown claim of having the Germans on the ropes by the beginning of 1917. Advances there had been, but Lettow-Vorbeck's darting forces had not been encircled and broken. By then, with Portugal having joined Belgium in what was turning into a minor European contest, fragmented command, poor co-ordination, interminable wrangling, and semi-deaf communication between Britain and its disdained colonial allies were creating a political headache to add to arduous fighting conditions. In particular, London as well as Pretoria wanted the East African arena to be kept free of the irritation of ineffectual Portuguese military intervention.

The problem of where Smuts had got to and where he imagined he had reached was resolved early in 1917 when he was drawn into the Imperial War Cabinet, a job for which he was evidently considered more suitable. By then, Britain's white troops were all but spent, with the evacuation of tens of thousands of Union infantry felled by sickness and half-rations. Limping back to Durban, they took with them lost South African hopes of a decisive demonstration of European military prowess.

From this oozed an inexorable African reality as the carrying of the British campaign was simply taken over, lock, stock and barrel, by large numbers of African troops—a massively expanded KAR along with West African forces propelled across from Nigeria and from the Gold Coast. In time, the Rhodesia Native Regiment also weighed in, as Lettow-Vorbeck's command weaved about downwards into central Africa, ducking into Nyasaland while constantly dragging British forces in its wake. By the time the Germans were obliged to capitulate, they had held Britain at bay for four-and-a half years and had bogged down over 160,000 troops, in addition to keeping the Royal Navy busy (see Fig. 14).

The misery and suffering of the campaign drained Britain's combatants, with some South Africans among them becomingly disillusioned by circumstances in the field. In part, imperial war in East Africa was making it difficult to bond as a national white Dominion fighting fraternity—men were shunted between British brigades, Rhodesian or Gold Coast African servicemen replaced lost white drivers in the South African Horse Corps, and, at times, the South African Motorcycle Corps even found itself riding with Indian regiments. Yet, far worse in a way than such unforeseen adaptations was the painful awareness of wishful thinking: instead of having marched out to some imagined European war of manly combat in open battle, they had ended up rotting away in a colonial African bush war that brought malaria and pneumonia rather than martial vindication. 'Ah, I wish to hell I was in France,' wrote one disconsolate British infantryman, compounding his illusions;

---

[42] 'With the British Forces in East Africa', *The Great War*, 148 (1917), 207.

Fig. 14. Botha's opponents: Imperial Germany's African troops.

'there, one lives like a gentleman and dies like a man, here one lives like a pig and dies like a dog'.[43]

By far the lion's share—and more—of that dying was done, not by the patriotic white volunteers from colonial collegiate schools, but by hundreds of thousands of conscripted rural African porters and carriers. Britain enlisted or forcibly requisitioned labouring auxiliaries from all its east and central African possessions—some 200,000 from Nyasaland alone, while by early 1917 around 230,000 men had been sucked from Northern Rhodesia. In total, it is estimated that the British alone employed at least one million army porters.

Riddled with respiratory and intestinal diseases, exposed to exceptionally harsh weather, and mostly malnourished, these neglected transport workers suffered appalling death rates, with losses among African porters and carriers exceeding 100,000 victims. It took until 1934 for the Colonial Office to recognize the catastrophic mortality of wartime, eventually acknowledging it as having been 'a scandal'.[44]

Nor had this been the end of it. Random plunder of local pastoral and arable economies was by no means confined to Lettow-Vorbeck's bony forces, obliged to sustain war on the cheap by subsisting on whatever could be seized. Locked in with its own immense supply problems, a hungry British camp requisitioned cattle, grain, and other edible crops, with its slogging columns maintaining themselves partly or sometimes wholly by the routine pillage of peasant settlements in their

[43] Angus Buchanan, *Three Years of War in East Africa* (London: Hammerton, 1919), p. xvi.
[44] Killingray, 'Africa', 124.

path. To deny sustenance to ravenous German units operating in the vicinity, villages were blasted and burned, leaving fields torched and livestock scattered. When it came to the implementation of scorched-earth, the British were, naturally, not short of pre-1914 colonial war experience upon which to draw. Most recently, it had been the wrecking of the republican Boer farmlands of the Orange Free State and the Transvaal in the South African War to deny sustenance to their guerrilla enemy. Once again, for whole populations warfare meant 'the war coming home'.[45]

Placed in a broader imperial context, there is possibly something here to suggest that Britain in South Africa in the early 1900s could be considered as a rough kind of stormy preamble to Britain in East Africa two decades later, where what could be witnessed was the unleashing of 'extreme forms of militarised brutalism against civilians'.[46] The inevitable consequence was not just enormous suffering and trauma for the hundreds of thousands of civilians whose lives were eaten by imperial forces. It was also a devastating food shortage after 1916, amounting, in the view of some general historians of Africa, to a crisis of survival that verged on 'outright famine'.[47]

INTERVENING TO KEEP A LID ON THINGS

Elsewhere on the continent, Britain's armed involvement amounted to a more light and more sophisticated enterprise. Politically, North Africa was more convoluted and required more than simply clearing the ground of a German enemy. In this region, the war saw Britain enmeshed in fluctuating actions to beat off some snarling challenges to its imperial position, holding out in disputed zones and coping with what, at times, seemed to be a constant swirl of minor rebellion and raiding by lurking Islamic bands. At the same time, though, wartime disorder also handed London the spur of necessity to tighten the screws of its colonial influence. Accordingly, in the enormous Anglo-Egyptian Sudan, the infidel British grew increasingly mindful of rocky circumstances north of the Sahara following the outbreak of war. For before long there was growing cause for a flexing of muscles to push their control further westwards.

There, Ali Dinar, the ruler of the Sultanate of Darfur, had been flirting brazenly with the Ottomans, the Germans, and the refractory Libyan Sanusiyya since 1915. Such nerve prompted the British governor of the Sudan, General Sir Reginald Wingate, to clamp down on a territory that was becoming intolerably wayward. Early in 1916, he despatched a punitive expedition to reel in the Sultan. A textbook imperial formation, this composite British Western Frontier Force included Australian, New Zealand, Egyptian, Sikh, and Ghurka soldiers. Soon dubbed 'the waterless fatigue force' by its grumbling British infantry, the

---

[45] Bill Nasson and Albert Grundlingh (eds), *The War Comes Home: Women and Families in the Anglo-Boer War* (Cape Town: Tafelberg, 2013).

[46] Jonathan Hyslop, 'The Invention of the Concentration Camp: Cuba, Southern Africa and the Philippines, 1896–1907', *South African Historical Journal*, 63/2 (2011), 263.

[47] Reid, *Modern Africa*, 192.

desert army duly subdued the upstart sultanate, killing Ali Dinar himself in the process.[48]

Yet, with this incursion Wingate had still to be wary of stepping on too many corns in what was sure to remain a potentially turbulent Muslim region. Not for nothing the proverbial canny Scot, he then steered clear of any further major showdowns, restoring a tenuous stability by breaking bread with the dominant Sufi orders of the Sudan. Keeping in step with relatively open-handed French conduct in Algeria and Morocco, the British pursued a similar sort of rapprochement with influential local chiefly forces. This did enough to blunt the menace of an otherwise rampant Islamic insurgency, as attacks such as the 1916 *jihad* launched by Abdullah Suhayni soon ran into the sand for lack of a mass momentum.

Keeping itself secure as the actual controlling power of the Anglo-Egyptian Sudan, Britain's imperial presence on the slab of north-east Africa came to rest on a sort of nervous stability, a delicate equilibrium that nonetheless ensured that its flag, alongside that of Egypt, would remain firmly aloft in the Sudanese condominium. That was also aided by Britain's bolstering of its position across the northern border in 1914 when, in reaction to Turkish entry into war, it formalized its occupying presence in Egypt by declaring a protectorate. Tipping colonial forces, especially the Indian army, into the Mediterranean edge of its African empire, Britain effectively shored up its 'existing strategic assets in the region, in particular the Suez Canal'.[49]

CONCLUSIONS: A SETTLING OF ACCOUNTS AND SOME LONGER SHADOWS

In their essentials, the motor forces that drove the British cause were fuelled from outside the continent. In one part, London's campaign of military conquest represented the termination of a German imperial Africa, an early twentieth-century postscript to the preceding colonial balance sheet of gains and losses. London strengthened its 'colonial globality' at Germany's expense, for whom colonies were in any event 'less important than was the case for Britain'.[50] It is, then, not without good reason that the impact of the war has been viewed by scholars as amounting to a second partition of Africa. In another part, Britain was pursuing an extramural war over Africa in the company of imperial European allies that it disliked and distrusted. Belgium presented a risk because of the possibility that it might use any enemy territory gained as a colonial bargaining chip if it ever came to underhand bilateral negotiations with Berlin for a separate peace. Then there was shaky Portugal, regarded by both London and Pretoria as impotent but nonetheless a

[48] John Slight, 'British Perceptions and Responses to Sultan Ali Dinar of Darfur, 1915–16', *Journal of Commonwealth and Imperial History*, 38/2 (2010), 241.

[49] Robert Aldrich and Christopher Hilliard, 'The French and British Empires', in Horne (ed.), *World War 1*, 533.

[50] Sebastian Conrad, *German Colonialism: A Short History* (Cambridge: Cambridge University Press, Cambridge, 2012), 185.

nuisance. In the end, there were no trade-offs with Lisbon, and South Africa's sub-imperial fantasy of powering north of the Limpopo came to nothing.

Certainly, there was considerable clarity of outcome after 1918. Britain acquired most of the former German East Africa as the desirable Tanganyika that would fill in the last piece of the great imperial arc from the Cape to Cairo. Having that prized extension of control made it easy to leave most of a marginal Togoland and Kamerun to French wants. In due course, the British incorporated their portion of Togo into the neighbouring Gold Coast. In southern Africa, South Africa's control over South West Africa, as in the case of other conquered enemy colonies, was mandated by the newly minted League of Nations under its mandate ranking system. Devised by Jan Smuts himself as a fig-leaf 'substitute for annexation to appease Woodrow Wilson on the rights of subject nations and self-determination',[51] mandate areas were accordingly 'not colonies'.[52] Yet, in practice, the former German South-West was steadily absorbed and administered as an additional province of the Union. An old white country of African empire, it now acquired its own protruding colonial teeth as it suppressed outbreaks of unrest such as the 1922 Bondelswarts uprising with aircraft inherited from the war, flown by bomber pilots who had earned a reputation as gifted 'colonial-born' airmen over both East Africa and France.

This was not exactly what had been in mind at the general allocation of mandate responsibilities, which, as a kind of neo-imperial trusteeship, bore the promise of a transition from an era of rampaging imperialism to a custodial order of colonial reform, less militaristic in ethos and with greater emphasis on the welfare and maturing political interests of Africans. And, while this may have been an extreme case of callous disregard for mandate expectations, in effect Britain's own new territories ended up being governed much like any other of its colonies, for all that the League of Nations inspected them for healthy progress.

In a way, it could hardly been otherwise. Being the single most powerful member of the League aside from France, Britain was also continuing as Africa's other large colonial power—it was able to call the shots.

Still, the intention of the mandate system was not without an outcome. That was the ushering-in of an atmospheric new era of international interrogation and international opinion, as a mandatory great power was subject to inspection by the League Secretariat and had to report to its Council on its discharging of trust responsibilities. As publicity spread in the 1920s, the issues affecting Britain as a mandatory regime came to weigh on consciousness and political discourse. The point, then, as has been argued, is that the mandates adoption can be viewed less as some new system of governance and far more as a gestation of critical international inquiry, 'a mechanism for generating talk'.[53]

---

[51] John H. Morrow Jr., *The Great War: An Imperial History* (Oxford: Routledge, 2004), 307.

[52] Michael D. Callahan, *Mandates and Empire: The League of Nations and Africa, 1914–1931* (Brighton: Sussex Academic Press, 2008), 13.

[53] Susan Pedersen, 'The Meaning of the Mandates System: An Argument', *Geschichte und Gesellschaft*, 32/4 (2006), 569.

Talk was, of course, widespread in the aftermath of the war. There is no doubting the release—even as half-hidden resentments—of restiveness among self-aware, modernizing African elites right across British colonial Africa. For those among them who had rallied to the war with subscription drives and offers to serve, the Great War had been something akin to a 'national experience' well before the much later imaginative construction of any of their nations. This, and their continually stunted political and social aspirations in peacetime, would have underpinned the mounting calls across parts of British West Africa for greater representation of the skilled and the literate in territorial government, as well as stirrings in southern and central territories over self-determination and freedom from discrimination and oppression.

How far did such more immediate post-war developments influence African decolonization movements in the longer term? In this respect, it is probably fair to say that the experience of the Great War, unlike that of the Second World War, did not represent some great cogwheel, which turned a modern nationalist challenge to British colonial authority. That, after all, continued to look virtually rock solid even at the end of the 1930s. Indeed, one of the older narratives of post-independence African history, one that accorded an influential and instrumental political role to war veterans after 1918, has long been discarded as too inflated and too premature.

At the same time, it remains no less important to take stock of what the Great War prefigured for later decolonizing African political movements. What it nudged along, as often as not, was a range of assertive attitudes and values that foreshadowed what would emerge as the fabric of modern anti-colonial nationalism. Assuming forms that were sometimes overlapping, sometimes distinct, they adopted a more confrontational tone in the voicing of grievances.

Those that broke out repeatedly came from militant urban workers and trade unionists, mutual aid and self-help associations, the small newspapers of the intelligentsia, progressive peasant farmers, and Christian movements that, having broken away from British mission tutelage, rejected the civilizing claims of colonial rule. In places the war had thrown a stinging light on Britain's African empire, and the rising anti-colonial disillusionment of the later inter-war years would have absorbed some of those rays. That said, in the more immediate aftermath of 1918 the trumpet blasts against colonial power were still tinny and of little danger to the walls of a London Jericho. For the war had witnessed the final consolidation of its African colonial structures, its planning legacy bringing stronger systems of ruling authority to administer subjects, to exploit economic environments, and to employ technologically and administratively more efficient ways of maintaining a stable colonial order. Granted, there would be strains to overcome and both urban and rural resistance to be snuffed out. But, at a fundamental level, the Great War 'probably marked the last high point of the reign of crude force'.[54]

That closing historical perspective may be as good a point as any to recall one reflex—and novel—resistance to British imperial war. Lacking a popular mandate for action in 1914, South Africa's declaration of an unprovoked offensive against German South West Africa was an inflammatory risk. Sure enough, it inflamed

---

[54] Bill Freund, *The Making of Contemporary Africa* (Basingstoke: Macmillan, 1998), 112.

a knot of disaffected and disloyal Afrikaner generals who stripped off their khaki and set out with around 11,000 poorer rural followers to topple the government and reclaim the Boer republican independence lost to Britain by 1902. That 1914 Afrikaner Rebellion, carried mostly by the landless white poor, rippled with anti-British imperialist, anti-Anglicized Union, and pro-German currents. Absorbed in doomed utopian dreams of a redeeming national republican independence, it was 'a desperate rebellion'.[55] Politely turning down as political suicide a Whitehall offer of Australian and New Zealand troops to assist in dealing with their troubles, Louis Botha and Jan Smuts used their Crown loyalist own to pacify their throwback republican own.

Radical Afrikaner resentment of a British imperial abomination smouldered on, clutching at straws, such as the Union's failings in East Africa, and the losses of its European forces on the Western Front. Final vindication—of a perversely vicarious kind—came at a most peculiar moment, November 1918. As the nationalist paper *Het Volk* reassured its readership, there was no need to be disheartened by the outcome of the war. After all, surely everything was not lost, as it had still ended 'in a victory for republicanism, as in any case America was really responsible for the victory'.[56] Such was the dreaminess of not living by empire when it was exactly that into which a great war had just locked British Africa's people more securely than before.

Yet something of that urge to take issue with a victorious British Crown persisted into the peace, and in some richly resonant ways. At the opening of South Africa's national war memorial at Delville Wood on the Somme in 1926, J. B. M. Hertzog, neutral in the war and now Nationalist prime minister of the Union, paid tribute to 'innocent Afrikaners' who had fallen in the world war for a true 'abiding' ally, 'in defence of France'.[57] Although no radical separatist, earlier in the decade he had been the first empire–commonwealth statesman to visit the newly formed Irish Free State, another smothered republic. By then there were also other spasmodic forces at work, such as the implantation of American Garveyism into some of the minds of rural southern Africa and West Africa. Beguiled by its preachings of a self-reliant universal black brotherhood, shrill adherents in South Africa declared that in the recent war America had supplanted King George V and his country, and that black Americans would be arriving 'by aeroplane and would release balls of burning charcoal on Europeans' as well as on faithless Africans.[58]

It was, in its chantingly hypnotic way, an understandably appealing legend. But it perhaps also went a little further than that, suggesting that, for some of British Africa's inhabitants, the war through which they had recently passed had certainly done something to blur and complicate the terms on which they were meant to resume their behaviour as colonial subjects and colonial citizens of the British Crown.

[55] Albert Grundlingh and Sandra Swart, *Radelose Rebellie? Dinamika van die 1914–1915 Afrikanerebellie* (Pretoria: Protea Boekehuis, 2009).

[56] *Het Volk*, 15 November 1918.

[57] *De Burger*, 29 October 1926.

[58] Philip Bonner, 'South African Society and Culture, 1910–1948', in Robert Ross, Anne Kelk Mager, and Bill Nasson (eds), *The Cambridge History of South Africa*, ii (New York: Cambridge University Press, 2011), 281.

8

The Dominions, Ireland, and India

Stephen Garton

The first soldier in British service to fire a shot in the First World War was an African scout in the West African Frontier Force, Alhaji Grunshi, attempting to capture Lomé, the capital of Togoland, in August 1914.[1] Australia's first military casualties of the First World War, medical officer Brian Pockley and Able Seaman Billy Williams, fell not charging up the beach at Anzac Cove, Gallipoli, but instead attacking a communication station at Kabakaul in German New Guinea (Kaiser-Wilhelmsland) on 11 September 1914. The German defences there were quickly overwhelmed, surrendering ten days later, ensuring that the colony was secured for Britain and its empire.[2] The initial engagement of New Zealand forces was likewise far from the shores of Gallipoli. Landing in Apia, German Samoa, on 29 August 1914, the small New Zealand force seized the German colony, meeting only token resistance and suffering no casualties.[3] India's awakening to the reality of war, however, was more traumatic. On 22 September the German cruiser *Emden* entered the Madras (Chennai) harbour and fired off 125 rounds, destroying a fuel tank storage area and sinking a merchant ship, causing casualties and creating widespread panic in the city. Thousands fled, fearing invasion.[4]

The First World War may have been a conflict between European powers, fought largely in Europe, the Middle East, and Africa, but it also involved people from all over the world and necessitated military engagements on many continents and most of the world's major oceans. The peoples of the numerous colonies, kingdoms, protectorates, and dominions in the British Empire were embroiled in this global conflict: some sent significant manpower resources to support Britain, over two million servicemen from the empire enlisted to serve overseas, others formed domestic militias to safeguard British possessions, while occupying forces returned home and many manned vital military, supply, and communication stations in support of Britain in the war against Germany and its allies. In the first year of the

---

[1] Hew Strachan, *The First World War: Volume I—To Arms* (Oxford: Oxford University Press, 2001), 495.

[2] University of Sydney, *Book of Remembrance of the University of Sydney in the Great War 1914–1918* (Sydney: Australasian Medical Publishing Company, 1939), 403.

[3] See Michael King, *The Penguin History of New Zealand* (Auckland: Penguin, 2003), 295–6.

[4] Strachan, *The First World War*, 479. For Madras, see Edwin P. Hoyt, *The Last Cruise of the Emden* (London: Andre Deutsch, 1967), 98–107.

war, when some of the most strategically important engagements were at sea, requiring the mobilization of naval, supply, and communication resources, conflict ranged widely around the globe, not just in the North Atlantic and the Mediterranean, but from the Falkland Islands and South America to the Pacific, the seas around Oceania and South East Asia, and into the Indian Ocean. Some in the British Empire found that the war came remarkably close to home, and in many instances colonial and dominion forces were vital to defending British interests far from Europe. It was the Australian HMAS *Sydney* that finally sank the German light cruiser the *Emden*, off the Cocos Islands, on 9 November 1914, after the German cruiser had sunk or captured over thirty allied merchant vessels and warships.[5]

How this fact has been represented in the prevailing historiography of the Empire at war has waxed and waned. In the immediate years after the war the idea that this was a conflict that engaged the whole empire, and was fought throughout the empire, was uncontentious and widely embraced. Popular accounts, such as Sir Charles Prestwood Lucas's five-volume history *The Empire at War* (1921–8), enthusiastically and proudly documented conflicts and engagements not just in Europe and the Middle East but in almost every corner of the globe, from the Sudan to the Cocos Islands, including chapters on China, Malaya, Ceylon (Sri Lanka), Burma, India, South America, and the Falkland Islands.[6] By the 1960s, however, in the shadow of a second great world conflagration, the focus had largely shifted to Europe and the Middle East.[7]

More recently, however, historians have once again begun to concentrate on the First World War as a truly global conflict. In some less sophisticated hands this entails a token chapter or two on Africa and the Pacific, and greater attention to Eastern Europe and the Middle East, while the overwhelming focus remains Western Europe.[8] In able hands, however, such as those of Hew Strachan, the clash of the European powers is seen in its full global context, as something fought throughout the world and involving many of the world's societies. More importantly, such studies chart the complex ways developments in, for example, the South Atlantic, Samoa, or West Africa had profound reverberations for the clash of European powers more generally, shaping as they did such vital factors as military

---

[5] Strachan, *The First World War*, 479–80.

[6] C. P. Lucas (ed), *The Empire at War* (London: Oxford University Press, 1921–28).

[7] See Barbara Tuchman, *The Guns of August* (New York: Macmillan, 1962), and Marc Ferro, *The Great War 1914–1918*, trans. Nicole Stone (London: Routledge and Kegan Paul, 1973). Also Robin Winks, *Europe, 1890–1945: Crisis and Conflict* (New York: Oxford University Press, 2003), and Michael Howard, *The First World War* (Oxford: Oxford University Press, 2002). There are even some histories of the naval campaigns that largely ignore the Pacific, while purporting to be global in coverage. See, e.g., Paul G. Halpern, *A Naval History of the World War I* (Annapolis: Naval Institute Press, 1994).

[8] See such classics as Martin Gilbert, *First World War* (London: Weidenfeld and Nicolson, 1994), and John Keegan, *The First World War* (New York: Knopf, 1990), or, more recently, Michael S. Neiberg, *Fighting the Great War: A Global History* (Cambridge, MA: Harvard University Press, 2005), and Lawrence Sondhaus, *World War One: The Global Revolution* (Cambridge: Cambridge University Press, 2011).

communications, trade and supply routes, control of the seas, and morale.[9] Nonetheless the primary viewpoint, even in the best of these studies, is essentially European. This is a story of European powers in conflict around the world. What is missing is the viewpoint of the peripheries of Empire. How did Australians, Canadians, Indians, South Africans, the Irish, New Zealanders, Cameroons, West Indians, Burmese, Tibetans, and many others experience, understand, and respond to the war? How did the colonies of empires, rather than European powers, experience the war? And, further, what were the consequences of this experience for their understanding of empire and its role in their future?

In exploring these questions, this chapter examines one slice of the larger British Empire—those countries that contributed significant manpower and resources to the war effort: the dominions, especially Canada, Australia, and New Zealand, and also India and Ireland. There are many other aspects of the British Empire experience of the Great War, some of them, notably Africa, covered elsewhere in this volume. But, in the dominions, India, and Ireland, the war effort had profound economic, political, and cultural effects. The settler dominions, Ireland and India, however, also afford an opportunity to explore the diversity and complexity of British imperial relations. While India was a colony subject to the dictates of Westminster, Ireland had representation there, despite its colonial status. Australia, Canada, and New Zealand, on the other hand, were independent nations within the empire, still subject to British dictates with respect to foreign policy, but nations that needed persuasion as much as command to ensure effective participation. The British Empire was not a centre and peripheries polity, where authority flowed from the heart of Empire out to the colonies and dependencies, but a polymorphous entity, necessitating the deployment of diverse strategies ranging from imperial authority, military command, political enticements, sentiment, and bonds of ethnicity, culture, and religion to mobilize for war. Moreover, in the far-flung corners of Britain's empire the experience of war sharpened and focused perceptions of the purpose of the empire itself. Finally, demobilization had a deep impact on these societies. The return of servicemen to troubled and divided cultures, suffering economic downturn, and seeking to manage deep personal grief and loss, fed manifest and latent nationalism within the empire. While the start of the Great War heralded widespread and enthusiastic commitment to the empire, the war and its aftermath created the conditions for an explosion of nationalist aspirations that were, in the end, profoundly to alter the nature of the empire, even presage its end.

MOBILIZATION AND ITS DISCONTENTS

When Britain declared war on Germany and its allies in August 1914, it did so in the name of the empire. In making this declaration, Britain expected that all parts

---

[9] Strachan, *The First World War*, 441–643.

of the empire, around seventy colonies, principalities, protectorates, kingdoms, and dominions, were perforce also at war. The British government did not seek, and never assumed it needed first to seek, permission or agreement from any part of the empire, even the self-governing dominions, although it observed the diplomatic protocols of immediately informing the governing authorities throughout the empire, and the dominion governments, of the decision. The far-flung empire, however, became a source of vital resources (food, clothing, supplies), defence materiel, communications, military intelligence, and manpower for the prosecution of the British war effort. The economic expectations and consequences of the empire war effort were profound. To establish imperial military forces and support their efforts, not to mention provision all the forces in Europe, the Middle East and other parts of the globe required massive war bond and treasury bill schemes ensuring that private and public funds were diverted to the war effort. While Britain itself raised £2 billion through these mechanisms, other parts of the empire, especially the dominions, also contributed: a further billion from Canada, Australia, and India alone. The long-term economic effects of massive indebtedness on the post-war economies of Britain and the empire were profound.[10]

Was Britain's confidence that in 1914 it spoke for the empire as a whole in committing the peoples under its sovereignty to war unwarranted? The mobilization of manpower in defence of British interests suggests not. The figures are noteworthy. India mobilized over one million men, nearly 900,000 of whom served overseas. Canada sent nearly 500,000 to Europe and the Middle East, Ireland 200,000, Australia, over 300,000 and New Zealand, 100,000. South Africa marshalled 100,000 for fighting on the African continent and sent contingents of 20,000–30,000 to Europe. The West Indies formed a regiment of over 15,000 that served largely in Africa and Egypt. There were also garrisons in India, Burma, Hong Kong, and Singapore. Similarly forces from what would later become Palestine, Egypt, Qatar, Oman, Saudi Arabia, and elsewhere in the Middle East were crucial to the success of the Middle East campaign. Many of these troops were front-line soldiers and died in defence of the empire's interests—around 60,000 Australians and a similar number of Canadians, 53,000 Indians, 35,000 Irishmen, nearly 20,000 New Zealanders, and over 1,000 West Indians.[11] Many more returned home with severe physical and psychological injuries. The sacrifice of the empire's forces in support of Britain was significant by any measure. In terms of the proportion of the forces in Europe and the Middle East, the Australian Imperial Force had the highest casualty rate (65 per cent) of any force on the side of Britain and its allies, but Canadians (50 per cent) and New Zealanders (59 per cent) were not far behind. While in terms of the total population mobilized for war a higher proportion of Britons (one in eleven) enlisted, than from anywhere in the empire, the

---

[10] Strachan, *The First World War*, 815–992. For particular parts of the empire, see David Meredith and Barrie Dyster, *Australia in the Global Economy: Continuity and Change* 2nd edn (Melbourne: Cambridge University Press, 2012), 100, and Vincent A. Smith (rev. by Percival Spear), *The Oxford History of India* (Oxford: Clarendon Press, 1958), 779.

[11] See F. W. Perry, *The Commonwealth Armies: Manpower and Organization in Two World Wars* (Manchester: Manchester University Press, 1988).

fact that 5 per cent of Canadians, 7 per cent of Australians, and nearly 9 per cent of New Zealanders enlisted was not insignificant.[12] Moreover, regardless of the proportion, the long-term burden of caring for many wounded and ill soldiers long after the conflict had ceased was still a heavy one, fuelling a widespread myth, particularly in Australia, of a 'blood sacrifice'.[13] Soldiers of the empire fought and died for Britain and the empire.

The overall extent of this mobilization should not be lost sight of in digging deeper into the evidence. Despite the evident empire enthusiasm for Britain's war effort, there were causes for concern in Westminster and in some of the major colonies and dominions. Would support for Irish home rule undermine the war effort there? Would Afrikaner resentments about the Boer War sap enthusiasm for enlistment, or worse encourage support for Germany? How would Québécois and Irish Catholic minorities in Canada and Australia respectively respond to the call to arms? Would Indians, especially leaders anxious to promote Indian home rule, throw their support behind the Empire? These were pertinent questions in 1914.

In the main, such fears proved groundless. The ideal of a benign empire in contrast to the brutish 'Hun' was useful war propaganda. Anxieties about the loyalty of ethnic minorities in the dominions or indigenous majorities in colonies were assuaged by early enthusiasm of groups such as the Québécois and West Indians for enlistment.[14] In South Africa, despite a small Afrikaner nationalist rebellion, led by Generals Koos De la Rey and C. F. Beyers, which was quickly crushed, there was no hesitation on the part of the Smuts and Botha government to mobilize to attack German colonies in South-West and East Africa.[15] Nonetheless, the alacrity with which governments, particularly in the dominions, embraced the war masks deeper tensions. Popular enthusiasm may have been high, but patterns of enlistment show that Canadian and Australian residents born in Britain were far more likely to enlist than those born in either dominion, and, after the initial enthusiasm of enlistment had faded, French Canadians and Irish Catholic Australians were more reluctant to volunteer than other Canadians and Australians. In part the commitment of the dominions to fighting overseas for Britain and the empire represented, as Jay Winter has argued, the presence of a significant British diaspora in the settler dominions.[16]

---

[12] A. G. Butler, *History of the Australian Army Medical Services in the 1914–18 War* (Sydney: Angus and Robertson, 1943), 863–905.

[13] Noel McLachlan, *Waiting for the Revolution: A History of Australian Nationalism* (Ringwood: Penguin, 1989), 197–8.

[14] J. M. S. Careless, *Canada: A Story of Challenge* (London: Cambridge University Press, 1953), 328–9. On the West Indian response, see Glenford Howe, *Race, War and Nationalism: A Social History of West Indians in the First World War* (Kingston: Ian Randle, 2002).

[15] T. R. H. Davenport, *South Africa: A Modern History*, 3rd edn (Basingstoke: Macmillan, 1987), 271–2.

[16] Jay Winter, *Remembering War: The Great War between Memory and History in the Twentieth Century* (New Haven: Yale University Press, 2006), 160–6. On the higher proportion of those of British descent among the volunteers, see Robert Bothwell, *The Penguin History of Canada* (Toronto: Penguin, 2006), 290–3, and L. L. Robson, *The First AIF: A Study of its Recruitment 1914–1918* (Melbourne: Melbourne University Press, 1970).

The most pressing loyalty question for the empire, however, given the strength of home-rule sentiments, was whether Irish and Indian nationalists would support the war effort. Empire loyalty could not be guaranteed, and this presented acute political problems for the Asquith Liberal government, which could ill afford internal revolts within the empire just at the moment when imperial unity was imperative. Equally, in mobilizing for confrontation, the British government believed it was vital to divert manpower and resources to the front line at the risk of imperilling peace on the peripheries of empire. This was a context that was equally challenging for nationalists in the colonies. Should they demonstrate their loyalty to Britain in the hope of securing post-war political gains or capitalize on the empire's vulnerability in a time of war to advance the home rule cause (see Fig. 15)?

Fig. 15. The appeal to sentiment: an Irish recruitment poster, 1915.

For the Asquith government there was little question that Edward Carson and the Ulster Unionists would support the war effort. The pressing question was the willingness of John Redmond and the Nationalist Volunteers to back Britain. Redmond was at heart a constitutional nationalist, who believed the nationalist cause stood more to gain by loyalty than rebellion, although he was not about to let the opportunity slip to secure concessions. He held off committing the Nationalists until September, when Asquith finally conceded, passing the Third Home Rule Bill, although Edward Carson insisted that the Act be postponed for the duration of the war. Carson also pressed for the exclusion of the Northern counties from this Act, another concession that Asquith had to make. Redmond may have secured commitment to home rule for Ireland at last, but in mobilizing Irish volunteers for the war effort he had to tread carefully. Rather than embracing loyalty as his rallying cry, he neatly sidestepped that trap, arguing instead that the Belgian atrocities demanded that Irishmen defend the 'rights of small nations'. His call was an effective one. Volunteers flooded recruiting stations in the early months of the war. Overall about 200,000 Irishmen volunteered for service and possibly another 30,000 served in British regiments.[17]

Redmond's triumph was a pyrrhic one. The British government failed to see that Irish nationalist politics was not determined merely by the actions of leaders such as Redmond and Carson. As John Horne has argued, there were really four varieties of statehood that split Irish political allegiances: Unionist, Ulster Unionist, nationalist, and republican.[18] The deal struck between Redmond, Carson, and Asquith unleashed political forces they were all unprepared for, providing fuel for the small, militant republican cause that ultimately led to the tragedy of Easter 1916. While the republicans did not command popular support in Catholic Ireland in the early years of the war, the ferocity of the British response to the rebels in 1916 and their martyrdom sapped enthusiasm for the war effort and ultimately sidelined Redmond. By the time of his death in 1918 he was a leader in name only; Irish politics had moved on from his constitutional approach.[19]

The situation in India was less volatile. The majority of the Indian National Congress leadership hoped that loyalty would be rewarded and supported the war effort, although, like Redmond, they pressed for concessions in a context where British rule was vulnerable. Both the Congress and the Muslim League were demanding signs of advance towards post-war self-government and in 1916 joined forces, signing the Lucknow Pact, in pursuit of home rule for India.[20] While British suppression of Indian nationalist movements had at times been repressive, notably crushing the Swadeshi protest movement over the partition of Bengal in 1905, and its response to home rule niggardly, through the 1909 Morley–Minto

[17] See Catriona Pennell, 'Going to War', in John Horne (ed.), *Our War: Ireland and the Great War* (Dublin: Royal Irish Academy, 2008), 37–48, and Keith Jeffrey, *Ireland and the Great War* (Cambridge: Cambridge University Press, 2000), 9–18.

[18] John Horne, 'Our War, Our History', in Horne (ed.), *Our War*, 1–14.

[19] Paul Bew, 'The Politics of War', in Horne (ed.), *Our War*, 97–107.

[20] See Judith M. Brown, *Modern India: The Origins of an Asian Democracy*, 2nd edn (Oxford: Oxford University Press, 1994), 194–207.

reforms, Indian nationalists hoped for more concessions at the outbreak of the Great War.[21] Britain gave them hope it would do so. In 1914 Prime Minister Asquith declared that 'henceforth Indian questions would have to be approached from a different angle of vision'.[22] Britain, however, also insisted that increased security provisions, enacted through the 1915 Defence of India Act, were the precondition of reform. Through increased censorship and powers to detain, Britain sought better to secure India in order to return more divisions to Europe for the war.[23]

British fears about internal security in India were not without foundation. War gave hope to small groups of Indian revolutionaries, inside and outside India, that the diversion of British occupying forces to Europe (Britain left a token force of 15,000 British and Sepoy soldiers in India during the war) offered an opportunity to overthrow British rule. These revolutionaries, particularly the Bengali Jungatar group, were supported by radical Indian independence groups in Burma, Singapore, and the Ghader Party in North America. They reached out to Irish Republicans for advice and support and also sought to establish relations with Germany in the hope that the German government would supply men and materiel to facilitate armed struggle. An Indian Independence Committee, led by Virendranath Chattopadhyaya, Champakaraman Pillai, and Abinash Bhattacharya, was established in Berlin, and together these diverse, but now united, radical Indian nationalists, planned a Christmas Day 1915 pan-Indian mutiny. In all about 4,000 Ghadarites slipped into India to support the armed overthrow of the British government in India, but the plot was easily thwarted by British intelligence. These radical groups continued to ferment dissent among Indians, with related efforts to incite outbreaks in Singapore, Lahore, and Afghanistan, but they never commanded the support of the mainstream nationalist movement.[24] Overall, the Indian political leadership committed itself to the war effort, believing there was more to gain through loyalty than disloyalty.

While serious organized rebellion against Britain and wider opposition to mobilization in support of Britain throughout the empire during the First World War was limited, as the war dragged on deeper social fissures became more obvious. Enthusiasm for enlistment flagged throughout the empire as the terrible human toll on the Western Front became more evident. While the high casualty rates fuelled the demand for more volunteers, rates of enlistment fell and the empire struggled to fill the quotas Britain demanded.[25] In this context, accusations about

---

[21] Sumit Sarkar, *Modern India 1885–1947* (Madras: Macmillan, 1983), 137–40.

[22] Quoted in Smith, *The Oxford History of India*, 780.

[23] See N. Gerald Barrier, 'Ruling India: Coercion and Propaganda in British India during the First World War', in DeWitt C. Ellinwood and S. D. Pradhan (eds), *India and World War I* (New Delhi: Manohar, 1978), 75–108, and Sarkar, *Modern India*, 149–50.

[24] See A. C. Bose, 'Indian Revolutionaries during the First World War: A Study of their Aims and Weaknesses', in Ellinwood and Pradhan (eds), *India and World War I*, 109–25; Thomas G. Fraser, 'Germany and Indian Revolution, 1914–18', *Journal of Contemporary History*, 12/2 (April 1977), 255–72; Giles Brown, 'The Hindu Conspiracy, 1914–17', *Pacific Historical Review*, 17/3 (August 1948), 299–310; and Sarkar, *Modern India*, 147–9.

[25] See Perry, *The Commonwealth Armies*, 1.

lack of imperial patriotism and allegations of cowardice flourished. White feathers and exhortations that Britain 'needs you' were two sides of the enlistment coin, unofficial and official. In Canada claims that French Canadians were shirking their duty by enlisting at a lower rate than British Canadians reflected some of the social and political tensions arising from declining rates of enlistment. French Canadians, on the other hand, pointed to the fact that Québécois volunteers had been put under the command of British Canadian officers, exacerbating ethnic tensions and undermining French Canadian morale.[26] In Ireland, Catholics enlisted at a lower rate than Ulstermen, but, despite the myth of lack of Catholic commitment to the war effort, more recent analysis has shown that the key differentials in rates of enlistment fractured along different lines, higher in the industrial north-east and more sluggish in farming districts and the impoverished Atlantic fringe.[27] Similar charges were laid against Irish Catholics in Australia, as the rate fell from 35,000 volunteers a month in 1915 to 6,000 by 1916, although, as in Canada and Ireland, the differences in rates of enlistment between urban and rural areas, the latter always lower, seem to have been significant factors.[28]

For Britain, however, the issue was not just the numbers of recruits but also their quality. Throughout the war there were concerns about the loyalty of Catholic Irish recruits, and stories circulated in Britain about their deficiencies as soldiers.[29] There were also concerns about the lack of discipline of colonial troops, particularly the Australians, although overall Australian battalions were seen as effective front-line soldiers.[30] A more pressing question, however, was the suitability of non-European soldiers both to fight for the empire and to defend British possessions, as occupying forces were reduced to a skeleton to bolster forces in Europe. Another consideration was the concern to avoid sending blacks into combat to fight against Europeans, a factor that meant that Indians, Africans, and West Indian troops more often fought in Africa and the Middle East than in Europe. Prevailing nineteenth-century ideas of the superiority of Europeans as a 'martial race', combined with suspicions about the loyalty of non-European peoples, grounded in experiences such as the 1857 First Indian War of Independence (for Britain the Indian Mutiny), meant Britain and the dominions were cautious about mobilizing large numbers of indigenous peoples. In Australia, where the Aboriginal population was small and the ideology that they were a 'dying race' particularly prevalent, there were in fact formal legislative provisions banning their enlistment. As the number of volunteers waned, however, desperate recruiting officers turned a blind eye to these restrictions, and over 500 Indigenous Australians eventually fought

---

[26] See Bothwell, *The Penguin History of Canada*, 290–3, and R. Matthew Bray, 'Fighting as an Ally: The English Canadian Response to the Great War', *Canadian Historical Review*, 61 (1980), 141–68.

[27] See David Fitzpatrick, 'Home Front and Everyday Life', in Horne (ed.), *Our War*, 133–4.

[28] See Stephen Garton and Peter Stanley, 'The Great War and its Aftermath, 1914–22', in Alison Bashford and Stuart Macintyre (eds), *The Cambridge History of Australia*, ii (Melbourne: Cambridge University Press, 2013), 51–2, and Robson, *The First AIF*, 62–81.

[29] Philip Orr, '200,000 Volunteer Soldiers', in Horne (ed.), *Our War*, 75.

[30] Peter Stanley, *Bad Characters: Sex, Crime, Mutiny, Murder and the Australian Imperial Force* (Sydney: Murdoch Books, 2010).

with distinction as fully-fledged members of Australian units in Europe and the Middle East.[31] In Africa blacks were the bulk of support forces—porters, guides, scouts, cooks—although, with the protracted campaign in East Africa, more Africans became front-line soldiers, and, as the war in Europe dragged on, some black units were sent to the Western Front.[32]

The exceptions were indigenous peoples in New Zealand and the peoples of northern regions of India. Maori enlistment was significant, and their long-standing reputation as a 'noble war-like people' encouraged recruiting authorities to accept and even encourage their enlistment. The status of Maori had long been far higher than that of Australian Aborigines, and Maori forces were an integral part of the New Zealand Force, with over 2,000 Maori serving overseas.[33] Indian enlistment was more contentious. Given the size of its population and the long tradition of Sepoy forces, there was no doubt that British authorities in India were going to need significant recruitment of Indian troops. Nevertheless, in this context prevailing stereotypes about the 'martial races' of the mountainous North-West, the Punjab, and the Himalaya regions, notably Afghans, Pathans, Baluchis, Sikhs, and Gurkhas, meant recruitment was focused largely in these regions. Many of these soldiers came from traditional warrior castes, although as the war progressed recruitment officers had to extend the net to other tribes and groups, such as Coorgs, Mahars, Telegus, Berads of Bombay (Mumbai), and Tiyars of Malabar. Improved pay and benefits encouraged enlistment, although British authorities continued to focus their recruitment efforts on the North rather than the South.[34]

Throughout the empire rates of voluntary enlistment began to decline and by 1916 represented a significant manpower crisis for Britain's imperial forces. Exhortations to enlist became more urgent, and increasingly the net widened to encompass groups previously thought unsuitable for combat. Manpower imperatives also trumped race sensibilities, and by 1918 there were Indians, West Indians, and Africans in France and Belgium fighting alongside British and dominion soldiers. Even the calibre of dominion soldiers waned as shortages became more acute. By early 1918, Sir Neville Howse, head of the Australian Imperial Force Medical Services in London, was complaining about the physical and mental condition of new Australian recruits. In 1917 alone he returned 16,000 to Australia as unsuitable as they were suffering variously from senility, deformed hands, missing fingers, flat feet, imbecility, epilepsy, and other debilitating conditions.[35] In the end many parts of the empire, with the notable exceptions of Australia, Ireland, and Newfoundland, resorted to conscription in a desperate effort to sustain the manpower required to prosecute the war effort, although conscription did not add significantly

[31] Alick Jackomos and Derek Fowell, *Forgotten Heroes: Aborigines at War from the Somme to Vietnam* (Melbourne: Victoria Press, 1993).
[32] Perry, *The Commonwealth Armies*, 187–202.
[33] James Cowan, *Maori in the Great War* (Christchurch: Willsonscott, 2011; first published 1926).
[34] See S. D. Pradhan, 'The Indian Army and the First World War', and DeWitt C. Ellinwood, 'The Indian Soldier, the Indian Army and Change, 1914–1918', in Ellinwood and Pradhan (eds), *India and World War I*, 49–67, 177–211.
[35] See Garton and Stanley, 'The Great War and its Aftermath', 55.

to the empire's military manpower, most of the conscript forces seeing action only by 1918.[36]

By 1917, from the perspective of Westminster, declining imperial enthusiasm for the war effort presented an acute political and manpower crisis. The Western Front appeared to be bogged down in stalemate, with little prospect of gain for either side. Breaking the deadlock seemingly involved greater manpower and resources at a time when enthusiasm was at its lowest. In this desperate context Westminster both increased pressure on President Wilson to bring the United States into the war, succeeding in April 1917, and sought to make concessions to nationalist forces in the empire to sustain commitment to the war effort. In June 1917 Edwin Montague, the new Secretary of State for India, proposed greater efforts towards the 'development of self-governing institutions in India', and later that year he travelled to India to meet Indian nationalist leaders to discuss this proposal. The subsequent 1918 Montagu–Chelmsford Report committed Britain to post-war reforms to promote gradual Indian self-government.[37]

Anxiety over President Wilson's commitment to peace, the worsening political situation in Russia, falling recruitment numbers, declining enthusiasm in the empire for supplying further men and materiel, and threats of open rebellion in parts of the empire, notably Ireland, fostered the belief that Britain needed to make more concessions to colonial sensibilities. If the allies were to break the stalemate in Europe, the British government needed to shore up support within the empire for a renewed war effort. In this context Britain hoped that support for the Zionist cause might radically shift the landscape, potentially strengthening support for the war in the USA and Russia and hopefully bringing additional financial aid for the war effort, although it ran the risk of alienating Arabic support, which it had actively courted since 1915. The Balfour Declaration of October 1917 proposed Palestine as a national home for Jewish peoples, setting in train post-war political tensions between Arabic nationalists and Zionists that were profoundly to affect Middle East politics for generations to come.[38] What seemed to be prudent diplomatic initiatives to sustain the war effort in 1917 eroded imperial bonds in the post-war era. While some dominions secured mandated territories as a consequence of Versailles, becoming minor imperial powers themselves, Britain's efforts to court both Arabic and Zionist support imploded. Furthermore, the 1919 Egyptian uprising against British rule was a visible manifestation of deep disquiet about British efforts to control former territories of the Ottoman Empire.

Combat also transformed the empire experience. While colonial contingents had fought in earlier campaigns (Sudan and South Africa, for example), the scale and enormity of the Great War was such as to bring many subjects and citizens of the empire together, physically and culturally, for the first time (see Fig. 16).

---

[36] Robson, *The First AIF*, 167–81; Keith Sinclair, *A History of New Zealand*, rev. edn with additional material from Raewyn Dalzeil (Auckland: Penguin, 2000), 249–50; Bothwell, *The Penguin History of Canada*, 305–6; Bray, 'Fighting as an Ally', 141–68; and Fitzpatrick, 'Home Front and Everyday Life', 141–2.

[37] Judith M. Brown, *Modern India*, 204–7.

[38] See Jonathan Schneer, *The Balfour Declaration: The Origins of the Arab–Israeli Conflict* (New York: Random House, 2010).

Fig. 16. The polyglot empire: soldiers from around the empire fight for Britain.

Soldiers of the empire served in all the major campaigns of the war and saw some of the most intense fighting—Gallipoli, the Somme, Paschendaele, Sinai and Palestine. Moreover, despite initial efforts to prevent black regiments from fighting in Europe, evident in the fact that initially West Indian and Indian regiments were largely deployed in Africa and the Middle East, the manpower shortages in Europe inevitably led to their participation on the Western Front, where they fought alongside British and dominion forces and against Germany and its allies. While most Indian regiments served in Africa and the Middle East, by 1918 over 100,000 Indian soldiers were stationed in Europe.[39]

The experience of the front line could both efface and reinforce race prejudice. Indian soldiers felt that they laboured under greater restrictions on leave than their British and dominion counterparts and complained at what they saw as unfair treatment by British officials.[40] Sometimes prejudice was overt. In 1918 the British West Indies Regiment was denied a pay rise granted to all other imperial troops. As a result, 180 sergeants in the regiment petitioned the Secretary of State, complaining about pay and also discrimination with respect to promotions. The tardy response from British authorities incited a mutiny by the regiment in December 1918 at Taranto in Italy, and West Indian soldiers were eventually granted a similar increase.[41] On the other hand, soldiers from around the empire bonded over their shared combat experience and contempt for the British High Command. Moreover, soldiers of colour often won new-found respect. Indian soldiers earned nearly

---

[39] Ellinwood, 'The Indian Soldier, the Indian Army and Change', 183.
[40] Ellinwood, 'The Indian Soldier, the Indian Army and Change', 202–3.
[41] W. F. Elkins, 'A Source of Black Nationalism in the Caribbean: The Revolt of the British West Indies Regiment at Taranto, Italy', *Science and Society*, 34/1(1970), 99–103.

Fig. 17. The pull of home: an Australian soldier in Egypt sustains his bond to the nation while fighting for the empire.

13,000 honours during the war, including twelve Victoria Crosses, and eventually a number were awarded Kings Commissions to command their own units.[42]

At the front line imperial forces found that, while they shared a language and a political heritage, there were differences of accent and idiom that marked them apart. Even though significant numbers of those in Australian, New Zealand, and Canadian units, for instance, had been born in the United Kingdom, time away from home had shaped them, sharpening their sense that things were different in the colonies. Soldiers could share stories of life in their part of the empire, highlighting the differences in the experience not only of the dominions but also between dominion soldiers and those in other parts of the empire. Moreover, British military disasters, particularly in the first three years of the war, punctured the image of British military might, something felt powerfully by Indian and Irish soldiers.[43] The exigencies of the war also fostered greater independence and autonomy among imperial forces. Indian officers experienced the pressures of command. At Gallipoli the Australian and New Zealand units served together as the Australian and New Zealand Army Corps, one part of the overall British Expeditionary Force, but on the Western Front they split into the Australian Imperial Force and the New Zealand Expeditionary Force and were increasingly under colonial rather than British command.[44] These experiences reinforced a sense of difference and independence from Britain (see Fig. 17). In some instances empire soldiers felt bonded more closely to each other than to the heartland of the empire

---

[42] Ellinwood, 'The Indian Soldier, the Indian Army and Change', 197–204.
[43] Ellinwood, 'The Indian Soldier, the Indian Army and Change', 197–204. See also Orr, '200,000 Volunteer Soldiers', 65–77.
[44] Garton and Stanley, 'The Great War and its Aftermath', 42–7.

they fought for. After demobilization, an Indian soldier in Bombay, for instance, wrote to the local paper quoting the views of an Australian officer friend that 'Empire be d—d. I have nothing in an Empire where I am not the equal of any other.'[45] For some the war experience represented a loss of faith in empire.

HOME-FRONT TENSIONS

The contribution of the British Empire, particularly the dominions, to financing, resourcing, and fighting the war in Europe and the Middle East, had significant economic, political, and cultural effects at home. On the peripheries of empire these were in part shaped by local circumstances, but, from a transnational perspective, what is noteworthy are the commonalities in home front experiences across diverse parts of the empire. In fundamental ways the commitment to support the war effort imposed significant financial and manpower burdens on those parts of Britain's empire most heavily involved, and the results were economic, social, and political stresses that frayed support for the war, divided these societies, and raised important questions about the future of the empire. The consequences for imperial relations varied enormously, largely dependent on how different parts of the empire came to interpret the meaning of the war, commemorate the war dead, and manage demobilization, but the experience of the war years was shaped by common strains and pressures. What began as 'innocent enthusiasm' ended in acrimony and recrimination.[46]

Economic pressures were acute. With the declaration of war, Britain needed funds, material resources, and manpower from its far-flung empire. In large part these were supplied by the economically powerful and prosperous dominions— particularly Canada, Australia, and New Zealand, as well as India. The effects were threefold. First, enlistment created acute labour shortages in some sectors. Secondly, significant funds had to be raised to support the war effort and this meant both long-term indebtedness, depressing post-war economies, but also the diversion of capital from broad-based economic development to war industries (clothing, arms, equipment) and primary production (particularly food). Thus some sectors of the economy experienced significant growth and others languished, unable to raise the capital to expand or maintain productivity. Finally, much of the productivity of primary and secondary wartime industry was sent overseas. Again this advantaged some sectors of the domestic economy, such as shipping and transport, but discouraged investment in others.[47] Where local capital was insufficient

---

[45] Quoted in Jim Masselos, 'Some Aspects of Bombay City Politics in 1919' in Ravinder Kumar (ed.), *Essays on Gandhian Politics: The Rowlatt Satyagraha of 1919* (Oxford: Oxford University Press, 1971), 145.

[46] The phase 'innocent enthusiasm' comes from John Herd Thompson, *The Harvests of War: The Prairie West 1914–18* (Toronto: McCelland and Stewart, 1983), 12.

[47] See Judith M. Brown, 'War and the Colonial Relationship: Britain, India and the War of 1914–18', in Ellinwood and Pradhan (eds), *India and World War I*, 33–5; Fitzpatrick, 'Home Front and Everyday Life', 137–8; and Stuart Macintyre, *The Oxford History of Australia*, iv. *1901–1942* (Melbourne: Oxford University Press, 1986), 154–5.

to meet wartime demands, governments sometimes stepped in to bridge the gap. In Australia the shipping industry was insufficient to supply the transport requirements of troops and materiel to Europe, and the government established the Commonwealth Shipping Line to meet the shortfall.[48]

These structural dimensions of the wartime economies of empire had a significant impact on everyday life on the home front. The most obvious effects were acute shortages of key goods and services, which in turn fuelled domestic inflation. Throughout the empire, notably Canada, Australia, and India, prices rose as much as 30 per cent throughout the war. Wage rises, however, lagged well behind, rising only 12 per cent in the same period in Australia, with a similar lag in Canada, New Zealand, and India. Added to this was an increased burden of taxation in many parts of the empire to fund the war effort. Indian land taxes had almost doubled by 1917 and import duties on textiles rose 7.5 per cent.[49] The result was considerable economic hardship at home, and, as the war dragged on the effect of these trends became more acute. From early 1917 onwards there were an increasing number of trade union strikes in many parts of the empire as those at home became increasingly frustrated at the burden they were bearing. Canada had 169 strikes in 1918, more than the total for the previous three years. In Australia the New South Wales General Strike of 1917, over wages and conditions in the railways, was merely the most disruptive of a series of strikes across a range of industries.[50] Protest, however, extended well beyond the bounds of organized labour. Food riots, lead by farming communities and tribes in parts of rural India, protested rising prices for such staples as salt, oil, and spices. In 1918 India's first major famine in a decade added to the widespread misery.[51] Protest was not confined to the countryside. In Australia Melbourne housewives, spurred on by feminists, led a major protest about rising prices and chronic food shortages.[52]

These grievances were exacerbated by evidence that others were prospering. While some industries suffered as a consequence of war, others thrived, supplying essential resources for the war effort or benefiting from the absence of British competition. In India, iron, steel, cement, chemical, and engineering manufacturing surged on the back of war demand, while merchants and manufacturers in cotton, wool, and paper industries, freed from competition from Lancashire mills, could both supply the domestic Indian market and exploit inflation to make considerable profits.[53] Irish farmers did well supplying food because of German blockades, but urban workers suffered shortages and significant inflation as a consequence, and rationing had to be introduced.[54] In many parts of the empire stories circu-

[48] Garton and Stanley, 'The Great War and its Aftermath', 50.
[49] Sarkar, *Modern India*, 170.
[50] Thompson, *The Harvests of War*, 160–1, and Lucy Taksa, 'Defence not Defiance: Social Protest and the NSW General Strike of 1917', *Labour History*, 60 (1991), 16–33.
[51] Krishnan G. Saini, 'The Economic Aspects of India's Participation in the First World War', in Ellinwood and Pradhan (eds), *India and World War I*, 162–3.
[52] Judith Smart, 'Feminists, Food and the Fair Price: The Cost of Living Demonstrations in Melbourne, August–September 1917', *Labour History*, 50 (1986), 117–29.
[53] Saini, 'The Economic Aspects of India's Participation in the First World War', 162–6.
[54] Fitzpatrick, 'Home Front and Everyday Life', 137–8.

lated about war 'profiteering', further fuelling anger, resentment, and the conviction that ordinary citizens were bearing the brunt while local capitalists were thriving.

Throughout the empire the maintenance of public order and the suppression of dissent during the war was a paramount consideration for colonial governments. In the dominions, India, Ireland, and other parts of the empire, legislation affording governments greater powers to detain citizens and censor publications were widely enacted. Vigorous censorship bureaucracies were established to police public discourse to ensure that anti-British or pro-German sentiments did not circulate freely. Books, articles, magazines, newspapers, and pamphlets that might undermine home front morale or question the war effort were rigorously scrutinized and stopped. Similarly, severe restrictions on rights of public assembly were imposed. In Australia and India, for example, gatherings of more than three to five people were outlawed unless police permission was obtained. Censorship and coercion were matched by propaganda. In India, the Central Publicity Board produced 4 million leaflets, 2.5 million war journals, and over 300,000 posters, and issued 275 communiqués, in an effort to sustain public support for the war effort.[55]

Increased powers of surveillance and coercion were essential in suppressing local opposition to the war. In India, revolutionaries associated with the Ghader movement were routinely imprisoned.[56] While the threat of revolt was far less serious in Australia, authorities were no less ruthless in utilizing wartime powers to stamp out radical movements. In 1917 leaders of a radical labour group, the Industrial Workers of the World, were sentenced to three years in prison on trumped-up arson charges.[57] The most dramatic incident of wartime suppression was the execution of the republican leaders of the Easter 1916 rebellion in Dublin. Within days of the quelling of the revolt the government arrested nearly 3,500 citizens and of these 90 were sentenced to death. In the end fourteen of the leaders were shot by firing squad within three weeks of the first shots being fired, for ever turning these rebels into martyrs for the republican cause.[58] Social regulation during wartime, however, also touched more mundane matters. There were increased regulations governing the sale of alcohol and hotel opening hours, restrictions on horse-racing, sport, and others leisure activities, all to maintain order and encourage enlistment—actions that circumscribed everyday life on the home front.[59]

Internment of immigrants went hand in hand with heightened policing of the home front, particularly in Canada and Australia, which both had substantial German communities. Australia interned nearly 7,000 supposed 'enemy aliens',

---

[55] Barrier, 'Ruling India: Coercion and Propaganda in British India', 93–101.

[56] Barrier, 'Ruling India: Coercion and Propaganda in British India', 75–6. See also Sarkar, *Modern India*, 148–50.

[57] Ian Turner, *Sydney's Burning: The Real Conspiracy* (Melbourne: Heinemann, 1967).

[58] See Michael McNally and Peter Dennis, *Easter Rising 1916: Birth of the Irish Republic* (Dublin: Osprey, 2007); Peter Hart, *The IRA at War, 1916–23* (Oxford: Oxford University Press, 2003); and Fearghal McGarry, *The Rising: Ireland, Easter 1916* (Oxford: Oxford University Press, 2010).

[59] Michael McKernan, *The Australian People and the Great War* (Melbourne: Collins, 1984), 94–115.

even though many were second-generation German Australians. In the climate of fear fostered by the discourse of internal threats, communities acted to prove their 'loyalty'. Over seventy towns and hamlets in Australia acted expeditiously to change their established German name to something more Australian—Steinfeld became Stonefield and Blumberg became Birdwood. In Canada, under the terms of the 1914 War Measures Act, 80,000 citizens of German, Austrian, Hungarian, and Ukrainian descent were registered as 'enemy aliens', and nearly 9,000 were placed in labour camps.[60]

Despite these measures repressing dissent and cultivating loyalty, social, ethnic, religious, and political fissures widened under the pressures of war mobilization. Some of these tensions crystallized around questions of recruitment. Conscription was a vexed question in many parts of the empire, particularly the dominions and Ireland. In 1916 and 1917, as the numbers of volunteers flagged, colonial and do-minion governments, under pressure from Whitehall to sustain troop numbers, proposed conscription, igniting broader social divisions over the war. Irish repub-licans and nationalists alike, the labouring classes more generally, and specifically French Canadians and Irish Catholic Australians were widely seen as the chief opponents of conscription. Anti-conscription leagues sprang up throughout the dominions and in Ireland, and there were riots and marches opposing conscription in many parts of the empire. While these campaigns suggest that opposition to conscription was indeed commonly along lines of class, ethnicity, and religion—especially working-class Irish Australians and French Canadians, in opposition to middle-class, Protestant, British born-loyalists—more recent research has compli-cated this picture, pointing to significant opposition in rural areas, which feared losing already scarce farm labour. In Australia working-class women voted differ-ently from their male counterparts, favouring conscription, on the basis that sons and husbands fighting overseas needed more support.[61]

The battle over conscription was bitterly fought, especially in Australia, where the government collapsed as a consequence. The Labor prime minister William Morris Hughes held a national referendum on conscription in 1916 in a desperate effort to overcome opposition to conscription within his own party. It failed. As a result he resigned from the Labor Party crossing the floor with a small group of like-minded members to join forces with the conservative opposition, forming a new Nationalist government, retaining the position of prime minister. He went to the people again on the conscription question in 1917. Mass demonstrations led by trade unions, the Catholic Church, and anti-Hughes factions in the Labor Party opposed conscription a second time, securing victory again, although Labor found itself in the political wilderness for almost two decades thereafter. While these bitter disputes cemented the image of working-class Irish Catholic Australians as

[60] See Gerhard Fischer, *Enemy Aliens: Internment and the Home Front Experience in Australia, 1914–20* (St Lucia: University of Queensland Press, 1989), and Larry Hannant, *The Infernal Machine: Investigating the Loyalty of Canada's Citizens* (Toronto: University of Toronto Press, 1995).
[61] See Thompson, *Harvests of War*, 150–2; Sinclair, *A History of New Zealand*, 249–50; and Both-well, *The Penguin History of Canada*, 305–7. On gender and conscription, see Glen Withers, 'The 1916–17 Conscription Referenda: A Cliometric Reappraisal', *Historical Studies*, 20/78 (1982), 36–47.

'disloyal', closer examination suggests that some Australians voted against conscription, not because they opposed the war but because they questioned the morality of sending men against their will, fearing 'blood on their hands'.[62]

On the peripheries of empire, especially in the dominions, India, and Ireland,
social, economic, ethnic, and political tensions worsened in the final years of the
war. The return of servicemen after the Armistice added another destabilizing element to what many feared was already a volatile mix. Returned servicemen, especially the injured, ill, permanently disabled and psychologically scarred, represented
not only a significant burden on the exchequer, but also a challenge in terms of
social reintegration. The joy of return was short lived when soldiers confronted
stagnant economies and divided civil societies. After an immediate spike in many
economies in the first few months after the Armistice, by mid-1919 the contraction in war production, the difficulties industries faced shifting from wartime to
peace-time manufacture, the contraction in world trade in part arising from shipping being engaged in demobilization, the post-war burden of extensive debt,
falling commodity prices, and in India bad harvests, propelled a sharp economic
downturn.[63]

Economic decline heightened widespread concern about the 'character' and
'temperament' of the men returning. Reports of the riots in the demobilization
camps overseas added to the general anxiety that war may have 'brutalized' veterans, making them unfit for civilian life.[64] Reports of roving bands of veterans, in
Canada and elsewhere, randomly attacking labour organizers, 'price-gouging' res-
taurants, shops, and factories run by profiteers, and immigrant businesses, fuelled
these perceptions.[65] These men were widely seen as emotionally scarred by years of
killing, which had robbed them of normal human sympathies.[66] Politicians, such
as former Australian prime minister John Watson, commonly remarked on the
'unsettled condition' of returned servicemen.[67] Such anxieties and fears underpinned the widespread desire to settle veterans on the land, especially in the dominions, where soldier settlement schemes in Canada, Australia, and New Zealand
were a favoured means of getting disgruntled veterans out of cities where they
might be prey to dissipation and onto the land where they could become sturdy
yeoman farmers. Britain also saw the potential of land settlement as a means of

[62] Robson, *The First AIF*, 82–141.
[63] See Bothwell, *The Penguin History of Canada*, 313–15; Careless, *Canada: A Story of Challenge*,
356–7; Sarkar, *Modern India*, 174–5; Jane Leonard, 'Survivors', in Horne (ed.), *Our War*, 215–17;
Garton and Stanley, 'The Great War and its Aftermath', 58–9.
[64] See Andrew Rothstein, *The Soldiers' Strikes of 1919* (Basingstoke: Macmillan, 1980), and Desmond Morton and Glenn Wright, *Winning the Second Battle: Canadian Veterans and the Return to
Civilian Life 1915–1930* (Toronto: University of Toronto Press, 1987), 110–12.
[65] See Desmond Morton, *When your Number's Up: The Canadian Soldier in the First World War*
(Toronto: Random House, 1993), 269–70, and Stephen Garton, *The Cost of War: Australians Return*
(Melbourne: Oxford University Press, 1996), 9–16.
[66] See Joanna Bourke, *An Intimate History of Killing: Face-To-Face Killing in Twentieth-Century
Warfare* (London: Granta,1999), 345–68.
[67] 'Report of the Conference of Representatives of the Commonwealth and State Governments in
Respect of the Settlement of Returned Soldiers on the Land', 1914–17, 1469–73.

easing the burden of reintegrating veterans, establishing an empire settlement scheme to send British veterans to the dominions to take up farms.[68]

Soldier settlement schemes, however, were part of a more comprehensive set of policy measures to ease the reintegration of veterans into civilian life. Generous re-establishment benefits included pensions, employment preference, educational and vocational schemes, housing loans, in some countries employment preference for government positions, and extensive hospital, medical, and convalescent services. Politicians in Britain and throughout the empire trumpeted the noble sacrifice of those who had served, and that of the families of those who had died for King and Country, as the condition for the debt that needed to be repaid. High-minded rhetoric, no matter how well meaning, created the potential for what Adam Seipp has called a 'crisis of reciprocity'.[69] Despite promises of compensation it was rarely enough in the eyes of veterans, who found the reality fell far short of expectations. Demeaning eligibility tests, long queues, parsimonious employers, officious bureaucrats, and sullen resentment from civilians created the conditions for veteran disillusionment. In Canada thousands marched in support of the 'Calgary Resolution', demanding a significant bonus for veterans to compensate them for lost income.[70] In Australia the prime minister, William Morris Hughes, despite his sympathies for returned servicemen, was driven to despair over their constant demands for more benefits, tartly commenting that he could not 'work miracles'.[71]

The economic and social strains on the home front during the war, exacerbated by the sharp economic downturn from 1919, along with the return of disgruntled soldiers, created a volatile climate that erupted in a series of strikes, riots, and other forms of social conflict in the immediate post-war years in Britain and throughout many parts of the empire. While many of these conflicts were more than veteran struggles, broader manifestations of deep social divisions and economic tensions, returned servicemen were often prominent participants in these tumultuous events. In June 1919 the most famous Canadian labour conflict of the twentieth century was fought on the streets of Winnipeg, where over 20,000 trade unionists clashed with police and militia over wages and conditions, resulting in two deaths and thirty seriously wounded.[72] Canadian veterans fought on both sides of this struggle. In the same year veterans were also prominent on both sides of a series of major strikes throughout New Zealand, and again the unions were crushed.[73] In India agrarian and labour unrest continued after the war, culminating

---

[68] See Kent Fedorowich, *Unfit for Heroes: Reconstruction and Soldier Settlement in the Empire between the Wars* (Manchester: Manchester University Press, 1995).

[69] Adam R. Seipp, *The Ordeal of Peace: Demobilization and the Urban Experience in Britain and Germany 1917–1921* (Farnham: Ashgate, 2009), 3–23.

[70] Morton, *When your Number's Up*, 269.

[71] 'Report of the Conference of League Delegates with the Prime Minister W. M. Hughes', Returned Soldiers', Sailors' Imperial League of Australia Conference, Melbourne, 1919, 3–9.

[72] Bothwell, *The Penguin History of Canada*, 310–11, and David Jay, *Confrontation at Winnipeg: Labor, Industrial Relations, and the General Strike* (Montreal and Kingston: McGill-Queen's University Press, 1990).

[73] King, *The Penguin History of New Zealand*, 308–13.

in the March 1921 agrarian riots in Karhaiya, where ex-sepoys were conspicuous in the leadership.[74]

Returned servicemen also rioted in defence of veteran rights and entitlements. In Australia between 1919 and 1921, mobs of returned servicemen, involving oftentimes hundreds of men, attacked shops, other businesses, and government offices when they felt they had not been paid due respect. In Darwin veterans rioted over the slow and the grudging manner of provision of their entitlements. They stormed the residence of the local administrator and took over government offices.[75] Veterans were also prominent in violent protests against 'disloyalty'. In Britain and the dominions, returned men found the extent of radical labour activism threatening, potentially undermining the society they had fought for. Fears of 'the Red Menace' created a context where veterans believed that they were the citizens best equipped to defend the social order from disloyal elements and foreign influences. Sometimes this degenerated into violent attacks on immigrants. Xenophobia was widespread. In this context some veterans were prepared to take matters into their own hands.[76] In Australia there were at least eleven major riots against disloyalty in cities and towns around the country. These disturbances often involved hundreds of rioters, many of them returned servicemen, who attacked those they deemed disloyal—usually Irish Catholics, trade unionists, supporters of Sinn Fein, supposed Bolsheviks, and prominent labour activists, often depicted as those who had failed to support the Anzacs during the war.[77] As the immediate post-war tumult receded, however, some of the more radical returned soldier groups formed the nucleus of paramilitary organizations and 'secret armies' that sought to defend the social order against working-class radicalism throughout the interwar years.[78]

Veterans presented governments with the challenge of maintaining the social order under the intense pressure of demobilization. With the exception of Ireland, however, the empire remained intact, and neither Britain nor its colonies fell into the category of failed states common across parts of Europe and the Middle East, seen by George Mosse as evidence of brutalization moving from the individual to the collective. British, dominion, and colonial authorities instead negotiated the threats posed by returning men in order to restore the social order.[79] Victory

[74] Sarkar, *Modern India*, 176–7.

[75] Fiona Skyring, 'Taking Matters into their Own Hands: Riots against Disloyalty, 1918–1920 in Australia', Ph.D. thesis, University of Sydney, 1996.

[76] See, e.g., Seipp, *The Ordeal of Peace*, 21–3; Bothwell, *The Penguin History of Canada*, 310; Morton and Wright, *Winning the Second Battle*, 119–24; and King, *The Penguin History of New Zealand*, 308–13.

[77] Raymond Evans, *The Red Flag Riots: A Study of Intolerance* (St Lucia: University of Queensland Press, 1984). See also Skyring, 'Taking Matters into their Own Hands'.

[78] See Robert Gerwarth and John Horne, 'Vectors of Violence: Paramilitarism in Europe after the Great War, 1917–23', *Journal of Modern History*, 83 (September 2011), 489–512. For Australia, see Andrew Moore, *The Secret Army and the Premier: Conservative Paramilitary Organisations in NSW, 1930–32* (Kensington: UNSW Press, 1989), and Michael Cathcart, *Defending the National Tuckshop: Australia's Secret Army Intrigue of 1931* (Melbourne: McPhee Gribble, 1988).

[79] George Mosse, *Fallen Soldiers: Reshaping the Memory of the World Wars* (New York: Oxford University Press, 1990).

helped, but much more was required to cement the successful reintegration of disgruntled veterans. In Britain itself, as Jon Lawrence has argued, ideas of a 'peaceable' people were propagated to tie the nation together and offset the threat of brutalization, at a time of deep division and discontent.[80] Similarly in the dominions, nationalism became the ideological glue that prevented these countries from collapsing under the economic, social, and political pressures of the post-war world, while at the same time transforming their relationship to the empire. In the case of Ireland and India, however, nationalism became a means to challenge British colonial authority, setting them on the path to independence.

REIMAGINING THE EMPIRE

With the signing of the Treaty of Versailles, the British Empire reached its apogee, covering more of the globe than at any other time in its history. Former German colonies became mandated territories under British or British Dominion control, while parts of the former Ottoman Empire, especially in the Middle East, were similarly annexed. Within forty years, however, the empire had become a commonwealth—a constitutional simulacrum shorn of might and meaningful majesty. India and Ireland were now independent nations, the former dominions similarly nations in their own right, although in the case of Australia, New Zealand, and Canada with the British monarch still as the Head of State, and many other parts of the former empire, particularly in Africa and Asia, had achieved nationhood or were locked in bitter independence struggles. The seeds of this transformation, from empire to commonwealth, in many instances had been sown well before the Great War; home rule in Ireland, Afrikaner nationalism, and Indian independence were all nineteenth-century movements that persisted into the twentieth century. But the Great War accelerated the evolution of these forces for change and created a context in which the bonds of empire could be reimagined.

Integral to this reimagining was a new language of self-determination, popularized by President Woodrow Wilson. In the Indian summer of the 'Wilsonian Moment' anti-colonial nationalists embraced this new rhetorical framework for pressing their campaigns, moving away from an older discourse of home rule to that of self-determination. These hopes were dashed by the outcome of the Versailles Treaty, which left questions of colonial relations unanswered or deferred them to be considered at a later date by the League of Nations.[81] In the context of the British Empire more generally, however, nationalism became both the cement for social and political stability and the weapon for undermining imperial relations. Integral to the success of nationalism in both situations was war and post-war instability. Nationalism became a means of binding societies torn apart by ethnic,

---

[80] Jon Lawrence, 'Forging a Peaceable Kingdom: War, Violence and Fear of Brutalization in Post-First World War Britain', *Journal of Modern History*, 75/3 (September 2003), 557–89.
[81] Erez Manela, *The Wilsonian Moment: Self-Determination and the International Origins of Anticolonial Nationalism* (Oxford: Oxford University Press, 2007).

social, and economic tensions and also a means of capitalizing on those tensions to shift nationalism in colonial contexts from an elite to a mass movement. Here the experience of the dominions diverged from that of Ireland and India.

Canadian historian J. M. S. Careless has argued that 'dominion nationalism' was the common outcome of the Great War for Britain's dominions.[82] While Britain had declared war in 1914 without formal consultation with the dominions, after their experience of sacrifice each demanded a seat in its own right around the table at Versailles, and some became minor imperial powers themselves as a consequence of gaining control over mandated territories such as German New Guinea and Samoa. The Australian prime minister William Morris Hughes constantly highlighted his '60,000 dead' as the moral ground on which to press his particular claims at Versailles, often to the annoyance of other delegates, especially when asserting the rights of the 'white dominions' over 'lesser' allies such as Japan.[83] Nonetheless, there were also domestic pressures propelling nationalism. Afrikaner and Québécois minorities in South Africa and Canada respectively were alienated by their experience of the war, both at the front line and on the home front. In the immediate post-war years South African and Canadian politicians faced the dilemma as appeals to empire to bind the populace were losing appeal. Political survival in the interwar years became dependent on appeasing these ethnic minorities through appeals to national rather than imperial unity. In Canada, for example, the newly elected Liberal Party led by Mackenzie King was heavily dependent on Québécois support, and appealed to Canadian nationalism and the sense that the war was over, cementing a long period of Liberal government from 1921.[84]

Jay Winter, however, has provided a more complex picture of post-war nationalism in the dominions. While highlighting the greater independence of the dominions after the war and the ways nationalism was deployed to stabilize these post-war societies, he also explores how the experience of sacrifice and collective mourning for the lost generation also bound the empire together through 'ties of remembering'.[85] In the interwar years, through the Imperial War Graves Commission, forms of transnational remembrance such as Armistice Day, and the extraordinary proliferation of local community war memorials in the dominions, bonds of shared sacrifice for the empire were acknowledged and reinforced. Realpolitik, however, also played a part in perpetuating older imperial bonds in an age of dominion nationalism. Canada was wary of the dominance of the USA, and Australia and New Zealand were anxious about their isolation close to a 'threatening' Asia. But the bonds were also genuinely deep, culturally and emotionally, facets polished

---

[82] Careless, *Canada: A Story of Challenge*, 339–41.

[83] See L. F. Fitzhardinge, 'William Morris Hughes', in Bede Nairn and Geoffrey Serle (eds), *Australian Dictionary of Biography*, ix. *1891–1939* (Melbourne: Melbourne University Press, 1983), 393–400.

[84] See, e.g., John Selby, *A Short History of South Africa* (London: George Allen and Unwin, 1973), 225–7; T. R. H. Davenport, *South Africa: A Modern History*, 3rd edn (Basingstoke: Macmillan, 1987), 274–5; Bothwell, *The Penguin History of Canada*, 306–20; and Careless, *Canada: A Story of Challenge*, 341–5.

[85] Winter, *Remembering War*, 154.

by the shared experience of sacrifice. In Australia an older empire loyalism was welded to an emerging nationalism, creating a distinctive form—empire nationalism, where allegiance to empire was simultaneously allegiance to the nation.[86]

Leading politicians and spokesmen for the returned soldier cause in Australia proclaimed the landing at Gallipoli as the birth of the nation, and by 1917 Anzac Day, commemorating the landing, had emerged as the pre-eminent national day in Australia. Australian commemoration stood apart in other ways. Where commonwealth war memorials commonly recorded the names of those who had died, many Australian memorials engraved the names of all those who had served.[87] The Anzacs were symbolically transformed from soldiers for the empire into the embodiment of Australian national virtues—egalitarianism, an endearing larrikinism, mateship, and reckless bravery—at the centre of nationalist iconography, where they remain to this day.[88] Ironically this made the 'crisis of reciprocity' particularly acute in Australia. Returned men, given their supposed symbolic importance, were particularly aggrieved at the failure of governments adequately to recompense them, fuelling the returned soldier riots of the post-war years and encouraging higher participation in returned services organizations than their counterparts overseas.[89] A second consequence was that empire loyalism was retained as a central element of Australian national identity. Australian servicemen had fought for king and country, and in this context disloyalty was seen as manifest in criticism of either the nation or empire.

The pressing need to quell discontent and sustain political and social order in the post-war years was acute throughout the empire. While nationalism in Britain and the dominions, often reconfigured and imagined anew, was a vital measure utilized to tie the social order together and diffuse returned services discontent, in other contexts it became the touchstone for opposition to Britain and Empire. War and commemoration might cement imperial bonds, but the experience could also undermine faith in empire. War and return sharpened perceptions of racial prejudice. Many West Indian, African, and Indian soldiers, like their African American counterparts, returned home with a deep sense of grievance that their sacrifice had not resulted in greater equality of treatment. Such discontents added fuel to nationalist and civil rights movements.[90]

[86] See Stephen Garton, 'Demobilization and Empire: Empire Nationalism and Soldier Citizenship in Australia after World War I—in Dominion Context', *Journal of Contemporary History* 50 (2015), 124–143.

[87] See K. S. Inglis, *Sacred Places: War Memorials in the Australian Landscape* (Melbourne: Miegunyah Press, 1998); Chris Maclean and Jock Phillips, *The Sorrow and the Pride: New Zealand War Memorials* (Wellington: GP Books, 1990); and Robert Shipley, *To Mark our Place: A History of Canadian War Memorials* (Toronto: NC Press, 1987).

[88] See McLachlan, *Waiting for the Revolution*, 197–8, and Graham Seal, *Inventing ANZAC: The Digger and National Mythology* (St Lucia: University of Queensland Press, 2004). For an important feminist critique, see Marilyn Lake, 'Mission Impossible: How Men Gave Birth to the Australian Nation: Nationalism, Gender and other Seminal Acts', *Gender and History*, 4/3 (1992), 305–22.

[89] See Garton, *The Cost of War*, 74–117. On Canada, see Morton, *When your Number's Up*, 270.

[90] See Richard Smith, *Jamaican Volunteers in the First World War: Race, Masculinity and the Development of National Consciousness* (Manchester: Manchester University Press, 2004); Melvin E. Page (ed.), *Africa and the First World War* (Basingstoke: Macmillan, 1987); and Ellinwood, 'The Indian

Equally important events on the home front could propel the disintegration of imperial ties. Ireland is the obvious case. The political context there had changed irrevocably since Easter 1916. The nationalists were in decline, and republicanism under the leadership of Sinn Fein was dominant outside Ulster and the northern counties. While Ulster Unionists proclaimed and celebrated returning servicemen, according them many of the benefits conferred on other veterans in the empire, in the south returning men were seen as representatives of a now discredited political effort to win home rule concessions. Many returned feeling they had fought for the wrong cause, and those on the home front reinforced these perceptions. While they received basic pension benefits, there was widespread prejudice against them. As a consequence, unemployment among Irish veterans outside of Ulster was nearly 50 per cent, five times higher than in Britain. Worse, the IRA feared that veterans might side with Britain in the post-war battle for independence, and at least 120 veterans were killed by republican supporters in an effort to stamp out British loyalty among returning soldiers. While Ulster veterans commonly joined the special constabulary to fight republicanism and maintain the Protestant ascendancy, other Irish veterans faced difficult choices—join the IRA or face persecution. Some enlisted in armies overseas to escape. Instead of efforts to reintegrate into a society where they were accorded a special place as a consequence of their sacrifice, Irish veterans were dragged into the bloody civil war for the creation of the Irish Free State.[91] The immediate post-war years were convulsed by a violent and bitter republican struggle that eventually led to the 1921 Anglo-Irish Treaty, which granted independence and afforded the new Irish Free State dominion status, with the six counties around Ulster remaining part of the United Kingdom.[92]

Elsewhere in the empire the effort to shore up British authority and maintain social order after the war also backfired. The 1918 Montagu–Chelmsford reforms may have been seen in Whitehall as a genuine gesture towards limited self-government, but they fell far short of Indian expectations in the light of Wilsonian aspirations to self-determination. Moreover, British authorities failed to grasp the significance of a new leader on the Indian political stage. Gandhi had returned to India in 1915, and, although he had supported the war effort, he was determined to pursue new methods of civil disobedience to advance the independence cause. Much ink has been spilt on the role of Gandhi, but at a fundamental level he succeeded in turning an aspiration of the educated middle classes into a genuinely

Soldier, the Indian Army, and Change', 177–211. For African American soldiers, see Chad Williams, *Torchbearers of Democracy: African-American Soldiers in the World War I Era* (Chapel Hill, NC: University of North Carolina Press, 2010).

[91] See Jane Leonard, 'Survivors', in Horne (ed.), *Our War*, 211–23, and 'Facing the "Finger of Scorn": Veterans' Memories of Ireland after the Great War', in Martin Evans and Ken Lunn (eds), *War and Memory in the Twentieth Century* (Oxford: Berg, 1997), 59–72. See also Jeffrey, *Ireland and the Great War*, 107–43.

[92] See, e.g., Joost Augusteijn (ed.), *The Irish Revolution 1913–23* (Basingstoke: Palgrave, 2002); Hart, *The IRA at War 1916–23*; D. G. Boyce, *The Irish Question and British Politics, 1868–1996*, 2nd edn (Basingstoke: Macmillan, 1996), 59–66; and Conor Kostick, *Revolution in Ireland: Popular Militancy 1917–1923* (London: Pluto, 1996).

mass movement. He was assisted by the pervasive economic crises of the war and post-war years that created the seedbed of social discontent in the countryside and the cities, fertilized by the miscalculations of British authorities seeking to impose order in the aftermath of war.

British efforts to maintain firm control in the immediate post-war years played into Gandhi's hands—moving him from the periphery to the centre of the nationalist movement, uniting many of the diverse factions of the old independence movement, and creating effective, if fragile, links between Hindu and Muslim nationalists. Fearing post-war social disruption and discontent, British authorities in India sought to extend wartime powers of arrest and detention beyond the Armistice. In 1917 the British government in India established a committee to advise on how to control terrorism during and after the war. The Rowlatt Committee recommended wider police powers to suppress terrorism, and in 1919 the so-called Rowlatt Act was passed by Parliament. The outcry from Indian nationalists was immediate. Britain had, in their view, given with one hand a miserly and inadequate form of local government power and, on the other hand, taken from them powers of liberty and free speech accorded to British subjects elsewhere. Gandhi galvanized the protest, instituting mass civil disobedience in many parts of India. In Bombay nearly 150,000 millworkers went on strike in support of Gandhi's Rowlatt Satyagraha, and similar disturbances occurred throughout the country, especially in major towns and cities. In Bombay (Mumbai) Sir George Lloyd demonstrated remarkable restraint, but in the Punjab General Reginald Dyer ordered troops to fire on protesters in Amritsar, killing nearly 1,000 demonstrators and wounding many more—thereafter great martyrs to the independence cause. It was to be another twenty-five years before the Indian nationalist movement succeeded, but the Rowlatt Satyagraha had transformed the Indian nationalist movement into a force that was genuinely nationalist in aspiration and mass in scope.[93]

The Great War brought the British Empire together in defence of British and imperial interests, involving peoples from around the world in a global conflict that left few societies in the empire untouched by the effects. The outcome of mobilization, and the experience of war on the imperial periphery, had contradictory effects. In some respects it bound the empire together in collective remembrance of its participation in this war to end all wars. In other respects it unleashed nationalist aspirations and sentiments that undid empire. Even in Australia and New Zealand, where the response to the Great War was the promotion of ideals of loyalty to Britain and Empire, such sentiments could not be sustained without yoking them to new nationalist aspirations, creating a unique political philosophy of empire nationalism. Participation in the war and the social and political tensions arising domestically among the participants in Britain's empire fuelled national

[93] See, e.g., Kumar, *Essays on Gandhian Politics*; Judith M. Brown, *Modern India*, 202–7; Sarkar, *Modern India*, 175–99; Judith M. Brown, *Gandhi's Rise to Power: Indian Politics, 1915–22* (Cambridge: Cambridge University Press, 1972); and Hari Singh, *Gandhi, Rowlatt Satyagraha, and British Imperialism: Emergence of Mass Movements in Punjab and Delhi* (Delhi: Indian Bibliographies Bureau, 1990).

sentiments and a sense that Britain was in decline and new nations would have to be more self-reliant in the future. Wilson's ideals of self-determination crystallized nationalist aspirations, giving them a more radical focus. In this context the Great War in many ways hastened and in some instances initiated nationalist movements and sentiments around the empire. The British Empire may have reached its greatest geographical extent and political reach at the end of the war, but this triumph also spelled its demise. In many instances it took a second great global conflagration to precipitate the final death throes of empire and its transformation into a commonwealth of equal partners, but the Great War gave considerable momentum to these profound political and cultural forces. In this sense the Great War became not just a war for empire and between empires but also one, in ways many participants may not have understood at the time, against empire.

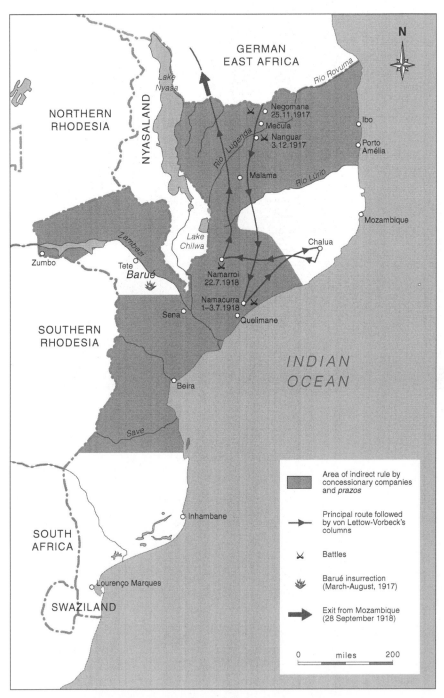

Map 7. Portuguese Africa at war. Allied forces were unable to trap and destroy General von Lettow-Vorbeck's columns in Mozambique (1917–18), leading to untold suffering for civilians and soldiers alike.

9

The Portuguese Empire

Filipe Ribeiro de Meneses

On 5 September 1923, Lisbon daily *O Século* described, on its front page, the previous day's commemorations of the Southern Angola campaign of 1914–15. During the event, attended by a large audience, the banners of the 1st Squadron of the Province of Angola Plateau Dragoons and the 1st Indigenous Machine-Gun Battery of Mozambique were decorated with the Military Valour medal, while that of the 5th Indigenous Infantry Company of Mozambique received the War Cross First Class. Metropolitan soldiers, white Angolan settlers, and black Mozambican soldiers were being rewarded for their bravery by a grateful and, as the newspaper saw it, common motherland. According to *O Século*, 'the whispering campaign which suggested that the glorious efforts of those who had fought in African lands, against men and against beasts, suffering from the inclement climate and the betrayal of so many blacks, had been forgotten, was defeated yesterday', in the face of the popular support evidenced in the streets of the capital. The article continued:

The meaning of the campaign currently being celebrated confers great prestige on the Republic. It was the first feat or arms carried out by the new regime and the blood that was shed was the first Portuguese blood shed on behalf of the cause for which, later, we would make so many sacrifices—the cause of the Allies, the cause of Law against injustice, the cause of Liberty and western culture against the militarist tyranny and barbarism of the Teutons.

This passage, and the event to which it refers, raise a number of immediate and important questions. Why was there fighting in the Portuguese colonies, even before the country was at war with Germany? What did the 'betrayals of so many blacks' consist of? And why was there a 'whispering campaign' against the memory of the military deeds now being commemorated? Answering these questions requires not only a summary of the events in wartime Portuguese Africa, but also a description of contemporary colonial policy, and a reflection on the nature of the Portuguese Empire. This was an enterprise in which myth usually trumped fact, and in which, by the twentieth century, metropolitan nationalist sentiment and aspirations obscured colonial realities with, unfortunately, tragic consequences. Charles Maier's definition of empire, summarized in the Introduction to this volume, is sufficiently wide to encompass Portugal and its colonies, an inchoate, if venerable, collection of territories scattered across three continents. Beginning with the First World War and culminating in the mass exodus of Portuguese settlers from Angola in 1975, as the once-prized colony slipped into civil war, Portuguese colonialism was marked by a tremendous misunderstanding, by the metropolitan population, of the nature of African life. A paradox thus emerges. It is true that, as Fernando Tavares Pimenta wrote recently, 'the "Portuguese Twentieth Century" was radically different from the "European Twentieth Century"' and that this 'difference resulted from the disproportionate weight of the colonial factor on Portuguese history'.[1] However, this does not mean that events in Africa permeated Portuguese consciousness, or that an 'imperial mentality' ever arose in Portugal; thus philosopher Eduardo Lourenço could describe, in 1974, the ongoing decolonization as a 'time-trial to get out of a colonial inheritance which does not touch us, which we do not even feel'.[2]

THE PORTUGUESE EMPIRE IN 1914

Portugal's constitutional monarchy embarked on a programme of colonial exploration and settlement towards the end of the nineteenth century, after long decades of neglect, as an attempt to compensate for a stalled modernization effort, known as *Regeneração*. The country, after a promising start, had shown itself incapable of catching up, by relying on its own resources, with other European powers in the economic, social, and political fields.[3] The monarchy and the political parties that served it then strived to reach a new compact with the people, built on the assumption that national glory and great wealth awaited in Africa—but it was ultimately the sight of others scrambling for that same Africa that woke Portugal from its colonial lethargy. Not much thought was given to the questions of why, or with what purpose, Portugal was about to act—but the sentiment that others were trespassing on lands the Portuguese had long seen as falling within their sphere spurred governments onwards. The Berlin Conference of 1884–5 hastened the realization that all this territory would be partitioned by other European powers, however long the history of Portugal's presence in Africa, if nothing was done quickly. And so, without much consideration for available resources, material and human, by 1887 Portugal, in the now famous *mapa cor-de-rosa* (pink map), was laying claim not only to Angola and Mozambique, whose borders had been more or less established, but to all the territory in between—the territory, roughly, of the future Federation of Rhodesia and Nyassland. This dizzying vision of a second Brazil in Africa, stretching from the Atlantic to the Indian Ocean, was quickly felled by the British, who, in January 1890, issued an ultimatum, forcing the Portuguese to withdraw their forces from what is today Zimbabwe.

---

[1] Fernando Tavares Pimenta, *Portugal e o século XX: Estado-império e descolonização (1890–1975)* (Lisbon: Edições Afrontamento, 2010), 8.
[2] Eduardo Lourenço, '"Requiem" por um império que nunca existiu', in Eduardo Lourenço, *O fascismo nunca existiu* (Lisbon: Dom Quixote, 1976), 97–115, at p. 99.
[3] Tavares Pimenta, *Portugal e o século XX*, 21.

What had begun as a venture into state-fomented nationalism by the Crown led to its, and the country's, humiliation; this failure was seized on by the rising Portuguese Republican Party, elements of which launched a first, unsuccessful, insurrection the very next year. Few, however, paused to ask why Portugal needed such vast tracts of territory, how it could occupy and develop them, and how it could impose its will on all their inhabitants. Thus, while lip service was paid to the general European colonial themes of the day—the spread of civilization and the Christian gospel—very little was done to ensure that this 'white man's burden' actually fell on the shoulders of the Portuguese who settled in the colonies, or who were sent there by the state, often as an alternative to custodial sentences at home.

The British Ultimatum did not spell the end of the monarchy's dalliance with Africa. Angola and Mozambique were still Portuguese, and British recognition of the fact was secured later that year; their borders with Belgian and German territories were also more carefully delineated (Belgium recognizing Portugal's right to the Lunda region of Angola, which turned out to be extremely rich, thanks to its plentiful diamond deposits). Moreover, their 'pacification' wars, long and costly, threw up many a hero—men such as Mouzinho de Albuquerque and Paiva Couceiro—for the Portuguese public to idolize, notably in the mid-1890s. But these were costly defensive campaigns, by which the Portuguese armed forces secured what diplomats had negotiated; they added nothing new to the territories, which were left, for the most part, untouched by the Portuguese, who simply did not have the funds required to transform their colonies. The inability to find Portuguese investors to amass and channel sufficient capital to the colonies led to the creation of Crown concessionary companies, which were active in Mozambique, but with disappointing results.[4] The colonies were also disdained by Portuguese emigrants, who continued to vote with their feet, crossing the Atlantic, notably to Brazil.

In October 1910 Portugal became a republic; power passed into the hands of a new governing elite, drawn from circles—urban middle classes—hitherto kept at arm's length. Although the Portuguese Republican Party would soon split into various warring parts, a reflection of the broad ideological spectrum it contained within its organization, all these factions agreed on the need for Portugal to continue as a colonial power. The Republicans were nationalists, with a peculiar but flawed reading of Portuguese history by which the national genius manifested in the past, notably at the time of the Discoveries, had been restrained, and then almost extinguished, by reactionary forces such as the Crown and the Catholic Church. It was the Republicans' mission to lead the people, through a process of self-discovery towards greatness, and the empire—still seen as a living link with that glorious past—had an important part to play in this process.[5] For them, then, the empire's

---

[4] On the subject of the Mozambique and Nyassa Companies, see, e.g., Leroy Vail, 'Mozambique's Chartered Companies: The Rule of the Feeble', *Journal of African History*, 17/3 (1976), 389–416, and Barry Neil-Tomlinson, 'The Nyassa Chartered Company', *Journal of African History*, 18/1 (1977), 109–28.

[5] Maria Cândida Proença writes: 'Aware of the strength of the empire in the formation of national unity and identity, republicans soon incorporated in their cultural and political discourse the defence, preservation and deveolopment of the overseas territories […]' 'A questão colonial', in Fernando Rosas

Fig. 18. Afonso Costa, the republic's leading statesman, understood the problems facing Portugal's colonies, but was powerless to bring about meaningful reform.

importance lay mostly in its didactic nature. The hope of extracting considerable wealth from Africa had also not been extinguished. When Afonso Costa, the undisputed leader of the Democratic Party, the regime's largest political formation, produced his first budget surplus, he allocated a significant part of the money left over to the navy, whose development was essential for the maintenance of Portugal's colonial ambitions (see Fig. 18). But that same Afonso Costa famously commented that what Portugal needed, for the sake of the empire, was not masses of poor people—it had plenty of those—to send as colonists to inhospitable lands, but rather a few men with lots of money to invest.[6] Since they were missing, investment had to come from the state, or the state had to become very involved in the running of the colonies to ensure that someone, somewhere, made a profit.

By then Costa and others had come to realize just how difficult it would be to turn their colonial aspirations into policy, and to implement that policy.

and Maria Fernanda Rollo (eds), *História da primeira república portuguesa* (Lisbon: Tinta da China, 2009), 205–28, at p. 205).

[6] This assertion was made in the context of Costa's application for a chair at Lisbon's Escola Politécnica, as a result of which he temporarily quit the cabinet. Selections from this thesis and other writings, speeches, and key pieces of legislation can be found in A. H. de Oliveira Marques, *Afonso Costa* (Lisbon: Arcádia, 1972).

The republic had a colonial programme, which its leaders believed would lead to a genuine transformation of Portugal's position in its overseas provinces. These were increasingly threatened by a host of enemies, animated by many and often contradictory sentiments; the most powerful of these, however, was Lisbon's inability to make the best possible use of the resources available to it in the colonies. Portugal's greatest sin, in the eyes of the rest of Europe, was its own poverty, which prevented it from carrying out the basic colonial mission of development. The wealth of Angola and Mozambique remained as untapped under Lisbon's authority as it had been under that of the local indigenous rulers. The republic's plans rested on the devolution of power to local authorities,[7] who would work alongside the population (that is, the local whites) to identify where and when reforms were needed in order to stimulate colonial life. Freed from the tutelage of the *Terreiro do Paço*, colonial authorities on the ground would take the decisions needed to develop the colonies rationally. It was the mirror image, in many ways, of the plan to devolve power in metropolitan Portugal to long-ignored municipal structures. Little was said that was new regarding the civilizing mission, and less still was done to make it come to life. In fact, by its opposition to the Catholic Church at home, the republic made the Church's cooperation in the colonies more difficult. Plans for 'lay missions' remained on the drawing board. Like the monarchy before it, the republic found it difficult to reconcile the interests of different groups involved in the colonial debate: metropolitan business interests, the (few) settlers on the ground, and the indigenous population.[8] Moreover, the republic could not afford to renounce the import and export duties applied to goods coming in and out of the colonies, even though these acted as yet another obstacle to the development of the colonies.[9]

---

[7] Article 67 of the 1911 Constitution read: 'The administration of the overseas provinces will be guided by the principle of decentralization, with laws especially designed to suit the level of civilization reached by each of them.' It would take until August 1914 for the first legislation—very broad, it must be said—to be passed laying out the republican vision for the future of the colonies, with guidelines established for the future 'organic charters' of each colony. Each colony was to have a governor, who would work alongside an elected/appointed *Conselho do Governo*, representing the local community. The more developed the colony, the deeper the presence of the administrative/political organs, with district governors/councils, and so on, down to the municipal and even parish level. This was the stuff of fantasy given conditions at the time. Instead of the forecast twelve months, it took nearly three years for the first Organic Charters to be drafted: Cape Verde (April 1917), Portuguese Guinea (31 May), Portuguese India (27 July), São Tomé e Príncipe (11 August), Timor (23 August), Macau (5 November), and Angola (28 November). Mozambique never received one. All were revoked by President Sidónio Pais in July 1918.

[8] Thus, while a May 1911 decree proclaimed that members of the the indigenous population were free to choose a job, they were obliged to work a certain number of days per year in order not to be considered a vagrant—a considerable loophole that allowed the state and private firms to secure free labour. Worse still, there was little enforcement of the laws that prohibited the physical punishment of workers in the colonies.

[9] Pedro Aires Oliveira writes: 'Renouncing the protectionist regime of 1892, thus allowing the colonial bourgeoisie to develop more vigorously, would entail significant losses for the metropolitan exchequer, something which was out of the question for the governing class in Lisbon'. P. Aires Oliveira, 'O factor colonial na política externa da Primeira República', in Filipe Ribeiro de Meneses and Pedro Aires Oliveira (eds), *A primeira república portuguesa: Diplomacia, guerra e império* (Lisbon: Tinta da China, 2011), 299–332, at p. 303.

Despite the change of regime, therefore, Portugal's central problem remained lack of money. Economic life, in the metropolis and in the colonies, remained sluggish; without adequate funds, there could be little administrative presence in Africa to enforce laws, however well meaning; without administration and material improvements (such as a working transport network), more settlers would not come. The financial life of the empire was entrusted to a single bank, the *Banco Nacional Ultramarino*. It was in a position to charge crippling interest rates, which it invariably did, to the detriment of the colonies. Military campaigns went on, as before, while the lack of sympathy across Europe's capitals for Lisbon's plight made foreign governments more receptive to complaints made by private groups against living and working conditions in Portuguese territories. Special attention was paid to the treatment of Angolan labourers shipped to the chocolate plantations of São Tomé e Príncipe, which became a *cause célèbre* in the years preceding the First World War.[10] All of these problems applied equally to the concessionary companies active in Mozambique, whose shareholders changed in accordance with interests and circumstances beyond Portugal's control, and whose performance, in terms of economic development and the defence of Portuguese sovereignty, fell well short of initial expectations.

Taking all of the preceding discussion into account, it is not surprising that the Portuguese Empire's experience of the First World War should have been completely original, and difficult to encompass in any generalization about empires in wartime. As Europe was dragged into the greatest war in living memory, Portugal was led by inexperienced and impractical politicians with little understanding of the realities of their international and colonial obligations. It is also not surprising that the very notion of mobilizing empire for war should be seen as alien when it comes to Portugal's war effort. Mobilization of human and material resources in order to affect the outcome of the fighting in Europe implied a material control over a territory, and a level of interaction with the population, that was simply beyond the ability of the Portuguese state and its agents to carry out. What limited mobilization took place was restricted to aiding the war effort in Africa, which consumed enormous European resources as well. René Pélissier, a French historian who had done more than anyone else to explain the Portuguese 'pacification' campaigns of the nineteenth and twentieth centuries, writes that 825 officers and 18,613 men were sent to Mozambique alone, to which must be added the 303 officers and 682 sergeants sent to command the 10,278 soldiers of the African units.[11] Uniquely, metropolitan Portugal was mobilized to secure the boundaries

---

[10] On labour abuses in São Tomé e Príncipe, see Lowell J. Satrem, *Chocolate on Trial: Slavery, Politics and the Ethics of Business* (Athens, OH: Ohio University Press, 2005); the relevant chapter in Kevin Grant, *A Civilized Savagery: Britain and the New Slaveries in Africa, 1884–1926* (New York: Routledge, 2005); and Catherine Higgs, *Chocolate Islands: Cocoa, Slavery and Colonial Africa* (Athens, OH: Ohio University Press, 2012).

[11] General Luís Augusto Ferreira Martins, in his *Portugal na grande guerra* (Lisbon: Ática, 1935–8), ii. 337, gives the following figures for Portugal's war effort in Africa: 32,000 officers and men sent to Africa; in Mozambique, Portuguese forces suffered 4,811 dead and 1,593 wounded, incapacitated, and missing; in Angola, the corresponding figures were 810 and 583. Coronel Freire de Andrade, in a report dated 25 February 1919, provided different figures for the various campaigns, totalling 1,128

of empire, at a difficult time, and with terrible human consequences, rather than the reverse. Remarkably, however, the defence of the empire was seen in Lisbon as a sideshow, with government efforts focused on the Western Front, to which a larger force, the *Corpo Expedicionário Português* (CEP), was sent. The scale of the promises made to the Allies in relation to both Africa and France resulted in the recruitment of wholly unsuitable men, as well as the placing of inexperienced, incompetent, or politically disenchanted officers in positions of great responsibility.[12]

What did mobilization of empire consist of, in the end, for Portugal? The largest colonies—Angola and Mozambique—were, as has been shown, greatly underdeveloped; Portuguese control, exercised ultimately by the threat of military force, was tenuous and only recently installed across much of these territories; the payment of a hut tax—often enforced not by official agents of the state but by simple travelling salesmen—was the sole point of contact between Africans and the Portuguese administration or its concessionary proxies. In the whole of Mozambique, and not employed by the state in one capacity or another, there were less than 1,000 settlers, concentrated mostly around Lourenço Marques, Manica, and Beira. The figures for Angola were comparable, although the number of mixed-race descendants of Portuguese, who formed a local elite, was much larger. As a result, both colonies served in peacetime as points of access to the African interior, notably Rhodesia, and as labour reservoirs. The colonial state had long participated in the securing of labour for private enterprise. Angola provided workers for the cocoa plantations in the São Tomé and Príncipe islands; Mozambique for the mines in the Rand and Rhodesian estates. Not surprisingly, then, it was labour that was most efficiently mobilized in the war, notably in the shape of porters for the campaigning armies, Portuguese and non-Portuguese alike. Full and accurate figures are hard to come by. Pélissier, based on an earlier work by E. Azambuja Martins, suggests that 30,000 porters were supplied to the British army, while 60,000 were used by the Portuguese.[13] The manner of their recruitment, and conditions endured while at the service of the armies, would have significant consequences. There were also, as we have seen already, units recruited throughout the empire, with Portuguese NCOs and officers leading African soldiers, who were, as a rule, deployed to any colony other than their own (the same not occurring to local

---

officers, 19,925 European soldiers, 10,778 indigenous soldiers, 116,381 porters, and thousands of animals. Ministério dos Negócios Estrangeiros (MNE), Arquivo Histórico Diplomático (AHD), Terceiro Piso, Armário 9, Maço 6B.

[12] British military authorities resisted the dispatch of the CEP to the Western Front, fearing that it would result in a weak spot in the Allied line. Portuguese insistence, allied to French pressure for men after the bloodlettings at Verdun and the Somme, overcame this resistance. See F. Ribeiro de Meneses, 'A grande aposta da república: O Corpo Expedicionário Português', in Ribeiro de Meneses and Aires Oliveira (eds), *A primeira república portuguesa*, 223–44.

[13] René Pélissier, *Naissance du Mozambique: Résistance et révoltes anticoloniales (1854–1918)*, ii. *La conquête* (Orgeval: Pélissier, 1984), 684. The figures were first advanced by E. Azambuja Martins, 'A campanha de Moçambique', in General Ferreira Martins (ed.), *Portugal na grande guerra*, ii (Lisbon: Ática, 1934). Azambuja Martins was General Ferreira Gil's chief of staff during the Mozambique campaign.

white troops). Finally, as we shall also see, and in line with previous practices, the Portuguese raised local 'auxiliaries'—friendly ethnic groups employed to devastate the areas held by those who rebelled against the state's authority.

In other words, while countries such as Great Britain and France (and even Belgium) used their colonies to strengthen their economic war effort, and to reinforce the armies fighting on the Western and other fronts, Portugal found itself having to commit European and African troops to the African battlefields; moreover, these were only in part deployed to face the small German forces arrayed against them. The greater part of the Portuguese war effort in Africa during the war was dedicated to fighting Africans.

MILITARY ACTIVITY IN ANGOLA AND MOZAMBIQUE, 1914–1918

Wrongly believing Portugal, England's oldest ally, to be at war with Germany, German military units carried out cross-border raids on Portuguese garrisons in southern Angola and northern Mozambique as soon as the war started in Europe. In December 1914, a subsequent border clash in southern Angola escalated, leading to a major German raid and the battle of Naulila, a Portuguese defeat.[14] The entire Portuguese defensive system in this recently 'pacified' region crumpled in the ensuing panic and a massive indigenous rebellion, involving the Kwanyama (Cuanhama, in Portuguese) people, began. The Portuguese then sought to re-establish control over Southern Angola, while the Allies conquered German South-West Africa. A new expedition sent by Lisbon was led by 63-year-old General Pereira de Eça. Uniting his troops with those still on the ground, he could count on 265 officers, 7,489 other ranks, and 60 cannon and machine guns. The occupation of the territory was carried out anew, alongside building of roads (800 kilometres), telegraph and telephone lines, and so on. This was an extremely brutal campaign, which saw the Portuguese pursuing a policy of terror, and there was widespread forcible conscription of men for labour, in both Angola and São Tomé. Allegations of war crimes carried out by these forces would be aired at the July 1917 secret sessions of parliament, in Lisbon.[15] And in the battle of Môngua, fought between 18 and 20 August 1915, the campaign witnessed one of the biggest ever ordered battles between African and European troops. One immediate consequence of Kwanyama King Mandume Ya Ndemufayo's defeat at Môngua was the massive flight of population into South-West Africa, by then under South African administration.

---

[14] For a recent account of these early clashes, see P. Southern, 'German Border Incursions into Portuguese Angola prior to the First World War', *Portuguese Journal of Social Science*, 6/1 (2007), 3–14.

[15] See F. Ribeiro de Meneses, 'Too Serious a Matter to be Left to the Generals? Parliament and the Army in Wartime Portugal, 1914–1918', *Journal of Contemporary History*, 33/1 (January 1998), 85–96.

Germany declared war on Portugal in March 1916. The Portuguese, who had strengthened their forces on the Mozambique–German East Africa border, quickly occupied the disputed territory of Kionga, on the right bank of the mouth of the Rovuma River,[16] but were repulsed later in April when they attempted to cross the river into the main portion of the German colony. In July General Ferreira Gil arrived, at the head of large expedition, with over 4,500 officers and enlisted men. He was under intense political pressure from the new Sacred Union government in Lisbon to produce a military triumph but, as Hew Strachan has shown, was a hostage to South African ambitions in Mozambique.[17] His eventual mission—to lead the Portuguese army into the interior of German territory, towards Masasi, away from the sea or any roads of note—was challenging; bereft of any meaningful experience of fighting in Africa, Ferreira Gil, who remained at his headquarters at Palma, on the coast of Mozambique, found it impossible to complete the mission. The Portuguese enjoyed a great numerical superiority but moved far too slowly. For the most part they were raw recruits, with little in the way of training for either battle or simply staying healthy in Africa. The logistical and medical support was poor, and Portuguese forces seemed to have no institutional memory of what campaigning in Africa entailed (incredibly, according to one account, their food consisted largely of salted cod, which required precious water to boil and which increased the men's thirst). They captured Newala, their first objective, on 22 October, but, already in a wretched state, could go no further. They were quickly surrounded by a smaller German force led by Captain Looff, commander of the sunk cruiser *Königsberg*, who brought with him one of the vessel's salvaged heavy guns. After a week-long siege, and after a relief effort had failed, the Portuguese escaped and fell back in disarray into Mozambique on the night of 28 November, converging on Palma in total disarray and being saved only from complete defeat by the rainy season and the timely intervention of British naval power. Casualties were very high, and Ferreira Gil was blamed for the debacle.[18] To make

[16] The retention of Kionga after the war's end quickly became a Portuguese war aim, but was by no means assured. The Committee of Imperial Defence's Sub-Committee on Territorial Changes, in its Second Interim Report, published on 22 March 1917, noted that the 'Portuguese have asked for a small rectification on the Southern border, which would give them the right bank of the River Rovuma to its mouth. The Committee consider that more precise information should be secured as to the value of the portion of German territory which lies south of the Rovuma, before it can pronounce an opinion on this point'. (TNA: PRO, Cabinet Papers).

[17] Hew Strachan establishes a link between Jan Smuts's desire, in 1915, to swap Mozambique south of the Zambezi River for putatively conquered German East African territory with Portugal, and his ambivalence, when installed as the overall commander of the British Empire forces in the area, about allowing Ferreira Gil to participate in the conquest of the German colony: 'If the Portuguese gained by their own efforts that which Smuts wished to give them, the case for getting them to hand over to South Africa Delagoa Bay and its adjacent territories would be considerably weakened'. Hew Strachan, *The First World War in Africa* (Oxford: Oxford University Press, 2004), 161–2.

[18] Von Lettow-Vorbeck would write: 'We took a really very considerable amount of booty, including four mountain guns, a number of machine guns, several hundred rifles, much ammunition, several automobiles, supplies and all kinds of equipment. During the following weeks we continuously found quantities of buried stores and ammunition'. General von Lettow-Vorbeck, *My Reminiscences of East Africa* (London: Hurst and Blackett, 1920), 166. Opposition deputy Tamagnini Barbosa portrayed Ferreira Gil as a negligent officer, playing bridge far behind his troops, neglecting to preserve

things worse, a massive revolt had broken out in Eastern Angola, usually referred to as the Luchazes revolt.[19] Payment of the hut tax—whose collection was the only function of the local authorities—was often marked by exploitative practices, and it provided the spark. This was a huge and sparsely populated area, whose tribal leaders were not fully convinced of the strength of the Portuguese. The revolt began in June 1916, but operations lasted until April 1917. It too resulted in the large-scale movement of the civilian population, this time into British-controlled Rhodesia.

The year 1917 was a long and drawn-out nightmare for the Portuguese in Africa. In April it was the turn of the Amboim and Novo Redondo coffee plantations, in Angola (the stage for terrible labour abuses and expropriation of lands by settlers, while the army remained impassive) to rise in revolt. The rebellious tribesmen could not get at the whites inside fortresses, but attacked their estates and coffee warehouses: settlers and families were killed, and an attempt was made to destroy their economic link to the land. This revolt occasioned the greatest European loss of life in Angola until 1961. The official report into the events noted the causal link between the exploitative practices of settlers and traders and the violence. It was eventually put down by Ovimbundo auxiliaries—a war of blacks against blacks, legitimized by the colonial authorities. This was in part because the Governor General of Angola, Massano de Amorim, did not want to cause a political crisis in Portugal by calling for more troops, and had to make do with what little he had. The fighting would last until the summer of 1918. Not far off, on the left bank of Cuanza River (the Libolo region), the Ambundo ethnic group also rebelled that year: the whole South Cuanza District was in a state of siege from 23 July onwards. The first military force sent in was beaten back; the area's whites were surrounded in a fort, Calulo. The revolt also lasted into 1918, being eventually defeated by forces involving 40 officers, 50 sergeants, 275 European soldiers, and 1,200 African soldiers, at great cost to the local population.[20]

The most serious rebellion, however, occurred on the other side of Africa, along the vital Zambezi River, which divides Mozambique into two. Strongest in the old Barué kingdom, the revolt lasted from March to September, spreading upstream to the Tete district and downstream along the southern bank of the Zambezi, being eventually defeated by European forces and African auxiliaries. It was caused by excessive taxation and the ever greater recruitment of men: to work on road projects (Tete to Salisbury) and as porters for the war effort. They were seized and dispatched

good lines of communication and to carry out effective reconnaissance. He qualified the general's performance at Newala as 'cowardly and unworthy of an officer', and claimed that the defeat had led to the loss of 1 radio transmitter, 4 artillery pieces, 500 shells, 8 machine guns, 1,500 rifles, 60,000 rounds, 5 lorries, and 100 ammunition carts. This and other accusations were made during the secret sessions of parliament held in Lisbon in July 1917. The original minutes can be consulted at the Assembleia da República's library or, alternatively (and with some reservations) at Ana Mira (ed.), *Actas das Sessões Secretas da Câmara dos Deputados e do Senado da República Sobre a Participação de Portugal na I Grande Guerra* (Lisbon: Assembleia da República/Afrontamento, 2002).

[19] René Pélissier calls it the Bundas revolt. See René Pélissier, *Les campagnes coloniales du Portugal, 1844–1891* (Paris: Pygmalion, 2004), 280–1.
[20] Pélissier, *Campagnes coloniales*, 293–7.

in chains to Quelimane, and thence to the north, amid scenes of great violence. There were considerable preparations in advance of the revolt, which included the setting-up of fortified stockades and negotiations between Nongwe Nongwe and Makossa, sons of a defeated former ruler, other local leaders, and even the British authorities in Rhodesia, who refused to provide support. The enterprise was aided by a spirit medium, and was fuelled by traditional medicine, which promised to turn bullets into water. One can argue that, if mobilization occurred here during the war, it was against the Portuguese, of whom there were very few in the area. Up to 15,000 warriors were assembled, but, lacking a clear objective other than to resist the Portuguese, the rebellion was ultimately doomed.[21] An important contribution to its eventual suppression was made by 10,000–15,000 Angune auxiliaries (from nearby Angonia). They were paid 10 shillings/month and were allowed to keep all the booty they could carry, including women and children. The ensuing struggle has been described as the last great slave campaign in Africa. Some 12,000 people sought refuge in Rhodesia, while the ensuing repression and suppression of the last remaining diehards lasted until the end of the First World War: terror was employed, alongside an attempt to keep operations and their nature secret.[22]

The spring of 1917 also saw a Makonde revolt in the north of Mozambique, ostensibly over taxation. Little is known about the event apart from the fact that it was put down with the help of Makua auxiliaries (a situation that, like the reliance of Angune auxiliaries in the Tete district, was to be reproduced in Mozambique's independence struggle in the 1960s). And, as if all this was not enough, 1917 saw the first German invasion of Mozambique, which brought the war to the Nyassa province, and lasted from April to September 1917. Led by Captain von Stümer, these 400 men (mostly, of course, African soldiers, or Askaris) were looking for supplies as well as carrying out reconnaissance activities. The Ajaua people welcomed them, and provided them with food. Some reports stress the establishment of links with Revd John Chilwembe's revolt in Nyassaland; others speak of the spread of *jihadist* propaganda by the Germans. The Portuguese naturally feared that the Germans might keep moving south, eventually joining up with the Zambezi revolt. British and Portuguese pressure forced the Germans out, and the Portuguese dealt with the revolt.[23]

The worst blow of all, however, was reserved for the year's end. German forces under General von Lettow-Vorbeck, under tremendous pressure in East Africa, defeated a large Portuguese position at Negomano, on the Rovuma river border,

[21] Malyn Newitt, *A History of Mozambique* (Bloomington and Indianapolis: Indiana University Press, 1995), 417–19. See also Pélissier, *Campagnes coloniales*, 284–9.

[22] This largely failed, with the revolt being mentioned at meetings of the British War Cabinet. Western and General Report n. 12, covering the week ending 18 April 1917, noted a letter from the High Commissioner for South Africa, who noted the threat to the Beira Railway, adding that an armoured train with 50 men, as well as a force of 125 Europeans, might be sent to protect this vital line of communication. He added, according to the report, that 'help should only be given to keep open railway communications with Beira and to protect Europeans, as further measures would lead the natives to conclude that the British were assisting the Portuguese to support their system of administration'. TNA: PRO, Cabinet Papers.

[23] Pélissier, *Naissance du Mozambique*, 695–7.

and crossed over into Mozambique, where they were to find rich pickings.[24] According to some accounts, the Portuguese commander, Major Teixeira Pinto, wounded at the start of the battle, committed suicide.[25] Von Lettow-Vorbeck would later write:

We buried 200 enemy dead, and about 150 European prisoners were released after taking an oath not to fight again during the war against Germany or her Allies; several hundred Askari were taken prisoner. Valuable medical; stores, so necessary to us [...] were captured, as well as several thousand kilos of European supplies, large number of rifles, six machine-guns and about thirty horses.[26]

Half of the German force re-equipped itself with Portuguese rifles, for which abundant ammunition was also seized. The disappointment among the Allies was great. On 6 January 1918 the British minister in Lisbon handed a Note to the Portuguese Ministry of Foreign Affairs which stated:

The information received by His Majesty's Government from Portuguese East Africa shows that the state of affairs there is very serious and that the present situation indicates the possibility of a grave disaster involving heavy losses of men and material. It appears that the German forces which have entered Portuguese territory have since subsisted on Portuguese supplies, arms and ammunition captured in different isolated posts which should have been withdrawn or energetically defended [...] In the opinion of His Majesty's Government it is essential on account of the situation as described above and if hostilities in East Africa are not to be prolonged indefinitely, that all the Portuguese forces in Nyassaland should be placed under the orders of General van der Venter [*sic*] for all purposes of military operations [...]

The recently installed Portuguese government, led by the anti-interventionist Sidónio Pais since his successful coup of December 1917, was eager for international approval, and acquiesced. Portugal's subordinate position in the East Africa campaign, obvious to all since 1916, now became official.

A prolonged game of cat-and-mouse was played out in Mozambique in 1918 as a massive Allied force attempted—unsuccessfully—to trap the von Lettow-Vorbeck's columns, which re-entered German East Africa in September. Portuguese troops, although numerous, were marginalized by the Allied commander under whom they now served, and were unable to participate in the active search

[24] That he should have done so was not completely unexpected. Jan Smuts had written in October 1916: 'The German commander is a tough fellow, determined to hold out to the very end and even to retire into Portuguese territory rather than surrender'. W. K. Hancock and Jean Van Der Poel (eds), *Selections from the Smuts Papers*, iii. *June 1910–November 1918* (Cambridge: Cambridge University Press, 1966), doc. 701, letter, Jan Smuts to J. X. Merriman, Morogoro, 27 October 1916, 409–10.

[25] This allegation is reproduced in Ricardo Marques's recent work on the Mozambique campaign, *Os fantasmas do Rovuma: a epopeia dos soldados portugueses em África na I Guerra Mundial* (Lisbon: Oficina do Livro, 2012), 224.

[26] Von Lettow-Vorbeck, *My Reminiscences*, 232. The German commander added: 'from captured dispatches we learned that the Portuguese European companies had only reached Negomano a few days before, in order to carry out the impossible English order to prevent a German crossing of the Rovuma. It was really a perfect miracle that these troops should have arrived so opportunely as to make the capture of the place so profitable to us. With one blow we had freed ourselves of a great part of our difficulties.'

for the Germans (although the Germans often brought the fight to them); they limited themselves to keeping the population in place and punishing those ethnic groups (Ajauas, Makondes) whom they suspected of collaboration with the enemy. In many cases the Germans were able to purchase supplies, something the Allies, given the hostility of the local population, could not do (hence their massive reliance on porters). They also helped themselves to the supplies afforded them by static Portuguese garrisons, largely seen as ineffectual. Hew Strachan goes as far as to consider the Portuguese one of the obstacles faced by theatre commander General Jacob van Deventer.[27] Von Lettow-Vorbeck explained that one of his collaborators, a Boer, described the war in the following terms: 'We chase the Portuguese, and the English chase us.'[28] As they moved around the colony, the Germans sparked off mini-revolts, promising to end the payment of hut tax and forced labour. But, in reality, the Germans were gang-pressing men as porters as well. At one point they threatened the Zambezi River before turning northwards. Their southernmost strike, at Namacurra, on 3 July 1918, allowed them to capture 350 modern rifles, endless ammunition, and vast food stocks. The mixed Portuguese–British garrison that guarded this treasure panicked and fled before the advancing German force. According to Von Lettow-Vorbeck, 'the English maintained that they had been infected by the example of the Portuguese'. Allied losses were heavy, not just in the battle but especially in the rout, as Europeans and Africans alike threw themselves into the Namacurra River, only to drown.[29]

AFTERMATH OF THE WAR: PARIS

Colonel Freire de Andrade, an officer with long-standing links with Mozambique, and a former foreign minister, wrote, in 1919, that 'everyone had disasters, especially in Africa, but no one can deny that it is good to have some successes'.[30] There had been none for the Portuguese (none, that is, that could be celebrated publicly), despite the massive investment made. Portugal was caught in a spiral of disappearing prestige, with its territory, already coveted by the other colonial powers before 1914, seemingly up for grabs. The indigenous population could sense the colonial state's weakness, and rebelled; Portugal's allies, who often had to pick up the pieces, sat up and took notice. Behind the scenes, France, Belgium (which had been nearly stricken from the map of Europe), and, most important of all, South Africa were staking their claims to Portuguese territory, as the opinion developed

---

[27] Strachan, *The First World War*, 179. According to Strachan, not only did the Portuguese inadvertently supply the Germans with most of their military materiel; they 'also antagonized the local population, making it increasingly hard for the British to recruit porters'.

[28] Von Lettow-Vorbeck, *My Reminiscences*, 264.

[29] Von Lettow-Vorbeck, *My Reminiscences*, 275–6.

[30] MNE, AHD, Terceiro Piso, Armário 9, Maço 6B, Report, Colonel Freire de Andrade, 25 February 1919.

that Lisbon was to blame for the failure to see out the war in Africa quickly.[31] On 25 July 1918, George Curzon wrote that Portugal was 'incurably incapable of ruling or keeping anything, except by virtue of her weakness'.[32] The Portuguese delegations—because, in reality, there were two, the first, under Egas Moniz, lasting only until March, before being replaced by a negotiating team headed by Afonso Costa—at the Paris peace talks in 1919 would have as their very first priority the preservation of the empire. This was threatened not only by the Allies' territorial ambitions but also by the emerging world order with its evolving notion of mandates, which suggested a level of responsible government and administration in Africa that Portugal might aspire to, but not deliver. There were also complaints at the peace talks over the abuses committed by the Portuguese as they struggled to keep control of their territories.

On 21 March 1919 Afonso Costa, now president of the Portuguese delegation to the Peace Conference, met Lord Milner in Paris to discuss African matters. The British colonial secretary enquired, among other matters, about the nature and future of the Mozambique and Nyassa companies, given that it was in their territory that the local populations had aided the German forces (in 1917–18), as a result of which the war in Africa—he asserted—had not ended sooner. Costa blamed everyone but Portugal for the situation, referring, for example, to the pre-war Anglo-German accords regarding the partition of Portuguese territory should Lisbon default on its loans, which had weakened his country's prestige; it had also been the case that the Nyassa Company had been, before the war, owned in part by German investors.[33] In April, a note was sent from the British delegation to its Portuguese counterpart expressing the view that Portugal's claim to Kionga would be backed by London only if the Portuguese were to embark on a 'complete and immediate investigation' regarding all cases of mistreatment of the natives of which the Portuguese government had been informed, and if those responsible for

[31] Franco-Belgian machinations regarding Portuguese territory, notably the Cabinda enclave, can be found in Archives des Affaires Etrangères, La Courneuve, Guerre 1914–1918, Possessions Portugaises, Dossier Général, 1613, notably in the 18 October report sent from the Ministère des Colonies to the Ministère des Affaires Etrangères. This more or less coincided with the reverberations in Portugal of a meeting of socialist parties in London, at which the creation of a large, neutral African state, to encompass, among other territories, Angola and most of Mozambique (the rest being assigned to South Africa), was discussed. The tiny Portuguese Socialist Party, which had been represented in London and had spoken out against the proposal, immediately denounced the spectre of an imposed partition of the empire, despite the sacrifices being made by the Portuguese in France and in Africa. South Africa's intentions towards Portuguese territory are clearly laid out in the correspondence between its leading political figures. As Louis Botha wrote to Jan Smuts, on 26 February 1918, 'I have only one desire and that is to be there when peace is discussed, for then I shall support you in person in getting many things and seeing difficulties solved for which we shall perhaps never have another chance—especially the question of Mozambique. Jannie, there is no doubt about it, this is a matter which we must bring up and settle in our favour. The region must be bought out and we must pay for it'. Hancock and Van Der Poel (eds), *Selection from the Smuts Papers*, document 815, English translation, 606–12, at p. 609.

[32] TNA: PRO, Cabinet Papers, G-218, Secret, 'Some Further Remarks on the German Colonies', printed for the War Cabinet, July 1918.

[33] MNE, AHD, Terceiro Piso, Armário 9, Maço 6b, Secret report, 'Conferência extra-oficial que teve lugar no Hotel Majestic às 11 ½ no dia 21 de Março de 1919'.

such mistreatment were punished. Costa, relaying this information to the Portuguese government, blamed the anti-interventionist President Sidónio Pais, who had removed him from power at gunpoint, for this display of British hostility. And when, at a meeting of the Mandates Commission, in July, Milner 'referred to the question of the protection of native races',[34] Afonso Costa replied that much was being done to correct the situation, but that not all reports were to be believed. According to the minutes of the meeting:

Complaints of this kind exist against all nations and press more heavily on us, a small country with large territories, than upon large countries with small territories. The British Government is well aware that many campaigns which have been raised over these matters are always more or less tendencious and are actuated by ulterior motives, above all where Germans were concerned. He referred to Morel and Casement, enemies at the same time both of Portugal and England. It is not possible to rely on assertions; it is necessary to investigate, and Portugal is doing so in many cases at present.[35]

Remarkably, the efforts of men such as Egas Moniz, Afonso Costa, Freire de Andrade, Álvaro de Castro, and others who negotiated Portugal's position with their British and South African counterparts paid off; even if working at cross purposes, they protected the empire from dismemberment. They were tireless in their efforts, alternating promises of reform (through the introduction of high-powered High Commissioners in Angola and Mozambique) and reminders of Portugal's principled entry into the war—born not out of hopes of territorial expansion but rather out of devotion to its ancient ally, Britain—with the exploitation of differences among the Allies. British fears of South Africa's intentions were certainly present, and helped Lisbon's designs.[36] Portugal's representatives in Paris eventually took to the offensive, hoping to use the losses suffered in the colonies to recover the costs incurred in fighting the war.[37] In May 1920 a memoir was circulated

[34] This is what is mentioned in the minutes. He was more detailed, in reality, stressing that he had seen 'very serious charges' brought against the Portuguese, by both enemies and friends, including British recruitment agents—something that essentially militated against Portugal receiving a mandate after the war's end. MNE, AHD, Terceiro Piso, Armário 9, Maço 6B, Most Confidential report by Afonso Costa, 27 September 1919.

[35] MNE, AHD, Terceiro Piso, Armário 9 Maço 6B, 'Conferência de 12 de Julho de 1919'.

[36] W. K. Hancock writes: 'They [the other dominions] were not willing, however, to underwrite every South African demand or desire; in particular, the Imperial War Cabinet had made it quite clear as early as 1917 that pressure would not be put upon Portugal to cede Delagoa Bay to the Union in exchange for territory in German East Africa'. W. K. Hancock, *Smuts: The Sanguine Years, 1879–1919* (Cambridge: Cambridge University Press, 1962), 498.

[37] When the full treaty was read out for the first time, on 6 May 1919, Afonso Costa argued against two of its provisions: the failure to make Germany pay for the Allied war effort, which would result, he claimed, in Portugal's bankruptcy, and neutral Spain's inclusion in the League of Nation's Executive Council, occupying a seat Costa had hoped would be Portugal's. As he put it: 'Let us compare the small nations which threw themselves into the fire to defend the rule of Law and those that remained neutral. The Treaty ruins the former, and gives the latter both the advantage of profiting from the wealth amassed while others were sacrificing themselves and the honour of being a part of the first government of the League of Nations [...] I request that my country, which sent its soldiers to France, be at the very least treated like those countries that sent only their travelling salesmen'. MNE, AHD, Terceiro Andar, Armário 6, Maço 20, 'Discurso do Dr Afonso Costa na Sessão Plenária das Preliminares da Paz de 6 de Maio de 1919'. Portugal was awarded the disputed Kionga triangle in September

to the principal bodies of the ongoing Peace Conference, detailing Portugal's reparations claims. Stressing that Portugal had entered the conflict out of solidarity with the Allies, and that the conflict had ruined an economy showing the first signs of recovery after decades of neglect, the memoir then spelled out the scale of Portugal's war effort: 34,457 soldiers sent to Africa and 63,062 sent to France; 3,800 killed in Africa, along with 40,000 wounded or rendered incapable of working (including locally recruited levies); 1,787 killed in France, along with 12,483 wounded or rendered incapable of work. All told, 273,547 African civilians had lost their lives in the colonies because of the war; and, since the conference seemed to be working to a figure of £1,050 ($5,000) for each civilian killed, the resulting payment for this item alone should be £287,225,000. All told, the Portuguese planned to ask for a reparations payment of £432,000,000.[38] The conference, not surprisingly, rejected the premiss behind the memoir,[39] which allowed Costa to accuse its leading figures of racial prejudice, valuing the life of Africans less than that of French and Belgian civilians.

AFTERMATH OF THE WAR: PORTUGAL

One of the most remarkable aspects of the Portuguese war effort in Africa was how little was known in Portugal about it during and immediately after the conflict. The debates of the July 1917 secret sessions of parliament remained closed to the public. As a rule, the official reports into each campaign were kept well away from public scrutiny; one exception was the report into the disastrous Newala campaign, released during the Presidency of Sidónio Pais (December 1917–1918) as a way of denigrating interventionists such as Afonso Costa. And when news of military reverses and dangers in Africa were indeed published, they were used not to question Portuguese colonialism and its aims, but rather as weapons with which to embarrass the government parties.[40] Soldiers (most of whom were illiterate) arrived

1919, an event celebrated by Afonso Costa's supporters as a great triumph in order to mask the disappointment of failing to secure a mandate (which made Portugal the sole Ally nation involved in African fighting to be denied ex-German territory).

[38] MNE, AHD, Terceiro Andar, Armário 11, Maço 20, 'Mémoire des reclamations introduites par le Portugal pour la réparation des dommages qui lui ont été causés par l'Allemagne et prévus à l'annexe 1 de la Partie VIII du Traité de Paix de Versailles'.

[39] MNE, AHD, Terceiro Andar, Armário 11, Maço 20, letter, Paris, 27 May 1920, Sir John Bradbury to Afonso Costa.

[40] See, e.g., the letters published under the pseudonym *Um Afrikander* in the summer of 1917 by the monarchist daily *O Dia*. These highlighted the danger posed by the German invasion of Nyassa province in Mozambique, which was already resulting in native uprisings similar to those of Angola in 1914, as well as new rebellions in Angola. On 3 July the author wrote: 'It is no longer a case of fighting blacks led by blacks. Now it is blacks led by whites using very sophisticated armament. I read in the newspapers that the Democratic [Portuguese Republican Party] politicians are of the opinion that a comprehensive military instruction be given to the expedition to be sent to Mozambique. This is good advice. *In a year's time* we will send an expedition to … photograph the ruins provoked by the war. Why did they not think this way in August 1914? […] Had we organized our expeditions intelligently, we would have been of much greater use to ourselves and to our rally, England. But Portugal preferred

in Portugal, were demobilized, and sent home. It would take many years before a veterans' organization, the *Liga dos Combatentes da Grande Guerra*, was established, but even when this league, dedicated to perpetuating the memory of the fallen soldiers while caring for the survivors, was at the most combative, its leadership never broke a golden rule that was observed in Portugal: never criticize publicly any occurrence that might damage the prestige of Portugal as a colonial power. Those who dared to do so were roundly criticized as traitors, and were denied a hearing—theirs were the 'whispering campaigns' mentioned at the start of this chapter. With Portugal under scrutiny by the League of Nations and the International Labour Organization over continuing abuses in its overseas territories,[41] the country's colonial lobby closed ranks and held fast, determined to see out another foreign 'conspiracy' designed to tear apart metropole and colonies. Thus it was possible for *O Século*, on 13 November 1924, to publish a highly implausible article by Álvaro de Castro, one of the regime's leading figures and, for a time, Governor General of Mozambique. Portugal, he wrote, had sent 40,000 men to Africa, while the colonies themselves supplied 20,000 soldiers and 25,000 porters, all of whom had given a very good account of themselves. Castro now argued, in entirely fanciful terms, that this experience made it possible to aspire to a huge colonial army led by Europeans, but manned by Africans, a force, if necessary, of 200,000 men, who might be brought to Europe in case of emergency. That year, in Oporto, during the Armistice Day celebrations, special attention had been paid to the war in Africa. Mass was said at Oporto Cathedral, while an Exhibit in Remembrance of the War in Africa (Exposição das Recordações da Guerra em África) was held: photographs, native costumes and weapons, war material, war literature, maps, and so on—all were exhibited in such a way as to reinforce the notion of an honourable and eventually victorious campaign waged primarily against a European enemy and those Africans who had been 'turned' by German gold and false promises. The huge battle at Môngua fell into the latter category.

Most Portuguese who followed colonial affairs closely knew this to be untrue. The conditions endured by Portuguese troops in Africa—if not quite who their enemy had been– had been laid bare in a number of important works published after the conflict's end. Carlos Selvagem's memoir of the campaign, *Tropa d'Africa (Jornal de Campanha dum Voluntário do Niassa)*, published in the early 1920s, still makes for harrowing reading. Another illuminating work was a doctoral thesis in medicine, presented in 1919 at the University of Lisbon by a doctor who had served in one of the expeditions, João Rodrigues Nunes da Costa.[42] According to this veteran, there had been no concern for the medical condition of the men sent to Africa, who, to make things worse, had not been furnished with the proper equipment (mosquito nets, quinine, proper uniforms, and hats). There had been

---

to concentrate on the action of the army in France, which was more eye-catching'. *O Dia* (Lisbon), 3 July 1917.

[41] See Aires Oliveira, 'O factor colonial', 317–21.

[42] *Do que eu vi e observei na expedição militar à província de Moçambique 1917–1919* (Lisbon: Faculdade de Medicina da Universidade de Lisboa/Tip. Casa da Cunha, n.d.).

no proper advice on how to cope with conditions, especially in terms of hygiene, and regulations on the subject were not enforced. Nunes da Costa wrote:

The word 'Africa' produced, in the minds of those sent there, a great terror. Going to Africa—[a place] of jungles and wild beasts, of savage blacks and mosquitoes, of illnesses and, possibly, death—was seen as a super-human enterprise. The atmosphere, the horror, generated by strange visions and the tales told by those who had just returned contributed to the depression, the demoralization, of those who saw themselves obliged to carry out their duty there. And as far as I know, no-one attempted to raise their morale!

Problems continued when the war ended, with soldiers crammed into ships for the return journey, whatever their medical condition, because the colonial government could no longer afford their upkeep: 'The voyage made by the *Mozambique* at the start of this year must be remembered by all. Like some phantom ship, it left hundreds of bodies in its wake.' As we have seen, however, this was only one—small—aspect of a much larger tragedy.

   Still, the Portuguese colonial empire survived. The League of Nations, which, in the light of the absence of the United States, was controlled by the leading European powers, proved itself toothless when it came to curbing abuses in the colonial sphere. Moreover, with the advent of Salazar's *Estado Novo*, political stability of a sort returned to Portugal and its overseas territories. The dictator's insistence that the colonies not prove a financial burden to the metropolis, combined with the former's clear-cut administrative and economic subordination to the latter, which Salazar imposed, ensured that little concrete development took place in Portuguese Africa (and Asia) until the late 1950s. For decades, Portuguese colonial authorities ruled over peaceful territories, their primary mission being to provide cheap and quiescent labour to existing enterprises, or to enforce the compulsory cultivation of cotton, on which Portugal's domestic textile industry depended. Reforms were limited to high politics, with overseas territories rebadged 'colonies' in the 1930 Colonial Act, and then returned to the more traditional 'overseas provinces' in the constitutional revision 1951. Later still, under Marcello Caetano, Angola and Mozambique would be promoted to 'states'. Only when other European powers embarked on decolonization did Portugal begin to invest in its colonies, and, after the outbreak of war in Angola in 1961, to allow others to invest in them, and only then did emigration to Angola and Mozambique begin in earnest. The colonies' backwardness and isolation were also reflected in the delayed appearance of African nationalism—but groups such as FRELIMO in Mozambique, and UPA and the MPLA in Angola, had no difficulty in connecting their struggle, begun in the 1960s, with older popular grievances, including those that dated back to the First World War and beyond.

10

The Japanese Empire

Frederick R. Dickinson

There is, perhaps, no better glimpse of the long-term chronological scope and widespread geographic expanse of the First World War than coverage of developments in East Asia. Long before the assassination of Archduke Franz Ferdinand in 1914, East Asia had become a critical arena of imperial struggle, competition that would both affect the course of the Great War and be irrevocably transformed by it. In 1895, historian and grandson of an American president, Brooks Adams, declared that "Eastern Asia is the prize for which all the energetic nations are grasping."[1] With the military defeat of the principal political, military, and cultural hegemon of Asia, Qing China, in that year, all eyes turned east to what was now the newest arena of imperial opportunity. Although the great European powers never colonized China, by the eve of the First World War they owned most of the Chinese economy.[2] And position in China had become a critical gauge of relative imperial might.

The Great War struck a fatal blow to nineteenth-century order not simply because of the physical destruction of Europe or the implosion of four empires near the European heartland. Rather, it exposed the limits of expansion in an area most recently celebrated as the "prize" of imperial competition. By the end of the war, the great European empires had lost substantial ground in the Asia/Pacific region to the meteoric rise of two very new empires, the United States and Japan. By resorting to major armed conflict, the long-term imperial rivalries that had spurred the Great War had, in other words, accelerated the shift of global power eastwards. Happily poised to assume a new leadership role in the region were statesmen of the vastly expanded empire of Japan.

---

[1] Cited in Akira Iriye, *Across the Pacific: An Inner History of American–East Asian Relations* (New York: Harcourt, Brace, & World, 1967), 77.

[2] According to Chi-ming Hou, foreign interests owned 84 percent of all steamer shipping (1907), 93 percent of railroads (1911), 90 percent of coal production (1914), and 100 percent of iron ore and pig iron production (1914) in China before the Great War. *Chi-ming Hou, Foreign Investment and Economic Development in China 1840–1937* (Cambridge, MA: Harvard University Press, 1965), 127–8.

OPPORTUNITIES OF THE EAST

Japan's 1895 military victory over China had spurred some, like German Kaiser Wilhelm I, to fear the rise of a "Yellow Peril" that would ultimately destroy European global hegemony.[3] In the immediate term, however, Brooks Adams appropriately captured the sense of opportunity raised by China's military defeat. Between 1895 and 1900, Beijing concluded a series of agreements with all of Europe's major empires granting exclusive rights to build and operate railroads, ports, mines, and military installations throughout China.[4]

Ironically, although its actions had precipitated this scramble for influence in China, Imperial Japan played a minor role in the competition itself.[5] Japan's imperial energies after 1895 were focused primarily upon exploiting its new territories acquired from China—Taiwan and the Pescadores Islands—and upon gaining an upper hand in the area over which the Sino-Japanese War had been fought: Korea. The latter enterprise, of course, ultimately led to war with Imperial Russia.[6] And, following its 1905 victory over the Tsar, the Japanese empire came to include Korea, southern Sakhalin Island, and Russia's former concession in southern Manchuria. From the end of the Sino-Japanese War until the eve of the First World War, in other words, East Asia became an area of opportunity for old and new empires alike. While the established empires of Europe exploited the commercial opportunities of informal empire in China, there were ample opportunities for both formal and informal empire for new arrivals Japan and the United States, as well.[7]

JAPAN ENTERS THE FIRST WORLD WAR

Japan's rapid acquisition of overseas territories between 1895 and 1905 was not, of course, without its detractors. Even friend of Japan American President Theodore Roosevelt worried in 1904 that a Japanese victory over Russia "may possibly mean a struggle between them and us in the future."[8] But the powers both facilitated Japanese imperial expansion and applauded the incorporation of both Taiwan and Korea in the Japanese Empire as an appropriate attempt by a "civilized" power to

[3] For details, see John C. G. Rohl, *The Kaiser and his Court: Wilhelm II and the Government of Germany*, trans. Terence F. Cole (Cambridge: Cambridge University Press, 1994), 203–4.
[4] For the classic study of these developments, see William L. Langer, *The Diplomacy of Imperialism, 1890–1902* (New York: A. A. Knopf, 1935).
[5] Japan did sign a "non-alienation" agreement with China reserving Fujian Province as an exclusive area for Japanese economic exploitation, but was very slow in following through with this privilege.
[6] For the most recent analyses in English of Japan in the Russo-Japanese War, see John W. Steinberg, et al. (eds), *The Russo-Japanese War in Global Perspective: World War Zero*, 2 vols (Leiden: Brill, 2005).
[7] Like Japan, the USA played a relatively minor role in the scramble for spheres of influence in China to concentrate on its new imperial territory acquired in the 1898 war with Spain, the Philippines. See Christopher Capozzola, Chapter 12, this volume.
[8] Quoted in Michael L. Cooper, *Theodore Roosevelt: A Twentieth Century Life* (New York: Viking, 2009), 208.

elevate a still backward Asia. Britain offered a powerful vote of confidence to the fledgling empire in 1902 when it ended its "splendid isolation" from entangling associations to conclude an alliance with Japan.[9] And not only did London and others not object to Japan's creation of a protectorate in Korea immediately following the Russo-Japanese War. The powers soon after granted full international citizenship status to Japan by raising their legations in Tokyo to full-blown embassies.[10]

The contrast between this acquiescence and the record of great power unease over Japanese initiatives during the Great War is stark. Great Britain invoked the Anglo-Japanese alliance formally to request Japanese assistance to destroy German raiders around Chinese waters on 7 August 1914, only three days after having declared war on Germany. But London worried immediately over the scale of Japan's proposed intervention and wrangled with Tokyo for over a week about the appropriate terms of Japan's engagement.[11] Analyses of US–Japan relations likewise stress heightened bilateral tensions during the war, from the long-winded American response to Japan's so-called Twenty-One Demands to Woodrow Wilson's attempt to deprive Japan of one of its principal wartime gains, Shandong, at the Paris Peace Conference.[12]

Historians typically characterize this new tension after 1914 as the consequence of a new level of Japanese belligerence.[13] But, aside from the Japanese takeover of German Micronesia (which had few Western detractors), Imperial Japan was not, unlike its activities from 1895 through 1905, adding to its formal empire between 1914 and 1919. Heightened Japanese tensions with the great powers after 1914, rather, mark one of the most tangible signs of the intimate connection between the Great War and imperial affairs. If defense of empire had ranked high among motives for the initial outbreak of war in Europe, the principal belligerents also realized that conflict jeopardized what had, since 1895, been an extraordinary opportunity for commercial expansion in China. Great power preoccupation with war in Europe left this key arena of informal empire suddenly vulnerable to a regional power that had hitherto not played a role in China commensurate with either its capabilities or its desires.

---

[9] For the classic study of the alliance, see Ian Hill Nish, *The Anglo-Japanese Alliance: The Diplomacy of Two Island Empires, 1894–1907* (London: Athlone Press, 1966).

[10] Oka Yoshitake, "Generational Conflict after the Russo-Japanese War," in Tetsuo Najita and J. Victor Koschmann (eds), *Conflict in Modern Japanese History: The Neglected Tradition* (Princeton: Princeton University Press, 1982), 202 n. 11.

[11] This wrangling continued through the infamous Japanese Twenty-One Demands. See Peter Lowe, *Great Britain and Japan, 1911–15* (London: Macmillan, 1969), chs 6–7. Although Lowe's book details British anxiety from 1911, this worry focused on Japanese initiatives in China, not in Japan's formal imperial territories.

[12] The March 1915 note sent by American Secretary of State William Jennings Bryan to Tokyo warned against any coercion of Beijing and the "assumption of political, military or economic domination over China by a foreign power." See Russell H. Fifield, *Woodrow Wilson and the Far East* (Hamden: Archon Books, 1965), 38. More recently, see Noriko Kawamura, *Turbulence in the Pacific: Japanese–US Relations during World War I* (Westport, CT: Praeger, 2000).

[13] Andrew Gordon speaks of a Japanese attempt at "colonization" of China during the war. Andrew Gordon, *A Modern History of Japan: From Tokugawa to the Present*, 2nd edn (New York: Oxford University Press, 2009), 173.

Indeed, Japan entered the war with little hesitation following Britain's formal request for aid. As elder statesman Marquis Inoue Kaoru exclaimed, war in Europe was the "divine aid of the new Taishō era for the development of the destiny of Japan."[14] Inoue had a variety of items on his wish list for the reign of the new Taishō Emperor, just begun in 1912. But among his priorities, and those of most Japanese policymakers in the autumn of 1914, was a systematic promotion of Japanese interests in China.

Despite the extraordinary record of expansion of the formal Japanese Empire from 1895 through 1905, dramatic political developments in China in 1911 had raised serious concerns about Japanese regional influence. Diverse Japanese interests from the Imperial Army to the Foreign Ministry to private revolutionaries had for several years endeavored to spur political change in Qing China.[15] But, rather than heed Tokyo's advice to refashion the Qing dynasty into a constitutional monarchy like Japan, Chinese general Yuan Shikai accepted the mediation of Britain and founded a republic on the model of the United States. Following the Sino-Japanese War, American educator John Stoddard had proclaimed Japan "the pioneer of progress in the Orient."[16] The rise of republican China, however, marked the first time after Japan's remarkable military victories over both China and Russia that Tokyo did not appear to be the most powerful agent of progress in the region. It was, warned General Terauchi Masatake, the Japanese governor general of Korea, "a serious matter for Japan's National Polity [*kokutai*]."[17]

Given this shocking setback, the outbreak of war in Europe in August 1914 triggered an immediate flood of appeals to the Ōkuma administration for prompt action in China—from an Inoue suggestion to send a high-level emissary to Beijing,[18] to elder statesman Yamagata Aritomo's call for an "inseparable spirit" between China and Japan,[19] to Terauchi's idea for an "Asian Monroe Doctrine."[20] Though disinclined to heed the words of any of these political rivals, Foreign Minister Katō Takaaki, in whose hands the principal Japanese decision for war rested in August 1914, likewise focused his attention on China. While originally requested

---

[14] Inoue Kaoru kō denki hensankai, *Segai Inoue kō den* (Biography of the Late Lord Inoue), 5 vols (Tokyo: Hara shobō, 1968), vol. v. 367.

[15] For the Saionji cabinet's attempt to create a constitutional monarchy in Beijing, see Usui Katsumi, *Nihon to Chūgoku: Taishō jidai* (Japan and China: The Taishō Era) (Tokyo: Hara shobō, 1972), 7–10. For an Imperial Army attempt to dispatch troops to Manchuria, see Kitaoka Shin'ichi, *Nihon rikugun to tairiku seisaku* (The Japanese Army and Continental Policy) (Tokyo: Tōkyō daigaku shuppankai, 1978), 93–4.

[16] John L. Stoddard, *John L. Stoddard's Lectures*, 10 vols (Chicago: George L. Shuman, 1897), iii. 116.

[17] In a 1911 memorandum to the cabinet. Cited in Shinobu Seizaburō, *Taishō seijishi* (Political History of Taishō), 4 vols (Tokyo: Kawade shobō, 1951), vol. ii. 349.

[18] In a 10 August memorandum to Prime Minister Ōkuma and Field Marshal Yamagata Aritomo. Inoue Kaoru kō denki hensankai, *Segai Inoue kō den* (Biography of the Late Lord Inoue), vol. v. 368.

[19] From Yamagata's "Opinion on China Policy," presented soon after the 15 August dispatch of an ultimatum to Germany. Ōyama Azusa (ed.), *Yamagata Aritomo ikensho* (Written Opinions of Yamagata Aritomo) (Tokyo: Hara shobō, 1966), 343.

[20] Terauchi shared this proposal directly with Japan's new minister to Beijing, Hioki Eki, in mid-August 1914. Akashi Motojirō monjo 32–11. Terauchi to Akashi, 22 August 1914; in Nihon seiji gaikōshi kenkyūkai, "Akashi Motojirō monjo oyobi kaidai" (Papers of Akashi Motojirō and Bibliography), *Keiō daigaku hōgaku kenkyū*, 58/9 (September 1985), 96.

by his British allies only to help destroy German raiders around Chinese waters, Katō sent an ultimatum to Germany on 15 August demanding that the Kaiser transfer to Japan the entire fruit of German expansion in China since the Sino-Japanese War, the Jiaozhou concession in Shandong Province.[21]

If there were those in Europe who plunged into war in August 1914 in defense of empire, Imperial Japan threw in its hat at the same time—in other words, very much anticipating both a defense *and* a formidable expansion of imperial might. Although the situation in China constituted informal, not formal, empire, as we have seen, the great power scramble for concessions in China since 1895 had marked one of the great frontiers of colonial activity from the latter nineteenth century. Japanese initiatives in 1914 constituted a first systematic entrance into this game.

WARTIME GAINS FOR IMPERIAL JAPAN

While Japanese leaders spied opportunity in 1914, they could not have anticipated the extraordinary prospects that war in Europe would actually bring. The conflagration would ultimately destroy four dynastic empires—Imperial Germany, the Austro-Hungarian Empire, Imperial Russia, and the Ottoman Empire. But it brought nothing but good fortune to Imperial Japan: in China, but also in the South Pacific, Siberia, and, most importantly, in global affairs.

In China, receiving no response following the 15 August ultimatum to transfer Jiaozhou, Japan declared war on Germany on 23 August and landed troops in Shandong Province by 2 September. After the fall of the German fortress at Qingdao on 7 November (see Fig. 19), Tokyo readied to take full advantage of its new position on the continent. Historians often describe the series of negotiations with Beijing from January 1915 and subsequent Sino-Japanese treaties of June 1915 as a sudden spurt of Japanese aggression that forecast the extraordinary violence of the 1930s.[22] But the Twenty-One Demands belong less in the company of subsequent Japanese military expansion than in the context of great power maneuvering for influence in China since the Sino-Japanese War. Conceived of first as an effort to obtain formal Chinese confirmation of Japan's newly established position in Shandong, the Demands became, more broadly, an opportunity to finally join the great power scramble for influence in China originally sparked by the Sino-Japanese War.

Tokyo had, as we have seen, watched from the sidelines as the great European empires established, through negotiations with a weakened Beijing, exclusive

---

[21] This comprised a 500-square-kilometer area around Jiaozhou Bay, including a series of forts and a modern harbor (with an enormous floating dry dock) at Qingdao (Tsingtao), and a railroad connecting Qingdao with Jinan (Tsinan) in central Shandong. The ultimatum asked for Jiaozhou, it will be noted, "with a view to the eventual restoration of the same to China." See Itō Masanori, *Katō Takaaki* (Biography of Katō Takaaki), 2 vols (Tokyo: Katō haku denki hensan iinkai, 1929), vol. ii. 83–5.

[22] Andrew Gordon, for example, argues that Japan's original aims with the demands "would have sent China far along the road toward colonization by Japan" (Gordon, *A Modern History of Japan*, 173).

Fig. 19. This cover of the monthly Japanese graphic journal *Tōkyō Puck* anticipates a quick Japanese victory at Qingdao and celebratory drink of Japanese sake out of a German helmet, October 1914.

economic zones and military bases throughout the continent after 1895. Having vanquished one of those new military bases in Shandong in 1914, Japan proceeded with negotiations of its own. And, given the formidable distraction of European attention away from Asia, Tokyo appropriately spied an opportunity to consolidate gains in all of its areas of continental interest. In addition to confirming its exclusive right to Germany's former concession in Shandong, therefore, the Twenty-One Demands consolidated Japan's long-time interests in Fujian Province, south Manchuria,

Eastern Inner Mongolia, and the Yangzi Valley.[23] With the Sino-Japanese Treaties of 1915, Japan leapt from being only a bit player in the competition for influence in China to becoming the principal arbiter of developments on the Asian continent. It is no wonder that even Foreign Minister Katō's greatest domestic political rival, Field Marshal Yamagata Aritomo, expressed "great satisfaction" at the negotiation of these terms.[24]

Even more surprising than this extraordinary boost to Japanese authority in China were the unexpected opportunities opened in areas never before contemplated as part of Japan's imperial orbit. Two months before the fall of Qingdao, the Imperial Navy joined the allied scramble for German territories in the South Pacific, ejecting the German navy and raising the Japanese flag in Jaluit, Yap, and Palau Islands in September 1914. By October, Tokyo and London had concluded a secret agreement establishing the equator as the operational divide between Japanese and British naval forces.[25] At the Paris Peace Conference, the powers granted Japan the Marshall, Mariana, and Caroline Islands as League of Nations Class C Mandates. Defined as lands that, owing to low population, small size, or geographic remoteness could best be governed by an authorized state "as integral portions of its territory,"[26] the C designation meant that Japan had, by 1919, formally become not only a continental but a Pacific empire.

The most substantial Japanese military operation during the First World War was the 1918 expedition to Siberia. Although often described as a defensive response by the powers to the Russian Revolution and spread of Bolshevik power east,[27] in the context of Japanese aims since August 1914, the Allied Intervention marked for Tokyo another golden opportunity to promote Japanese continental expansion. Just as a variety of Japanese interests had on the eve of the Chinese Revolution aimed to capitalize upon continental unrest to expand their orbit of influence, many in Japan considered the Russian Revolution another extraordinary opportunity. Foreign Minister Motono Ichirō urged prompt action in Siberia and North Manchuria to establish a "predominant position in the Orient."[28] Home

---

[23] Tokyo had originally obtained exclusive rights in Fujian at the same time that China ceded Taiwan, just across the straits from Fujian, to Japan. In south Manchuria, although Japan had taken over Russian leases on ports and railroads following the Russo-Japanese War, it had never negotiated lease agreements directly with China. Japan had laid claim to Eastern Inner Mongolia in the Third Russo-Japanese Convention of 1912, but China had never recognized these rights. In the Yangzi Valley, Japanese concerns had purchased coal and iron ore from the Daye iron mines near Hanyang since 1899 and Tokyo had tried to negotiate Sino-Japanese joint management of the company in 1912, only to face a Chinese attempt to nationalize iron ores in 1914. For details of these arrangements, see Frederick R. Dickinson, *War and National Reinvention: Japan in the Great War, 1914–1919* (Cambridge, MA: Harvard University Asia Center, 1999), ch. 3.

[24] Untitled Miura Gorō memorandum of 1915. In Yamamoto Shirō, *Miura Gorō kankei monjo* (Papers relating to Miura Gorō) (Tokyo: Meiji shiryō kenkyū renrakukai, 1960), 17.

[25] Francis X. Hezel, *Strangers in their Own Land: A Century of Colonial Rule in the Caroline and Marshall Islands* (Honolulu: University of Hawai'i Press, 2003), 148.

[26] Hezel, *Strangers in their Own Land*, 155.

[27] For the classic treatment, see James W. Morley, *The Japanese Thrust into Siberia* (New York: Columbia University Press, 1957).

[28] In a series of memoranda drafted with the aid of secretaries Matsushima Hajime and Matsuoka Yōsuke between November 1917 and the Treaty of Brest-Litovsk in March 1918. Morley, *The Japanese Thrust into Siberia*, 53–5.

Minister Gotō Shinpei in December 1917 called for one million Japanese troops to occupy Russia east of Lake Baikal at a cost of five billion yen a year.[29] And special adviser to Prime Minister Terauchi Masatake, Nishihara Kamezō, began formulating plans in November 1917 for an "independent" Siberia under Japanese tutelage.[30]

By far the most influential champions of action in Siberia were, however, elder statesman Yamagata Aritomo and his protégés in the Imperial Army. Although these men had played a central political and military role in Japan's wars against China and Russia, Foreign Minister Katō Takaaki and the civilian cabinet had, with their swift declaration of war against Germany and successful negotiation of rights in China, decisively outmaneuvered the Yamagata faction in the first year of the Great War.[31] As prime minister from October 1916, Yamagata protégé General Terauchi Masatake had, himself, seized the reins of Japan's continental policy in 1917 by negotiating a series of loans to Beijing totaling 145 million yen (the so-called Nishihara Loans). Members of the Yamagata faction viewed intervention in the Russian Far East, therefore, as an ideal opportunity both to expand Japanese authority in East Asia *and* to shore up military–bureaucratic authority at home.[32] By January 1918, a Joint Committee on Military Affairs began General Staff–War Ministry discussions for a dispatch of troops to Siberia.[33] In April 1918, the War Ministry decided on support for White Russian Generals Dimitry Leonidovich Horvath and Grigory Mikhailovich Semyonov, who were fighting from Manchuria for an independent Siberia.[34] By May 1918, Vice Chief of the Army General Staff Tanaka Giichi negotiated a military agreement with China that laid the groundwork for an immediate dispatch of Japanese troops to the core of Russia's presence in Manchuria, the Chinese Eastern Railway.[35] By the first arrival of Japanese troops in the Russian Far East in August 1918, in other words, the Siberian Intervention had become an overwhelmingly Imperial Army show, and Yamagata Aritomo and his army protégés would use the occasion to flood the Russian Far East with 72,000 troops.[36]

Despite the scale of its operations in Siberia, Tokyo's most significant gain in the First World War was the cumulative effect that all of its activities had upon its

---

[29] Tsurumi Yūsuke, *Gotō shinpei* (Biography of Gotō Shinpei), 4 vols (Tokyo: Keisō shobō, 1965–7), vol. iii. 886–8.

[30] Nishihara was promoting the agenda of the newly formed Committee for the Development of the National Destiny. Yamamoto Shirō, *Nishihara Kamezō nikki* (Diary of Nishihara Kamezō) (Kyōto: Kyōto joshi daigaku, 1983), 232–4 (diary entry of 6–23 December 1917).

[31] For more on the politics of Japan's declaration of war against Germany and the Twenty-One Demands, see Dickinson, *War and National Reinvention*, chs 2, 3.

[32] For the politics of Japan's Siberian Intervervention, see Dickinson, *War and National Reinvention*, ch. 5. For the connection between the intervention and the future of representative government in Japan, see Paul E. Dunscomb, *Japan's Siberian Intervention, 1918–1922: "A Great Disobedience against the People"* (Lanham, MD: Lexington Books, 2011).

[33] Usui, *Nihon to Chūgoku: Taishō jidai*, 128.

[34] Morley, *The Japanese Thrust into Siberia*, 102–3.

[35] Dickinson, *War and National Reinvention*, 183–7.

[36] This figure according to Major K. F. Baldwin, Office of the Chief of Staff, War Department, Military Intelligence Division, "A Brief Account of Japan's Part in the World War" (16 September 1921), 5. Stanley K. Hornbeck papers, Box 255, "Japan: War Costs and Contributions" file, The Hoover Institution on War, Revolution, and Peace, Stanford, CA.

international status. Although it had entered the war as a rising regional power, by the Paris Peace Conference Japan had joined the ranks of world powers. Japanese delegates joined the official governing body of the conference, the Council of Ten, to participate in discussions of the most weighty issues of world peace. As Prime Minister Hara Takashi proudly proclaimed in January 1920, "as one of five great powers, the empire [Japan] contributed to the recovery of world peace. With this, the empire's status has gained all the more authority and her responsibility to the world has become increasingly weighty."[37]

Japan's new authority at Paris rested, of course, upon a record of Japanese participation in the Entente going back to the earliest days of war in August 1914. While Japan had, as we have seen, jumped at the opportunity to vastly expand its own interests and authority in the Asia/Pacific region, its record of military operations from 1914 through 1918 highlights an unprecedented level of Japanese cooperation with an allied cause. Japan's siege of Qingdao was carried out in the autumn of 1914 by 29,000 Imperial Army troops in tandem with 2,800 British imperial forces.[38] Two task forces of the Imperial Navy chased ships from the German East Asiatic Squadron and ultimately occupied German islands north of the equator on their own in September 1914. But Imperial Navy operations in the Indian Ocean exemplify the critical reliance of the far-flung British Empire on allied aid. Japanese ships played a key role in the mobilization of the British Empire between 1914 and 1918, conveying Australian and New Zealand troops from the Pacific through the Indian Ocean to Aden in the Arabian Sea. And, following attacks on Japanese merchant vessels in the Mediterranean, three Japanese destroyer divisions and one cruiser (thirteen ships in all) in February 1917 joined the allied fight against German submarines there.[39]

Where Japanese troops were not directly involved, substantial Japanese aid flowed. Several Japanese Red Cross units operated in allied capitals throughout the war, and Japan supplied badly needed shipping, copper, and monies to the allies, including 640 million yen in loans. To the Russians, Japan sold 600,000 desperately needed rifles.[40] According to one contemporary Western observer, "if this help had been denied, the collapse of Russia would have come long before it did."[41]

Indeed, the lengths to which members of the Entente *and* the Central Powers eagerly sought Japanese aid and support from the outset of the war is astonishing and exemplifies, again, the incredible global stakes of the conflict. The German ambassador to Japan, Count Graf von Rex, was so distressed by the prospect of Japanese support of the Entente in early August 1914 that, in an audience with Japanese Foreign Minister Katô Takaaki, he broke the chair upon which he was

---

[37] Hara Takashi, "Hara shushō no tsūchō" (Announcement of Prime Minister Hara Takashi) (January 1920); cited in Kawada Minoru, *Hara Takashi: Tenkanki no kōsō* (Tokyo: Miraisha, 1995), 150.

[38] Eguchi Keiichi, *Futatsu no taisen* (Two Great Wars) (Tokyo: Shōgakukan, 1989), 20.

[39] Letter from Secretary of the Navy Edwin Denby to American Secretary of State, 23 September 1921. Stanley K. Hornbeck Papers, Box 255, "Japan: War Costs and Contributions" file, Hoover Institution on War, Revolution, and Peace, Stanford, CA.

[40] Baldwin, 'A Brief Account of Japan's Part in the World War' (16 September, 1921), p. 6.

[41] Payson Jackson Treat, "Japan, America and the Great War," *A League of Nations*, 1/8 (December 1918), 7.

sitting and almost tumbled to the floor.[42] German and Austrian representatives in European capitals approached Japanese representatives several times in the first two years of war over the possibility of a separate peace.[43]

Given Japan's early commitment to the Entente, expectations among Japan's allies were even greater. Despite initial misgivings about the scope of Japanese actions in Asia in early August 1914, Britain petitioned in September 1914 for troops from Japan to the Western Front.[44] With the fall of Qingdao, allied requests for aid snowballed. On 6 November 1914, British Foreign Secretary Edward Grey urged Britain's ambassador to Tokyo to ask that a Japanese force "take part in the main operations of war in France, Belgium and Germany in the same way as our Army is doing, and to fight alongside of our soldiers on the continent of Europe."[45] Soon after, French newspapers reported informal French requests for 500,000 Japanese troops to join Serbia in operations on the Balkan Peninsula.[46] As late as July of 1918, the US Navy declared it a "matter of vital necessity" that Japanese battle cruisers help protect US troop transports across the Atlantic.[47]

Given the constant wrangling between Japan and its allies over the Siberian Intervention, historians have viewed the operation as the most egregious example of autonomous Japanese action during the First World War.[48] In the context of incessant allied requests for Japanese aid from 1914, however, the expedition should be recognized, as well, as another glimpse of the enormous global reach of the First World War. The Russian Revolution of November 1917 and conclusion of a separate peace with Germany the following March marked a serious strategic blow to the Entente. Not only did it mean the collapse of the Russian front, given the rabidly anti-Western Bolshevik regime newly ensconced in Moscow; the future of the entire Russian Empire was thrown into question. Stretched to the limit on the Western Front, Britain and France turned to the United States to lead the effort to shore up allied-friendly elements within the Russian Empire. But in the context of four years of allied calls for more Japanese aid, the Entente held high hopes for Japanese participation, as well. At the very moment that the American Secretary of the Navy approached Japan's ambassador to the US about possible Japanese battle cruisers to the Atlantic, Washington formally invited Japanese troops to join British, French, Italian, American, and Canadian forces in Siberia.[49]

---

[42] In an audience of 9 August 1914. Matsui Keishirō, *Matsui Keishirō jijoden* (Autobiography of Matsui Keishirō) (Tokyo: Kankōsha, 1983), 79.

[43] Frank Iklé, "Japanese–German Peace Negotiations during World War I," *American History Review*, 71 (October 1965), 62–76.

[44] Sir Edward Grey to Japanese Ambassador to Britain, Inoue Katsunosuke, 2 November 1914. Japanese Foreign Ministry archives, File 5–2–2–51, "Papers related to Appeals for a Japanese Expedition on the Occasion of the European War," Tokyo.

[45] Sir Edward Grey to British Embassy, Tokyo, 6 November 1914. Japanese Foreign Ministry archives, File 5–2–2–51, "Papers related to Appeals for a Japanese Expedition on the Occasion of the European War," Tokyo.

[46] Treat, "Japan, America and the Great War," 8.

[47] Secretary of the Navy, Edwin Denby to American Secretary of State, 23 September 1921.

[48] See, e.g., the classic study by John Albert White, *The Siberian Intervention* (Princeton: Princeton University Press, 1950).

[49] Leonard A. Humphreys, *The Way of the Heavenly Sword: The Japanese Army in the 1920's* (Stanford: Stanford University Press, 1995), 25.

Fig. 20. "The European Girls Still Courting the Japanese Soldiers," cover of *Ōsaka Puck*, 15 September 1917.

Long before the Paris Peace Conference, in other words, the enormous global ramifications of the Great War had spurred desperate pleas for Japanese help and had catapulted Japan to a prominent position on the world stage. As depicted in a political cartoon on the front cover of the 15 September 1917 issue of the monthly Japanese graphic journal, *Ōsaka Puck*, Japan was a noble soldier beseeched by a young lady representing the allied powers. Inclining toward the soldier, one hand on his left shoulder, the women whispers "it can only be you" (see Fig. 20).[50]

---

[50] "The European Girls Still Courting the Japanese Soldiers," *Ōsaka Puck*, 12/18 (15 September 1917), cover.

THE GREAT WAR AND THE FATE OF THE JAPANESE EMPIRE

In the history of the Second World War, Japan is well known for marshaling the full resources of its expansive empire. This included, among others, 240,000 Korean nationals in Japan's armed forces,[51] 38,935 Chinese males in Japanese factories,[52] 200,000 "comfort women" from Japan, China, Korea, the Philippines, and Holland,[53] and four million Koreans dispersed beyond their borders working in various capacities in the Japanese Empire by 1944.[54] Having only just come together in the early twentieth century, the Japanese Empire during the First World War did not mobilize significant numbers of subject peoples. But the outbreak of major conflict raised critical questions about the control of subjects in the Japanese Empire.

Although China was never a part of Japan's formal empire, Tokyo, as we have seen, considered the country the principal arena of opportunity from the outbreak of hostilities in August 1914. Japanese leaders, therefore, remained particularly vigilant from the start about Chinese actions during the global conflict. Tokyo resisted all Chinese efforts to maintain the neutrality of its territory by promptly engaging German power in Qingdao.[55] And China's notification of Britain in November 1915 that it was prepared to join the allied cause prompted an immediate Japanese objection circulated to all allied ambassadors on 6 December 1915.[56] Beijing maneuvered to join the war informally through the first dispatch of Chinese laborers to France in August 1916.[57] But formal belligerence had to wait a change of administration in Tokyo and a determination by the new prime minister Terauchi Masatake and his hand-picked negotiator, Nishihara Kamezō, that China's entrance into the war would work to Japan's benefit. China declared war on Germany on 14 March 1917 as part of Terauchi's effort to strengthen Japanese influence over the new cabinet of Duan Qirui in Beijing.[58] Japanese leaders were ultimately unable to prevent a substantial flow of Chinese laborers to Europe.[59] But they could minimize the diplomatic impact of such Chinese sacrifices by virtue of their own substantial military aid to the allied cause. Japanese naval aid to the Mediterranean from February 1917 garnered explicit recognition

---

[51] Utsumi Aiko, "Lee Hak Rae, the Korean Connection and 'Japanese' War Crimes on the Burma–Thai Railway," trans. Herbert P. Bix., *The Asia-Pacific Journal: Japan Focus*, 26 August 2007 <http://japanfocus.org/-Gil-Heong_yun/2505> (accessed 14 January 2014).

[52] This figure covers the years 1943–5. William Underwood, "NHK's Finest Hour: Japan's Official Record of Chinese Forced Labor," *The Asia-Pacific Journal: Japan Focus*, 8 August 2006 <http://www.japanfocus.org/-William-Underwood/2187> (accessed 14 August 2006).

[53] See George Hicks, *The Comfort Women: Japan's Brutal Regime of Enforced Prostitution in the Second World War* (New York: W. W. Norton & Company, 1995).

[54] Carter J. Eckert, Ki-Baik Lee, Young Ick Lew, Michael Robinson, and Edward W. Wagner, *Korea Old and New: A History* (Seoul: Ilchokak Publishers, 1991), 322.

[55] Xu Guoqi, *China and the Great War: China's Pursuit of a New National Identity and Internationalization* (Cambridge: Cambridge University Press, 2005), 88.

[56] Xu, *China and the Great War*, 110.

[57] Xu, *China and the Great War*, 120.

[58] Dickinson, *War and National Reinvention*, 169.

[59] For the full story, see Xu, *China and the Great War*.

from Britain, France, and Italy of Japanese rights to Germany's former concession in Shandong Province.[60] Given the assiduous overtures of the Central Powers for a separate peace with Japan, the Entente also hoped that its support for Japanese continental interests would help keep Japan within the allied camp.[61]

If Japanese leaders strove to control Chinese actions during the war, they were much more methodical in their guidance of subject peoples in formal colonies Taiwan and Korea. Through the First World War, Tokyo systematically introduced the critical political, economic, and social institutions of a modern nation state into both territories *and* pursued policies that severely restricted the opportunities of Japanese subjects. Between 1910 and 1919, Japan choked off Korean publications by refusing to issue permits for Korean language newspapers outside the governor general's newspaper, the *Daily News* (*Maeil sinbo*).[62] During fifty years of colonial rule in Taiwan, Japan allowed only one newspaper to be owned and operated by the Taiwanese.[63]

As Alexis Dudden has adroitly shown, incorporating territories into the Japanese Empire involved more than simply introducing modern political, economic, and social institutions and maintaining a lid on local dissent. It necessitated, as well, an elaborate strategy to define, under widely accepted terms of international law, the subject status of Japan's colonized peoples.[64] As we have seen, the great powers readily acquiesced to Japanese colonization of both Taiwan and Korea. Three representatives of Korean King Kojong sent in June 1907 to the Second International Conference on Peace at The Hague to contest Korea's new post-Russo-Japanese War status as a protectorate could not even receive an airing. Following Japan's 1905 protectorate treaty with Korea, the Koreans did not, in the eyes of all other great power attendees at The Hague, have a legal right to participate in deliberations.[65]

While Japanese authorities could before 1919 fairly readily control subject peoples within its colonial territories *and* the international terms of their subject status, they struggled to maintain a handle upon subject peoples outside colonial borders. Even before the November 1905 protectorate treaty, Tokyo had successfully compelled Korean King Kojong to appoint a Japanese national as honorary Korean consul in Honolulu. From this vantage point, Japanese authorities could keep a close watch on a burgeoning Korean population in Hawai'i. But the local Korean community never accepted the fait accompli. By 1909, it had established the Korean National Association (*Kook Min Hur*, or *KNA*), which became the core

[60] Dickinson, *War and National Reinvention*, 177.

[61] Iklé, "Japanese–German Peace Negotiations during World War I," 70–1. The Fourth Russo-Japanese Convention of July 1916 also reflected, in part, an allied desire to strengthen Japan's fidelity to the fight against Germany and can be reasonably considered, in part, as a reaction to these peace feelers. See Dickinson, *War and National Reinvention*, 138–48.

[62] Michael E. Robinson, "Colonial Publication Policy and the Korean Nationalist Movement," in Ramon H. Myers and Mark R. Peattie (eds), *The Japanese Colonial Empire, 1895–1945* (Princeton: Princeton University Press, 1984), 320.

[63] Robinson, "Colonial Publication Policy," 323.

[64] Alexis Dudden, *Japan's Colonization of Korea: Discourse and Power* (Honolulu: University of Hawai'i Press, 2005).

[65] Dudden, *Japan's Colonization of Korea*, 7.

of a Hawai'i-based independence movement. During the First World War, the Japanese Foreign Ministry in Tokyo and governor general in Seoul continued to receive reports of local American support for the *KNA*.[66]

Of even greater concern for both Tokyo and Seoul were activities of Korean subjects in Jiandao, South Manchuria, the portion of China contiguous with Japan's Korean colony. Korean migration to this area had increased after the 1905 Japanese protectorate treaty, prompting an expedition of Japanese troops in 1907. By 1909, Japanese forces had withdrawn and the Jiandao Treaty had recognized Chinese legal jurisdiction over the community. But the annexation of Korea in 1910 raised renewed hopes for Japanese control in the region, and the outbreak of war in Europe in August 1914 was viewed, in part, as an opportunity to establish that control. Group Two of the 1915 Twenty-One Demands aimed expressly to define South Manchuria as unambiguously a Japanese sphere of influence, politically, economically, and legally. Despite a Japanese cabinet decision in August 1915 that the recently concluded treaties with Beijing superseded the Jiandao Treaty, however, local Chinese authorities continued to exercise their former legal rights.[67] Tokyo established full control over the Jiandao Korean community only after the Imperial Army invasion of Manchuria in 1931.

Japan's greatest problem with its subject peoples, of course, erupted in the context of a powerful new wartime and post-war slogan, "self-determination." At the very moment that Japan had begun to celebrate at the Paris Peace Conference the new global scale of Japanese authority, Asia seemed to explode in hopes of a complete overhaul of the acceptable parameters of national and imperial power. First, following an initially small-scale declaration of independence by a group of Korean patriots in a Seoul restaurant and simultaneous assembly of students in a Seoul park on 1 March 1919, disturbances spread by the beginning of April to fifty locations in eleven provinces across the peninsula and mobilized up to 40,000 demonstrators.[68] Just one month later, on 4 May, 3,000 Chinese students held a mass rally in Tiananmen Square in central Beijing to protest against the transfer of Germany's Shandong Province concession to Japan. When the burning of a pro-Japanese cabinet minister's house and beating of the Chinese minister to Japan spurred a police crackdown, the initial small-scale demonstration erupted into a nationwide rally in 200 cities. By June, local merchants and labor unions had joined a nationwide series of boycotts, some lasting up to one year.[69]

[66] For example, the American governor of Hawai'i had expressed hope for the realization of *KNA* aims, the mayor of Honolulu had attended an anniversary celebration of the *KNA*'s founding, and a *KNA* leader had been able to acquire pineapple fields on Windward Oahu expressly to establish a military school to "prepare for revolution in Korea." In 1917, rumors circulated of a *KNA* plot to destroy the Japanese warship Izumo on its tour of Hawai'i. For fascinating coverage of this Korean community in Hawai'i, see Wayne Patterson, *The Ilse: First-Generation Korean Immigrants in Hawai'i, 1903–1973* (Honolulu: University of Hawai'i Press, 2000), ch. 7.

[67] Usui Katsumi, "Nanman, Tōmō jōyaku no seiritsu zengo" (Around the Conclusion of the South Manchuria and Eastern Inner Mongolia Treaties), in Kurihara Ken (ed.), *Tai-Manmō seisakushi no ichimen* (Tokyo: Hara shobō, 1966), 127.

[68] Takakura Tetsuichi, *Tanaka Giichi denki* (Biography of Tanaka Giichi), 2 vols (Tokyo: Tanaka Giichi denki kankōkai, 1958), vol. ii. 158.

[69] Usui, *Nihon to Chūgoku: Taishō jidai*, 146.

Although unrelated to mushrooming demands for "self-determination," the enormous wartime expansion of Japanese power spurred violent protest against Japan farther afield than anyone in Tokyo could have imagined in 1914. Between February and May 1920, Russian partisans loosely tied with the Bolshevik Red Army surrounded Japanese and White Russian garrisons in the Siberian town of Nikolayevsk on the Amur River and proceeded to slaughter them. By the end of the Nikolayevsk Massacre, several hundred Japanese Army regulars and civilians had lost their lives.[70]

Imperial Japan had little difficulty meeting violence with violence. Japanese troops and gendarmes brutally suppressed the 1 March Movement in two months after killing 2,000 Koreans and arresting 20,000 protesters.[71] And the Nikolayevsk Massacre was used by the Imperial Army to prolong its occupation of Siberia for two more years. The incident, in fact, spurred the last expansion of Imperial Japanese power of the Great War. Having been bitterly disappointed by the acquisition of only southern Sakhalin Island after the Russo-Japanese War, the army leadership used the Nikolayevsk Massacre as justification to occupy northern Sakhalin in 1920.

The Paris Peace Conference did not, in other words, bring immediate peace to East Asia. On the contrary, by confirming all of Japan's wartime gains—in China, the South Pacific, and Siberia—the conference sanctified for Japan a very nineteenth-century trajectory of war and imperial conquest. What the powers failed to accomplish at Paris, however, came front and center to Washington in 1921–2. Convened most explicitly to tackle the naval arms race raging among Britain, the USA, and Japan after the Great War, the Washington Conference more broadly dealt with the most pressing post-war geopolitical issue in East Asia, the incredible wartime rise of Japanese power.

If the First World War and the Paris Peace Conference had exceeded Japanese expectations for imperial conquest, the Washington Conference marked a decisive turning point toward a new national trajectory. Japanese delegates at Paris took a first critical step toward participation in a new post-war internationalist order by accepting membership in the League of Nations and its governing body, the League Council. But commitment to the Five-, Four-, and Nine-Power Treaties at Washington reflected a widespread general Japanese embrace of the new order.[72] Tokyo had become the "pioneer of progress in the Orient" in the latter nineteenth century by adopting the trappings of a modern nation state and empire. Its new post-Versailles status of world power was secured, by contrast, by determined investment in a new global culture of peace. After having swiftly expanded its military power from the founding of the modern state, Japan at the Washington Conference committed for the first time to naval arms reductions and, by 1925, to slashing its

---

[70] Dunscomb, *Japan's Siberian Intervention, 1918–1922*, 115–26.

[71] E. Patricia Tsurumi, "Colonial Education in Korea and Taiwan," in Myers and Peattie (eds), *The Japanese Colonial Empire, 1895–1945*, 302.

[72] Compare this positive portrayal of Washington with the more sardonic view of Kenneth Pyle, who declares that "the Washington System was a house built on sand" (Kenneth B. Pyle, "Profound Forces in the Making of Modern Japan," *Journal of Japanese Studies*, 32/2 (2006), 410).

ground forces by four divisions. After having steadily expanded the scope of its empire from the Sino-Japanese War, Japan, again for the first time, withdrew ground forces from Shandong and Siberia in 1922 and from northern Sakhalin Island by 1925.

These dramatic changes constituted the core of what contemporaries called a "New Japan," a new national polity adapted to the lessons of the Great War and structured to sustain a new era of peace marked by multi-lateralism, commercial over military expansion, and democracy.[73] Interwar Japan participated whole-heartedly in all major multi-lateral conventions of the interwar era (the Paris Peace Conference, League of Nations, Washington Naval Conference, Geneva Naval Conference, Kellogg–Briand Pact, and London Naval Conference), actively pursued naval and ground force reductions and imperial retraction, and stood upon the foundation of universal male suffrage (1925) and political party cabinets (1924–32).[74] As Japanese plenipotentiary to Paris, Saionji Kinmochi declared in September 1919, Japan after Versailles would secure its new world status by becoming a major contributor to the global "peace project" (*heiwateki jigyō*).[75]

CONCLUSION

Fought in Europe in part as a defense of empire, the Great War would mark the beginning of the end of the age of empires. Like Japan, the core of the winning Entente, particularly Britain and France, made out well after the war in terms of territory and authority. The two most expansive empires before 1914, both Imperial Britain and France would reach their territorial peak between 1919 and 1939, following the break-up and distribution of former lands of Imperial Germany, Austria–Hungary, and the Ottoman Empire. We are familiar with the story of how two key British territories—Ireland and India—would plunge into turmoil after 1919 in a manner that would presage the end of the British Empire after 1945. But the greatest blow to the age of empires, and, especially, to European global hegemony in 1919, came arguably from East Asia.

Following the Sino-Japanese War of 1894–5, East Asia had come to be viewed as the ultimate "prize" of imperial competition. The First World War dramatically revealed, however, that the great European empires would no longer control events in the Asia/Pacific region. Desperate from the start to obtain Japanese aid, the war's principal belligerents worried just as fervently about the potential for complete Japanese domination of the Asian continent and the western Pacific. Indeed, from the

---

[73] As Prime Minister Katō Takaaki declared in 1925, "the Japanese people [...] must come together in a grand resolution and effort to build the foundations for a New Japan" (Katō Takaaki, "Meika no sakebi" (Pronouncement of a Celebrity), *Kingu*, 1/5 (May 1925), 1).
[74] For more on the decisive liberal internationalist turn of interwar Japan, see Frederick R. Dickinson, *World War I and the Triumph of a New Japan, 1919–1930* (Cambridge: Cambridge University Press, 2013).
[75] In a speech on 8 September 1919. Quoted in Ritsumeikan daigaku Saionji Kinmochi den hensan iinkai (ed.), *Saionji Kinmochi den* (Biography of Saionji Kinmochi), 6 vols (Tokyo: Iwanami shoten, 1993), vol. iii. 323.

occupation of German Micronesia to the Twenty-One Demands to the Siberian Intervention, Japan took full advantage of the distraction of great power attention to Europe to control events in Asia. While historians often stress the subordinate nature of Japan's participation at Paris,[76] Woodrow Wilson's inability to contain any of Japan's wartime expansionist energies at the conference demonstrates the enormity of the new authority in Japanese hands. Indeed, the number of issues left unaddressed by the rise of Japanese regional and global power necessitated an entirely new international assembly in 1921.

The Great War finally ended in Asia after the United States, Britain, Japan, and six other powers convened the Washington Conference. But, while Washington effectively calmed Japan's expansionist energies, it did little to stem the general shift of global power from Europe to the United States and Japan. Indeed, the trauma of the Second World War may fully be understood only when we recognize the extent to which the new framework of global security depended upon the support of one of the most powerful newcomers to the world stage after 1919, Japan. Japan's active subscription to the global peace culture guaranteed a solid foundation for peaceful international intercourse in the 1920s and after 1945. Alternatively, the Japanese challenge between 1931 and 1945 greatly expedited the retreat of European power from the Asia/Pacific region, the end of empire, and the rise of American global hegemony.

[76] See the classic characterization of Japan as a "silent partner" at Paris in Thomas W. Burkman, "'Sairento patina' hatsugen su" ("The Silent Partner Speaks"), *Kokusai seiji*, 56 (1976), 102–16.

11

China and Empire

Xu Guoqi

The First World War was a war between empires, both dynastic and imperial. In the wake of that war, four of the existing empires (the German, Russian, Austro-Hungarian, and Ottoman empires) were destroyed and two (the British and French empires) expanded while also being fundamentally weakened. But a rising empire in Asia (the Japanese Empire) had emerged substantially strengthened. Although China may not be considered an important factor in the war, or even in the history of modern imperial history, the war nonetheless deeply affected China's national fate. The ghosts of China's own imperial past were released by the First World War in many strange and surprising ways. Furthermore, while China was not an empire, it could be argued that "empire" or, more accurately still, the avoidance of becoming part of a Japanese Empire, played a decisive role in China's decision to join the Allied war effort, ultimately making a substantial and often overlooked contribution of no less than 140,000 workers to the war on the Western Front. Moreover, the modern fate of China was deeply affected by the collapse of Russian Empire and the regime that replaced it. Few scholars of the First World War have paid attention to the twisted history of China and empire. This chapter will attempt to close that gap.

THE YEAR 1895 AND THE FATES OF TWO EMPIRES

To examine the problem of China and empire in the wake of the Great War, one must go back to the year 1895. China had been one of most powerful empires in the world for many centuries. Although the Chinese Empire's fortune and influence had declined substantially in the late eighteenth and early nineteenth centuries with the rise of the West, and although China had suffered one defeat after another at Western hands since the Opium Wars, only their defeat in the Sino-Japanese War of 1894–5 really compelled the Chinese to think seriously about their future destiny and the value of their civilization. More importantly, it caused them to question their traditional identity. The outcome of that war, moreover, was responsible for bringing both countries into the Great War when it broke out in 1914.

The war of 1895 meant many things for China. It subjected the country to much greater foreign control than before. With the huge indemnity imposed by Japan subsequent to the war and penalties such as the Boxer Indemnity levied by major powers in 1901, a burden of foreign debt effectively crushed almost every opportunity for self-directed modernization and nation-building. But the psychological impact of the war was even greater. As Liang Qichao (1873–1929), an influential author and thinker of late Qing and early Republican China, noted, the war "awakened China from the great dream of four thousand years."[1] Yan Fu (1853–1921), Liang's contemporary and the famous translator of many influential foreign works by authors such as Adam Smith, Thomas Huxley, and others, wrote in 1895 that the impact of the Sino-Japanese War on China "will be so serious and significant that one might argue that China has not experienced an equivalent upheaval since the Qin dynasty [221–206 BC]." Yan was perhaps the first Chinese to use the phrases "national salvation" and "sick man of Asia" to awaken his countrymen to the seriousness of the situation.[2] The devastating defeat at the hands of Japan was both a turning point and shared point of reference for Chinese perceptions of themselves and the world. The war set into motion developments that would lead to the complete collapse of the Chinese Empire and sealed the fate of the Qing dynasty.

After the 1895 war, Chinese elites, no matter what their attitudes toward Chinese tradition and civilization, agreed that, if China were to survive, it had to change. Change became the buzzword of the era. The famous reformer Kang You-wei observed that China "would not have been willing to reform so wholeheartedly if it had not experienced the 1895 war, which hurt it so badly and caused such nerve-wracking pain."[3] According to Kang, China had to undertake political and constitutional reforms, similar to those of the Meiji era in Japan, in order to survive.[4] Many Chinese also began to doubt the traditional Chinese conception of the world order.

The 1911 Revolution drew inspiration from new ideas, was driven by a new public, and drew on the widespread motivation to set up a brand new political system that had gained strength after the 1895 war. If the Sino-Japanese War had jolted China into a nationwide quest for change and new thinking about world affairs, the 1911 Revolution finally achieved that social, cultural, and political transformation.[5] One of the most important legacies of the revolution was the rapid dismantling of a 2,000-year-old dynastic system and traditional notions

[1] Liang Qichao, "Gai Ge Qi Yuan (the Origins of Reform)," in Liang Qichao, *Yinbing shi he ji* (Beijing: Zhonghua shuju, 1989), 113.

[2] Wang Shi (ed.), *Yan Fu Ji (Collections of Yan Fu's Writings)*, iii (Beijing: Zhong hua shu ju, 1986), 521.

[3] Tang Zhijun (ed.), *Kang Youwei Zheng Lun Ji (Collections of Kang Youwei's Writings on Politics)*, i (Beijing: Zhong hua shu ju, 1981), 239.

[4] Kang Youwei, "Shang qing di di liu shu" (The Sixth Letter to the Qing Emperor, January 29, 1898), in Tang Zhijun (ed.), *Kang Youwei Zheng Lun Ji*, i. 211–12.

[5] Mary Backus Rankin, "State and Society in Early Republican Politics, 1912–18," in Frederic Wakeman and Richard Louis Edmonds (eds), *Reappraising Republican China* (Oxford: Oxford University Press, 2000), 6–27.

about a "Chinese empire." The new polity the Chinese embraced was republic-anism, which accorded with the expectations of the newly energized Chinese public that gradually took shape after 1895. The Chinese cry for nation-state status, the obsession with establishing a credible international position, and the rise of a new conception of citizenship all paved the way for China's burying its own empire in 1912.

By declaring China a republic, Chinese leaders signaled that a new nation had been born and was ready to join the world. After the 1911 Revolution, nationalism became a defining and most powerful political force. Chinese nationalism emerged in tandem with the desire to transform the country into a modern nation state and the appearance of a new public. Until the turn of the twentieth century, the Chinese had not shown a real sense of nationalism. Nationalism arose only after the Sino-Japanese War had provided a strong motive for them to pay attention to national and international affairs. Moreover, the Chinese approach to world affairs was strongly conditioned by the fact that, since the turn of the century, foreign powers had almost completely dominated its economy and key sections of its ter-ritory. Chinese domestic politics could not but be closely linked to the foreign presence.[6] The general perception of *neiyou waihuan* (troubles from within and threats from without) colored republican thinking and strategies. The Great Powers' demands and attitudes toward China also limited the options of the new public and its government.

China in the period between 1895 and 1914 had experienced profound changes. Its new public had given up on the old *Tianxia* concept and overcome the Middle Kingdom syndrome that had proved so disastrous in recent decades. For many centuries, Chinese considered their civilization was the best civilization in the world (*all under Tianxia*) and China was the Middle Kingdom. The modern Chinese state for a time straddled the usual polarity of nationalism and inter-nationalism, since Chinese internationalism was undergirded by and predicated on a strong nationalism. The quest for a new national identity was promoted in this period by a curious mixture of political nationalism, cultural anti-traditionalism, and a strong desire for active engagement in world affairs. Although this combin-ation created contradictions and ambiguities in Chinese efforts to assert national legitimacy, it had set the stage for China to socialize within the new world order by the eve of the First World War.

While the 1895 war paved the way for the disintegration of Chinese Empire, that same war helped Japan to promote its own new and ambitious imperial pro-ject. With its defeat, China was forced to pay Japan an indemnity of 360 million yen, an amount that not only defrayed Japan's war expenses (about 247 million yen), but also provided funds for the construction of the Yawata Iron Works, the first modern factory built in the Meiji era.[7] More importantly, the war made Japan a major power in East Asia and an empire with its first colony, Taiwan and the

---

    [6] Zhang Yilin, *Xin taiping shi ji* (Taipei: wen hai chu ban she, 1966), 64.
    [7] Akria Iriye, *Japan and China in the Global Setting* (Cambridge, MA: Harvard University Press, 1992), 19.

surrounding small islands, which China was forced to cede. The war also laid the groundwork for Japan to acquire a second colony by forcing China to abandon Korea, traditionally a Chinese tributary state. Japan seemed to be bound for a major international military game.

Indeed, the Sino-Japanese War planted the seeds for Japan's direct entry into the Great War nearly twenty years later. Germany had played a leading role in the so-called triple intervention subsequent to the Sino-Japanese conflict in which the Germans "advised" the Japanese to return to China the Liaodong Peninsula, another territory Japan had forced China to cede. This infuriated the Japanese, who became determined to avenge themselves against Germany. One Japanese newspaper headline—"Wait for Another Time"—clearly conveys this sentiment.[8] In preparation for its showdown against Germany, Japan achieved a major diplomatic coup in 1902 when it signed an alliance treaty with Britain, which at that point was also preparing for war with the Germans. This treaty eventually set the diplomatic stage for Japan's entry into the Great War. On the basis of the relationship this treaty created, when war broke out in 1914, Japan managed to insert itself into the war effort.

Japan was becoming a recognized imperial power as antagonism between the Entente and the future Central Powers began to intensify. The Japanese were determined to be a leading player in international politics, but their plans faced some resistance from the Western powers. Lacking external help, the obstacles to Japan fulfilling its growing ambitions were real, and so the crisis of war's outbreak in August 1914 was considered by many Japanese to be the "opportunity of a thousand years." After waiting years for their chance, with the European war, the Japanese time had come. No wonder elder statesman Inoue Kaoru hailed the news as "divine aid of the new Taisho era for the development of the destiny of Japan."[9] Four days after Britain's entry into the war, on 8 August 1914, the Japanese decided to declare war on Germany, though the official declaration was not announced for another week.

Taking revenge for being forced to give up the Liaodong Peninsula was, of course, a convenient excuse. Japan's real goal was to expand its interests in China while the major powers were busy killing each other in Europe. The biggest payoff for Japan would be kicking the Germans out of Asia and establishing itself as the dominant power in China. As I argued above, China at this point was in the process of becoming a republic as a way to renew and strengthen itself in the face of modern threats. Japan was determined to make China a dependent before that transformation could be completed. The Okuma cabinet declared that "Japan must take the chance of a millennium" to "establish its rights and interests in Asia."[10] The European war also served a purpose in Japanese domestic politics,

[8] S. C. M. Paine, *Sino-Japanese War of 1894–1895* (Cambridge: Cambridge University Press, 2003), 290.

[9] Frederick Dickinson, *War and National Reinvention: Japan in the Great War, 1914–1919* (Cambridge, MA: Harvard University Press, 1999), 35.

[10] Ikuhiko Hata, "Continental Expansion, 1905–1941," in John W. Hall (ed.), *The Cambridge History of Japan* (Cambridge: Cambridge University Press, 1988), vi. 279.

because the war could be used as a national rallying point.[11] The death of the Meiji emperor in 1912 meant the end of an era and the weakening of the existing political order. Japan lost its national purpose in the post-Meiji years, and its entry into the war would instill in the Japanese people some sense of higher purpose. It would allow them to return to "simplicity and purity," and redefine Japan as a nation. Joining the Great War thus would help Japan achieve three goals: avenging itself on Germany, expanding its interests in China, and rejuvenating its domestic politics.

THE TWENTY-ONE DEMANDS AND THE DREAM OF A NEW CHINESE EMPIRE

When the Great War broke out, Japan immediately seized the opportunity to declare war on Germany, citing its alliance with Great Britain. In November 1914, Japan took control of Qingdao—a Chinese territory under German control since 1898. Interestingly, the German defeat in Qingdao as early as 1914 represented the beginning of the German Empire's demise, although at that time nobody knew it. But Japan's real intention was not to bury the German Empire or simply to take Qingdao. By taking this step, which demonstrated its intention and capability to pursue control of China, Japan could reasonably assert itself as the leading empire in Asia. Thus, on 18 January 1915, Japan directly presented Chinese president Yuan Shikai with the Twenty-One Demands. The demands consisted of five sections with a total of twenty-one articles. These demands were so severe that George E. Morrison, then an adviser to the Chinese government, called them "worse than many presented by a victor to his vanquished enemy."[12] Obviously, the Japanese meant to make China a vassal state while the other powers were engaged in European battles.

Japan's demands presented the biggest challenge yet to China's survival as a fledgling nation state. In his interview with Samuel G. Blythe on 15 April 1915, Yuan Shikai commented on Sino-Japanese negotiations over the Twenty-One Demands: "Whatever China can concede will be conceded, but she cannot help remaining firm on those articles which encroach on China's sovereignty or infringe the treaty rights of other Powers."[13] Yuan's government was forced to accept under the Japanese ultimatum all the demands but those in Section 5, which were the most damaging.[14] The Twenty-One Demands sharpened China's interest in the Great War and its concerns with long-term Sino-Japanese relations. More importantly they also prompted President Yuan Shikai's attempt to restore the old Chinese polity by declaring himself emperor in early 1916. Why would Yuan want to restore the empire that the Chinese had recently buried? The conventional wisdom

[11] For the best study on this issue, see Dickinson, *War and National Reinvention*.
[12] Cyril Pearl, *Morrison of Peking* (Sydney: Augus and Robertson, 1967), 307.
[13] Samuel G. Blythe, "The Chinese Puzzle: A Talk on Policies and Conditions with the President of China," *Saturday Evening Post*, 187/46 (1915), 4.
[14] In August 1916 Japan tried to use the so-called Zhengjiatong Incident to get what it wanted in No. 5 of the Twenty-One Demands.

suggests Yuan's personal ambition and his lack of understanding of republicanism. Without denying the role of Yuan's selfish interest and the chaos of China's internal affairs, it is possible to suggest that other factors, the Twenty-One Demands in particular, loom large in his monarchical scheme. Clearly the ongoing Great War and Japan's unchecked ambitions and aggression may have forced Yuan to consider extraordinary measures to stave off total national disintegration and China's becoming a dependent of Japan. The demands presented to Yuan fully revealed Japanese intentions and just how hopeless the Chinese position was in dealing with a foreign threat. Japan left China no choice. The Chinese had either to yield or to face invasion while the major powers abandoned them to focus on their own affairs or survival. The conventional wisdom that Yuan gave in to Japanese demands in exchange for Japan's support for his scheme has quite possibly got things the wrong way around. Yuan's plan to institute monarchy was in direct response to Japanese demands, as he tried to figure out how China could survive under the difficult circumstances it faced domestically and externally. Jerome Chen, an expert on Yuan Shikai, noted this point in his very critical biography of Yuan. According to Chen, Yuan "wanted a strong China. Strength came from unity; unity from obedience to him." For Yuan, a polity such as republicanism or monarchy was only a means to an end—national wealth and power. Yuan's conviction that a strong center was required for modernization, national strengthening, and maintaining order was shared by other political leaders, including Sun Yatsen, who believed that too much democracy would impede the "rapid, peaceful and orderly" mobilization of resources.[15] Liang Qichao, a leading reformer, wrote to Yuan and advised him to "be the servant in appearance but be the master in reality."[16] This explains why Yuan was "more interested in national strength than in republicanism."[17] To achieve national strength, he could not hesitate to establish a different polity if he thought republicanism was not working.

After the humiliation of the Twenty-One Demands, Yuan believed even more strongly that a strong central government under a strong leader was the only formula to help China avoid similar problems in the future. Wellington Koo, who had worked closely with Yuan before being appointed minister to the United States, explained in January of 1916 that the decision in favor of a monarchy reflected the need for a "government able to hold the country together, develop its wealth and strength, and help realize the intensely patriotic aspirations of its people."[18] As contemporary scholar Li Jiannong noted, one of the major justifications for restoration of the monarchy was that "republicanism does not suit the national condition. [...] Unless there is a great change of policy, it is impossible to save the nation."[19] Even John Jordan, the top British diplomat in China who

[15] Edward Friedman, *Backwards toward Revolution: The Chinese Revolutionary Party* (Berkeley and Los Angeles: University of California Press, 1974), 169, 78.
[16] Ding Wenjiang (ed.), *Liang Rengong Xiansheng Nianpu Chang Bian Chu Gao* (Life Chronology of Mr Liang Qichao) (Taipei: Shijie shuju, 1959), 579–620.
[17] Jerome Chen, *Yuan Shih-Kai* (Stanford: Stanford University Press, 1972), 164, 201, 210.
[18] *Peking Daily News*, 14 March 1916.
[19] Li Jiannong, *The Political History of China* (Princeton: D. Van Nostrand Co., 1956), 309.

maintained close contacts with Yuan, noted this rationale. He reported to his boss in the Foreign Office in London: "One driving motive behind the Chinese is that they will be in a better position to withstand Japanese aggression under a monarchy than under a Republican form of government."[20] Jordan, who was not happy with Yuan's monarchical scheme, still wrote highly of him after Yuan's death, calling him "a great man and a true patriot."[21]

Moreover, it is telling that key people who supported Yuan's monarchical scheme included strong nationalists such as Yang Du and a leading constitutional scholar, the American political scientist Frank Goodnow. Yang Du (1874–1932) was a political reformer who later became a major figure in Yuan Shikai's monarchical scheme. He was perhaps the first Chinese to coin the term "internationalist nationalism" (*shijie de guojia zhuyi*). Starting in late 1906, Yang published a series of articles under the rubric "Jintie zhuyi shuo" (the theory of gold-ironism) in a new journal (*Zhongguo xinbao*), of which he was editor-in-chief. According to his own definition, the theory of gold-ironism was concerned with how to make China economically rich and militarily powerful, with gold standing for wealth and iron for power. In this long treatise on the theory of gold-ironism, he devoted much space to his idea of internationalist nationalism, arguing that, since the new world order was based on economic and military power, if China wanted to survive in this new environment, it had to play the same game as the great powers. Yang claimed that his approach provided a blueprint for China's joining the new system successfully. Only by achieving both wealth and power could China become an active member of the world system, and Yang argued that China already had the resources to put his ideas into practice.[22] For Yang and other advocates of this approach, participating in international affairs as an equal member was the key to nationalist internationalism. It seemed to Yang and his allies that China's national interests might be best served with Yuan as emperor. In a long essay entitled "National Salvation by a Constitutional Monarchy," published in April 1915, Yang strongly argued that a republic had proved inefficient for China. If China wanted to be rich and powerful, it had to change its polity, and only a constitutional monarchy could save it.[23]

Frank Goodnow (1859–1939), an eminent American constitutional scholar, served as Yuan's constitutional adviser from 1913 to about 1915. He was president of Johns Hopkins University from 1914 to 1929. Goodnow was keenly interested in adapting constitutional provisions to Chinese social and cultural realities. He believed in Yuan, seeing him as "honestly desirous of saving his country," and bought Yuan's idea that China could be saved only by a "practically

[20] Jordan to Langley, 20 October 1915, TNA: PRO WO350/13/101–3.
[21] For Jordan's general appraisal of Yuan, see Jordan to Langley, 13 June, 6 October 1916, TNA: PRO, Jordan Papers, FO350/15.
[22] Yang Du, "Jingtie zhuyi shuo" (Theory of Gold-and-Iron Doctrine), *Zhongguo xinbao*, 1–6 (1906, 1907).
[23] For the complete essay, see Yang Du, *Yang Du Ji* (Collections of Yang Du's Writings) (Changsha: Hunan remin chubanshe, 1986), 566–84.

autocratic government."[24] Serving as Yuan's constitutional adviser provided Goodnow with an opportunity to put his theory into practice. In the summer of 1915, at Yuan's request, he prepared a memorandum on the relative merits of republicanism and monarchism for China. Goodnow declared that a monarchy "is better suited than a republic to China" because republicanism did not suit the country's present conditions. For Goodnow, "China's history and traditions, her social and economic conditions, her relations with foreign powers all make it probable that the country would develop that constitutional government which it must develop if it is to preserve its independence as a state, more easily as a monarchy than as a republic."[25]

Having the backing of such a distinguished scholar from an influential republic justified Yuan's move and greatly enhanced the respectability of his monarchical scheme. Liang Qichao suggested that Yuan's monarchical campaign started with Goodnow's view, or at least that seemed to be the case "on the surface."[26] No matter what his original motivation for writing the memorandum, Goodnow's name and its prestige were used to great advantage to promote Yuan's dream of empire.[27] Certainly, other foreigners had voiced the same or similar ideas, but no one had received the same degree of attention or was as influential. If his ideas and actions did not necessarily represent official American policy, Goodnow nonetheless represented various elite American groups' interests in China. He had been nominated for his advisory position by the Carnegie Foundation, at the recommendation of a Harvard president emeritus.

But even with support from people such as Yang Du and Goodnow, Yuan's monarchy scheme ended in disaster, with Yuan personally suffering the biggest defeat of his life. He died soon after, humiliated. After the 1911 Revolution, no one could legitimately declare himself emperor in China. As Mary Wright reminds us: "Even at the height of the reaction around 1915, China was a vastly different country from what it had been fifteen years earlier."[28] If Yuan's scheme grew out of a Chinese desire for national strengthening, his fall was caused by those same forces. Among those who opposed Yuan's restoration scheme, concern for China's international status was paramount. The main reason Liang Qichao opposed Yuan's scheme was his conviction that a sudden change of polity would negatively affect China's quest to join the world as an equal member. He argued that the monarchy scheme would derail China's efforts to attend the crucial post-war peace conference and so provide further opportunities for Japan to thwart Chinese

[24] Goodnow to Nicholas Murry Butler, 26 February 1914, quotation from Noel Pugach, "Embarrassed Monarchist: Frank J. Goodnow and Constitutional Development in China, 1913–1915," *Pacific Historical Review*, 42/4 (November 1973), 507.
[25] "Dr Goodnow's Memorandum to the President," *Papers Relating to the Foreign Relations of the United States (FRUS): 1915* (Washington: Government Printing Office, 1924), 53–8.
[26] Liang Qichao, "yi zai suo wei guo ti wenti zhe," in Liang Qichai, *Dun bi ji* (Tapei: Wenhai chubanshe, 1966), 138.
[27] "A Statement by Dr Goodnow," *Peking Gazette*, 18 August 1915, repr. in *FRUS 1915*, 59–60.
[28] Mary C. Wright, *China in Revolution: The First Phase, 1900–1913* (New Haven: Yale University Press, 1968), 51.

interests.[29] Liang attacked what he called Yuan's seven major mistakes, the first being his lack of a conception of the modern nation state.[30] To Liang and General Cai E, the first general to take military action against Yuan, an anti-monarchical war had to be waged to recover the human dignity of four hundred million Chinese.[31]

Liang attached such importance to the implications of Yuan's scheme that he risked his life to write an extremely powerful article entitled "How Strange is This So-Called National Polity Problem" (*Yi zhai suowei guoti wenti*). Liang told his daughter: "Unless heaven takes away my pen, I will write and denounce Yuan and his cronies."[32] Liang not only used his pen, he also joined the military action against Yuan by traveling south to work with Cai E, who was leading the fight. That trip south would be dangerous and difficult. "I will go though I risk my life, because the whole nation's fate and destiny might rely on this trip," Liang wrote to his daughter.[33]

One direct result of the open military opposition to Yuan was that China became divided internally. Yuan's death also deprived the northern Beiyang faction of a leader and "caused internal dissension," and so even dead he still played a role in the birth of warlordism.[34] This may be his single most powerful legacy. As Ernest Young has noted, it was in the wake of the Yuan government's collapse in 1916 that "military men, without significantly sharing power with civilian politicians, were asserting their predominance and independence in the provinces."[35]

Unfortunately Yuan's failure did not prevent others from trying to restore the Chinese empire. If the Great War indirectly contributed to Yuan's monarchical scheme by freeing the Japanese to deliver the Twenty-One Demands, the 1917 scheme to restore the Qing Empire grew directly from the consequences of that war.

A SECOND ATTEMPT TO RESTORE THE CHINESE EMPIRE

Perhaps no single foreign-policy initiative had a stronger impact on China's domestic politics and society than its policy on the First World War. Instead of enjoying the fruits of its first major independent diplomatic program, China tasted bitter social disorder, political chaos, and national disintegration. Disputes over the war participation policy exacerbated factionalism, encouraged warlordism, and

[29] Liang Qichao, "Yi zai suo wei guo ti wen ti zhe" (How Strange is this So-Called Polity Issue), in Liang Qichao, *Dun bi ji*, 156; see also Liang Qichao, *Yinbing shi he ji: zhuang ji*, 33.

[30] Liang Qichao, *Yinbing shi he ji: wenji*, 34.

[31] Liang Qichao, *Yinbing shi he ji: wenji*, 39, 89.

[32] Zhang Pinxing (ed.), *Liang Qichao Jia Shu* (Family Letters of Liang Qichao) (Beijing: Zhong guo wen lian chu ban she, 2000).

[33] Zhang Pinxing (ed.), *Liang Qichao Jia Shu*.

[34] Li, *The Political History of China*, 345.

[35] Ernest Young, *The Presidency of Yuan Shih-k'ai, Liberalism and Leadership in Early Republican China* (Ann Arbor: University of Michigan Press, 1977), 242.

led to civil war. In the wake of its war entry policy of 1917, China was a stage set for a tragic drama. A series of bizarre episodes—the dissolution of parliament, the restoration of the Qing emperor, the frequent comings and goings of new governments, the dismissal and return of Prime Minister Duan Qirui, and the resignation of President Li Yuanhong—all took place in the wake of Duan's push for China to participate in the First World War.

After the Chinese had protested to Germany about its submarine policy in February 1917, China's direct participation in the war seemed imminent. The formal declaration of war did not come until the middle of August, six full months later, however. Prime Minister Duan did not anticipate that publication of his protest note would set off a tremendous debate over his war policy. The debate led to near derailment, not only of what was expected to be a smooth entry into the war, but, more importantly, of Chinese society itself. As President Li Yuanhong observed: "Upon the diplomatic rupture suddenly taking place, political crises have followed each another."[36] Policy debates, especially regarding major issues, can be a natural and healthy process. But in early twentieth-century China, whose society and political structure were not yet prepared to withstand controversy, political debate was dangerous and destabilizing. In the past, this level of policy-making had been carried out easily by top leaders without consultation. And, when debates did take place, the emperor had had the final say. But, in the era of the First World War, and especially after the death of Yuan Shikai, no Chinese leader enjoyed such paramount power; moreover, a broader Chinese public had become interested and active in politics. Yet, to judge by its reaction to political crises that grew out of the war issue, Chinese society was not yet ready for this role. The new republican political structure, so fragile and unstable that any crisis might crush it, made the situation more acute. If the politicians in charge could not deal with this new multidimensional political culture, or know how to make compromises, or have the skill to steer China through uncharted waters, disasters could not but follow.

Despite the existence of opposition groups, the majority of the Chinese social elite supported the idea of China's participation in the war. After the official protest had been delivered to Germany, most Chinese supported the government's move to declare war, arguing that no country could maintain neutrality while trying to enhance its international status. As one contemporary pointed out: "Every politically important element in China's limited but energetic sphere of public life was in favor of breaking off with Germany." As to declaring war: "Scattered elements opposed it, such as a group of radicals led by the famous ex-president Sun Yatsen, but the southern parties as a whole approved and backed it."[37] Jiang Tingfu, who

---

[36] Li Yuanhong, "Declaration by the President of his Policy," *Peking Gazette*, 1 June 1917.

[37] "Zhong de jie jiao shi mu ji qi li hai" (the inside story of China's breaking off its diplomatic relations with Germany and its implications) (no author, presumably written by a high official within the government), 18 March 1917, in Zhang Bofeng et al. (eds), *Bei Yang Jun Fa, 1912–1928* (Wuhan: Wuhan chu ban she, 1990), iii. 61; "Feng Guozhang li zhong de jie jiao shi mu ji qi li hai yi jiang shu gao" (Draft Memorandum from Feng Guozhang regarding China's Breaking off Diplomatic Relations with Germany and its Impact) (18 March 1917), in Zhong guo li shi di er dan an guan (ed.), *Zhong*

observed the debate closely, insisted that, when Chinese military and civilian factions were debating war policy in 1917, "most of them argued that [China] should join the Allied side. Few insisted on neutrality. None suggested joining the German side."[38] The fact that a majority supported China's rupture with Germany and even its participation in the war explains why, on 11 March, the parliament supported Duan Qirui's policy, voting 158 to 37 in the Senate and 331 to 87 in the House. This gave the Duan government an immediate mandate to break off relations with Germany.[39]

But this consensus on the war policy was soon to be dashed, and a personal clash between Prime Minister Duan and President Li Yuanhong would deal it the first blow. Duan was obsessed from the start with using the European war as a vehicle for China's renewal, and he harbored a secret wish that China had entered the war at its outbreak. Liang Qichao might have been the moving force behind China's drive to participate in 1917, but it was up to Duan to carry out the policy. In early 1917, with the American invitation to issue a protest and pushed by Liang Qichao, Duan believed the time for quick action had arrived. But from the very start the prime minister found himself clashing with President Li Yuanhong over how to handle the war. When the Duan cabinet decided to break off relations with Germany, it decided to ascertain Japan's response to China's war aims. This made sense to Duan, since China had failed twice before in its efforts to join the war because of Japanese opposition. When Duan and all his cabinet members visited Li Yuanhong in early March, asking for his signature on a telegram to the Japanese government, Li suggested that these were important issues and advised them for an opinion from the parliament. In fact, President Li thought it improper to inform a foreign country of such vital decisions before parliament had given its approval. Since such a proposal meant a definite step toward China's declaration of war, Li insisted that it must have the prior approval of parliament, which alone had the power to declare war. In response, Duan resigned as protest against Li's lack of cooperation and mistrust of his cabinet's judgment.[40]

Why did Duan choose to resign rather than negotiate with Li? Duan's personality and his relationship with Li perhaps explain his decision. Duan had never respected President Li and considered his refusal to sign a personal insult. Moreover, at this juncture there was enormous confusion regarding the Chinese government's political structure. In Duan's mind, presidential functions were mainly

Hua Min Guo Shi Dan an Zhi Liao Hui Bian: Di San Ji: Zhengzhi (Collections of Archival Materials on the History of Republican China, iii. Politics[2]) (Nanjing: Jiangsu guji chubanshe, 1991), 1172.

[38] Jiang Tingfu, *Jiang Tingfu Hui Yi Lu (Memoirs of Jiang Tingfu)* (Taipei: Zhuang ji wen xue chu ban she, 1979), 65.

[39] "Zhong de jie jiao shi mu ji qi li hai" (the inside story of China's breaking off its diplomatic relations with Germany and its implications) (no author, presumably written by a high official within the government), March 18, 1917, in Zhang Bofeng et al. (eds), *Bei Yang Jun Fa, 1912–1928*, iii. 61; "Feng Guozhang li zhong de jie jiao shi mu ji qi li hai yi jiang shu gao" (Draft Memorandum from Feng Guozhang regarding China's Breaking off Diplomatic Relations with Germany and its Impact) (18 March 1917), Zhong guo li shi di er dan an guan (ed.), *Zhong Hua Min Guo Shi Dan an Zhi Liao Hui Bian: Di San Ji*, 1172.

[40] *Min Guo Ri Bao*, 8 March 1917.

ceremonial and symbolic, and the president had no call to intervene in cabinet decisions. But Li Yuanhong thought and acted differently. A cautious man, Li insisted that the war question was so important it should be considered with great care. As president, he believed he should insist on handling the war policy legalistically, by briefing parliament and getting its approval. Li was also appalled by the political nature of the debate over the war. He once commented to reporters that "today's fellow Chinese have a tendency to look at the issue [of China's joining the war] as an issue of different parties and party relations. This is not good." Li declared: "If China wants to join, it should do so for the national interest," and he warned that "we Chinese should never enter into the war in a spirit of risk-taking opportunism."[41] Duan, however, did not worry about these legal issues, so long as he could achieve his goal. Because of his personal confidence, Duan believed that, if something should be done, he should pursue it despite any risks. Li might have had his own ambitions and principles but, unlike Duan, he knew his weaknesses and when to compromise. Indeed, his capacity to compromise allowed this first political obstacle to a Chinese war policy to be hurdled. Two days after Duan had resigned, through the mediation of Vice-President Feng Guozhang, Li acceded to the condition set by Duan before he would once again assume his duties as prime minister: that Li not interfere in diplomatic affairs and the cabinet's foreign policy. Duan returned immediately to Beijing to resume his duties. On 10 and 11 March, the parliament passed Duan's policy of breaking relations with Germany by a large margin. Everything seemed to be working in Duan's favor and moving along smoothly. But another problem soon arose.

To ensure that his war policy would pass, Duan began soliciting support from military governors in April. He assumed that, if he could win their support, he could use it to put pressure on his opponents, especially those in the parliament as well as the president. To this end, Duan called a conference of military governors, which convened officially on 25 April, with more than twenty military governors or their representatives attending. Duan himself chaired the opening session. Once Duan had assured them that war participation was in both their own and national interests, these *dujun* or provincial military governors became advocates of Duan's war policy and did what they could to support it. But, during their sojourn in Beijing, they also started to intervene in national politics by attending a cabinet meeting and even in foreign affairs by collectively visiting ministers from the Allied countries.[42] Given the intimidating power of the *dujun*, Duan's advocacy of participation in the war against Germany stirred strong passions within Chinese political circles in general and within the Beiyang military clique in particular. This controversy soon shook the whole fragile political system. The problem of participation in the war led to intrigues inside the parliament, conflicts between the president's office and the Duan's cabinet, and a dispute over the constitution.

[41] *Zhong Hua Xin Bao*, 3 March 1917.
[42] *Dujun* literally means "supervisor of military affairs," a post that was first used in 1916. For details, see Arthur Waldron, "The Warlord: Twentieth-Century Chinese Understandings of Violence, Militarism, and Imperialism," *American Historical Review*, 96/4 (October 1991), 1073–1100.

With support from the *dujun*, Duan's cabinet felt confident enough to decide to declare war on Germany on 1 May. Under pressure from Duan and the military governors, President Li agreed to pass Duan's war declaration on to the parliament for consideration. On 8 May, the House of Representatives started to debate the declaration of war. Given the prior support of both houses, parliament could easily have passed this bill. According to Tao Juyin, a scholar on politics in early Republican China, a majority of members supported Duan's declaration of war on Germany.[43] Indeed, as Wang Zhengting, vice-president of the Senate and a leading member of the Nationalist Party (GMD), wrote in July 1917: "The severance of diplomatic relations with Germany was approved by both houses with a large majority. An equally large majority would have voted for war against Germany had there been no interference from these military governors."[44] Li Jiannong, a leading scholar in the political history of early Republican China, also suggested that, "if the Peiyang military clique had not used harsh methods, the bill [for participating in the war] would have passed without trouble." Li wrote that in the parliament "all parties (except the 1916 Club, a leftist wing) intended to pass the bill."[45]

But Duan and his cronies miscalculated the situation and tried to get the bill passed immediately in their own way. The *dujun* took matters into their own hands and chose to use threats to assure its passage. On 10 May, while the House of Representatives was holding a committee meeting on the issue, a mob of several thousand people calling themselves the "Citizens' Petition Corps," the "Petition Corps of Military, Political and Commercial Circles," and other names, gathered in front of the House. Secretly under the direction of army generals, their goal was to "persuade" representatives to pass the war declaration immediately. They distributed circulars to members containing veiled and not-so-veiled threats such as "we are ready to sacrifice our person" and "we will deal with you eventually." A delegation of six persons declaring themselves to be citizen representatives even approached the Speaker of the House and demanded that the war declaration should be passed that day; otherwise, they would burn down parliament and murder the members. Three thousand members of various "petitions corps" surrounded the building and refused to disperse until the bill had been passed. Ten or more congressmen were beaten and harassed. Was Duan involved in this fiasco? Although his enemies attacked him for direct involvement, some evidence suggests that the incident was organized without Duan's knowledge. According to one source, Duan's close assistant General Fu Liangzuo orchestrated the whole episode without Duan's authorization.[46] Whether Duan was involved in the planning or not, he could not avoid direct and full responsibility. After all, his assistants and associates had acted

---

[43] Tao Juyin, *Du Jun Tuan Zhuang* (Biographies of Corps of Military Governors) (Taipei: Wenhai chubanshe, 1971), 61.

[44] *Millard's Review*, 14 July 1917, 150.

[45] Li, *Political History of China*, 365–6.

[46] Zeng Yujuan, "Li Duan Mao dun yi fu yuan chun tu" (Clashes between Li Yuanhong and Duan Qirui and the Conflicts between the Presidential Office and the Cabinet), in Du Chunhe, Lin Binsheng, and Qiu Quanzheng (eds), *Bei Yang Jun Fa Shi Liao Xuan Ji* (Selected Materials on Beiyang

for him, and he was the one who encouraged the military intervention in civil politics in the first place.

Many congressmen were so angry at Duan and the *dujun* that they decided to delay voting on the war question and demanded that Duan explain the spectacle of mobs surrounding the parliament building. The GMD members of parliament refused to attend further sessions until they had been guaranteed protection against mob violence and intimidation. But Duan continued to play a dangerous game, getting the military governors involved in central policy and foreign affairs on an ever-greater scale. In mid-May, the *dujun* made further threats at a reception they gave for the members of the parliament. These ongoing threats outraged the members of parliament, and, on 19 May, the House of Representatives passed a resolution stating that the war bill would be passed only if Duan's government were reorganized. This action was actually a no-confidence vote for Duan and in effect called for his dismissal. It soon became clear that the gridlock between parliament and Duan Qirui would not easily be resolved. As Tao Juyin indicates, after Duan's terrible handling of the so-called public groups fiasco and his continuing use of the military governors, the parliament decided it had to target his cabinet before passing the war act.[47]

This was an enormous blow to Duan. The war act was stalled, and his government was itself in grave danger. Duan's cabinet members resigned in protest over his embarrassing handling of the public groups fiasco, leaving the Duan government a "one man cabinet" consisting only of himself, the prime minister. Standing alone with only the *dujun* to back him, Duan was faced with a terrible situation. In response to this crisis, Duan resorted to further threats and the dissolution of the parliament to secure his political survival and his war policy. More than ten of the military governors or their representatives voiced support for this move, and, because the cabinet lacked the power to dissolve parliament, the *dujun* openly pressured President Li to do so.[48] This immediately brought Li back onto a collision course with Duan. Li, unmoved by the *dujun*' pressure, claimed that the president had no constitutional power to dissolve the parliament. On the evening of 21 May, with no prospect of any progress with Li, all the *dujun* left Beijing for their own respective power bases. Two days later, President Li took the bold action of dismissing Duan and appointing Wu Tingfang to act temporarily in his stead in order to break the gridlock between Duan and parliament. Refusing to accept his dismissal and calling Li's action illegal, lacking the endorsement of the prime minister—namely himself—Duan declared he would take no responsibility for any consequences that might arise from this action.[49] This was tantamount to calling

Warlords) (Beijing: Zhongguo she hui ke xue chu ban she, 1981). See also Ji Yu, *Duan Qirui Zhuan* (Hefei: Anhui ren min chu ban she, 1992), 272–3.

[47] Tao Juyin, *Du Jun Tuan Zhuang*, 61.

[48] "Bei fang ge sheng dujun cocheng qing Li Yuanhong jie shang guo hui wen" (Memorandum from the Northern Provinces' Military Governors asking Li Yuanhong to Dissolve the Parliament) (*Dong Fang Zazhi*, 14/7 (1917)).

[49] *Zhong Hua Xin Bao*, 24 May 1917.

on the military governors to stage a rebellion. Accordingly, eight of the military governors in late May declared independence from Li's central government.

Thus a new and even more serious crisis emerged, putting Li Yuanhong on the hot seat. The northern government was faced with division and disintegration. Li found, ironically, that the only source to whom he could turn for help was a warlord, Zhang Xun (1854–1923), who had not declared independence and had in fact volunteered his services. Zhang, a determined enemy of the republican system and the very conservative military governor of Anhui province, was known as the "pigtail general" because his army still wore the queue as a gesture of loyalty to the Qing. On 1 June, Li officially asked Zhang to mediate. Li's reliance on Zhang turned out to be a terrible mistake, like Duan's earlier soliciting of help from the *dujun* collectively. In Zhang, Li found no savior but rather a destroyer of the republic. On 7 June, even before he and his army had reached Beijing, Zhang demanded that the president dissolve the parliament immediately; otherwise he would not take on the responsibility of mediation. Li, now on the back of a tiger, reluctantly agreed. After much confusion and haranguing, the president dissolved parliament on 13 June 1917. But this move did not satisfy Zhang, because Zhang's real goal from the moment he accepted the role of mediator was the restoration of the Manchu emperor. On 1 July, by Zhang Xun's arrangement, a reassembled Qing court declared a restoration. While Yuan's monarchical dream had lasted less than three months, the Qing restoration proved even shorter, about one week. Zhang Xun had clearly misread his time. He insisted that the 1911 Revolution had been the result of agitation from intellectuals who were "deeply engrossed in Westernization" and was not the people's choice.[50] The quick collapse of Zhang's scheme proved the widespread presence of republican thinking, the real source of the revolution. But the Zhang restoration fiasco did serious damage to republican politics. Li Yuanhong had not only failed to solve the problem of the *dujun* rebellion; he had unwittingly helped to unleash a most unlikely ghost—that of the old Qing empire. He resigned immediately in great shame and embarrassment. Furthermore, the restoration scheme provided Duan with an excellent opportunity to return to power as a defender of the republic, by defeating Zhang militarily. But Duan again fumbled the opportunity, and soon he and his opponents in the southern provinces were entangled in a serious dispute over the constitution that led to the further breakdown of consensus on his Great War policy.

When Duan finally managed to get China into the First World War on 14 August 1917, the country was in worse shape domestically, having weathered political crises brought on in the course of sorting out the institutional basis of a war policy.[51] President Li had gone, parliament had been dissolved, and the nation was divided. The goal of the war declaration had subsequently changed. Before the political crisis, Duan's motive for joining the war was to advance China's national interest,

---

[50] Sun Yao (ed.), *Zhong Hua min guo shi liao* (Taipei: Wenhai chubanshe, 1966), ii, pt 4, 3.

[51] Interestingly, Chinese parliament finally approved China's declaration on Germany and Austria on 6 November 1918, five days before the war was over. For details on this, see Nan hai yin zi, *An fu huo guo ji* (Beijing: Zhong hua shu ji, 2007), 76–9.

but after all that had happened Duan's main attention and focus were shifted to fight his opponents domestically.

THE GREAT WAR AND ITS GREAT IMPLICATIONS

The broadly defined First World War years coincided with a period of tremendous change within China as the old Confucian civilization began to collapse and China struggled to become a nation and sought to assume equal relations with the West. Although the Great War triggered enormous domestic unrest in China, we should not discard the war's long-term positive impact on its national development and China's contributions to the war. With the Great War, China embarked on a new journey—namely, that of internationalization and national renewal. China's new course and great contribution to the war began with the journey of 140,000 Chinese laborers to Europe during the Great War.

The Great War was a total war, fought on both the battlefield and the home front; it consumed fighting forces and other human resources. It was also a great trench war. The Chinese played a crucial part in the trench warfare. These laborers were recruited by the governments of France and Britain to help both countries in their Great War against the Germans; later, when the United States joined the war, the Americans took advantage of their labor as well. South Africans, Indians, Vietnamese, and many other laborers went to France during the war to support the British and French. Many went because they came from colonial countries and had to answer the call from their imperial masters. But China, no country's colony, sent by far the largest number of men, and its laborers worked in Europe the longest. The Chinese came voluntarily and their contributions were the most significant (see Fig. 21). Although most of the Chinese laborers were illiterate farmers with no clear ideas about China or the world when they were selected to go to Europe, they had a part in developing that new national identity and would play an important role in China's internationalization. As a result of their personal experiences in Europe and daily work with Americans, British, French, and fellow laborers from other countries, the Chinese developed a unique perception of China as a nation and as a member in the family of nations. During the Great War, laborers from many countries served in France. They came to answer the call from their colonial masters or to seek personal material gain. But none of them had a direct link to their nations' grand strategy and substantially affected national developments as the Chinese laborers did in China, which was then facing a great historical turning point. Unlike China, no country where these laborers came from had attached so much importance to (or had such high expectations for) the Great War. To be sure, Chinese laborers had gone abroad before to places such as California, South Africa, and Cuba. But the Chinese in France during the First World War were completely different from previous groups. First, their journey was directly linked to national policies of three countries—China, Britain, and France—that were collectively involved in the laborers' recruitment and treatments in France. Second, their arrival in France represented China's major drive for internationalization

Fig. 21. A parade of Chinese volunteers before their departure for France.

and equal status in the world. All these characters had been missing in previous groups' journeys. Their labor, their sacrifices, and their lives provided Chinese diplomats in Paris with a critical tool in their battle for recognition and inclusion on the world stage.

The Chinese laborers not only made important contributions to the war; they also contributed enormously in terms of what happened at the post-war peace conference and in China's subsequent development. It is important to keep in mind that the Chinese government and social elites were deeply involved in the laborers' journey to France. From the beginning, Chinese elites, whether government officials, independent thinkers, or educators, considered the idea of sending laborers to Europe from a broad perspective. First, the laborers were crucial and coherent parts of the grand plan to have China join the community of nations as an equal member. The thinking went that having Chinese laborers work side by side with Westerners in France would forge a crucial link between China and the West, and would be a daily reminder to the world of the strategic relevance of China's "laborers as soldiers" program. The key to understanding the intensity of Chinese interest in the European war is that it was seen as an effective vehicle by which the Chinese could push for internationalization at home and establish their nation anew abroad. Their journey to France thus symbolized China's active participation in world affairs and provided support for China's powerful demand in the post-war world arena for equal treatment of China and its people. The laborers' success is also reflected in the fact that, although nobody has given them this credit, they are an important part of China's own "greatest generation," the generation of the 1910s and 1920s that fundamentally changed China's direction of development during and after the Great War (see Fig. 22).

Without sending its laborers to Europe and eventually joining the war, China would have had more difficulty being invited to the post-war peace conference and therefore would not have had the opportunity to bring its case to the world audience. Without its membership at the post-war peace conference and through the

Fig. 22. Chinese laborers in France.

conference the opportunity to bring China's cases to the world's attention, China would not have recovered Shandong in the soon to come Washington Conference. Given all the misfortunes and mishaps China experienced in the course of its attempts to engage in the First World War, it is perhaps surprising that the Chinese people were genuinely excited and even jubilant when the fighting ended with the Allies' victory. Nonetheless, when the news arrived, the government in Beijing immediately declared a three-day national holiday to commence upon the Armistice. Thirty thousand people gathered before the Presidential Palace in Beijing on 17 November to celebrate the victory; they cried out with one voice, "Long live justice! Long live national independence!" The excitement and high expectations derived from Chinese adulation over Woodrow Wilson's many pronouncements regarding a new world order. Although not every Chinese believed in him, feelings ran high at the dramatic conclusion of the war. One of the major sources of Wilson's appeal for the Chinese was the new world order idea, especially his plan for a League of Nations and national self-determination. Thus, trusting Wilson and enthralled with the idea of a League of Nations, the Chinese had extremely high hopes for the coming peace conference, especially when the news came that Wilson himself would go to Paris.

The official Chinese goals for the Paris Peace Conference fell into three major categories: first, territorial integrity, or restoration to China of the foreign concessions and leased territories; secondly, restoration of national sovereignty, or the abolition of restrictions imposed upon China by the Protocol of 1901; third, economic freedom, or the exercise of complete tariff autonomy.[52] To be sure, the Chinese delegation's immediate focus was on the recovery of Shandong. But Chinese expectations for the peace conference met with disappointment when Japan's claims to Shandong were supported by Britain, France, and Italy, thanks to a secret arrangement Japan had made with them in early 1917. The Chinese cause was further compromised by treaties China had signed with Japan in 1915 and 1918, respectively, regarding Shandong. At a meeting of 22 April 1919, British prime minister Lloyd George, after admitting that "he had never heard of the Japanese Twenty-One Demands, let alone the ultimatum" Japan presented to China, pressed Wellington Koo to choose between allowing Japan to accede to Germany's right to Shandong, as stated in the treaty between China and Germany, or recognizing Japan's position in Shandong, as stipulated in the Sino-Japanese treaties. The major reason the Big Four pressed China to concede was the treaties China had signed with Japan in 1915 and 1918. Even Wilson, an advocate of open diplomacy in his Fourteen Points, now joined the other powers. At the session of 22 April, he told the Chinese that the war "has been fought largely for the purpose of showing that treaties cannot be violated," and advised that "it would be better to live up to a bad treaty than to tear it up."[53] On 30 April, the United States, Britain, and France decided to allow Japan to retain former German interests in China, including Shandong. On 28 June 1919 members of the Chinese delegation all decided not to sign the treaty and absented themselves from the signing ceremony. Koo remembered this day as more than merely sad. "It was a memorable day for me and for the whole delegation and for China. China's absence must have been a surprise if not a shock to the Conference, to the diplomatic world in France and to the entire world beyond."[54]

Koo was right. Many, including Wilson, were surprised by the Chinese move. Wilson was "greatly disturbed at the absence of Chinese." He told American secretary of state Robert Lansing that this was "most serious. It will cause grave complications."[55] "The betrayal at Versailles" indeed led many Chinese elites to doubt the value, and even the possibility, of China's identifying with the West. The moral and practical attraction of Western ideas in China's quest for national stature lost weight among many influential Chinese elites. Yan Fu, the famous scholar and translator of many Western books, declared that the behavior of the West in 1919 showed that "three hundred years of evolutionary progress have all come down to nothing but four words: selfishness, slaughters, shamelessness, and corruption."[56]

<hr>

[52] Department of State (ed.), *Papers Relating to the Foreign Relations of the United States, 1919, the Paris Peace Conference*, ii (Washington: Government Printing Office, 1942), 492, 509–11.

[53] Wensi Jin, *China at the Paris Peace Conference in 1919, Asia in the Modern World, No. 2* (Jamaica, NY: St. John's University Press, 1961), 14–15.

[54] Koo Memoir (Columbia University Oral History Project), reel 2, vol. 2.

[55] "Memorandum by the Secretary of state, the signing of the treaty of peace with Germany at Versailles on June 28th, 1919," in Department of State (ed.), *Papers Relating to the Foreign Relations of the United States, the Paris Peace Conference, 1919*, xi (Washington: Government Printing Office, 1945), 602.

[56] James Pusey, *China and Charles Darwin* (Cambridge, MA: Harvard University Press, 1983), 439.

Some concluded that Paris Peace Treaty testified to a "failure of Wilsonianism and victory of imperialism." The new world system, based on the exploitation of Germany and China, could not last long.[57] Some even warned that the League of Nations could do China no good. China must rely on itself.[58]

By forcing the whole world to take notice of China's situation, the Chinese refusal to put its signature on the Versailles treaty also set the stage for resolution of the Shandong problem at the Washington Conference in 1921. In his 1920 annual report to Earl Curzon, Jordan's successor in China Alston wrote:

The rising tide of international esteem began to flow when China refused, weak as she was, to be bullied into signing the treaty of Versailles. Though the momentary political victory at that time went to Japan, the moral victory remained with China, and has since culminated in her obtaining one of the temporary seats on the Council of the League of Nations.[59]

Moreover, China's refusal to sign the Versailles peace treaty directly led to a new treaty between China and Germany in 1921, to legitimize the abolition of rights and establish a new relationship. The new Sino-German treaty was the first equal treaty China signed with a major European country after the Opium War. China and Germany, both very disappointed with the Versailles Treaty and the new world order, and both having shared the bond of a sense of betrayal, were determined to turn a new page in their mutual relations after 1921. To a great extent, this explained why Germany enjoyed good relations with China in 1920s and 1930s.

Another direct influence of the war and the post-war peace conference on China is that they were directly responsible for the May Fourth Movement, a major movement in Chinese history. When the news of the big powers' refusal to return Shandong to China broke, Chinese students started to protest on 4 May 1919. Throughout the month of May, while the Chinese delegation was hard at work in Paris, students across China demonstrated, shouting and carrying banners that read "Down with the traitors!," "Give China Justice!," "Buy National Goods!," and "Give us back our Qingdao!" "Externally, struggle for national sovereignty; internally, punish national traitors" was a very popular slogan in 1919. The May Fourth Movement marked the end of Chinese all-out efforts to join the liberal Western system, efforts begun by China's seeking to join the First World War, and prompted a Chinese search for a third way, a way between Western ideas and Chinese traditional culture. The movement was an expression of the new foreign policy public's disillusion with the Western powers after their refusal to return Shandong. "Young China's faith in Wilsonian idealism has been shattered to dust. 'The New World Order' is no more," wrote one Chinese.[60] For Chen Duxiu, the pro-West liberal scholar and later a co-founder of the Chinese communist party, Wilson had turned

[57] *Taipingyang (Pacific)*, 2/1 (1919), 9.
[58] *Taipingyang (Pacific)*, 2/2 (1919), 2–4.
[59] TNA: PRO FO405/229/2.
[60] Hu Shih, "Intellectual China 1919," *Chinese Social and Political Science Review*, 4/4 (December 1919), 346–7; quotation from Zhang Yongjin, *China in the International System, 1918–20: The Middle Kingdom at the Periphery* (New York: St Martin's Press, 1991), 74.

out to be an "empty cannon" whose principles were "not worth one penny."[61] Students across China openly expressed their disappointment at the failure of Wilsonianism. Those at Beijing University cynically joked that Wilson had discovered a jolting new formula for the idealistic world order: "14 [referring to Wilson's 14 Principles] = 0."[62] The humiliation China had suffered in Paris put a dampener on the pursuit of a Westernized national identity. The practical failure of the Paris Peace Conference alienated Chinese intellectuals, many of whom had been exposed to ideas about the decline of West generated by the likes of Oswald Spengler. The May Fourth Movement, another turning point in China's quest for national identity, prompted a search for a third way, a way between Western ideas and Chinese traditional culture. After their heart-breaking experience at the Paris Peace Conference, the Chinese perceived the Bolshevik Revolution as the only successful model for state-building, and Bolshevik Russia was the only power that appeared sympathetic to their aspirations. At that point, Mao Zedong, then just another young educated youth, concluded that Russia was "the number one civilized country in the world."[63]

It is only from the perspective of this "double betrayal" that we can fully appreciate China's sudden interest in the Russian Revolution and the Soviet Empire that followed. When the Bolshevik Revolution had occurred in 1917, the Chinese had not seemed interested. Few if any in China paid serious attention to Marxism at that point. Only after 1919, after being betrayed by the West, did the Chinese start to think about the Russian political system and initiate serious studies of Marxism. The results of the First World War planted the seeds of destruction for the Japanese Empire in the Second World War and eventually led to the rise of a red empire in China (communist dictatorship), but that is a different story to be told another time.

[61] *Meizhou Ping lun*, 20, 4 May 1919.

[62] Zhong Guo She hui ko xue yuan Jing dai shi yan jiu so (ed.), *Wu Si Yun Dong Hui Yi Lu* (Recollections of the May Fourth Movement) (Beijing: Zhong guo she hui ko xue chu ban she, 1979), i. 222.

[63] John King Fairbank and Albert Feuerwerker (eds), *The Cambridge History of China: 1912–1949*, (Cambridge: Cambridge University Press, 1986), xiii, pt 2, 802.

12

The United States Empire

Christopher Capozzola

PROLOGUE: THE PANAMA CANAL, 1914

On 16 August 1914, newspapers noted the official opening of the Panama Canal. Early the previous morning, the steamship *Ancon* left Cristóbal on the Caribbean Sea on a day-long voyage to the Pacific Ocean, completing in nine hours a journey that usually took weeks. But one canal engineer, noting the absence of fanfare, reflected that "a strange observer coming suddenly upon the scene would have thought the canal had always been in operation." News from Panama that day was eclipsed by headlines recounting events thousands of miles away in Europe, where diplomatic controversies had escalated into war between the major powers, a conflict that commentators at the time, and historians contemplating it since, have understood as a war between imperial rivals.[1]

Two and a half years later, in April 1917, the United States formally joined the war in Europe, and its armed forces played a critical role in the war's final stages. By the time of the Armistice, the United States would have recruited and trained nearly four million men and women in its armed forces, and sent nearly two million of them to France. America mobilized its empire—of which the newly constructed Panama Canal was the crown jewel—as part of the global war effort. But that empire, like the canal's opening day, has remained in history's shadows, in part because the US empire played only a small part during the critical 1917–18 intervention in Europe. While the United States did not deploy large armies of colonial soldiers to the trenches of the Western Front—as did Britain and France—it nonetheless deployed its empire in war, and rethought the terms of colonial control along the way. If territorial empire mattered little to the US war effort during the First World War, the wartime era nevertheless transformed the US empire as a set of political institutions and mindsets. In particular, looking at practices of military and police training across both the territorially incorporated US empire and its

---

[1] Julie Greene, *The Canal Builders: Making America's Empire at the Panama Canal* (New York: Penguin, 2009), 337–8, 344–5; David McCullough, *The Path between the Seas: The Creation of the Panama Canal, 1870–1914* (New York: Simon and Schuster, 1977), 608–17 (quotation at p. 609). For news coverage, compare "The Panama Canal Officially Opened," *New York Times*, 16 August 1914, 14, and "Big Armies Ready on 248-Mile Battle Front," *New York Times*, 16 August 1914, 1.

sites of military occupation reveals shifts in colonial arrangements that had consequences for a generation to come, even if they rarely made newspaper headlines.

Between 1914 and 1924, the United States established, armed, trained, and at
times directly administered the military or police forces of nearly a dozen dependent territories and nominally sovereign nations. An imperial perspective on
the First World War—and a chronology that extends beyond the strict 1914–18
period—uncovers the long-term significance of wartime events in the periphery of
the US empire. World war strained the US military's capacity for imperial administration, both by drawing experienced soldiers to service in Europe and by calling
into question the authority of the United States to exercise sovereign control over
other nations. As American soldiers clamored to get to France, as global unrest
made political order and stability a pressing issue, and as Latin Americans, Carib-
beans, and Asians pointed out the contradictions of US imperialism in an age that
cherished the rights of national self-determination, it became increasingly clear
that military and police training was a practical, rhetorical, and timely solution to
a crisis the war had generated.[2]

America's ambitious policing policy also had consequences, in both the short
and long terms. It drew many of these countries more firmly into a US-centered
orbit. It distorted the political and budgetary priorities of small nations that were
ill-equipped simultaneously to field large armed forces and pursue economic development. And it created enduring relationships between the security apparatuses of
these nations and those of a US empire that after 1918 wielded power more globally at the same time as it retreated from the acquisition of territory. Formal colonial control continued, but informal cooperative arrangements proliferated. The
military base replaced the coaling station; the joint exercise supplemented the lone
gunboat.

THE UNITED STATES EMPIRE AT THE OUTSET OF WAR

By 1914, the United States empire had undergone a generation of transformation,
in its physical size, strategic value, and constitutional rationale. Devastating wars
against Native Americans in the 1890s completed the century-long military conquest of the North American continent. War with Spain in 1898 and with the
Philippines from 1899 to the early 1900s had led to the annexation of Puerto Rico,
Guam, Hawai'i, American Samoa, and the Philippines. The US also wielded effective control over other parts of the Caribbean and Central America through

---

[2] Few scholars have traced the long histories of US efforts to train foreign military forces. For over-
views, most of them focused on the post-1945 period, see Lesley Gill, *The School of the Americas:
Military Training and Political Violence in the Americas* (Durham, NC: Duke University Press, 2004),
esp. 59–89; Jeremy Kuzmarov, *Modernizing Repression: Police Training and Nation Building in the
American Century* (Amherst: University of Massachusetts Press, 2012), esp. 21–52; Chester J. Pach, Jr,
Arming the Free World: The Origins of the United States Military Assistance Program, 1945–1950 (Chapel
Hill, NC: University of North Carolina Press, 1991), esp. 7–28; and Mark Peceny, *Democracy at the
Point of Bayonets* (University Park, PA: Pennsylvania State University Press, 1999).

coercive trade relations, repeated short-term military interventions and long-term occupations in Haiti and the Dominican Republic, Cuba, Nicaragua, and Mexico. The United States was thus not new to territorial conquest and expropriation, but it was nevertheless a relative latecomer to imperial rivalry in the geopolitical sense. Along with these sovereign assertions, a nascent imperial outlook had also emerged, shaped by the Spanish– and Philippine–American wars and, not least, the construction of the Panama Canal. Theodore Roosevelt's 1904 corollary to the Monroe Doctrine announced an "international police power" that "some civilized nation" would exercise in "flagrant cases of wrongdoing," which Roosevelt and his successor, William Howard Taft, used to justify US military and economic interventions in the Caribbean basin. And, in a series of decisions known as the Insular Cases, the US Supreme Court elaborated the notion of an "unincorporated territory," authorizing the federal government to wield sovereign power over regions that would never become part of the territorial United States.[3]

This is not to say that these changes were universally accepted. The 1900s and 1910s also witnessed a contentious debate about the long-term future of America's imperial possessions and the citizenship status of their residents. President Woodrow Wilson's election in 1912 led to several initiatives to reverse the course of US imperial policy. In a speech on 28 December 1912, in his home town of Staunton, Virginia, Wilson announced that "the Philippines are our present frontier, and we [...] are presently, I hope, to deprive ourselves of that frontier," a position that the Democratic Party had held in its platform without interruption since the election of 1900. Sponsored in Congress by Virginia representative William

---

[3] Theodore Roosevelt, *Presidential Addresses and State Papers* (New York: Review of Reviews Co., 1910), iii. 119–89 (quotations at pp. 176, 177). On the US empire in this period, see Julian Go, *American Empire and the Politics of Meaning: Elite Political Cultures in the Philippines and Puerto Rico during U.S. Colonialism* (Durham, NC: Duke University Press, 2008); Alfred W. McCoy and Francisco Scarano (eds), *Colonial Crucible: Empire in the Making of the Modern American State* (Madison: University of Wisconsin Press, 2009); Bartholomew H. Sparrow, *The Insular Cases and the Emergence of American Empire* (Lawrence, KS: University Press of Kansas, 2006); Lanny Thompson, *Imperial Archipelago: Representation and Rule in the Insular Territories under U.S. Dominion after 1898* (Honolulu: University of Hawai'i Press, 2010). For more on American interventions in Central America and the Caribbean, see George W. Baker, Jr, "The Wilson Administration and Cuba, 1913–1921," *Mid-America*, 46 (January 1964), 48–63; Mark T. Gilderhus, *Pan-American Visions: Woodrow Wilson and the Western Hemisphere, 1913–1921* (Tucson, AZ: University of Arizona Press, 1986); Michel Gobat, *Confronting the American Dream: Nicaragua under U.S. Imperial Rule* (Durham, NC: Duke University Press, 2005), 73–201; Lester D. Langley, *The Banana Wars: An Inner History of American Empire, 1900–1934* (Lexington, KY: University Press of Kentucky, 1983); Carlos Pereyra, *El Crimen de Woodrow Wilson* (Madrid: Impr. de J. Pueyo, 1917); Mary A. Renda, *Taking Haiti: Military Occupation and the Culture of U.S. Imperialism, 1915–1940* (Durham, NC: Duke University Press, 2001); Joseph H. Tulchin, *The Aftermath of War: World War I and U.S. Policy toward Latin America* (New York: New York University Press, 1971). Whether to include sites such as the Caribbean in this chapter would in the past have generated disagreement. Here I follow a recent consensus that breaks down the rigid distinction maintained between "formal" and "informal" empires, and follow Paul A. Kramer's encouragement of "thinking with the imperial," asking not what empire is, but "what it does, what kind of analyses it enables or forecloses" (Kramer, "Power and Connection: Imperial Histories of the United States in the World," *American Historical Review*, 116 (June 2011), 1348–91 (quotations at pp. 1349, 1350)).

Jones, bills proposing the independence of Puerto Rico and the Philippines none-theless languished for lack of bipartisan support.[4]

But, by 1915, Wilson was explaining to Congress that its handling of the colo-nial question constituted part of larger "great policies" that war in Europe had made particularly urgent. "Our treatment of [US territorial subjects] and their at-titude towards us are manifestly of the first consequence in the development of our duties in the world and in getting a free hand to perform those duties." This was, Wilson insisted, "very intimately associated with the question of national safety and preparation for defense."[5]

For Wilson, this meant putting the Philippines on a path toward eventual (but not immediate) independence. The outbreak of war in August 1914 heightened uncertainties about the Philippines' status. In early 1915, Philippine Governor General Francis B. Harrison warned Secretary of War Lindley Garrison that failure to pass the Jones bill could lead to "disturbances." Woodrow Wilson urged Senate action, citing "the general world situation, from which I think it is our duty to re-move every element of doubt or disturbance." Not all agreed. Ohio senator Warren G. Harding won national attention for his speech on the floor of the Senate in January 1916. "I do not want it said that this great nation, aspiring to a place in the councils of the world [...] is so miserably afraid that it wants to cast aside some of its possessions to avoid some of the dangers of war." Elihu Root, the architect of America's Philippine policy and serving then as a Republican senator from New York, dismissed Jones's proposals as "chuckle-headed." But a bill promising greater self-government for the Philippines passed, Wilson signed it on 29 August 1916, and 40,000 gathered in Manila to celebrate.[6]

War in Europe also changed the place of the US territorial empire in American military and naval strategy. During the war years, the US flexed its diplomatic muscle in Central and South America with several aims in mind: to assert US dominance while Germany and Britain were engaged in war with each other; to

---

[4] Woodrow Wilson, "An Address at a Birthday Banquet in Staunton," 28 December 1912, in *The Papers of Woodrow Wilson*, ed. Arthur S. Link et al. (Princeton: Princeton University Press, 1966–94), xxv. 635.

[5] Woodrow Wilson, "An Annual Message on the State of the Union," 7 December 1915, in *The Papers of Woodrow Wilson*, ed. Link et al., xxxv. 293–310 (quotation at p. 303).

[6] Francis Burton Harrison to Lindley Garrison, 20 January 1915, Box 42, Papers of Francis Burton Harrison, Library of Congress Manuscript Division, Washington; Wilson, quoted in Roy Watson Curry, *Woodrow Wilson and Far Eastern Policy, 1913–1921* (New York: Bookman Associates, 1957), 86; Warren G. Harding, "The Philippine Islands," in Frederick E. Schortemeier (ed.), *Rededicating America: Life and Recent Speeches of Warren G. Harding* (Indianapolis: Bobbs-Merrill, 1920), 236–7; Elihu Root, quoted in Whitney T. Perkins, "The New Dependencies under McKinley," in Paolo E. Coletta (ed.), *Threshold to American Internationalism: Essays on the Foreign Policies of William McKinley* (New York: Exposition Press, 1970), 276. For more on the implementation of the Jones Act, see Roy W. Curry, "Woodrow Wilson and Philippine Policy," *Mississippi Valley Historical Review*, 41 (December 1954), 435–52; Frank H. Golay, *Face of Empire: United States-Philippines Relations, 1898–1946* (Quezon City: Ateneo de Manila University Press, 1997), 201–6; Maximo M. Kalaw, *The Case for the Filipinos* (New York: Century Co., 1916); Arthur S. Link, *Wilson: Confusions and Crises, 1915–1916* (Princeton: Princeton University Press, 1964), 350–6; Michael P. Onorato, "The Jones Act and the Establishment of a Filipino Government, 1916–1921," *Philippine Studies*, 14 (July 1966), 448–59.

create a sense of hemispheric unity with the US as its leading voice; and to keep Germany from gaining a foothold in the Caribbean basin that might threaten America's free hand over the newly constructed Panama Canal. From 1910 to 1916, the US Navy assumed that war against Germany would culminate in a massive naval battle in the Caribbean, and indeed ever since 1913 had made such a contingency part of War Plan Black, its plan for war against Germany. (The Germans, for their part, had made similar preparations for naval war against the United States.) Wary of German expansion and informed by grand strategies laid out by naval theorist Alfred Thayer Mahan—who saw the Panama Canal as a turning point in the history of geopolitics—the United States made moves to assert and defend its military supremacy in the Caribbean well before it entered the war, and continued to do so during and after the 1917–18 period of US intervention.[7]

Nowhere did German actions seem more menacing than in Mexico, where the overthrow of dictator Porfirio Díaz had sparked revolution and civil war on the southern border of the United States. Drawing on the Roosevelt Corollary, Woodrow Wilson committed troops to a brief occupation of the Caribbean port city of Veracruz in April 1914. During the next two years, German officials sought to curry favor with leading factions of the Mexican revolution, and offered support to the revolutionaries' Plan de San Diego, which sought to recover Mexican territories lost to the United States in the US–Mexican War of 1846–8. Long before the January 1917 Zimmermann Telegram—in which German diplomats were instructed to seek a wartime military alliance with Mexico—the US government (and Americans who lived in the south-west) believed that German intrigue would unsettle border relations and drag the United States into the European war.[8]

Another important step in the consolidation of US hegemony in the Caribbean was the acquisition of the US Virgin Islands from Denmark in 1916. The idea had been on the table for decades, but it was the world war that made it happen: the USA feared that Germany might conquer Denmark or pressure the Danes to grant Germany territorial concessions in the Danish West Indies, which would threaten US interests in the region generally and at the Panama Canal more specifically. Indeed, in September 1915, Secretary of State Robert Lansing went so far as to tell the Danish government that, if it ceded the islands to Germany (either by consent

---

[7] Greene, *Canal Builders*, 350–1; Dirk Bönker, *Militarism in a Global Age: Naval Ambitions in Germany and the United States before World War I* (Ithaca, NY: Cornell University Press, 2012), 125–48; Holger H. Herwig, *Politics of Frustration: The United States in German Naval Planning, 1889–1941* (Boston: Little, Brown, 1976); Alfred T. Mahan, "The Panama Canal and Sea Power in the Pacific," *Century Magazine*, 82 (May–October 1911), 240–8; Donald A. Yerxa, "The United States Navy in Caribbean Waters during World War I," *Military Affairs*, 51 (October 1987), 182–7.

[8] Patrick L. Cox, "'An Enemy Closer to Us than Any European Power': The Impact of Mexico on Texan Public Opinion before World War I," *Southwestern Historical Quarterly*, 105 (July 2001), 41–80; Benjamin Heber Johnson, *Revolution in Texas: How a Forgotten Rebellion and its Bloody Repression Turned Mexicans into Americans* (New Haven, CT: Yale University Press, 2003); Friedrich Katz, *The Secret War in Mexico: Europe, the United States, and the Mexican Revolution* (Chicago: University of Chicago Press, 1981); James A. Sandos, *Rebellion in the Borderlands: Anarchism and the Plan of San Diego, 1904–1923* (Norman, OK: University of Oklahoma Press, 1992); Barbara W. Tuchman, *The Zimmermann Telegram* (New York: Viking, 1958).

or coercion), the US would invade and seize them. Negotiations for transfer were smooth—the Danish had little interest in maintaining their economically unviable island empire—but the purchase of the Virgin Islands came with a catch: the Danish government (pressured both by colonial officials and by island residents) insisted that the islands' residents must become US citizens. Lansing assented, and the deal was sealed on 4 August 1916, ratified soon thereafter by the two nations, and the Danish flag hauled down on 31 March 1917. The New York *World* editorialized that the islands' $25 million price tag was high, "but as an insurance against the menace of an inimical power it is cheap enough."[9]

Decisions made regarding the Virgin Islands had consequences in Puerto Rico, just 50 miles west of America's newest territory. Puerto Rican political leaders had pressed for greater political autonomy ever since annexation in 1898, but the threat of war prompted the Wilson administration to press for reforms that would clarify the status of the island and its residents. During congressional debate on Puerto Rico's status in February 1917, Secretary of War Newton D. Baker told Congress that passage of legislation was "of the utmost importance if we are to soon face an international crisis." The second Jones Act, signed on 4 March 1917, marked the culmination of four years of partisan conflict and legislative maneuvering on the Puerto Rican question. Members of Congress had objected to earlier bills that granted US citizenship to Puerto Rican residents, but, after American concessions to Denmark in negotiations for the US Virgin Islands, it became politically impossible for the US to deny to Puerto Ricans what Virgin Islanders had just won. Wilson was pleased with the Act's passage, as was Brigadier General Frank McIntyre, who headed the War Department's Bureau of Insular Affairs. "The wisdom of these acts has been vindicated as measures of preparation for the present emergency," he explained in his annual report. "They have been accepted by the people most concerned as a timely recognition of their rights to self-government and as an additional evidence of the unselfishness of the American people in their relations with their newest territory."[10]

---

[9] New York *World*, quoted in George W. Baker, "Robert Lansing and the Purchase of the Danish West Indies," *Social Studies*, 57 (February 1966), 68. See also "Buying Islands for Defense," *Literary Digest*, 53 (30 December 1916), 1697–8; "Buying More Islands," *The Nation*, 103 (3 August 1916), 99–100; "Buying the Danish West Indies," *Independent Review*, 87 (7 August 1916), 175 ff.; Wilfrid H. Callcott, *The Caribbean Policy of the United States, 1890–1920* (Chicago: Octagon Books, 1966 [1942]), 426–9; Maurice Francis Egan, *Ten Years near the German Frontier: A Retrospect and a Warning* (New York: George H. Doran, 1919), esp. 261–4; Robert S. Lansing, "Drama of the Virgin Islands Purchase," *New York Times*, 19 July 1923; "New Islands under the Flag," *Literary Digest*, 53 (5 August 1916), 290–1; Charles Callan Tansill, *The Purchase of the Danish West Indies* (Baltimore: Johns Hopkins Press, 1932), 373–516. For more on pressures from Virgin Islanders, see Gregory LaMotta, "Working People and the Transfer of the Danish West Indies to the United States, 1916–1917," *Journal of Caribbean History*, 23/2 (1989), 178–95.

[10] Baker, quoted in Arturo Morales Carrión, *Puerto Rico: A Political and Cultural History* (New York: W.W. Norton, 1983), 198; McIntyre, quoted in United States Bureau of Insular Affairs, *Report of the Chief of the Bureau of Insular Affairs* (Washington: Government Printing Office, 1917), 21. See also César J. Ayala and Rafael Bernabe, *Puerto Rico in the American Century: A History since 1898* (Chapel Hill, NC: University of North Carolina Press, 2007), 57–9; Truman R. Clark, *Puerto Rico and the United States, 1917–1933* (Pittsburgh: University of Pittsburgh Press, 1975); Frank Otto Gatell, "The Art of the Possible: Luis Muñoz Rivera and the Puerto Rican Jones Bill," *Americas,*

Changes in US colonial policy might have occurred with or without world war—Woodrow Wilson and his fellow Democrats were insistent on rolling back policies that had been in place since the full-throated imperialism of William McKinley. But, even before the US had entered the war, events in Europe changed two key factors that then accelerated any timetable of reform Wilson may have had in mind in Staunton, Virginia, in 1912: the war created concern about German motives and actions in Latin America and the Pacific, and the war opened a space for colonized subjects to demand reforms of US imperial rule.

MOBILIZING THE EMPIRE

The US declaration of war against Germany on 6 April 1917 also brought the US empire into the war. The Philippine Legislature—recently established by the previous year's Jones Act—announced its support of US policy, although the decision had already been made for the Filipinos. In the Dominican Republic, then under military occupation, there was no legislature, and thus the US declaration effectively brought that country into the war as well. In Central America, close US allies such as Cuba and Panama declared war immediately; others such as Nicaragua and Honduras delayed in the hope of writing diplomatic concessions from their powerful neighbor to the north, but soon fell in line. Only Mexico and El Salvador steadfastly maintained their neutrality.[11]

Few colonial soldiers were mobilized to serve in combat; the only colonial subjects who saw military service in Europe were those who were already living in the continental United States in April 1917 and joined up or were drafted thereafter. The Philippine Scouts—a colonial unit of the US Army established in 1901— never saw service outside the islands. In Manila, colonial officials and Filipino elites pressed for the formation of a Philippine National Guard, and hoped that it would serve in combat in Europe and as a training school for future officers of the army of an independent Philippines. Many Filipinos expressed an eagerness to serve: near Manila, Crisanto Guevara wrote that "I did not hesitate a moment in volunteering [...] to defend the right of the noble American nation." Others were less enthusiastic. In Honolulu, Pablo Manlapit, a Filipino member of the Hawai'ian National Guard, questioned the enthusiasm that accompanied the announcement that military service might be rewarded with US citizenship. "I have my own country to serve," he gruffed. In any case, delay, opposition, and distance prevented the Philippine National Guard from formal service. The war did substantially increase Filipino recruitment into the US Navy, where small numbers

17 (July 1960), 1–20; Morales Carrión, *Puerto Rico*, 173–99. Modest expansions of self-government also took place in Guam in 1917. See Don A. Farrell, *The Pictorial History of Guam: The Americanization, 1898–1918* (Tamuning: Micronesian Productions, 1986), 163.

[11] William D. McCain, *The United States and Panama* (Durham, NC: Duke University Press, 1937), 190–205; Emily S. Rosenberg, "World War I and 'Continental Solidarity,'" *The Americas*, 31 (January 1975), 313–34, esp. 321.

Fig. 23. Territory of Hawai'i registration day, 31 July 1917.

had served since 1901. In 1917, Navy Secretary Josephus Daniels began increasing the recruitment of Filipinos into bottom-rung positions as messmen and stewards (quietly eliminating African American sailors from those grades), a policy that would remain in place until the end of the twentieth century (see Fig. 23).[12]

[12] Christopher Capozzola, "Minutemen for the World: Empire, Citizenship, and the National Guard, 1903–1924," in McCoy and Scarano (eds), *Colonial Crucible*, 421–30; "Filipino Offers His Services to Defend 'Noble American Nation,'" *Philippines Free Press*, 14 April 1917, 13; Ricardo Trota Jose, "The Philippine National Guard in World War I," *Philippine Studies* 36 (Third Quarter 1988), 275–99; Pablo Manlapit, quoted in "Thinks Filipinos Not Inclined to Citizenship," *Honolulu Star-Bulletin*, 28 March 1916, 2; Ronald H. Spector, "Josephus Daniels, Franklin Roosevelt, and the Reinvention of the Naval Enlisted Man," in Edward J. Marolda (ed.), *FDR and the US Navy* (New York: St Martin's Press, 1998), 24–6.

A Puerto Rican regiment provided some 18,000 soldiers to the US military, most of whom were shipped across the Caribbean to guard the Panama Canal. Nearly as many Puerto Ricans were recruited as civilian laborers to build the two dozen military training camps hastily constructed after the US entry into war in April 1917, and thousands more were funneled into agricultural programs set up to respond to labor shortages during the war years. Trapped in substandard working conditions, they lodged a protest after the Armistice. "I think that the protection of the American flag belongs to us," Bacilo Rivera wrote from an Arizona cotton farm, "because we Porto [*sic*] Ricans have shed our blood for it." Naval authorities in Guam likewise recruited a few hundred Chamorros to serve in the Guam militia, later formally incorporated into the US armed forces as the Marine Corps Native Auxiliary.[13]

War recruited few colonial soldiers, but it did mobilize US soldiers serving in colonial locations, who moved in large numbers to new formations heading for France. Soldiers in the Philippines were some of the army's only experienced troops, and call-ups quickly summoned these men for redeployment in Europe. The number of American soldiers in the Philippines declined from 13,795 in 1917 to 5,255 just two years later; colonial subjects serving in the Philippine Scouts expanded from 5,702 to 8,159 in the same years, but they hardly made up the difference. John J. Pershing, who would serve as commanding officer of the American Expeditionary Forces (AEF) in France, had already left the Philippines in December 1913, while Europe was still at peace; he headed the US intervention in northern Mexico before being tapped for the top job in the AEF.[14]

In Mexico and again later in France, Pershing consistently tapped former Philippine comrades as advisers and subordinate officers. As a young marine officer in 1903, James G. Harbord had helped establish the Philippine Constabulary, the colonial paramilitary police force. He duly impressed his boss, John J. Pershing, who remembered the young officer and appointed Harbord Chief of Staff of the AEF in May 1917; later Harbord ran the US military supply chain. Harry Hill Bandholtz, the AEF's Provost Marshal General, had been head of the Philippine Constabulary from 1907 to 1913; the Constabulary's founding commander, Henry T. Allen, brought his policing experience to bear as the commanding officer of the American occupation of the Rhine after the war. Even Bishop Charles Henry Brent, the former Episcopal bishop of the Philippines

---

[13] John Whiteclay Chambers II, *To Raise an Army: The Draft Comes to Modern America* (New York: Free Press, 1987), 231–2; Farrell, *Pictorial History of Guam*, 158; Robert McGreevey, "Borderline Citizens: Puerto Ricans and the Politics of Migration, Race, and Empire, 1898–1948" (Ph.D. dissertation, Brandeis University, 2008), 182–223 (quotation at p. 213); Ché Paralitici, *No quiero mi cuerpo pa' tambor: El servicio militar obligatorio en Puerto Rico* (San Juan: Ediciones Puerto, 1998), 118–53. A small number of Virgin Islanders served in a naval band at the St Thomas Naval Station, but were otherwise excluded from the armed forces altogether. See William W. Boyer, *America's Virgin Islands: A History of Human Rights and Wrongs* (Durham, NC: Carolina Academic Press, 1983), 116–17.

[14] Edward M. Coffman, *The Regulars: The American Army, 1898–1941* (Cambridge, MA: Harvard University Press, 2004), 324–71; Brian McAllister Linn, *Guardians of Empire: The U.S. Army and the Pacific, 1902–1940* (Chapel Hill, NC: University of North Carolina Press, 1997), 253.

who had converted Pershing to the Episcopal Church, became head of the AEF's chaplain corps.[15]

If all these important figures—and hundreds of lower-ranking officers—knew each other from the Philippines, what is most remarkable is that they did not seek to replicate their Pacific experiences at the Western Front, but rather tried to leave them behind. "The principles of warfare as I learned them at West Point remain unchanged," Pershing explained in his two-volume memoirs of the war, which mentioned the Philippines just once. Pershing's assertion notwithstanding, the war in Europe—and the National Defense Act of 1916 that put US armed forces on a quasi-war footing—did fundamentally transform the US Army, from a small-scale "frontier" fighting force to a large standing army with global responsibilities and technologically sophisticated capacities to match.[16]

The war also brought changes in the relationship between the United States and its Allied powers. At meetings on 10–11 April 1917, the Americans met with British and French naval officers and agreed that the US Navy would take command of naval defense in the Caribbean. The newly established Atlantic Fleet Patrol Force was the embodiment of the Monroe Doctrine that James Monroe had never imagined and the Roosevelt Corollary that Roosevelt had only dreamed of, giving the USA free rein in the region, whereas before the war it had always had to tread lightly for fear of stepping on British toes. During the war, the anticipated massive naval battle with Germany never materialized and the Canal Zone was never in danger. The anticipated German U-Boat assaults rarely took place; false alarms far outnumbered actual attacks. Naval service in the Caribbean or Pacific was what one officer later described soon after the war as "deadly dull," but it had important long-term consequences.[17]

Politicians and strategists in Washington believed the most important contribution the US empire could make was economic. The war upended transatlantic

[15] Henry T. Allen, *My Rhineland Journal* (Boston: Houghton Mifflin, 1923); Henry T. Allen, *The Rhineland Occupation* (Indianapolis: Bobbs-Merrill, 1927); George Yarrington Coats, "The Philippine Constabulary, 1908–1917" (Ph.D. dissertation, Ohio State University, 1968), 10–11; Henry Gilhouser, "The Moro Province," *Bulletin of the American Historical Collection*, 1 (May 1973), 46; James G. Harbord, *Serving with Pershing: An Address Delivered before the University Club of Port Chester, Port Chester, New York, May 26, 1944* (n.p., n.d.), 5, 7; Michael C. Reilly, "Charles Henry Brent: Philippine Missionary and Ecumenist," *Philippine Studies*, 24 (Third Quarter 1976), 303–25; Heath Twichell, Jr, *Allen: The Biography of an Army Officer, 1859–1930* (New Brunswick, NJ: Rutgers University Press, 1974), 215–52.

[16] John J. Pershing, *My Experiences in the World War* (New York: Frederick A. Stokes, 1931), i. 11. James G. Harbord, *Leaves from a War Diary* (New York: Dodd, Mead, 1925), is similarly silent on the Philippines. On changes in the US army, see Coffman, *The Regulars*; John Dickinson, *The Building of an Army: A Detailed Account of Legislation, Administration and Opinion in the United States, 1915–1920* (New York: Century, 1922), esp. 3–56; Mark E. Grotelueschen, *The AEF Way of War: The American Army and Combat in World War I* (New York: Cambridge University Press, 2007).

[17] Carroll Storrs Alden, "American Submarine Operations in the War," *U.S. Naval Institute Proceedings*, 46 (June 1920), 820; Yerxa, "United States Navy," 183. See also Dean C. Allard, "Anglo-American Naval Differences during World War I," *Military Affairs*, 44 (April 1980), 75–81; Thomas G. Frothingham, *The Naval History of the World War: The United States in the War, 1917–1918* (Cambridge, MA: Harvard University Press, 1926); David F. Trask, *Captains and Cabinets: Anglo-American Naval Relations, 1917–1918* (Columbia: University of Missouri Press, 1972).

trade patterns just as the US economy moved onto a war footing; colonial territories that had lurched in boom-and-bust agricultural cycles now experienced a boom in commodity prices that Cubans would later recall as the *Danza de los Millones*. Wages, though, rarely kept up with spiraling prices, and, despite stringent anti-radical laws across the US empire, labor activism mounted both during the war and after. Increasingly, protest took on a more self-consciously anti-colonial cast, voicing internationalist resistance to US exploitation, whether through pan-Asianism, Garveyism, or an anti-colonialism inflected with Wilsonian rhetoric. Through their military service and their labor organizing, subjects of the US colonial empire increasingly used the wartime context to change the terms of political debate. What they saw as an opportunity, colonial officials understood as a threat, engineered by Germany and demanding a vigorous response.[18]

KEEPING ORDER: POLICING THE US EMPIRE

Within a few short years, the terms of US colonial policy in its largest territories had been remade, a response to Democratic ascendancy, global events, and pressure from Filipino and Puerto Rican political movements. The US declaration of war on Germany in April 1917 heightened fears of German subversion and concerns about the loyalty of America's imperial subjects. Compared to other wartime empires, there was relatively little political unrest, but colonial officials did not rest easily, particularly as military mobilization for war in Europe took the US armed forces out of their colonial posts. Writing from the US Virgin Islands, Governor Rear Admiral James Oliver explained to Navy Secretary Daniels that "it must be borne in mind that these islands, like the Isthmus of Panama, are a nest and focus of intrigue and although it has not been possible, up to this time, to connect any of the disturbances that have occurred with German propaganda, it is considered not unlikely that they have such connection." War required a rethinking of the patterns of military control in both the formal and the informal portions of the US empire. More than ever, empire became something that needed to be policed to keep extractive economies running smoothly, and indigenous police—rather than the US military—would be the ones to do the policing.[19]

Military intervention and occupation were hardly new elements of US foreign policy in the 1910s, although they did increase markedly under the administration of President Woodrow Wilson. What was different was the dramatic expansion of the policy of staffing and training military, paramilitary, and police forces that

[18] César J. Ayala, *American Sugar Kingdom: The Plantation Economy of the Spanish Caribbean, 1898–1934* (Chapel Hill, NC; University of North Carolina Press, 1999), 71, 85, 87; Jason M. Colby, *The Business of Empire: United Fruit, Race, and US Expansion in Central America* (Ithaca, NY: Cornell University Press, 2011), 118–45; Norwell Harrigan and Pearl I. Varlack, "The U.S. Virgin Islands and the Black Experience," *Journal of Black Studies*, 7 (June 1977), 394–8; Erez Manela, *The Wilsonian Moment: Self-Determination and the International Origins of Anticolonial Nationalism* (New York: Oxford University Press, 2007).

[19] Quoted in Boyer, *America's Virgin Islands*, 115.

nominally marched under other flags. This approach cannot really be called a policy, which would suggest a global vision masterminded from Washington. It was rather a series of improvised responses to global pressures and local politics across Latin America and the Pacific. Nominally, the stated aim of police training in most locales was to create modern, professional, and non-political forces that would train young men in a process of nation-building, establish a politically stable balance between civil and military arms of the state, and yield a domestic order favorable to economic investment. In practice, the unstated aims included the expansion of US military authority and surveillance capabilities around the globe through the unofficial incorporation of subsidiary forces that were trained to act like the US military and at times were even officered by the US military, yet remained outside the political spotlight and off the books of the US budget.[20]

The model for almost all of these policing formations was the Philippine Constabulary, a quasi-military colonial police force established in the Philippines in 1901 as part of the US effort to suppress the Philippine revolution. The constables—most of whom were Filipinos serving under white American officers detailed from the US Army—were nominally subject to civilian control by the colonial government, but could be ordered to serve alongside the US Army, and in practice they functioned as a paramilitary counter-insurgency force throughout the islands, with close connections to US. military intelligence units. The Philippine Constabulary kept order on the cheap, and served a publicity function in the metropole, as news articles boasted of its role as a school for civilization and citizenship for Filipino colonial subjects.[21]

During the First World War, structures and practices developed in the Philippine Constabulary spread across the Pacific, particularly as concerns about labor radicalism, anti-colonial agitation, and Japanophile pan-Asianism frightened colonial officials. By war's end, the Philippine Constabulary had expanded in size (even as the Jones Act installed Filipinos in its top brass positions). Military and paramilitary surveillance forces kept watch on Japanese labor leaders in Hawai'i, Chamorro naval base workers in Guam, and South Asian anti-colonial radicals in the Pacific north-west.[22]

[20] For earlier efforts, see Donald M. Bishop, "Shared Failure: American Military Advisors in Korea, 1888–1896," *Transactions of the Royal Asiatic Society, Korea Branch*, 58 (1983), 53–76; John P. Dunn, "Americans in the Nineteenth Century Egyptian Army: A Selected Bibliography," *Journal of Military History*, 70 (January 2006), 123–36; Robert C. Harding II, *Military Foundations of Panamanian Politics* (New York: Transaction Publishers, 2001), 29–30; Pach, *Arming the Free World*, 7–9; Thomas L. Pearcy, *We Answer Only to God: Politics and the Military in Panama, 1903–1947* (Albuquerque: University of New Mexico Press, 1998), 37–43.
[21] George Yarrington Coats, "The Philippine Constabulary, 1901–1917" (Ph.D. dissertation, Ohio State University, 1968); Charles Sumner Lobingier, "The Peacekeepers of the Philippines," *Review of Reviews*, 42 (September 1910), 310–14; Alfred W. McCoy, *Policing America's Empire: The United States, the Philippines, and the Rise of the Surveillance State* (Madison: University of Wisconsin Press, 2009).
[22] Kornel S. Chang, *Pacific Connections: The Making of the U.S.–Canadian Borderlands* (Berkeley and Los Angeles: University of California Press, 2012), 117–46; Moon-Ho Jung, "Seditious Subjects: Race, State, Violence, and the U.S. Empire," *Journal of Asian American Studies*, 14 (June 2011), 221–47; McCoy, *Policing America's Empire*, 293–346; Gary Y. Okihiro, *Cane Fires: The Anti-Japanese Movement*

More by accident than by design, the Wilson administration replicated the Pacific policing model in the Caribbean, particularly in Haiti and the Dominican Republic. On 28 July 1915, US marines landed in Haiti to intervene in economic and political unrest. The situation on the ground, though, was not as dire as the geopolitical context or the threat of German infiltration. As Secretary Lansing explained to the Haitian ambassador, if the United States had not intervened, "in all probability some other nation would have felt called upon to do so," and reflected that "intelligent Haitians should feel gratified that it was the United States rather than some other power whose motives might not be as unselfish as ours."[23]

The US military government soon established a national police force, the Gendarmerie d'Haiti, under the direct control of the US marines. Commanded by a young Major Smedley Butler, an imperial enthusiast, the gendarmerie functioned as a tool of counter-insurgency, viciously suppressing anti-colonial movements in Haiti's rural provinces such as the 1918 Cacos rebellion. The gendarmerie made little effort to pose as a school for citizenship. Marines brought the Jim Crow mindsets of the US armed forces to their roles supervising inexperienced Haitian gendarmes. For their men, they had little respect; for peasant insurgents, even less. Butler himself recalled that he and the gendarmes "hunted the *Cacos* like pigs."[24]

Not longer after US intervention in Haiti, US marines occupied the other side of the island of Hispaniola. On 5 May 1916, a sizable force landed at the Dominican capital of Santo Domingo in the midst of civil unrest and established a military government that would remain in place until 1924. Among the government's first actions were the dismantling of the existing Dominican army and the creation of a new force to replace it. On 7 April 1917, the day after the US had declared war on Germany, Military Governor Harry S. Knapp issued an executive order setting up the Guardia Nacional Dominicana. As elsewhere, the new force would entirely replace existing military and police units, and would be officered by American marines "for the purpose of training the Guardia and bringing it to a high state of efficiency."[25]

in Hawaii, 1865–1945 (Philadelphia: Temple University Press, 1991), 102–28. On Guam, see Henry P. Beers, *American Naval Occupation and Government of Guam, 1898–1902* (Washington: Office of Records Administration, Navy Department, 1944); Paul Carano and Pedro C. Sanchez, *A Complete History of Guam* (Rutland, VT: C. E. Tuttle, 1964); L. M. Cox, *The Island of Guam* (Washington: Government Printing Office, 1917); Farrell, *Pictorial History of Guam*, 152; Penelope Bordallo Hofschneider, *A Campaign for Political Rights on the Island of Guam, 1899–1950* (Saipan: Division of Historical Preservation, 2001); Roy E. James, "Military Government: Guam," *Far Eastern Survey*, 15 (11 September 1946), 273–7; Robert F. Rogers, *Destiny's Landfall: A History of Guam*, rev. edn (Honolulu: University of Hawai'i Press, 2011).

[23] Lansing, quoted in Lars Schoultz, *Beneath the United States: A History of U.S. Policy toward Latin America* (Cambridge, MA: Harvard University Press, 1998), 232.

[24] Butler, quoted in Hans Schmidt, *The United States Occupation of Haiti, 1915–1934*, rev. edn (New Brunswick, NJ: Rutgers University Press, 1995), 85. See also Michel S. Laguerre, *The Military and Society in Haiti* (London: Macmillan, 1993), 69–83; James H. McCrocklin, *Garde d'Haiti, 1915–1934: Twenty Years of Organization and Training by the United States Marine Corps* (Annapolis, MD: US Naval Institute, 1956); Renda, *Taking Haiti*, 147–64.

[25] Bruce J. Calder, *The Impact of Intervention: The Dominican Republic during the U.S. Occupation of 1916–1924* (Austin, TX: University of Texas Press, 1984), 55.

But—again like elsewhere—the policy did not work out in practice as it was announced. The Guardia Nacional was always a hybrid mix of an army and a police force, "never large enough to discharge the military functions incumbent on the national army and [...] too military to devote itself, except spasmodically, to its police duties," as Colonel Rufus Lane, one of its officers, later reflected. Poorly funded from the outset, the Guardia Nacional was not well trained, especially after qualified US marine officers left the Dominican Republic for reassignment in France. Those who stayed behind had little enthusiasm for the police training work. As one of them, Joseph H. Pendleton, noted, it was disheartening "when the first real war of one's service came, to be shelved down here" (see Fig. 24).[26]

With US sovereignty over the Virgin Islands came a military government administered by the US Navy that mirrored similar set-ups in Haiti and Guam. The Virgin Islands authorizing legislation, passed by Congress on 3 March 1917, described naval administration as "a temporary government," and the impending war emergency (the US had already broken off diplomatic relations with Germany and would soon declare war) provided all the justification needed to give the Navy a free hand in day-to-day control. The military governor established a new police force, exacerbating ongoing tensions between islanders and police forces that had existed during the Danish colonial period. In 1907, the Danes had eliminated the native police and substituted Danish soldiers as police officers; island residents resented the loss of jobs and what they experienced as a police state atmosphere. The Navy returned Virgin Islanders to the ranks, but subjected them to US control and the same dynamics of racial segregation and subordination that operated in nearby Haiti.[27]

The undertakings continued. The US sent a small number of troops in February and March 1917 to Cuba to intervene in a contentious election there, less concerned about the outcome than fearful the situation could open a door for German naval action. Within a year, the US had made a commitment to train, equip, and for all practical purposes command the Cuban navy, under a euphemism of "naval cooperation." In Puerto Rico, US colonial officials expanded the Policía Insular and took steps to connect its officers with the US Army's Military Intelligence Division.[28]

[26] Rufus Lane, quoted in Calder, *The Impact of Intervention*, 55; Pendleton, quoted in Valentina Peguero, *The Militarization of Culture in the Dominican Republic, from the Captains General to General Trujillo* (Lincoln, NE: University of Nebraska Press, 2004), 37. See also Stephen M. Fuller and Graham A. Cosmas, *Marines in the Dominican Republic, 1916–1924* (Washington: History and Museums Division, US Marine Corps, 1974), 45–52; Melvin M. Knight, *The Americans in Santo Domingo* (New York: Vanguard Press, 1928), esp. 86–118.

[27] Boyer, *America's Virgin Islands*, 118; Knud Knud-Hansen, *From Denmark to the Virgin Islands* (Philadelphia: Dorrance, 1947), 103–9; LaMotta, "Working People," 184, 194 n. 26. See also Boyer, *America's Virgin Islands*, 110–38; Isaac Dookhan, "Changing Patterns of Local Reaction to the United States Acquisition of the Virgin Islands, 1865–1917," *Caribbean Studies*, 15/1 (1975), 67–72; Dookhan, "The Search for Identity: The Political Aspirations and Frustrations of Virgin Islanders under the United States Naval Administration, 1917–1927," *Journal of Caribbean History*, 12 (May 1979); Luther Harris Evans, *The Virgin Islands, From Naval Base to New Deal* (Ann Arbor, MI: J. W. Edwards, 1945); J. Antonio Jarvis, *Brief History of the Virgin Islands* (St. Thomas, VI: Art Shop, 1938), 124–5.

[28] José E. Martínez Valentín, *La Presencia de la policia en la historia de Puerto Rico, 1898–1995* (San Juan: José E. Martínez Valentín, 1995), 23, 70–1, 214–16; Louis A. Perez, Jr, "The Military and Electoral Politics: The Cuban Election of 1920," *Military Affairs*, 37 (February 1973), 5–8; Yerxa, "United States Navy," 185.

Fig. 24. Marines landing at Santo Domingo during US occupation of the Dominican Republic, 1916.

In June 1918, political violence and labor actions in Panama made the stability of the Panama Canal appear uncertain, and the United States intervened there again. That October, US and Panamanian officials launched a full-scale reorganization of the Panamanian national police. In fact the Policía Nacional was already under US control. Following an April 1915 riot in the Canal Zone, Secretary of State William Jennings Bryan strong-armed the Panamanian government into disarming the police force and placing it under the effective control of US military forces stationed in the Canal Zone. US troops would remain in the province of Chiriquí until 1920.[29]

The development of police forces in the Pacific and Caribbean allowed the USA to extend its own efforts elsewhere. After the Armistice, the US committed 250,000 troops to the occupation and reconstruction of the German Rhineland. Under the command of Major General Henry T. Allen, himself the former head of the Philippine Constabulary, American troops brought practices of occupation and imperial control into the European front.[30]

The most visible and contentious exception to this emerging pattern was in Mexico, where soldiers in the revolutionary nationalist armies and leaders of successive regimes uniformly rejected US interference. Instead, US policing focused on the security of the border itself, first through the Punitive Expedition, a 1916 troop build-up and series of raids on revolutionary leader Pancho Villa, and then, after the war's end, through a large-scale militarization of the US–Mexico border. Soldiers returning from service in Europe sometimes found themselves reassigned to the border region, where the army had built twenty-four posts in Texas alone and after 1919 maintained a border air patrol. A civilian wing, the US Border Patrol, was established in 1924.[31]

America's preoccupation with colonial policing, social order, and surveillance was not unique to the era of the First World War, but the war—and its twin threats of German invasion and anti-colonial subversion—gave policing an intensity and urgency it had not had before. That would have resonated with the experiences of Americans on the home front as well, where the war accelerated long-term trends toward the professionalization of policing, the expansion of federal policing power,

[29] "America Assumes Control in Panama," *New York Times*, 29 June 1918, 3; George W. Baker, Jr, "The Wilson Administration and Panama, 1913–1921," *Journal of Inter-American Studies*, 8 (April 1966), 279–93; Callcott, *Caribbean Policy*, 449–50; Michael L. Conniff, *Panama and the United States: The Forced Alliance*, 2nd edn (Athens, GA: University of Georgia Press, 2001), 71–88; Carlos H. Cuestos Gómez, *Soldados Americanos en Chiriquí* (Panama: Litografía Enan, 1990); Narciso Garay, *Panamá y las Guerras de los Estados Unidos* (Panama: Imprenta Nacional, 1930), 56–7, 61; Harding, *Military Foundations*, 28–33; John Lindsay-Poland, *Emperors in the Jungle: The Hidden History of the U.S. in Panama* (Durham, NC: Duke University Press, 2003), 11–43; McCain, *United States and Panama*, 202–3; Norman J. Padelford, *The Panama Canal in Peace and War* (New York: Macmillan, 1942), 123–46; Renato Pereira, *Panama: Fuerzas armadas y politica* (Panama: Ediciones Nueva Universidad, 1979), 8–11; "Troops Police Cities in Panama," *New York Times*, 30 June 1918, 8.

[30] Erika Kuhlman, "American Doughboys and German Fräuleins: Sexuality, Patriarchy, and Privilege in the American-Occupied Rhineland, 1918–23," *Journal of Military History*, 71 (October 2007), 1077–1106; Margaret Pawley, *The Watch on the Rhine: The Military Occupation of the Rhineland, 1918–1930* (New York: Palgrave Macmillan, 2007); Twichell, *Allen*, 215–52.

[31] Jürgen Buchenau, *In the Shadow of the Giant: The Making of Mexico's Central American Policy, 1876–1930* (Tuscaloosa: University of Alabama Press, 1996), 128–39; Don M. Coerver and Linda B. Hall, *Texas and the Mexican Revolution: A Study in State and National Border Policy, 1910–1920* (San Antonio, TX: Trinity University Press, 1984); Kelly Lytle Hernández, *Migra! A History of the US Border Patrol* (Berkeley and Los Angeles: University of California Press, 2010); Edwin Lieuwen, "The Depoliticization of the Mexican Revolutionary Army, 1915–1940," in David Ronfeldt (ed.), *The Modern Mexican Military: A Reassessment* (San Diego, CA: Center for US–Mexican Relations, 1984), 51–62; Thomas Rath, *Myths of Demilitarization in Postrevolutionary Mexico, 1920–1960* (Chapel Hill, NC: University of North Carolina Press, 2013), esp. 18–30; Eileen Welsome, *The General and the Jaguar: Pershing's Hunt for Pancho Villa* (New York: Little, Brown, 2006).

and the deployment of military intelligence capabilities in domestic anti-radical surveillance. When Attorney General Thomas W. Gregory noted in the 1918 annual report of the Department of Justice that "it is safe to say that never in its history has this country been so thoroughly policed," he was describing the continental United States. But his comments could have applied just as well to the US empire and its sites of military occupation.[32]

Opponents of US policies abounded, even if wartime anti-radical legislation silenced many critics, both in the United States and in its empire. Late in the war, Dominican writer Américo Lugo attacked the US for destroying the pre-1916 Guardia Republicana and replacing it with an American-oriented copy that little reflected Dominican traditions and utterly failed to capture the loyalties of the Dominican people. Filipino nationalists denounced the establishment of colonial military institutions that served the security needs of the colonizer rather than the military aims of a future independent Philippines. Puerto Rican popular culture looked askance at the close timing of the Jones Act that granted US citizenship and the Selective Service Act that drafted Puerto Ricans into the US Army, generating a folkloric insistence that Washington had engineered "citizenship for conscription." And, after the war, US pacifists and anti-imperialists would launch a series of investigations—culminating in congressional hearings—into occupation policies in Haiti and the Dominican Republic. Testimony documented widespread violence perpetrated by the novice police forces, but violence that had been carried out by Haitians or Dominicans drew little criticism and even less oversight.[33]

Did policing initiatives work? The answer to that question depends on what they were intended to achieve. As a school for citizenship, a training ground for sovereign nationhood, and a method of separating the military and civilian sectors, these efforts were failures. But they accomplished other aims: they played important roles in suppressing insurgency and anti-colonial activism. They simultaneously saved money and allowed the United States to withdraw its armed forces and redeploy them in Europe. They replaced indigenous armies that had popular support and nationalist goals that were often antagonistic to US interests. And these forces proved useful to emerging dictators, who found that US-led training oriented the military and police forces of these nations around US models for the rest of the twentieth century. D. P. Calixte, the commandant of the Garde d'Haiti, noted in 1939 of his force that "its spirit, morale, and military training are American." While the British colonial Gurkhas and French *tirailleurs* fought at the Western Front, US colonial troops did not. But the two million American soldiers

[32] United States Department of Justice, *Annual Report of the Attorney General, 1918* (Washington: Government Printing Office, 1919), 14–15, 37–9; Christopher Capozzola, *Uncle Sam Wants You: World War I and the Making of the Modern American Citizen* (New York: Oxford University Press, 2008), 117–43.

[33] Lugo, quoted in Peguero, *Militarization of Culture*, 42; Callcott, *Caribbean Policy*, 478; Schoultz, *Beneath the United States*, 253–71; Lorrin Thomas, *Puerto Rican Citizen: History and Political Identity in Twentieth-Century New York City* (Chicago: University of Chicago Press, 2010), 65; United States Congress, Senate, *Inquiry into the Occupation and Administration of Haiti and Santo Domingo*, 77 Cong., 1st and 2d sess. (Washington: Government Printing Office, 1922).

in Europe depended in part on the soldiers of the Panamanian army and the sailors of the Cuban navy, the Philippine Scouts, and the Dominican Guard. And nearly a century later, they still do.[34]

EPILOGUE

The war's end in November 1918 hardly brought an end to the practices of military and police training or to the US military's insistence on its strategic importance. Post-war events—labor unrest in the continental United States, revolution in Russia, radical nationalist movements in the Caribbean, anti-colonial revolts in Ireland and India—confirmed authorities' belief in the need for colonial policing and folded US efforts into an emerging global network of anti-anti-colonial practices.

In 1921, Warren G. Harding and the Republicans replaced the Democratic administration of Woodrow Wilson, but little changed in the policing of the US empire. In 1924 the US government announced a quick withdrawal of the occupation force in Nicaragua and its replacement with a US-focused, US-trained force that would act in US interests without flying the US flag. As Acting Secretary of State Joseph Grew explained to his Nicaraguan counterpart in 1925: "The Constabulary is to be armed, equipped, and trained as a military police force with the object of entirely replacing the existing national police, navy and army of Nicaragua. This force is to be trained free from political influence as a national institution and used only to maintain peace, law, and order."[35] But unrest in 1926 brought another occupying army of US marines to Nicaragua.

The US withdrew from the Dominican Republic in 1924, from Nicaragua in 1933, and from Haiti in 1935. In 1934, the US established a commonwealth government on the path to independence for the Philippines; in 1936 it ended its quasi-protectorate status over Panama, and that same year transferred political control of the Virgin Islands from the Navy to a civilian government, all the while speaking of good neighborliness. Among those neighbors were: Harmodio and Arnulfo Arias, who came to power in Panama in 1931 and pressed US officials to relinquish control of the Policía Nacional so that they could use it as a political force aimed at suppressing their opponents; Nicaraguan dictator Anastasio Somoza García, who headed the Guardia Nacional soon after US troops had departed in 1933 and three years later used the force to topple the government of Juan B. Sacasa; Manuel Quezon, the first president

---

[34] D. P. Calixte, *Haiti: The Calvary of a Soldier* (New York: W. Malliet and Co., 1939), 29.

[35] Joseph C. Grew, "Plan for the Establishment of a Constabulary in Nicaragua," 17 February 1925, in *Papers Relating to the Foreign Relations of the United States: 1925* (Washington: Government Printing Office, 1940), ii. 624. See also Leo J. Daugherty III, *The Marine Corps and the State Department: Enduring Partners in United States Foreign Policy, 1798–2007* (Jefferson, NC: McFarland and Co., 2009), 54–7; Gobat, *Confronting the American Dream*, 205–21; Bernard C. Nalty, *The United States Marines in Nicaragua*, rev. edn (Washington: Historical Branch, US Marine Corps, 1961).

of the Philippine Commonwealth, who rose to power within the US colonial regime as an informant for the secret division of the Philippine Constabulary; Rafael Trujillo, who as a young man gave up his dead-end job as a sugar mill security guard in January 1919 to join the Guardia Nacional Dominicana, then rose to the head of the Guardia, and used the force to seize power in 1930. The Second World War would see far more mobilization of colonial soldiers and long-term transformations in US military power, both in the Caribbean and the Pacific. And in the twenty-first century, from Haiti, East Timor, and Kosovo to Iraq and Afghanistan, police training programs—newly rechristened as "disarmament, demobilization, and reintegration"—continue to function in the toolkit of imperial powers, who rely on patterns of policing, military training, and military cooperation that were set firmly in place during the First World War.[36]

[36] Gobat, *Confronting the American Dream*, 262–6; Jeffrey L. Gould and Aldo A. Lauria-Santiago, *To Rise in Darkness: Revolution, Repression, and Memory in El Salvador* (Durham, NC: Duke University Press, 2008); Harding, *Military Foundations*, 33; McCoy, *Policing America's Empire*, 96; Stephanie Hunter McMahon, "You Pay for What You Get: The U.S. Virgin Islands, 1917–1936," *Journal of Caribbean History*, 41/1–2 (2007), 109–41; Richard Millett, *Guardians of the Dynasty* (Maryknoll, NY: Orbis Books, 1977), esp. 15–83; Peguero, *Militarization of Culture*, 44–6; Steve C. Ropp, *Panamanian Politics: From Guarded Nation to National Guard* (New York: Praeger, 1982), 25–6.

13

Empires at the Paris Peace Conference

Leonard V. Smith

Were empires in the Great War simply nation states writ large, or something else? Categories drawn from the realist school of international relations theory have long encouraged us to think the former. Like nation states, empires under realism have human-like characteristics.[1] As realists would have it, empires have appetites and aversions. They crave unconquered territories, and covet domains of rival empires. Above all, they live in perpetual fear for their own safety in a zero-sum quest for "security." An empire can be safe only if its rivals are less safe. Like nation states, empires find themselves thus locked in the dysfunctional security dilemma, competing when cooperating would more suit their self-interest.[2] Indeed, the structural stress of empires under realism gives them a sort of life cycle. They are born, they grow strong, they overextend, they age, they weaken, and, ultimately, they die.[3]

Realism has long counseled a certain interpretation of the history of empire in the Great War. The war accelerated the aging process of empire, not just among the defeated, but also among the victors. The apparent outcome of the war appeared to prove the advanced decrepitude of empires based on dynastic loyalty. The multinational land empires of the Habsburgs, the Romanovs, and the Ottomans disintegrated, along with that of the Hohenzollerns. On the other hand, the "blue water" empires based in trade and extraction beyond Europe survived, including those of marginalized Portugal and occupied Belgium. The British, French, and Japanese empires even expanded under the fig leaf of League of Nations Mandates. Yet the glory of imperial aggrandizement after the Great War would prove fleeting. Post-war Britain and France could ill afford their restive new domains in the Middle East, particularly given that their real security threat would come from an inevitably resurgent Germany. Japanese expansion in Shandong and the Pacific islands would encourage overambitious dreams of dominance over Great East Asia.

---

[1] Although he does not specifically address empire, Alexander Wendt has interrogated the notion of humanizing states in "The State as Person in International Theory," *Review of International Studies*, 30 (2004), 289–316.

[2] For the classic explanation of the "security dilemma," see John Herz, "Idealist Internationalism and the Security Dilemma," *World Politics*, 2 (1950), 157–80.

[3] See, among many other works, Paul Kennedy, *The Rise and Fall of the Great Powers: Economic Change and Military Conflict from 1500 to 2000* (New York: Random House, 1987).

Empires at the Paris Peace Conference

255

These dreams, in turn, would only deepen the security suspicions of another Great Power with imperial interests, the United States. To realists, the lesson of history seemed to be that victory in 1918 had exacerbated the overreach that aged empires. The war had simply sped up empire's life cycle.

Rethinking a realist explanation of empire in the Great War must begin by not thinking of empires as people. The definition put forward by Charles Maier cited in the Introduction to this volume provided a more disembodied definition, based in a subordinated relationship of the imperial periphery to the center, and on imposed and/or co-opted intermediaries. Jane Burbank and Frederick Cooper have described empires as "large political units, expansionist or with a memory of power extended over space, polities that maintain distinction and hierarchy as they incorporate new people."[4] In these sorts of depersonalized, almost mechanical definitions, empires exist as ostensibly permanent structures for the hierarchical management of difference. Difference could have dynastic, economic, racial, or various other kinds or origin. Empires could combine varieties of difference in a practically unlimited number of ways. The permanent nature of politically significant difference distinguishes empire from a nation state writ large. Depersonalized empires can remain intrinsically dynamic. Empires are always expanding or contracting, though the reasons can go well beyond realist notions, security, or pecuniary gain (the material underpinning of security). As Burbank and Cooper have noted, empire has proved one of the most durable forms of political organization in human history. Indeed, empires have a much longer history than the territorial nation state, largely a creation of nineteenth-century Europe.

Empires in the Great War were not one species of agent, but several, as the chapters in this volume have shown. Each was an amalgam of lands and loyalties. For some, the dynasty was certainly the essential feature. Imperial Russia, the Habsburg Monarchy, and the Ottoman Empire meant nothing without their imperial houses. The German Empire was likewise dynastic, through the House of Hohenzollern. Yet "Germany" reinvented itself as a nation state virtually from the moment Kaiser Wilhelm crossed the border to the Netherlands in November 1918. Loss of its "blue water" dominions in Africa, China, and the Pacific never made Germany less German, if anything the reverse. Generations of German historians seemed barely to remember that Imperial Germany even had an empire.

"Blue water" empires were likewise diverse composites. Even the British Empire, the world's largest empire in 1919, existed as such through a variety of personal political links to the House of Windsor. Strictly speaking, the only "imperial" title held by George V was Emperor of India. As we will see, self-governing dominions could pull in separate ways at a highly problematic moment for the metropole. Just what held the French empire together never seemed altogether clear, as generations of domestic critics from the political Left, Right, and Center never ceased to point out. The Third Republic, of course, had no dynasty, and just what the sovereign

---

[4] Jane Burbank and Frederick Cooper, *Empires in World History: Power and the Politics of Difference* (Princeton: Princeton University Press, 2010), 8. Whether the "memory" is held by the empire itself or by the individuals in charge of it is not of primary analytical importance here.

people thought the colonies contributed by way of profit or security remained a matter of contention. The Japanese Empire, ostensibly dynastic, expanded across water and land, with generally more assimilationist aims than its European counterparts. The United States, originally a collection of British colonies, presented an official disdain for formal empire. Yet in 1919 it exercised various forms of sovereignty over lands as diverse as Alaska, Hawai'i, Puerto Rico, Panama, and the Philippines, to say nothing of powerful influence over independent states as diverse as Cuba, Haiti, and Mexico.

By definition, realism or any other theory must simplify. To be sure, the sadder-but-wiser position afforded by realism adequately explains "what happened," if the point of studying empires in the Great War is determining just how they walked down the road to the inevitable. This chapter, in contrast, takes neither the characters in the story nor its outcome as self-evident. Empires in the Great War were both the sites over which peace was made, and the actors making it. Empires and peace-making disrupted and shaped each other, and the reciprocal nature of this encounter is key to understanding it.

Further, the chapter argues that the Paris Peace Conference contributed to the normalization of the nation state, through legitimizing successor states to the multinational empires in Europe and Anatolia, and through the creating of nation states-in-the-making under the League of Nations Mandates. Yet the Great Powers in charge of the conference were also themselves empires in one form or another. As peace-making extended beyond what had been the Western Front, victorious empires found themselves supporting new and restive political entities that would undermine their coherence as empires. As peace-making in the Great War came to an end, successor states would demarcate the limits of the "victorious" empires, at precisely the moment that the victorious empires appeared geographically to be at their zenith. Empires became what states made of them.

THE RISE OF THE SUCCESSOR STATE IN POST-IMPERIAL EUROPE

The complex and unstable amalgam of ideas known as "Wilsonianism" implied a radical transformation of the international system, from the time of the armistice with Germany. Wilsonianism would legitimize a specific kind of agent as the successor to empire in Europe. In announcing the results of an extended correspondence between the Imperial German government and President Woodrow Wilson, Secretary of State Robert Lansing declared on 5 November 1918 that the governments of the Allied and Associated Powers declared "their willingness to make peace with the Government of Germany on the terms of peace laid down in the President's Address to Congress of 8 January 1918, and the principles of settlement enumerated in his subsequent addresses."[5] Wilson's January 1918 address, known

---

[5] Quoted in Frederick Maurice, *The Armistices of 1918* (London: Oxford University Press, 1943), 51–2.

by then around the world as the "Fourteen Points" speech, soon became shorthand for the entire Wilsonian program. The "subsequent addresses" referred to a number of other speeches, among them Wilson's castigation of realism, scorned as "the great game, now forever discredited, of the balance of power." Wilson's speeches left little doubt that the conference would have two equal and simultaneous objectives—writing specific treaties with defeated powers and redesigning the international system itself.

The adoption of Wilsonianism as the ideological foundation for the peace radicalized existing institutional structures. During the war, the Great Powers had established the Supreme War Council, comprising representatives of Britain, France, the United States, Italy, and Japan, to coordinate military operations against the Central Powers.[6] After the armistices with the various Central Powers, the Supreme War Council provided the nucleus of a conference of Great Powers that would make the peace. As it morphed into the Supreme Council of the Paris Peace Conference, it declared itself a provisional world sovereign—with full authority to determine what there was to decide as well as how to decide it. But the Great Powers had done all this under a radically new discursive structure, a kind of Wilsonian global imperium. This discursive structure would shape both the agents and the formal structures of peace-making, down to the Treaty of Lausanne with republican Turkey in 1923. The conference became the institutional expression of what Erez Manela has called the "Wilsonian moment," unique in the history of international relations. The conference, in Manela's words, "launched the transformation of the norms and standards of international relations that established the self-determining nation-state as the only legitimate political form throughout the globe."[7]

The rise and ignominious fall of the League of Nations has loomed so large in the historiography of the Paris Peace Conference that we can easily forget how much the conference as a whole did to affirm the nation state as the locus of sovereignty. To be sure, had the League ever functioned as it was supposed to, national sovereignty in external affairs would have been circumscribed. Collective security guaranteed by collective intentionality was supposed to replace formal alliances, and mandates were not supposed simply to rebrand colonial acquisitions.[8] But, even at its most expansive, the Wilsonian imaginary sought to provide a new moral compass and a transnational source of legitimacy for the nation state. Wilsonianism never sought to replace it.

Paradoxically, the conference provided no clearer evidence of the sanctity of the nation state than its treatment of post-Imperial Germany. The Treaty of Versailles certified simultaneously the demise of the German Empire and the affirmation of

---

[6] See F. S. Marston, *The Peace Conference of 1919: Organization and Procedure* (London: Oxford University Press, 1944), ch. 1, "The Supreme War Council," 1–12; and Maurice Hankey, *Diplomacy by Conference: Studies in Public Affairs, 1920–1946* (New York: G. P. Putnam's Sons, 1946), 10–39.

[7] Erez Manela, *The Wilsonian Moment: Self-Determination and the International Origins of Anticolonial Nationalism* (Oxford: Oxford University Press, 2007), 5.

[8] See Leonard V. Smith, "The Wilsonian Challenge to International Law," *Journal of the History of International Law*, 13 (2011), 179–208.

Germany as a nation state. The Germans themselves had seen off the Hohenzollern imperial house, even before the Armistice of 11 November. The treaty would deprive Germany of the material attributes of empire—its overseas colonies and the high seas fleet necessary to protect them.

But the peacemakers of 1919 had gone to considerable lengths to preserve German unity and independence, notably in opposing French efforts to detach the Rhineland. Indeed, the loss of territories to a re-established Poland was supposed to make Germany more "German" than ever, though in the event an "impossible border" between Germany and the successor states to its east kept the Weimar Republic a multinational polity.[9] As the Poles would later point out with considerable bitterness, the Treaty of Versailles included no protections for minorities in Germany. Even the criminalized national identity provided for by Article 231 (the *Kriegsschuld* or "war guilt" clause) served the cause of German national unity. Whatever else divided post-imperial Germans, a shared hatred of the Treaty of Versailles united them as a self-determining national community.

Above all, the Paris Peace Conference legitimized ethnically demarcated successor states to replace the multinational dynastic empires on the European continent. In the end, this meant legitimizing an impossible kind of agent, in effect mini-empires structuring ethnic difference within the same nation state. The construction of the successor state began during the war itself—frequently toward imperial ends. As early as August 1914, Imperial Russian Commander-in-Chief Grand Nicholas appealed to the Poles of Germany and Austria to fight for a "united" Poland under the tsar.[10] This inaugurated a virtual bidding war, for a quasi-sovereign Poland integrated into one or more of the multinational empires.[11] As early as 1915, British colonial entrepreneurs in Egypt saw to the establishment of an Arab Bureau to foment nationalist uprisings in the Ottoman domains.[12] Through T. E. Lawrence, better known as Lawrence of Arabia, the British imperial project of Arab nationalism reached popular culture.

As Arno Mayer noted many years ago, V. I. Lenin and Woodrow Wilson competed to provide a new discursive structure for international relations.[13] While much divided the Bolshevik and liberal visionaries, they shared the aim of undermining formal empire, whether dynastic or "blue water." Put together, the Bolshevik Revolution and the Fourteen Points radicalized the identity of the successor state. As Erez Manela and others have argued, Wilsonian "self-determination"

[9] Annemarie H. Sammartino, *The Impossible Border: Germany and the East, 1914–1922* (Ithaca, NY: Cornell University Press, 2010).
[10] See Robert Machray, *Poland, 1914–1931* (London: George Allen & Unwin, 1932), 51.
[11] See the decree from the German and Habsburg emperors of 5 November 1916 establishing an "autonomous" Polish state in Stanislas Filasiewicz (ed.), *La Question polanaise pendant la guerre mondiale*, 2 vols (Paris: Section d'Études et de publications politiques du comité national polonais, 1920), ii. 57–8.
[12] See Aaron Kleiman, "Britain's War Aims in the Middle East in 1915," *Journal of Contemporary History*, 3 (1968), 237–51; and Bruce Westrate, *The Arab Bureau: British Policy in the Middle East, 1916–1920* (University Park, PA: Penn State University Press, 1992), 14–21.
[13] Arno Mayer, *Political Origins of the New Diplomacy, 1917–1918* (New Haven, CT: Yale University Press, 1959), especially "Epilogue: Wilson vs. Lenin," 368–93.

morphed partly under Bolshevik pressure into "national self-determination"—the Pandora's Box of peace-making in the Great War.[14]

The Bolshevik "Peace Decree" of 26 October 1917 was a call not so much for peace as for a transformation of the war. Discursively, the decree proclaimed a Bolshevik empire, and in its way continued the wartime practice of using nationalism toward imperial objectives. In the short run, the Bolsheviks sought to instrumentalize nationalism toward the disruption of imperial sovereignty everywhere, be the imperial sovereign the House of Habsburg, the House of Hohenzollern, the House of Osman, the House of Windsor, the Japanese imperial house, or the citizens of the French or American republics. The decree posited that the world owed liberation to any nation that did not possess "the right to determine the form of its State life by free voting and completely free from the presence of troops of the annexing or stronger State and without the least pressure."[15]

Wilson's Fourteen Points constituted what Mayer called a "countermanifesto"—if a more cautious and less consistent one than its Bolshevik counterpart.[16] German-speaking majority Alsace and Lorraine (before 1918 an imperial territory directly ruled by the Kaiser and his government) were to be restored to France (Point VIII). Point XIII called for an "independent Polish State" that would comprise "territories inhabited by indisputably Polish populations" but with "free and secure access to the sea." The impossibility of combining these characteristics, given the German population along the Baltic, made Poland the archetype successor state from the outset. Nevertheless, Wilson's countermanifesto never explicitly called for the break-up of either the Habsburg Monarchy or the Ottoman Empire. Rather, it evoked nebulous terms such as the "freest opportunity of autonomous development" (Point X). The Fourteen Points maintained a studied silence on the victorious empires, beyond a less than lucid claim in Point V that the interests of colonized persons and colonial states were to be considered equally.

Bolshevism and Wilsonianism cast the successor state as the Other of Empire. In so doing, they had helped naturalize the doctrine of, in the words of Stéphane Pierré-Caps, "to each nation, its state."[17] Under "national self-determination," "nation" came to mean ethnicity, defined primarily by some combination of language, culture, and religion. Post-imperial states would need geographic boundaries. "National" boundaries determined who could belong to the political community under what circumstances, and were thus cultural as well as territorial. "Historic" boundaries were territorial, and mostly dynastic and/or imperial in origin, such as "Bohemia" or "Hungary." By definition, "national" and "historic" boundaries were constructed—the former by politicians, ethnographers, and activists; the latter by

[14] Manela, *The Wilsonian Moment*, particularly part II, "The Internationalization of Nationalism."

[15] "The Declaration of Peace (November 8, 1917)," in John W. Wheeler-Bennett, *Brest-Litovsk: The Forgotten Peace, 1918* (London: Macmillan and Co., 1938), 376.

[16] Mayer, *Political Origins of the New Diplomacy*, ch. 9, "Wilson Issues a Countermanifesto," 329–67.

[17] Stéphane Pierré-Caps, "Karl Renner et l'état multinational: Contribution juridique à la solution d'imbroglios politiques contemporains," *Droit et société*, 27 (1994), 423. See also Ernest Gellner, *Nationalism* (New York: New York University Press, 1997).

royal and imperial houses. As such, all boundaries were subject to mutually incon-
sistent interpretations.

By the time the victors met in Paris, the "successor state" in multinational Central
and Eastern Europe had come to mean an agent structured by an impossibility—a
unitary, sovereign state that reconciled national and "historic" boundaries. For example, any Poland rebuilt over the ruins of the Romanov, Hohenzollern, and
Habsburg imperial projects could comprise a large majority of ethnic Poles, or
could reclaim territorial boundaries preceding the partitions of eighteenth century.
But, by definition, self-determining Poland could not do both. In any regional
system, constructing successor states would thus prove a zero-sum game. A successor state could fully realize its national and historic boundaries only at the expense of its neighbors—a specific variety of the realist security dilemma.

As the Other of Empire, a proper successor state logically would seek to eradi-
cate politically significant difference within its borders. A Wilsonian solution to
the perils therein involved the protection of ethnic minorities under the surveillance of the League of Nations. Post-imperial Poland was supposed to provide the
model as the Polish Minorities Treaty or the "Little Versailles" treaty, signed the
same day as its namesake.[18] Through a variety of very specific provisions, for example, Jews could become political Poles and remain culturally and religiously
Jewish. As Carole Fink has shown, the Polish treaty would guide all subsequent
statements from the conference on the subject, and similar agreements would bind
no fewer than seven additional successor states.[19]

In the event, successor states became mini-empires internally. They hierarchically
structured ethnic difference with increasing zeal as the interwar years continued.
Inevitably, the denial of the liberal solution to ethnic difference fed irredentism.
Successor states sought expansion to include lands inhabited by "exiled" ethnic minorities across Central and Eastern Europe. For Germany under the Third Reich,
the attributes of the successor state laid the groundwork for a new and overtly exter-
minationist imperial project.[20] For all its hatred of the Paris Peace Conference, Nazi
Germany owed much to the logic of the successor state created there.

THE COVENANT OF THE LEAGUE OF NATIONS AND
THE DISCURSIVE ASSAULT ON EMPIRE

The Covenant of the League of Nations, published as a preamble to all five treaties
produced by the Paris Peace Conference, provided a blueprint for the redesigned

[18] For the text, see "Treaty of Peace between the United States of America, the British Empire,
France, Italy, and Japan and Poland," *American Journal of International Law*, 13, Supplement, Official
Documents (October 1919), 423–40.

[19] Carole Fink, "The Minorities Question at the Paris Peace Conference: The Polish Minority
Treaty, June 28, 1919," in Manfred Boemeke, Gerald Feldman, and Elisabeth Glaser (eds), *The Treaty
of Versailles: A Reassessment after 75 Years* (Cambridge: Cambridge University Press, 1998), 249–74.

[20] See Mark Mazower, *Hitler's Empire: How the Nazis Ruled Europe* (New York: Penguin Press,
2008).

system of international relations. As I have argued elsewhere, the covenant as written implied a radically new interpretation of sovereignty.[21] Indeed, the covenant as written designed a true "imperium" of a specific notion of popular sovereignty applicable across the globe. The rational, morally accountable individual of nineteenth-century liberalism would become the building block of sovereignty everywhere. This individual was the proper "self" of "self-determination." Ultimately, "world government" would thus exist at the level of the individual, through a global community of commensurable, self-sovereign citizens. All configurations of sovereignty, from the village to the international system itself, would be accountable to one version or another of this community.

This said, nation states, Great Powers, and even empires did not need ipso facto to disappear. The powers had won the victory of 1918, this view held, because of their historic combination of might and right. The peace conference both asserted and affirmed the "greatness" of the powers in this sense. The League of Nations would institutionalize their central role through the League Council. But in the Wilsonian Promised Land, all nation states, including the Great Powers and the empires directed, would operate in accordance with the will of the liberal individuals included in the political community. Liberalism was always about the inclusion of everyone eligible for inclusion, which was not always everyone. Collectively, the global community of liberal individuals had a sovereign will beyond that of the nation state or empire.

As with any other form of empire, the global imperium imagined by Wilsonianism preserved politically significant difference. Wilson himself, like so many American presidents before and after him, universalized the American example. Some forms of difference, such as religion and ethnicity, could be recognized and legitimized, but would remain bounded by the values of the covenanted community. Other forms of difference, notably race, could determine whether individuals or categories of individuals were eligible to make a covenant at all. Its "successful" management of difference, Wilson believed, had made the United States a universal example to inspire the world. No American president more overtly supported racial segregation at home. The international corollary was that racial difference could determine whether a given community merited "self-determination."

Nonetheless, the liberal imperium imagined under the covenant shook the very foundations of existing empires—a point not lost on its supporters or detractors. The silence in the covenant on victorious empires in fact spoke loudly. The Mandate System outlined in Article 22 challenged the very notion of empire. Sovereignty in the mandates became a "sacred trust of civilization." To be sure, just where sovereignty lay in this trust was never specified.[22] But the covenant certainly did not imply unrestricted sovereignty on the part of the mandatory power.

---

[21] See Smith, "Wilsonian Challenge." See also Leonard V. Smith, "Les États-Unis et l'échec d'une seconde mobilisation," in Stéphane Audoin-Rouzeau and Christophe Prochasson (eds), *Sortir de la Guerre de 14–18* (Paris: Tallandier, 2008), 69–91.

[22] See Quincy Wright, "Sovereignty of the Mandates," *American Journal of International Law*, 17 (1923), 691–703.

The covenant established the former imperial domains of Germany and Ottoman Turkey as lands "inhabited by peoples not yet able to stand by themselves under the strenuous conditions of the modern world." The very term "not yet able" indicated that with time these peoples would acquire not just the ability but the right to stand by themselves. In the meantime, the "sacred trust" of their sovereignty over themselves was to be administrated on provisional basis by the mandatory powers accountable in some way to the League. Mandatory rule, in short, had within it a presumption of independence and thus an implicit expiration date.

To be sure, the mandatory system under the liberal imperium preserved racial difference. Only Jan Smuts of South Africa had supported something that looked like mandatory authority in Europe.[23] Other peacemakers in Paris agreed that white Europeans, by definition, could self-determine immediately. The covenant included a clear racial hierarchy among non-Europeans in the future mandates. "Certain communities formerly belonging to the Turkish Empire," what would become Class A Mandates, were held "to have reached a stage of development where their existence as independent nations can be provisionally recognized." Mandatory rule there was supposed to be purely administrative, and presumably of short duration. Others, notably "those of Central Africa, are at such a stage that the Mandatory must be responsible for the administration of the territory under conditions which will guarantee freedom of conscience and religion." The mandatory power would be responsible for prohibiting the slave trade, the traffic in arms and liquor, and the militarization of the territories in question. Independence in Class B Mandates would occur at some indefinite point in the future. Still other territories, notably the former German South-West Africa (today Namibia) and the South Pacific islands formerly occupied by Germany, became Class C Mandates. These would most closely resemble colonies of old, "best administered under the laws of the Mandatory as integral portions of its territory."

The mere existence of Class A Mandates posed uncomfortable questions about empires, because they implied that non-white peoples were eligible for self-determination. Even before 1914, the acceptance of the Empire of Japan as a Great Power showed that empire did not need to be a uniquely Western political construct. Mandates further undermined Western racial assumptions of empire. What was it about the imperial territories of the defeated empires that made them eligible for the Mandate System, whereas the territories of the victorious empires were not? The matter became particularly difficult for the Arab-speaking former Ottoman domains of the Middle East. The French had annexed Algeria (with a huge Arab and Berber majority), and ruled over protectorates in Morocco and Tunisia before the Great War. After it, they acquired mandates in Syria and Lebanon. Just why should some Arabs be put on a fast-track toward independence and others not? The British Empire ruled India, and acquired mandates in Palestine and Transjordan. What was the rational for presuming perpetual British rule in the former and not in the latter? Were Arabs racially superior to Indians? Imperial

[23] J. C. Smuts, *The League of Nations: A Practical Suggestion* (London: Hodder and Stoughton, 1918), esp. 11–12.

sovereignty had never been unitary. But the covenant made its irregular character a matter of international relations.

The covenant threatened the disruption of imperial authority even where it seemed unproblematic. Article 1 stipulated simply that "any fully self-governing State, Dominion, or Colony" was eligible to become a member of the League. This provision plainly had in mind the British Empire, which comprised five polities sovereign enough to sign the Treaty of Versailles in their own names.[24] It also further normalized the nation state as the principal agent in international relations. But, in that case, what exactly did imperial authority constitute over self-governing dominions?

Racial unity could not be guaranteed even among the "white" governing units of the British Empire. As Naoko Shimazu has shown, the Japanese proposal for a "racial equality" clause in the covenant had already created a rift within the British Empire delegation, based on strident opposition in the dominions to Japanese immigration. The Australians, fixated on maintaining Australia as a "white" dominion, managed to win the debate within the British Empire delegation.[25] The dominions had also asserted their independence in foreign policy during the Paris Peace Conference. Though little noted at the time, Article V of the security treaty between Britain and France signed the same day as the Treaty of Versailles specifically spared the dominions any obligation to participate in the enforcement of the security treaty without the approval of their parliaments.[26] By the time of the Chanak Crisis of 1922, this exemption would have immediate relevance.

"EMPIRE IS WHAT STATES MAKE OF IT"

In a famous 1992 article, international relations theorist Alexander Wendt interrogated "anarchy," the foundational assumption of realism underpinning the security dilemma.[27] "Anarchy," meaning the lack of a central authority strong enough to keep the peace among states, carried within it the logic that states would by nature compete rather than cooperate, whatever their objective self-interest. In contrast, Wendt argued that "there is no 'logic' of anarchy apart from the practices that create and instantiate one structure of identities and interests rather than another; structure has no existence or causal powers apart from process." In other words, in one of Wendt's signature phrases, "anarchy is what states make of it."[28] This chapter makes an analogous claim for empire. Beyond a generally haphazard presumption

---

[24] The United Kingdom, Canada, Australia, New Zealand, South Africa, and the Government of India.

[25] Naoko Shimazu, *Japan, Race and Equality: The Racial Equality Proposal of 1919* (London: Routledge, 1998), esp. ch. 5, "Australia Overwhelms the British Empire Delegation," 117–36.

[26] "Agreement between England and France Providing for Assistance to France in the Event of Unprovoked Aggression by Germany," *American Journal of International Law*, 13/4, Supplement: Official Documents (October 1919), 416.

[27] Alexander Wendt, "Anarchy is what States Make of It: The Social Construction of Power Politics," *International Organization*, 4 (1992), 391–425.

[28] Wendt, "Anarchy," 394–5.

of expansion, "empire" did not have a consistent logic. As peace-making moved beyond Europe, empires could evoke state identities for imperial ends, and states could demarcate the limits of empires.

No empire more skillfully exploited the discursive structure of international relations of 1919 than Japan—to a degree that "empire as person" language creeps back in to describe how it did so. No empire more successfully appropriated the construct of the nation state toward imperial ends, at least in the short term. Japan, the one Asian Great Powers, had not been involved in negotiating the armistice with Germany, though it had been a member of the Supreme War Council. Historians of Japan have tended to emphasize its marginalization at the Paris Peace Conference.[29]

But more interesting perhaps was the inclusion of Japan in the conference as one of the Great Powers in the first place, given its limited military contribution to the war. In realist terms, Japan merited inclusion because of its Great Power status before the war. Japan had made a naval alliance with Britain in 1902, and of course had won the Russo-Japanese War of 1904–5. Moreover, the imperial army had been fighting the Bolsheviks in Siberia since the summer of 1918. No viable settlement in Asia could be made without Japan. As the council of Great Powers morphed into the sovereign body of the conference before its first plenary session, it noted Japan's future inclusion in the minutes almost in passing and without explanation.[30]

But the fact remained that Japan had never formally accepted Wilsonianism as the ideological foundation for the peace. President Wilson had to be reminded of this fact by Baron Makino Nobuaki, head of the Japanese delegation, at a meeting on 22 January.[31] In response, Wilson contended that Japan would accept Wilsonianism implicitly after the fact, notably through inclusion in the future League of Nations. In so doing, according to Wilsonian logic, Japan would join the other pre-war Great Powers in becoming "great" in a moral as well as a material sense.

The Empire of Japan had been contemplating its imperial peace aims for some time. As early as September 1915, the Japanese established the Kôwa Junbi Iinkai (Peace Preparation Commission) to coordinate planning among the military, the cabinet, and the Diet.[32] The Japanese delegates to an inter-allied conference in late 1917 received instructions for peace aims that largely concurred with what

---

[29] See Frederick R. Dickinson, *War and National Reinvention: Japan in the Great War, 1914–1919* (Cambridge, MA: Harvard University Asia Center, 1999), ch. 6; and Thomas W. Burkman, *Japan and the League of Nations: Empire and World Order, 1914–1938* (Honolulu: University of Hawai'i Press, 2008), ch. 4.

[30] "Secretary's Notes of a Conversation Held in M. Pichon's Room at the Quai d'Orsay on Sunday, January 12, 1919, at 4 p.m.," in *Papers Relating to the Foreign Relations of the United States, 1919: The Paris Peace Conference*, 13 vols (Washington: Government Printing Office, 1942–7), iii. 506. Subsequently cited as *FRUS: PPC*.

[31] "Secretary's Notes of a Conversation Held in M. Pichon's Room at the Quai d'Orsay, Paris, January 22, 1919, at 15 Hours 15," in *FRUS: PPC*, iii. 678–9.

[32] See Thomas W. Burkman, *Japan and the League of Nations: Empire and World Order* (Honolulu: University of Hawai'i Press, 2008), 30–1.

transpired—cessation of the German rights in Shandong, China; the German Pacific islands north of the equator; and general cooperation with the Western Allies on all issues that did not directly concern Japanese interests. As Shimazu has noted, debates about the future course of the empire revolved around whether Japan as a Great Power should pursue a *datsu A ron* ("escape Asia" or pro-Western) policy or an *ajia shugi* (pan-Asian) policy.[33] The aftermath of the Great War seemed to present Japan with the opportunity to pursue both policies simultaneously. The empire could expand in Asia through the Mandate system, with the approval of the Western allies. Its uncontroversial acquisition of Class C Mandates in the Pacific islands north of the equator affirmed this notion.[34]

The problematic nature of sovereignty under the mandate system helps explain why the valuable German concessions at Shandong were pointedly left outside it—at least unless China itself became a mandate. Japan occupied Shandong after its only significant ground engagement in the Great War, the siege of the German enclave that came to a successful conclusion in November 1914. Maintaining control after the war became a matter of straightforward, realist imperial expansion, toward the end of the continued ascendance of Japan as a regional and global Great Power. As Shimazu has argued, from this point of view, the racial equality clause was no more than an imperial bargaining chip, easily enough surrendered when Japan achieved its aims in Shandong.[35]

But all of the protagonists—Japan, China, and the other Allied and Associated Powers—agreed that Shandong was part of "China." In determining the fate of the former German concessions, the Japanese skillfully pitted against each other two assumptions of the new international order, toward very familiar imperial ends. "Self-determination" collided with the sanctity of international agreements among recognized nation states. The covenant affirmed "a scrupulous respect for all treaty obligations in the dealings of organized peoples" as essential condition for "international peace and security." Through the collision of these two principles, the Shandong affair made the awkward silence in the covenant speak on existing imperial arrangements.

Wartime treaties between Japan and China codified most of the Twenty-One Demands of 1915, and accorded Japan "all rights, interests and concessions, which Germany, by virtue of treaties or otherwise, possesses in relation to the province of Shantung."[36] Throughout the peace conference, the Japanese delegation would insist that these agreements constituted binding agreements between two sovereign states. All the Great Powers had maintained for decades the same principle in their own quasi-imperial arrangements in China. The Japanese position thus exposed

---

[33] Naoko Shimazu, *Japan, Race and Equality: The Racial Equality Proposal of 1919* (London: Routledge, 1998), 92–5.

[34] Mark. R. Peattie, *Nan'yô: The Rise and Fall of the Japanese in Micronesia, 1885–1945* (Honolulu: University of Hawai'i Press, 1988), 56.

[35] Shimazu, *Japan, Race, and Equality*, especially ch. 4, "Japan's Status as a Great Power," 89–116.

[36] Document No. 1, "Japan's Twenty-One Demands," in *The Shantung Question: A Statement of China's Claim together with Important Documents submitted to the Peace Conference in Paris* (San Francisco: Chinese National Welfare Society in America, 1919), 33.

the uncomfortable nature of all such arrangements in the new world order. As Viscount Chinda Sutemi of the Japanese delegation put the matter: "The question is simple: a definite agreement exists between China and Japan; so there is no cause for a long discussion, and we cannot be convinced that a dilatory solution can be of any advantage at all."[37]

Of course, the Chinese delegation in Paris, and a good bit of the world opinion as envisioned according to the Wilsonian imaginary, saw the matter quite differently. Wellington Koo told the Council on 22 April 1919: "The Treaty we signed was the forced consequence of the ultimatum [the Twenty-One Demands]. Consequently it is very different from a treaty freely consented to."[38] Moreover, he held that, with the defeat and overthrow of the Kaiserreich, the concessions no longer had moral force, whatever their legal standing. Everyone, including the Japanese, had agreed that Shandong was "China." Any reasonable notion of self-determination had to require that sovereignty over the province return undivided to the struggling Chinese republic. Koo concluded: "the principles on which the Peace must be founded are incompatible with Japanese ambitions."[39]

The uncomfortable choice between the legality of signed agreements among allegedly sovereign states and more abstract Wilsonian notions of morality called into question the entire imperial enterprise in China. If the council denied claims by the Japanese Empire that had been acccepted according to the formal procedures of international diplomacy, what would become of very similar arrangements made with China by other council members? Just why would "unequal" treaties between Japan and China prove any less legitimate than any number of unequal treaties made since the nineteenth-century Opium Wars? Baron Makino phrased the matter succinctly: "In the past, international relations with China have not always been conducted according to principles of justice. It is better not to try to search for the first guilty party; one began, the other followed."[40] Woodrow Wilson himself, the prophet of the new diplomacy, felt compelled to assure the Japanese: "I respect all international agreements, even when I should prefer that they had not been signed, and that I am not at all proposing to hold them null and void."[41] But if the new diplomatic order remained bound by unequal agreements made under the old diplomatic order, then what exactly was new about it? In the end, Article 156 of the Treaty of Versailles accorded Japan the German concessions as a cessation of sovereignty

[37] "Conversation between President Wilson and MM. Clemenceau and Lloyd George," 22 April 1919, 11 a.m., in Arthur Link (ed. and trans.), *The Deliberations of the Council of Four (March 24–June 28, 1919): Notes of the Official Interpreter, Paul Mantoux*, 2 vols (Princeton: Princeton University Press, 1992) [originally published in French in 1955], i. 322. Hereafter referred to as *Deliberations*.
[38] "Conversation between President Wilson and MM. Clemenceau and Lloyd George," 22 April 1919, 4 p.m., *Deliberations*, i. 331.
[39] "Conversation between President Wilson and MM. Clemenceau and Lloyd George," 22 April 1919, 4 p.m., *Deliberations*, i. 334.
[40] "Conversation between President Wilson and MM. Clemenceau and Lloyd George," 22 April 1919, 11 a.m., *Deliberations*, i. 325.
[41] "Conversation between President Wilson and MM. Clemenceau and Lloyd George," 22 April 1919, 11 a.m., *Deliberations*, i. 323.

without an expiration date.[42] In short, empire in China remained what states made of it.

If the Shandong affair showed how empire could appropriate the ideological foundations of peace-making, the disposition of the former Ottoman domains showed how peace-making could disrupt empire. During the war, the Great Powers had made a variety of deals with each other to share the spoils, much in the manner of realist nation states writ large. The Sykes–Picot Agreement of May 1916 divided much of the Arab domains of the Ottoman Empire between the British and the French, with the Italians later included as part of the St Jean de Maurienne Agreement of April 1917.[43]

But the motivations behind imperial expansion went well beyond a realist concept of security. The French attachment to Syria and Lebanon, inexplicable if "security" meant protection from a resurgent Germany, had much to do with affective attachments rooted in religion and the concept of a "Mediterranean" France.[44] As the hollowness of the victory of 1918 became clearer, "France" as a nation state had to have something to show for its victory, somewhere. Imperial symbolism became strategic preoccupation. The dilemmas of what Marjorie Farrar has called "victorious nationalism beleaguered" became still more acute under Alexandre Millerand, who succeeded Georges Clemenceau as president of the Council of Ministers in January 1920.[45]

Even the famously coherent British Empire proved not immune to concerns beyond realist notions of security. Whatever else it may have done, the Balfour Declaration of November 1917 further interjected transnational politics of European Jews into the region (see Fig. 25). At least part of the motivation for doing so revolved around a sincere, transnational desire for a homeland for Jews in Palestine.[46] Had the British cared only about "security," including the endlessly expansive concern with protecting access to India through the Suez Canal, and the extraction of oil from the Arabic-speaking lands, would it not have made more sense to abandon a Jewish homeland, and make terms with the Arabs?

The millenarian fervor that infused the last weeks of the Great War deepened the ideological confusion around the disposition of the Ottoman domains.

[42] As a result of the Washington Naval Conference of 1921–2, Japan returned sovereignty to China, amid the chronic political instability of the Warlord Era. See Brian T. George, "The State Department and Sun Yat-Sen: American Policy and the Revolutionary Disintegration of China, 1920–24," *Pacific Historical Review*, 46 (1977), 387–408.

[43] On the Sykes–Picot Agreement, see David Fromkin, *A Peace to End All Peace: The Fall of the Ottoman Empire and the Creation of the Modern Middle East* (New York: Henry Holt and Company, 1989), 188–99. The text of the St Jean de Maurienne Agreement appears in René Albrecht-Carrié, *Italy at the Paris Peace Conference* (New York: Columbia University Press, 1938), 345–6. This agreement also accorded the Italians an unspecified portion of German colonies in Africa.

[44] For a deeply felt contemporary justification of the French presence, see Comte Roger de Gontaut-Biron, *Comment la France s'est installé en Syrie, 1918–1919* (Paris: Plon, 1922), esp. 1–10.

[45] Marjorie M. Farrar, "Victorious Nationalism Beleaguered: Alexandre Millerand as French Premier in 1920," *Proceedings of the American Philosophical Society*, 126 (1982), 481–519.

[46] On the competition of interests behind the Balfour Declaration, see Jonathan Schneer, *The Balfour Declaration: The Origins of the Arab–Israeli Conflict* (New York: Random House, 2010).

Fig. 25. Empire in action: British checkpoint in Palestine, 1920.

The Anglo-France Declaration of 7 November 1918 certainly claimed to endorse self-determination throughout the region.

The goal envisaged by France and Great Britain in prosecuting in the East the war let loose by German ambition is the complete and final liberation of the peoples who have for so long been oppressed by the Turks, and the setting up of national governments and administrations deriving their authority from the free exercise of the initiative and choice of the indigenous populations.

Woodrow Wilson himself could not have put the matter more expansively. Like most of the Fourteen Points and the Balfour Declaration, the Anglo-French Declaration avoided an explicit promise of full national sovereignty. But how could competing imperial interests be reconciled with the new structure of international relations that the peace conference set itself the task of building? As in the case of Shandong, what would be the status of old agreements in the new order?

In resolving these issues as peace-making moved beyond Europe proper, the formal structure of the Paris Peace Conference lived on. The Supreme Council continued to approve treaties as provisional world sovereign. But the identities of the agents operating under this structure changed, particularly as peace-making moved to the Ottoman lands. The extension of peace-making beyond Europe proper meant that different preoccupations reached center stage. The departure of President Wilson on the very day of the signing of the Versailles Treaty signaled the beginning of the long departure of the United States from the peace process. In any event, the United States had never declared war on the Ottoman Empire. Eventually, the conference morphed more or less explicitly into a conference of empires, motivated by imperial preoccupations. Yet states would determine the limits of imperial authority.

If the person of Woodrow Wilson left peace-making after the signing of the Treaty of Versailles, Wilsonianism did not. Above all, the conference operating under Wilsonianism had legitimized the self-determining successor state as a category of identity. The Anglo-French Declaration of November 1918 and the Covenant of the League of Nations still provided a very public discursive structure for the new international order that the empires could not discard lightly. Article 22 of the covenant had explicitly identified at least some of the peoples of the Middle East as worthy of full independence, and sooner rather than later. These mostly Arabic-speaking peoples would not hesitate to remind the mandatory powers of the promises made. But the conference would find that it had evoked an identity that it could not wholly control. Self-determination on largely ethnic grounds would open a Pandora's Box, as various entities sought to brand the "self" worthy of self-determination in ways not foreseen in the soaring rhetoric of President Wilson in 1918. In Anatolia, Turkish and Greek successor states would demarcate the limits of imperial sovereignty. Empire thus became what successor states as well as imperial states made of it in the former Ottoman domains.

In the Arabic-speaking lands, imperial states sought to create client pre-states in the mandates, through siding with powerful notables who were then supposed to provide a manageable indigenous elite. Yet the reliability of indigenous partners would remain suspect, and it remained far from certain to the mandatory powers whether bargains struck between the new imperialists and their collaborators would suffice to appropriate sovereignty in the mandates. While in the short run empire could assert sovereignty through military force, the imperial and state sovereignty in the Middle East would become an ever more muddled affair.

During the war, the British had subsidized two rival families in the Arabian Peninsula in the hope of subverting Ottoman rule—the Hashemites of Mecca and the House of Saud.[47] As the fortunes of the former came to wane in favor of the latter in the spring of 1919, British attention turned to using the Hashemites as an instrument of nationalism toward imperialist ends in the Levant. However, enthroning Faysal, son of the Hashemite Emir of Mecca, potentially conflicted with French claims under the Sykes–Picot Agreement. Faysal, who had spent some months in Paris pleading the Arab case, came to an arrangement with Clemenceau in April 1919, according to which Faysal would rule a nominally independent Syria including Lebanon under a loose French mandate.[48] The British accepted these arrangements, provided the French in return endorsed a British mandate in Palestine that would help fulfill the Balfour Declaration.

[47] Hussein at one point complained that he had to spend half of his £12,000 per month subsidy fending off attacks from Saudi forces. Fromkin, *Peace to End All Peace*, 424.
[48] Meir Zamir, "Faisal and the Lebanese Question, 1918–1920," *Middle Eastern Studies*, 27 (1991), 409–10.

But it soon became clear that matters were not wholly under the control of the French, the British, or even Faisal. A Syrian National Congress called by Faisal in June 1919 endeavored to sort out the complex relationship among religion, geography, ethnicity, and nationalism in the region.[49] While divided along sectarian and other political lines, the congress did agree upon a completely independent "Syria" comprising the whole Levant. This put Faysal (in any event a native of Mecca, not Syria) in an untenable position. He could antagonize either his European patrons or his Syrian subjects. In March 1920, the congress declared Syrian independence with Faysal as king. Shortly thereafter, the Conference of San Remo of April 1920 agreed on a French mandate in Syria (including Lebanon) and a British mandate in Palestine and Trans-Jordan. At least for the moment, the two imperial allies had enough military force to decide the locus of sovereignty in Syria. In July 1920, the French Armée du Levant occupied Damascus and forced the exile of Faysal.[50] The League of Nations approved the French mandate for Syria in July 1922. But the matter could hardly end there. France had acquired a costly imperial trophy of debatable strategic or even commercial significance. Moreover, this new spoke in the French imperial wheel was programmed for independence on the date of its manufacture.

The British acquired a valuable if awkward mandate in Mesopotamia/Iraq, previously at the edge of the Ottoman world. There, the British asserted long-held imperial interests—an expansive notion of secure passage to India and access to oil. Then as now, names for the region draw from geography rather than nationality, and encompass peoples divided against each other. The term "Mesopotamia" comes from ancient Greek, meaning "land between rivers," the Tigris and the Euphrates. The Arabic term "Iraq" means simply "fertile" or "deep-rooted" land. Then as now, a fault line existed between Sunni and Shia Arabs. Many more fault lines existed among tribes. In addition, a large Kurdish population considered itself entitled to self-determination.

Susan Pedersen has argued that the British mandate in Iraq began and ended for much the same reason—a continuing struggle to find a cost-effective means satisfying competing imperial interests.[51] The post-war United Kingdom had fiscal concerns at odds with post-war expansion of the British Empire. The prospective cost of maintaining some 100,000 troops to secure Mesopotamia gave rise to ferocious debates, both inside Westminster and between Westminster and the Government of India.[52] As the mandate took shape, the political solution involved setting the then-unemployed Faysal on an Iraqi throne under a British mandate. Technological innovations such as airplanes, tanks, and armored vehicles, military

---

[49] For a broad overview, see Moshe Ma'oz, "Attempts at Creating a Political Community in Modern Syria," *Middle East Journal*, 26 (1972), 389–404.

[50] Dan Eldar "France in Syria: The Abolition of the Sharifian Government, April–July 1920," *Middle Eastern Studies*, 29 (1993), 487–504.

[51] Susan Pedersen, "Getting Out of Iraq—in 1932," *American Historical Review*, 115 (2010), 975–1000.

[52] See Briton Cooper Busch, *Britain, India, and the Arabs, 1914–1921* (Berkeley and Los Angeles: University of California Press, 1971), esp. chs 8–9.

officials reasoned, created cost-effective means of imperial rule based on terrorizing the indigenous population.[53] As Pedersen argued, the British construed a very dependent form of "independence" for Iraq in 1931 as a still more economically frugal means of reconciling imperial and state interests in Britain, in the throes of the Great Depression.

In the end, and as represented on a map, the peace made in the predominantly Arabic-speaking domains of the Middle East more or less resembled that envisaged by the Sykes–Picot Agreement. But the imperial settlement would raise more issues than it would solve. These mandates all became "Class A," meaning that they were expected shortly to become independent states. The mandate hardly provided a stable political structure, even one presumed to be transitional. Imperial French and British authorities found themselves in permanent competition, often violent, for sovereignty in these states-in-the-making. Arab–Jewish riots in Jerusalem and a major tribal revolt in Iraq in 1920,[54] followed by a revolt in Syria and Lebanon in 1925,[55] meant that the peoples of these lands would pursue the various contradictory meanings of "self-determination" with all the means at their disposal. The Wilsonian discursive structure put forward in the Anglo-French Declaration turned out to have much more import in the long run than the formal disposition of mandates in the region might have suggested.

Empire became what states made of it in quite a different way in Anatolia. On 19 August 1920, the conference signed the Treaty of Sèvres with Ottoman Sultan Mehmet VI. Sèvres was the last treaty of the Paris Peace Conference as such. But, from the moment of its signing, the treaty literally papered over quite a different reality. Real sovereignty in Anatolia had shifted away from the regime of the sultan toward two mutually antagonistic successor states. Like successor states in Central and Eastern Europe, successor Greece and successor Turkey sought to reconcile ethnic and "historic" boundaries in what after the Balkan Wars had become the Anatolian heartland of the Ottoman Empire. War between the two successor states would decide the relative position between them. Successor Turkey would demarcate French power in its new mandate in Syria. For the British Empire, constructing post-Ottoman Anatolia would have more serious implications. A near-war with successor Turkey would call into question the existence of the British Empire as a unitary agent in the international system.

After the Mudros armistice of 30 October 1918, a modest force of some 3,500 Allied (mostly British) troops entered Constantinople, as an unofficial occupying

[53] On the role of the Royal Air Force, see David E. Omissi, *Air Power and Colonial Control: The Royal Air Force, 1919–1939* (Manchester: Manchester University Press, 1990), and Priya Satia, "The Defense of Inhumanity: Air Control and the British Idea of Arabia," *American Historical Review*, 111 (2006), 16–51. The British seriously considered the use of poison gas, though, contrary to widespread belief on the part of posterity, they did not do so. R. M. Douglas, "Did Britain Use Chemical Weapons in Mandatory Iraq?," *Journal of Modern History*, 81 (2009), 859–87.

[54] John J. McTague, Jr, "The British Military Administration in Palestine," *Journal of Palestine Studies*, 7 (1978), 55–76.

[55] Joyce Laverty Miller, "The Syrian Revolt of 1925," *International Journal of Middle East Studies*, 8 (1977), 545–63.

Fig. 26. Empire under siege: removing a French mailbox in wartime Turkey.

force.[56] The sultan and the formal structures of the Ottoman government remained in place. The Sèvres treaty would cast post-Ottoman "Turkey" under the sultan as a criminalized agent. Consequently, it lost its imperial domains and owed reparations. As empires, Britain, France, and Italy rushed to define post-Ottoman Turkey according to their own imperial interests—guaranteeing access to the straits of the Dardanelles, and expansion in the Arabic-speaking lands.

The Treaty of Sèvres laid the foundation for an inter-allied protectorate in Anatolia. Like the four other treaties produced by the conference, it began with the Covenant of the League of Nations (see Fig. 26). Thereafter it drove Wilsonian principles unashamedly in imperial directions.[57] Post-imperial Turkey would fall into Allied receivership through losing control over its finances. According to Article 231 of the Treaty of Sèvres, by joining the war on the side of Germany and Austria–Hungary, Turkey had caused "losses and sacrifices of all kinds for which she ought to make complete reparation." As with the German *Kriegschuld* clause, the Allies recognized that this would be well beyond the capacity of the post-imperial Turkey to pay, particularly given the loss of the Arabic-speaking lands. Accordingly, in order "to afford some measure of relief and assistance to Turkey," the treaty set up a Financial Commission comprising one representative each from

[56] Andred Mango, *Atatürk: The Biography of the Founder of Modern Turkey* (Woodstock: Overlook Press, 1999), 196.
[57] For a summary of the diplomacy leading up to the treaty, see A. E. Montgomery, "The Making of the Treaty of 10 August 1920," *Historical Journal*, 15 (1972), 775–87.

France, the British Empire, and Italy, with a Turkish representative serving in a consultative capacity. This commission had vast powers, such as more or less complete control over the government budget (Article 232), and authority over future government loans (Article 234). No other defeated Central Power had to subject itself to such a compromise of its sovereignty, in the name of reparations or anything else.

While the treaty preserved at least nominal Turkish sovereignty over Constantinople and did not interfere in the position of the sultan as caliph, it set in motion a process that would probably have resulted in the partition of the Anatolian peninsula.[58] A French, British, and Italian commission would make recommendations for an autonomous Kurdistan within six months of the signing of the treaty (Article 62). Sovereignty around Smyrna (technically still Turkish, as per Article 69) would finally be determined by a plebiscite after five years of direct rule by Greece (Article 83). The treaty immediately established an independent, if amorphous, Armenia (Article 88). Its eventual boundaries would be determined through arbitration, improbably enough, by the president of the United States.[59] Minorities in vestigial Turkey proper would enjoy protections similar to those in the other treaties (Articles 140–51), except that ultimate sovereignty on minority protection would rest with the Allies in consultation with the League Council, rather than with the League itself.

The emergence of mutually antagonistic Greek and Turkish successor states gave the Treaty of Sèvres a surreal quality from the outset. As early as May 1919, Mustafa Kemal (later known as Atatürk), the hero of the Gallipoli campaign, took up the innocuous-sounding position of inspector of the 9th Army. He placed his headquarters in Samsun along the Black Sea, well beyond Allied military power. In February 1920, the last Ottoman parliament had adopted the Misak-i Millî (National Pact), a declaration of national independence that directly challenged Allied sovereignty. Meanwhile, Greece morphed into a successor state determined to realize what Michael Llewellyn Smith called the "Ionian Vision,"[60] which made ethnic and historic claims on the Anatolian peninsula. This vision saw pre-1914 boundaries as simply what Eleftherios Venizelos called the "backbone" of a much greater Greece, which would encompass most of the remaining Ottoman territory in Europe (including Constantinople), the territories on both sides of the straits, and the Anatolian peninsula itself up to the Central Plateau.

Of some 160,000 Allied troops in all of Anatolia at the signature of the Sèvres treaty, some 90,000 were Greek.[61] British, French, and Italian forces were

---

[58] The all-important straits would become internationalized, open to all vessels in peace and war (Article 36).

[59] On the tangled politics of Armenia in the late Wilson administration, see Lloyd E. Ambrosius, "Wilsonian Diplomacy and Armenia: The Limits of Power and Ideology," in Jay Winter (ed.), *America and the Armenian Genocide of 1915* (New York: Cambridge University Press, 2004), 113–45. The United States, not having declared war on the Ottoman Empire, did not sign the Treaty of Sèvres.

[60] Michael Llewellyn Smith, *Ionian Vision: Greece in Asia Minor: 1919–1922* (London: Allen Lane, 1973).

[61] Paul C. Helmreich, *From Paris to Sèvres: The Partition of the Ottoman Empire at the Paris Peace Conference of 1919–1920* (Columbus, OH: Ohio State University Press, 1974), 279–80.

concentrated around the straits and Constantinople, which the powers still considered the strategic center of gravity. In effect, this configuration of military power tied Allied imperial fortunes in Anatolia to the outcome of the conflict between Greek and Turkish successor states. After the failed London Conference of February 1921, the Great Powers consented to, or even encouraged, a renewed Greek offensive in Anatolia. This campaign sought to topple the competing republican regime and to consolidate successor Greece in the peninsula.[62] While the initial success of this campaign brought the Greeks to within some 60 miles of Angora (later Ankara), their badly overextended forces shortly found themselves in retreat. By September 1922, the Turks had put Greek-dominated Smyrna to flames. It would later rise as Izmir. The violent exchanges of population between the Greek and Turkish successor states had begun.

Along the way, the conference of empires essentially disintegrated. As early as October 1921, the French made an agreement with the Kemal, in effect granting his regime recognition by a Great Power. This agreement resolved the border between Cilicia and the French mandate in Syria.[63] Italian imperial interests contracted to the Dodecanese islands, a policy unaltered by Benito Mussolini's March on Rome in October 1922. By the time of the Chanak crisis, both France and Italy had for some months actually been delivering war material to the Ankara regime.[64] Their small contingents of troops had been withdrawn to Constantinople, leaving the British Empire as the sole defender of "Allied" sovereignty in the straits.

The Chanak Crisis of the fall of 1922 showed that the British Empire had ceased to function as a unitary imperial agent. As Kemal's forces closed in on the straits after the defeat of the Greeks, Westminster sent a telegram to the dominions on 15 September requesting military support in the event of war with Turkey. Colonial Secretary Winston Churchill released the telegram to the British press on a Saturday, which, allowing for the time difference, meant that it reached most of the dominions through local newspapers before it could be officially decoded the following Monday.[65]

The little noted though long-remembered Article 5 of the 1919 security treaty between Britain and France, which established the requirement of prior consultation with dominion parliaments, had sudden relevance. Canada and Australia declined military assistance. Newfoundland agreed with the policy of confronting Kemal, but did not agree to send troops. South Africa under Prime Minister Jan Smuts chose silence. New Zealand offered assistance, but only a battalion with the possibility of a brigade later. In the end, the agreement at Mundania on 11 October 1922 headed off armed conflict between the British and Turkish forces, and paved the way for renewed peace negotiations for a revised treaty. The last of the great

[62] For an efficient narrative account, see Peter Kincaid Jensen, "The Greco-Turkish War, 1920–1922," *International Journal of Middle East Studies*, 10 (1979), 553–65.

[63] See Yücel Güçlü, "The Struggle for Mastery in Cilicia: Turkey, France, and the Ankara Agreement of 1921," *International History Review*, 23 (2001), 580–603, esp. 593–603.

[64] Nur Bilge Criss, *Istambul under Allied Occupation, 1918–1923* (Leiden: Brill, 1999), 141.

[65] David Walder, *The Chanak Crisis* (London: Hutchinson, 1969), 215–16.

wartime leaders still in power, David Lloyd George, fell on October 19.[66] The Treaty of Lausanne, signed on 24 July 1923, was not the product of the Paris Peace Conference proper. It concluded a settlement with the Turkish successor state, which could largely determine its relations with the still-present empires in the Middle East on its own terms. In Anatolia, the reach of imperial states became what successor states made of it.

CONCLUSION

To return to the original question of this chapter, then, what *were* empires at the Paris Peace Conference? Daniel Nexon and Thomas Wright have argued that, in the international system, empires do not behave as states, still less as people. Rather, they exist as interacting networks. Each empire is constituted through "*heterogeneous contracting* between imperial cores and constituent political communities."[67] As we have seen, in a given situation, different communities within an empire could pull in different directions. Following Alexander Motyl, Nexon and Wright have posited an analogy of a "rimless hub-and-spoke" system, in which each spoke is linked to the hub, but there is no rim to tie the spokes to each other.[68] The "rimless wheel" metaphor also emphasizes the lack of a permanent external boundary. Different empires can interact in so many ways for so many different reasons that they can seem unpredictable or irrational. They can act in ways consistent with the security preoccupations of realism, but these actions are not reducible to those preoccupations.

This chapter has sought to think broadly about empire as a category of analysis at the Paris Peace Conference. Empires were both agents making peace and the sites over which peace was made. The successor state, with its imperative to reconcile such volatile legitimizing categories as "history" and "ethnicity," proved both the solution to empire and the problem of empire. In Central and Eastern Europe, self-determining successor states created a regional subsystem to replace empire, though in so doing they created a cauldron of irredentism and toxic ethnic hatreds. In the Middle East and Anatolia, successor states showed the limits of empire.

More implicitly than explicitly, this chapter has also explored the "agent/structure problem" from international relations theory. More than twenty-five years after Alexander Wendt's foundational article reformulating the problem, it no longer seems controversial to assert in the abstract that agents and structures in international relations build each other in an ongoing dialogue.[69] At the end of 1918, the Great Powers accepted Wilsonianism as a discursive structure for making

---

[66] See J. J. Darwin, "The Chanak Crisis and the British Cabinet," *History*, 65 (1980), 32–48.

[67] Daniel H. Nexon and Thomas Wright, "What's at Stake in the American Empire Debate," *American Political Science Review*, 101 (2007), 253 (emphasis in original).

[68] See the definition of empire in Alexander Motyl, *Imperial Ends: The Decay, Collapse, and Revival of Empires* (New York: Columbia University Press, 2001), 4.

[69] See Alexander Wendt, "The Agent-Structure Problem in International Relations Theory," *International Organization*, 41 (1987), 335–70.

peace. While Wilsonianism had the most to say about Europe, the structure it provided was clearly meant to apply around the globe. Wilsonianism authorized and legitimized the identity of the successor state. Successor states would challenge empire everywhere. In accepting Wilsonianism, the Great Powers had accepted a structure that reshaped and circumscribed their capacities as empires.

In the contested terrain of sovereignty in the international system after the Great War, empire became what states made of it in a dual sense. The Japanese as a state exploited the opportunities of the system so skillfully that the temptation to describe its intentionality in human terms is difficult to resist. In Shandong and the Pacific, the Japanese Empire became what the Japanese state made of it. In an opposite sense, empire became what successor states made of it in the Middle East and Anatolia. League mandates authorized troublesome states-to-be in Palestine, Syria, Lebanon, and Iraq. Implicitly, Wilsonianism as a discursive structure also legitimized successor Turkey. In Anatolia, this new Turkey saw off not just its Greek successor state rival, but also the European empires that sought to make post-Ottoman Anatolia an inter-allied protectorate. Furthermore, during the Chanak Crisis successor Turkey provoked, if temporarily, the fracturing of the British Empire as a unitary agent.

Yet it would be a mistake to underestimate the resilience of empire during and after the Great War. For better or worse, Great Powers remained the backbone of empire between the wars. Whatever the ethical issues at stake, they proved remarkably adroit at hierarchically structuring difference, both in the mandates and in the pre-existing imperial domains. Colonial bureaucracy and brute force were effective tools in the twentieth century, just as they had been in the nineteenth. Interwar nationalist movement in would-be successor states might have won eventually, whether the Great Powers went to war with each other again or not. But independence movements were largely contained not just before Europe's next Great War beginning in 1939, but during it. The Second World War and its aftermath broke European and Japanese imperial power. Even so, proper decolonization was a product mostly of the late 1950s and 1960s, and many traces of empire persist today. The cold war and post-cold war Pax Americana opened up new chapters in the history of empire. As Burbank and Cooper have argued, empire as a political structure is nothing if not durable. Perhaps as long as there is politically significant difference to structure, empire will be there to structure it.

Index

Abdülhamid II, Sultan 21, 23
Abdurahman, Abdullah 137
Abu Hatir Efendi, Ibrahim 28
Adams, Brooks 197, 198
Adana 18, 20
Addis Ababa 44, 45, 46
Adowa 34, 36, 39, 44
Afghanistan 1, 62, 130, 159, 253
Africa 15, 134
    conscription in 8–10, 37–8
    effects of war in 146–7, 149–51
    war and 135–7, 138–45, 147–8
    see also France; Germany; Great Britain; Italy;
        Ottoman Empire
Agafonov, Ivan 94, 95, 96
Alaska 256
Albuquerque, Mouzinho de 181
Allen, Maj. Gen. Henry 243, 250
Aleppo 29, 32
Alexander III, Tsar 92
Algeria 7, 39, 51, 120, 122–3, 125; *see also* France
Alsace-Lorraine 54, 56
Alston, Beilby 233
Amendola, Giovanni 51
Amorim, Massano de 188
Anatolia:
    imperialism and 19, 24, 32, 33, 103, 269,
        271–6
    war and 4, 11, 22, 26, 27, 49–50, 98, 256
Angola 15, 140; *see also* Portugal
Arias, Arnulfo 252
Arias, Harmodio 252
Aritomo, Yamagata 203, 204
Armenia 6, 20, 24, 68
    war and 25–7, 29, 32, 96
    see also Russia
Askari, the 6, 67, 138, 143, 189, 190
Asmara 44, 45, 46
Asquith, (Earl) Herbert H. 158, 159
Atatürk, Kemal, *see* Kemal, Mustafa
Australia 3, 8, 9, 14, 164, 167–9
    effects of war in 165–6, 170–1, 174
    war participation of 152, 154–6, 160–1
    see also Great Britain
Austria 11, 34, 36, 41
Austria-Hungary 4, 5, 6, 11, 19, 23, 34, 37
    Balkans and 74–6, 85
    Czechoslovaks and 82, 85
    economy of 81, 83
    Germany and 66, 69, 77–8
    monarchy before/after 1914: 73–9
    Poland/Serbia and 77–8

    revolution and 86–9
    war and 79–82, 85, 90

Baker, Newton 240
Balkans, the 5, 11, 21, 38, 74–6
Bandholtz, Harry Hill 243
Baratov, Gen. 98
Beirut 28, 29, 37
Belfield, Sir Henry Conway 133
Belgium 19, 91, 254; *see also* Germany; Great
    Britain
Beneš, Edvard 79
Berchtold, Count Leopold 76, 77
Berend, Ivan 86
Berlin 64, 75, 80, 140, 159
    government in 24, 62, 130, 132, 133, 148
    Ottomans and 27, 44, 68, 109
Bethmann-Hollweg, Theobald von 55
Bevan, Edwyn 69
Bevione, Giuseppe 37
Beyers, Gen. C. F. 156
Beyrau, Dietrich 80
Bhattacharya, Abinash 159
Bismarck, Otto von 52, 57
Bobrinskii, Count Georgii 97
Bonaparte, Napoleon 1, 18, 54
Bosnia-Herzegovina 19, 74–6
Botha, Louis 8, 63, 140, 142, 151, 156
Brent, Bishop Charles Henry 243
Brusilov, Gen. Alexei 98, 99
Bryan, William Jennings 249
Bulgaria 5, 20, 27–8, 69, 89
Bülow, Bernhard von 52
Burbank, Jane 255, 276
Burma 1, 153, 155, 159
Butler, Maj. Smedley 247
Buxton, Lord Sydney 144

Cadorna, Luigi 42
Caesar, Julius 35, 50
Caetano, Marcello 196
Cai, E 222
Cambodia 122
Cameroon 8, 61, 63, 154
Canada 3, 8, 9, 14
    effects of war in 165–6, 170
    maintenance of order in 167–9
    nature of soldiers 164–5
    war participation of 154–6, 160
    see also Great Britain
Caporetto 42, 43
Careless, J. M. S. 173

Caroselli, Francesco 41
Carson, Edward 158
Casement, Roger 62
Castro, Álvaro de 195
Catherine the Great 18, 91
Caucasus 11, 25, 32, 62, 94, 103–4
Cemal, Pasha 22, 24, 25, 27, 29, 32
Charles I, Emperor 78, 81, 82, 85, 86
Chattopadhyaya, Virendranath 159
Chen, Duxiu 234
Chen, Jerome 219
Chilembwe, John 136, 189
China 91
    impact of war on 229–34
    imperialism and 214–16
    nationalism and 215, 220–2
    war, policy and 3, 10, 13, 41, 153, 197–204,
        208, 211, 222–8
    1911 revolution and 215–16
    see also Germany; Japan; Korea; Paris Peace
        Conference; Wilson, Woodrow
Churchill, Winston 274
Clairin, Georges 125
Clemenceau, Georges 120, 267, 269
Clifford, Sir Hugh 133
Colli di Felizzano, Giuseppe 46
Colosimo, Gaspare 41, 42
Conrad, Sebastian 54, 57
Constantinople 18, 31, 35, 43
Cooper, Frederick 255, 276
Corradini, Enrico 36, 40
Costa, Afonso 182, 192, 193, 194
Costa, João Rodrigues Nunes da 195–6
Couceiro, Paiva 181
Cuba 229, 252; *see also* United States
Curzon, George 192
Cyrenaica 42, 43
Czechoslovakia 11, 85, 89

Dalmatia 36, 41, 76
Damascus 19, 29, 32, 127, 128, 270
Daniels, Josephus 242
D'Annunzio, Gabriele 36, 40, 41
Dardanelles 10, 31, 38, 102, 272
Del Boca, Angelo 39
Denikius, Gen. Anton 105
Deventer, Jaap van 143, 191
Deventer, Gen. Jacob van, *see* Deventer, Jaap van
Diagne, Blaise 12
Díaz, Porfirio 239
Dickinson, Frederick 3
Diehl, James 88
Dinar, Ali 147–8
Di San Giuliano, Antonino 36
Dodecanese islands 38, 42, 49, 50, 274
Doering, Maj. Kurt von 133
Dominican Republic 13, 237, 242, 247, 248,
    251, 252
Donson, Andrew 59

Duan, Qirui 223, 224, 225–8
Dudden, Alexis 209
Dyer, Reginald 176

Eça, Gen. Pereira de 186
Edib, Halide 17, 32, 33
Edirne/Adrianople 21
Egypt 21, 49
    Germany/Turkey and 25, 29, 40, 42, 45
    Great Britain and 1, 4, 11, 12, 23, 25, 147,
        148, 155, 162, 258
Enver Bey, Pasha 21, 22, 23, 24, 29, 32, 38,
    40, 104
    Italy and 15, 39, 40, 44, 47, 48, 51
Ethiopia 44–5, 48; *see also* Italy
Evans-Pritchard, Edward 43

Faysal ibn Husayn 12, 269, 270
Ferreira Gil, Gen. 187
Filonardi, Eugenio 46
Fink, Carole 260
Finland 11, 83, 89, 102, 103, 108
Fischer, Fritz 55, 60
France:
    Africa and 12–13, 46, 132
    Algeria and 1, 110, 112, 113, 115, 118, 119,
        148, 262
    colonial labour and 118–23
    colonial policy of 1, 109–11, 127–9
    Germany and 52, 55, 56, 57, 61, 62, 64, 68,
        109, 117
    imperial economy of 113–15, 117
    Italy and 37, 41, 44
    Ottomans and 25, 28, 109–110
    racist policies of 117, 123, 129
    Syria and 1, 12, 29, 127, 128, 262, 267,
        269, 274
    war and 2, 7, 9, 19, 26, 109–11, 125–6
    women and 123–4
    see also Great Britain
Francis Joseph I, Emperor 74, 75, 77, 78, 80, 81
Franz Ferdinand, Archduke 18, 19, 75, 77,
    78, 197
Frémeaux, Jacques 114
Freud, Sigmund 67
Frobenius, Leo 46
Fu Liangzuo, Gen. 226

Gallipoli 25, 32, 61, 152, 163, 164, 174, 273
Gandhi, Mohandas K. (Mahatma) 10, 11, 175–6
García, Somoza 252
Garibaldi, Giuseppe 41
Garrison, Lindley 238
Gasar Hamad 40
Gasr Bu Hadi 40
George V, King 12, 142, 151, 255
Germany:
    Africa and 45, 52, 53, 57, 63, 64, 65, 67,
        68, 132–3, 136, 138, 139

Belgium and 55, 59, 145
China and 54, 63, 159, 223–6, 232–3, 255, 265
continental wartime empire and 2, 3, 24, 58–60, 94, 103, 105
effects of imperialism on 70–2
global empire of 8, 9, 15, 25, 37, 38, 44, 46, 48, 60–5
imperialism of 4, 7, 11, 14, 52–4, 67–70, 255, 257, 258, 260
Italy and 37, 44, 46
Japan and 199, 201, 202, 204, 206, 208–10, 217, 218, 264, 265
Kaiserreich of 54–7
Poland and 53, 54–5, 56, 60
Portugal and 186, 187, 190
race and 65–7
Russia and 58, 62, 63, 103
United States and 239, 241, 244, 245, 248, 256
see also France; Great Britain; Ottoman Empire
Gerwarth, Robert 86
Giichi, Tanaka 204
Giolitti, Giovanni 38
Goltz, Gen. Colmar von der 23, 24
Goodnow, Frank 220, 221
Graziani, Rodolfo 51
Great Britain:
African colonies of 8, 44, 46, 130–51, 133, 173
Australia and 155–6, 165, 171, 172, 173, 176
Belgium and 54, 132, 139, 148, 161, 181, 186, 206
Canada and 155–6, 160, 165, 170, 172, 173
China and 229, 232
conscription and 9–10
dominions, nationalism and 172–7
France and 127, 132
Germany and 1, 13, 52, 54, 56, 57, 61, 62, 64, 68, 69, 71, 131, 132, 139, 141, 143, 148, 152, 154, 156, 159, 209
India and 1, 4, 11, 12, 25, 42, 50, 68, 132, 154, 155, 158–9, 162, 165, 172, 176, 262, 267, 270
Ireland and 1, 4, 8, 10, 71, 154, 158, 172, 175, 212
Italy and 42–3
Japan and 199, 200, 206, 208, 217, 218, 264
South Africa and 8, 9, 61, 132–5, 137, 138, 149, 150, 151
Turkey and 40, 45–6, 69, 162, 271–2
see also New Zealand; Ottoman Empire; Wilson, Woodrow
Greece 1, 5, 6, 26, 32, 50, 271, 273, 274
Gregory, Thomas 251
Grew, Joseph 252
Grey, Sir Edward 131, 206
Grunshi, Sgt.-Maj. Alhaji 63
Guchkov, Aleksandr 102

Habsburg Empire 6, 19, 260
imperialism of 1, 3, 14, 16, 23, 25, 41, 254, 255
pre-war monarchy of 73–90
Haile Selassie, Emperor 45
Haiti 13, 237, 247, 248, 251, 252, 253, 256
Harbord, James 243
Harcourt, Lewis 140, 144
Harding, Warren 238, 252
Harrar 45
Harrison, Francis 238
Hassan, Mohammed Abdullah 45, 47, 48
Hatlie, Mark 86
Hawai'i 241, 256
Hentig, Werner Otto von 62
Hercegovina, *see* Bosnia-Herzegovina
Herero, the 52, 53, 56, 61, 65, 66, 132, 140
Hertzog, J. B. M. 151
Herzegovina, *see* Bosnia-Herzegovina
Ho, Chi Minh 12, 128–9
Hohenzollern Empire 1, 19, 254, 255, 258, 259, 260
Horne, John 86, 158
Hoskins, Brig.-Gen. Reginald 143
Hrushevsky, Mykhailo 102
Hughes, William Morris 168, 170, 173
Hull, Isabel 53
Hungary:
post-war 11, 87, 88, 89, 94, 259
pre-war history of 74, 76, 77
al-Husri, Sati' 22
Husayn, ibn Ali, Sharif of Mecca 31, 32

Ianushkevich, Gen. Nikolai 96
İhsan, Pte. 30
India 167, 169
effects of war in 165–6, 170–1, 175–6
race and 65, 67, 140, 163–4
war in 3, 8, 9, 10, 31, 56, 62, 139, 143, 145, 148, 152, 154–9, 161
see also Great Britain
Indochina
France and 1, 5, 12, 109, 110, 111
war in 113, 114, 118, 120, 121, 122, 124, 128
Inoue Kaoru, Marquis 200
Iraq 1, 4, 12, 31, 130, 253, 270, 271, 276
Ireland 2, 164, 167–9
effects of war in 165–6, 175
war participation of 62, 154–8, 160
see also Great Britain
Istanbul 18, 31, 32
war and 19, 20, 23, 24, 25, 26, 27, 28, 29
Italy:
Africa and 35–51
imperialism of 1, 5, 15, 20, 24, 34–5
Turkey and 43, 47
see also Ottoman Empire
Iudenich, Gen. Nikolai 98, 99, 105

Ivan the Terrible 91, 104
Iyasu, Lij 44–5, 46, 47, 48
Izmir 20, 33, 274

Jabavu, D. D. T. 137
Japan:
China and 63, 197–8, 200–3, 214–22, 224, 232, 233, 234, 266
Germany and 63, 201, 203
imperialism of 1, 3, 5, 13, 208–9, 254, 256, 259, 262–6, 276
post-war power of 211–13
Russia and 91, 92, 199, 203–4
Siberia and 5, 203, 204, 206, 212, 213, 264
war and 24, 44, 173, 198–9, 205–7
see also Korea; Paris Peace Conference; Wilson, Woodrow
Jenkins, Jennifer 69
Jiang, Tingfu 223–4
Jones, William 238, 240, 241, 246, 251
Jordan, John 219–20

Kang, Youwei 215
Kaoru, Inoue 217
Kazakhstan 99–100
Kemal, Mustafa 19, 25, 26, 32, 38, 50, 273, 274
Kennedy, Paul 5
Kenya 45, 132, 133, 143
Kinmochi, Saionji 212
Kirsche, Emil 48
Knapp, Harry 247
Kolchak, Gen. Aleksandr 105
Koo, Wellington 219, 232, 266
Korea 1, 5, 13, 92, 198, 199, 200, 208, 209, 210, 211, 217
Korošec, Anton 85
Kosovo 20, 253
Kramář, Karel 81
Kramer, Alan 89

Lansing, Robert 232, 239, 240, 247, 256
Lawrence, Jon 172
Lawrence, T. E. 258
Lederer, Ivo 76
Lenin, Vladimir 3, 101, 103, 106, 107, 115, 258
Lettow-Vorbeck, Gen. Paul von
Africa and 6, 64, 67, 68, 143–6
Portugal and 178, 189–90, 191
Levant, the 5, 269, 270
Li, Jiannong 219, 226
Li, Yuanhong 223, 224, 225, 227, 228
Liang, Qichao 215, 219, 221, 222, 224
Libya:
Italy and 15, 20, 21, 35, 36, 37, 38, 40, 41, 42, 44, 47–52
Ottomans and 21, 38, 40, 110, 147
see also Tripoli

Liulevicius, Vejas Gabriel 60
Lloyd George, David 131, 232, 275
Lohr, Eric 96
Lourenço, Eduardo 180
Lucas, Sir Charles Prestwood 153
Lugo, Américo 251

Mackenzie King, W. L. 173
McIntyre, Brig. Gen. Frank 240
McKinley, William 241
Mahan, Alfred Thayer 239
Maier, Charles 3, 53, 92, 110, 179, 255
Maji-Maji, the 52, 53, 132
Makonnen, Tafari, *see* Haile Selassie, Emperor
Manela, Erez 256, 258
Mangin, Gen. Charles 7, 56, 110, 119
Mao, Zedong 234
Marinetti, Filippo Tommaso 35
Martini, Ferdinando 39, 41, 44
Marx, Karl 115
Masaryk, Tomáš Garrigue 79
Masatake, Gen. Terauchi 200, 204, 208
Mayer, Arno 258, 259
Mazzini, Giuseppe 41
Mehmed VI, *see* Mehmet VI, Sultan
Mehmet VI, Sultan 19, 271; *see also* Osman, House of
Menelik, Emporer 34, 44, 46
Mesopotamia 10, 12, 270
Messimy, Adolphe 119
Mexico 13, 237, 239, 241, 243, 250, 256
Miani, Col. Antonio 39
Mikael, Ras 45
Miliukov, Pavel 101, 102
Millerand, Alexandre 267
Millo, Enrico 38
Milner, Lord Alfred 131, 192, 193
Minh, Ho Chi, *see* Ho, Chi Minh
Mıntzuri, Hagop 27
Misrata 40, 51
Moniz, Egas 192, 193
Monroe, James 200, 237, 244
Montague, Edwin 162
Montenegro 5, 76, 78, 87
Morrison, George E. 218
Morocco 1, 61, 68, 109, 110, 112, 113, 120, 148, 262
Moscow 16, 102, 107, 206
Mosse, George 171
Motyl, Alexander 275
Mount Lebanon 28–9
Moyd, Michelle 67
Mozambique 186–96; *see also* Portugal
Murav'ev, Mikhail 106
Mussolini, Benito 1, 34, 36, 40, 43, 50–1, 274

Nama, the 52, 53, 132
Namibia 8, 262
Napoleon, *see* Bonaparte, Napoleon

Newfoundland 9, 161, 274
New Guinea 61, 63, 131, 152, 173
New Zealand:
    effects of war in 165–6, 169, 170
    imperialism and 8, 9, 14, 154, 155, 156,
        172, 173, 176, 274
    war and 63, 147, 151, 152, 161, 164, 205
Nexon, Daniel 275
Nguyen, Ai Quoc, *see* Ho, Chi Minh
Nicaragua 13, 237, 241, 252
Nicholas II, Tsar 81, 99, 258
Niedermayer, Oskar von 62
Nieszawa 94–5
Nitti, Francesco 89–90
Nobuaki, Baron Makino 264
Nunes da Costa, João Rodrigues 195–6

Ohannes, Pasha 29–30
Oliver, Gov. James 245
Oppenheim, Max von 62
Osman, House of 19, 25, 259
Ottoman Empire 10, 127, 201
    Africa and 38, 44, 52, 123, 147
    Germany and 61, 62, 68, 75, 131, 141
    Great Britain and 12, 162, 172, 258, 270
    imperialism of 1, 3, 14–15, 17, 18, 26,
        32–3, 255, 258–9, 262, 267, 269,
        271, 272
    Italy and 2, 4, 5, 15, 35, 37, 41, 42, 110
    Russia and 6, 98, 99, 103–4
    spring of 19–23
    war and 4, 18, 19, 23–32, 76, 254

Pais, Sidónio 190, 193, 194
Palestine:
    post-war 10, 12, 162, 262, 267, 269,
        270, 276
    war and 61, 131, 155, 163
Panama Canal 235, 237, 239, 245, 249
Pantano, Gherardo 43
Paris 7, 88, 111, 117, 124, 129, 139, 140
Paris Peace Conference 1, 14, 15, 50, 85, 191,
        192, 193, 262–3, 268–9
    China and 230–4, 266
    imperialism and 254–6, 258, 260, 261, 267,
        271, 275
    Japan and 13, 199, 202, 205, 207, 210–13,
        264, 265
    Wilson and 257, 269
Pedersen, Susan 270, 271
Pélissier, René 184
Pershing, John 243, 244
Peter the Great 91
Philippines:
    colonialisation and 13, 236, 237, 238, 241,
        246, 251, 252, 256
    war and 208, 243, 244
Pillai, Champakaraman 159
Pimenta, Fernando Tavares 180

Pinto, Maj. Teixeira 190
Pius XI, Pope 34
Poland 254
    Africa and 179–82
    economy of 183–4
    effects of war in 191–6
    war and 11, 184–6
    war in Angola/Mozambique and 186–91
    see also Germany; Portugal
Portugal:
    Angola and 179–80, 183–6, 188, 196
    imperialism and 191–3
    Mozambique and 15, 64, 143, 144,
        178–85
    Poland and 15, 132, 145, 148
    war and 187, 190, 194, 195, 254
    see also Germany
Pratap, Mahendra 62
Princip, Gavrilo 19
Puerto Rico 13, 236, 238, 240, 248, 256
Punjab, the 4, 161, 176

Quezon, Manuel 252–3

Redmond, John 158
Rex, Count Graf von 205
Rey, Gen. Koos De la 156
Riza, Ali 26
Romania 6, 60, 78, 85, 87, 88
Romanov Empire 1, 3, 6, 19, 100, 254, 260
Rome 35, 39, 44, 85
    fascism in 15, 43, 274
    imperialism of 1, 34, 37, 41, 48, 49, 50
Roosevelt, Theodore 198, 237, 244
Root, Elihu 238
Rumpler, Helmut 73
Russia:
    Armenia and 97–8, 103–4
    Bolshevism in 3, 10, 102–4, 106–8
    economy of 96–7, 99
    ethno-politics of 96–7, 105, 107
    imperialism/nationalism of 91–6, 98–102, 104
    Red imperialism 106–8
    'Russification' of 92–3
    Siberia and 105, 106, 211
    war and 5, 6, 11, 15, 19, 24–8, 32, 93–5,
        97–9, 102
    'White' Russians and 104–5, 107
    see also Germany; Ottoman Empire, Ukraine

Said Halim, Grand Vezir 24
Salandra, Antonio 41
Salazar, António de Oliveira 196
Salgari, Emilio 36
Salonica 20, 21, 32
Salvago Raggi, Giuseppe 44, 45–6
Salvemini, Gaetano 36, 40
Sami, Bekir 28
Sammartino, Annemarie 59

Samoa 54, 61, 63, 131, 152, 153, 173, 236
Sanders, Gen. Liman von 61
Sandino, Augusto 252
Sarajevo 18, 38, 77
Sarıkamış 25, 26, 27
Sarraut, Albert 109, 111, 113, 114, 115, 117, 118, 127, 128
Schmidt, Gen. Rochus 59
Schnee, Heinrich 70, 133
Schwerin, Friedrich von 58
Seipp, Adam 170
Seitz, Theodor 133, 141
Selvagem, Carlos 195
Senghor, Léopold Sédar 117, 128
Senussi (Islamic order) 40, 43
al-Senussi, Ahmad al-Sharif 40, 42, 43;
    see also Senussi (Islamic order)
al-Senussi, Mohamed Idris 42, 43, 50
Serbia 5, 19, 20, 76, 77, 78, 81, 82, 86, 206
Sèvres 32, 271, 272, 273
Shakib Arslan, Amir 22, 29
Shcherbinin, Pavel 80
Shimazu, Naoko 263, 265
Shoufani 28
Showalter, Dennis 79
Siberia 3, 92, 97, 104, 201; *see also* Japan;
    Russia
Simon, Henry 117
Sirte 39, 40
Skoropadskii, Hetman Pavel 105
Smith-Dorrien, Gen. Sir Horace 144
Smuts, Jan 63, 68, 142, 144, 145, 149, 151, 156, 263, 274
Somalia 15, 45, 46, 47, 48
Sonnino, Sidney 41
South Africa 10, 14, 173
    war and 63, 140–7, 154–6, 162, 229, 224
    see also Great Britain
Spee, Maximilian Graf von 140
Spengler, Oswald 234
Stalin, Joseph 107
Steinbach, Daniel 57
Stevenson, David 33
Stoddard, John 200
Stolypin, Petr 93
Strachan, Hew 153, 187, 191
Stümer, Capt. von
Suez 11, 23, 25, 27, 29, 141, 148, 267
Suhayni, Adbullah 148
Sun, Yatsen 219, 22
Supilo, Franjo 76
Sutemi, Viscount Chinda 266
Syria 270, 271, 276
    war and 29, 31, 32, 33
    see also France

Taft, William Howard 237
Takaaki, Katō 200–1, 203, 204, 205
Takashi, Hara 205

Talat, Mehmet 27, 29, 32
Tamari, Salim 31
Tanzania 8
Tao, Juyin 226, 227
Tarhuna 40
Tarsus 18, 19
Ther, Philipp 55
Thrace 22
Tisza, István 77
Togo 8, 61, 63, 131
Townshend, Gen. Charles 31
Toynbee, Arnold 35
Trento 40, 41
Trieste 40, 41
Tripoli 20, 36, 37, 39, 42, 43, 44, 50, 51
Trotsky, Leon 19
Trujillo, Rafael 253
Tsereteli, Irakli 101
Tunstall, Graydon 79
Turkey:
    imperialism 4, 19, 20, 24, 48, 262, 271–2
    post-war in 257, 262, 273, 274, 276
    war and 25, 33, 38, 48, 50, 94
    see also Great Britain; Italy; Ottoman
        Empire

Ukraine 11, 60, 62, 71, 83, 93, 94, 97, 102–3, 105, 108
United States of America 206, 219, 235–6, 257
    China and 200, 229, 232
    Cuba and 13, 237, 241, 245, 248, 256
    imperialism of 1, 13, 14, 245–52, 255, 256, 261
    post-war in 16, 196, 197, 198, 213, 252–3, 269, 273
    pre-war empire and 235–41
    war and 85, 162, 236, 241–5, 252–3
    see also Germany
Uzbekistan 99–100

Vatican, the 34, 35
Venice 35, 49, 51
Victor Emmanuel III, King 48, 51
Vietnam 129, 229
Vollenhoven, Joost Van 112
Volpi, Giuseppe 38, 51

Wandycz, Piotr 77
Wang, Zhengting 226
Washington Conference 3, 14, 211, 212, 213, 132, 233
Washington D.C. 13, 14, 88, 206, 211, 213, 244, 246, 251
Watson, John 169
Wendt, Alexander 263, 275
Wilhelm I, Kaiser 198
Wilhelm II, Kaiser 25, 77, 255
Wilson, Woodrow 43, 50, 83, 90, 149

American government and 162, 237–8,
    240–1, 252, 261
China and 231–4, 266
Great Britain and 175, 177
Japan and 199, 213, 264
policy of 12–16, 32, 33, 172, 245, 256–60,
    268, 269, 271, 272, 275, 276
Wingate, Gen. Sir Reginald 147, 148
Winter, Jay 156, 173
Wright, Mary 221
Wright, Thomas 275
Wu, Tingfang 227

Yan, Fu 215, 233
Yang, Du 220, 221
Young, Ernest 222
Yuan, Shikai 200, 218–20, 221,
    222, 223
Yugoslavia 85; *see also* Balkans, the;
    Bosnia-Herzegovina; Serbia

Zahla 28, 29
Zewditu 46
Zhang, Xun 228
Zückert, Martin 77

Printed and bound by CPI Group (UK) Ltd, Croydon, CR0 4YY